The Transplanted

Interdisciplinary Studies in History

HARVEY J. GRAFF, *General Editor*

The Transplanted

A History of Immigrants

in Urban America

JOHN BODNAR

Indiana University Press

BLOOMINGTON

First Midland Book Edition 1987
© 1985 by John Bodnar

MANUFACTURED IN THE UNITED STATES OF AMERICA

Library of Congress Cataloging in Publication Data

Bodnar, John E., 1944–
  The transplanted.

  (Interdisciplinary studies in history)
  Bibliography: p.
  Includes index.

  1. Minorities—United States—History. 2.
City and town life—United States—History. 3.
United States—Social conditions. I. Title. II.
Series.
E184.A1B59 1985   305.8'00973   84-48041
CL. ISBN 0-253-31347-3
PA. ISBN 0-253-20416-X

6 7 8 9 10 99 98 97 96 95 94

For

D O N N A

*A social interpretation of history places ideas, events
and behavior as well as institutions in the larger
context of the overall social system.*
                                        —Robert F. Berkhofer, Jr.

Contents

[*ix*

Contents

Illustrations

Maps

Acknowledgments

A work of synthesis rests primarily on the efforts of hundreds of other scholars who have mined the vast array of source material documenting a particular historical experience. The footnotes in the text reveal some of my debts to others. More directly I would like to thank those individuals and institutions who have been so generous with their support. The John Simon Guggenheim Foundation provided a fellowship which allowed me time to complete the writing of the book. The American Philosophical Society also provided a timely grant. At Indiana University, Roger Newton, Charlene Fears, Robert Byrnes, and Lewis Perry supported me by making available the resources of the university's Institute for Advanced Study. A long list of scholars have shared their thinking with me on subjects relevant to this book over a long period of time and a few read all or parts of the manuscript. I am especially grateful to June Alexander, Josef Barton, John Buckowczyk, Al Camarillo, Milton Cantor, Howard Chudacoff, Kathleen Conzen, Ronald Cohen, Herbert Gutman, John Higham, William Hoglund, Fred Luebke, Raymond Mohl, Ewa Morawska, Moses Rischin, William Reesce, Peter Stearns, Stephan Thernstrom, Rudolph Vecoli, and Olivier Zunz. My former colleague Walter Nugent has always been a fertile source of ideas, and David Montgomery has been supportive for nearly a decade. Karen Gatz helped me with some translation from German, and Jeannie Harrah and Pauline Gliessman were extremely helpful in expediting the completion of the manuscript. Valuable typing services were provided at one stage through the Indiana University Department of History and I would like to thank Libby Gitlitz and Debra Chase. Harvey Graff proved to be both a cooperative and incisive editor. Beyond the walls of professional concerns, my life was made more enjoyable by my children, Eric and Brenna, and by my wife, Donna, who has always done more than her share.

Introduction

In every time and place men and women must make some effort to adjust to the economic realities which confront them. Nowhere is this lesson more obvious than in the industrial cities and towns of the United States in the final quarter of the twentieth century. Residents faced with transformations in the labor market which demand skills unlike the ones they possess or industries faced with new forms of competition from abroad all scurry to adjust, adapt, and reorient themselves to new demands and new realities. Young people contemplating their futures must reconsider the value of skills and patterns of life useful to their parents and look in new directions while realizing that even a partial abandonment of all that they previously knew—neighborhoods, values, associations, and even dreams—cannot be accomplished without some pain. Americans coming of age in the 1980s are realizing a lesson their grandparents and great-grandparents knew fully well: The imperatives of capitalism must be served. The continual shift in capital and market conditions stirred by the ceaseless drive for profits and economy still demands a response from ordinary individuals who live under its influence. The fragile link between the generations of the last century and the current one is not necessarily cultural or emotional as much as it is the shared need to respond to an evolving capitalism, the need to choose from available but limited life paths, and the powerful drive to preserve something of one's inheritance even while acquiescing in a changing economic order—a drive which can sometimes influence the larger economic system itself.

The earlier generations, which left behind lessons of confronting American capitalism, were largely immigrants. They were usually young people themselves and their confrontation involved movement over long distances as well as compromises, acceptance of things unfamiliar, and stubborn resistance to change. After the second decade of the nineteenth century and prior to World War II, over 40 million of these individuals left homelands in Asia, North America, Europe and elsewhere to find a place in the new economic order of capitalism. This book looks to make something of a summary statement of that incredible and wide-ranging movement for at least the majority who moved to American cities and towns. Millions, of course, settled in rural America, mostly before the 1880s, and that story is a rich and important one, which eventually should be told. But for the larger portion, capitalism was encountered in urban neighborhoods, factories, mills, offices, mines, and homesteads. It is their story which speaks to the generations today.

The people who moved to American cities and industrial towns during the first century of American capitalism have been chronicled and described by an abundant number of scholars, novelists, journalists, and other writers and have been ascribed an array of characteristics. Often their flight to America has been seen as the act of desperate individuals fleeing poverty and disorder only to be further weakened by back-breaking labor and inhospitable cities in America. Their fate was one of a life in insulated ethnic ghettos, continual struggle, and an eventual but precarious attachment to the new economy. Others have celebrated these humble newcomers as bearers of proud, long-established traditions which helped to organize their lives amidst the vagaries of the industrial city and served as a context in which they organized their transition, rather successfully, to a new land. A third school of thought has advanced the argument that these newcomers were aspiring individuals whose ties to tradition were loosened in their homelands and who moved to America eager for opportunity, advancement, and all the rewards of capitalism. In this final framework, immigrants moved from tradition-bound peasants to modern, acquisitive individuals.[1]

Most previous descriptions of immigrants assume that the immigrant experience was a common experience shared equally by all; the transition to capitalism is either entirely difficult, conducted entirely within the confines of a traditional but apparently adaptive culture, or entirely rewarding over a given period of time. But even the most cursory glance at an immigrant community or stream will suggest that not all newcomers behaved in a similar fashion, that varying degrees of commitment to an assortment of cultures and ideologies were evident, and that not everyone faced identical experiences. Some individuals pursued modern forms of life and livelihood while others valued more traditional patterns. Workers existed who championed socialism and others died for their attachment to Catholicism. Some immigrants came to America and acquired large fortunes, and many more simply went to work everyday with no appreciable gain. What they actually shared in common was a need to confront a new economic order and provide for their own welfare and that of their kin or household group. They all did this but they did so in different ways and with divergent results.

Because this work seeks to focus on the common experience of confronting capitalism and because it attempts to synthesize the entire immigrant encounter with urban-industrial America for over a century, it necessarily transcends older categories of "old" and "new" immigration and the traditional focus on group life which has dominated previous understanding. The need now is to move beyond the restricted field of vision offered by studying one or more ethnic groups. This is not a book about the Irish in Boston, the Germans of Cincinnati, or the Chicanos of Los Angeles. It is about the entire immigrant saga comprised of all these groups and cities and other groups and cities. In its reach for the general, it does not seek to render unimportant ethnic or even class analysis but only to suggest that a meaningful level of analysis exists beyond the older view that immigrants were members of a particular ethnic group or that they were only humble workers.

The desire to move beyond the older framework of analysis is especially stimulated by the suspicion that immigrants were not clinging together as clusters of aliens or workers but were, in fact, badly fragmented into numerous enclaves arranged by internal status levels, ideology, and orientation. The important implication of group fragmentation is that the real dynamic which explained immigrant adjustment was not simply at the nexus of immigrant and American culture or at the point where foreign-born workers met industrial managers, but it was at all the points where immigrant families met the challenges of capitalism and modernity: the homeland, the neighborhood, the school, the workplace, the church, the family, and the fraternal hall. Both within groups and outside of them an array of leaders and orators offered solutions and life paths to deal with the overpowering reality of social change. Socialists, clerics, entrepreneurs, politicians, and labor organizers all made their pitch to immigrant families who listened, sometimes followed but seldom abandoned the central requirement in their lives: to secure the welfare and well-being of their familial or household base. Groups of families would even take different paths as some moved rather quickly into business and middle-class pursuits and other struggled to achieve steady work in factories and mills. But the final product of this disparity was a whole range of competing ideologies, leaders, and models of life which promised to shape the ultimate pattern of immigrant adjustment. The suspicion is that the immigrant response to capitalism was conditioned less by group culture or by American urban culture and economic structures and more by the interaction of classes, ideologies, and culture within and outside of communities of newcomers.

It is impossible, moreover, to treat this immigrant experience without relating it to the evolution of world capitalism after 1800. Capitalism is a system of market-directed production for profit based on wage-labor. In its earliest stages it was best characterized by its emphasis on commercial ventures and networks. By the third and fourth decades of the nineteenth century, it began, however, to evolve into the advanced stage of industrial capitalism. Transcending the simple profit goals of mercantilism, the drive for profit now fused financial resources with machinery, raw materials, and labor power to produce wealth. In other words, wealth was generated not by simple trade but by combining human and technological power often in a circumscribed workplace such as a factory. As capitalism, especially in its industrial stage, subsumed both the means of production and labor power, it began to transform not only nature but society. Admittedly, capitalism is a rather abstract term and cannot be ascribed material characteristics. It can, however, serve as a valuable interpretive device to discuss a framework in which economic actors played out their roles in specific times and places.[2]

Capitalism proved to be an agent of social change not only in the societies in which it flourished but in underdeveloped regions as well. At home in countries such as the United States and England, ideologies emerged which honored the pursuit of profit and success in the business and secular world. Unstable social relations between divergent classes and competition between companies, both viewed by capitalist leaders as potentially disruptive to the cause of profits, efficiency, and stability, were mitigated by extending capital's control over the state. While the attempt to manage the political economy was never completely successful, it did achieve meaningful results. In the United States regulatory statutes for various industries and union activity began to proliferate by 1900. Abroad less developed regions were pulled into the orbit of capitalism by becoming suppliers of raw materials, foodstuffs, and manpower. The growth of world capitalism, in fact, resulted in both the emergence of a worldwide market for labor and a heightened cultural exchange between the dynamic new order of concentrated wealth and power and the more stolid ways of life in less developed regions.[3]

In essence neither immigration nor capitalism as it emerged in the United States would have been possible without each other. Prior to the 1830s American economic growth was extremely slow as little investment in material capital took place and technology advanced slowly. A virtual absence of productivity-raising activity characterized the nation and small populations, low levels of per capita income, and primitive technologies of transportation and communications existed. By 1840, however, this picture was changing as economic growth and output per capita were showing signs of increasing. Stimulated by a growing foreign demand for American staples, the economy began to expand and offer greater incentives for investments in material capital, inventions, and acquisition of skills, and, of course, inexpensive labor. Manufacturing sectors grew and stimulated the growth of cities. Dependent upon economies of scale, manufacturers had to locate where transportation routes facilitated the acquisitions of raw materials and the presence of population concentrations could easily meet demands for larger supplies of labor. American population growth led to expanded markets which made possible the exploitation of economies of large-scale production. These economies were realized from specialization and the division of labor within firms and from increased specialization among firms as well as technological innovation. Slowly the merchant capitalism which predominated prior to the Civil War gave way to an industrial capitalism which rationalized production under the factory system and looked for an ever-increasing supply of labor to fill the growing number of simple tasks it created and keep labor costs somewhat depressed. By 1870 the United States had a manufacturing output equal to that of France and Germany combined. By 1913 American manufacturing output equaled that of France, Germany and the United Kingdom, and it was the chief producer of foodstuffs in the world. In 1870 over one-half of all workers were farmers or farm laborers. Forty years later over two-thirds were industrial toilers, many of whom had come from regions as diverse as Japan, Mexico, Ireland, Germany, and Italy.[4]

Immigrants were quite important to the entire industrial transformation. Without European immigration to America, for instance, it has been estimated that wages in Eastern industries would have been 11 percent higher than they were in 1910. Immigrants also brought a sizable body of skills and knowledge which were absolutely indispensable for the growth of some industries, and the presence of a large pool of unskilled labor attracted further investment. Additionally, the fact that the cost of rearing and training a huge labor force was largely borne outside the United States allowed for even greater levels of investment and growth. Without immigration in the first century of American capitalism, the United States work force would have been only 70 percent of what it was by 1940.[5]

Finally, by going beyond vague dichotomies of preindustrial immigrants and American culture and looking precisely at the specific points of contact between capitalism as both an economic system and a way of life and specific categories of newcomers, the entire scope of immigration history is rescued from a model of understanding which has dominated scholarly and popular understanding for decades. Whether immigrants were upwardly mobile achievers or dispirited peasants they were always assumed to move in a linear progression from a premodern, holistic community to a modern, atomistic one. Such a framework presented immigration as a clash of cultures. But if the entire experience is broken down into innumerable points of contact between various categories and beliefs, what emerges is a clearer portrait of the process of social change stimulated almost incessantly by the changing imperatives of the marketplace and the diverse responses of human beings themselves. Their response, conditioned by their social station, familial status, and ideological orientation, becomes a variable itself helping to structure not only their own life path but even somewhat the all embracing economic system. Ordinary individuals are rescued from the status of victims; they are not simply manipulated by leaders, their class standing, or their culture, but active participants in an historical drama whose outcome is anything but predictable.[6] This view further accentuates a process hidden from sight in previous accounts. Immigrants now are no longer confronting an amorphous mass called America or modern society but specific leaders and ideologies which evoke acceptance, resistance, and divergent paths into the capitalist economy. Agents of tradition preaching ethnic culture, conservatism, and religious devotion appear alongside champions of assimilation, education, and even worker militancy. Spokesmen for what Fernand Braudel calls the "material life," the old routines handed down from time immemorial, compete against advocates of modernization and protest. Occasionally an ideology of tradition will be used in the service of social change. The point is that instead of linear progression, immigrants faced a continual dynamic between economy and society, between class and culture. It was in the swirl of this interaction and competition that ordinary individuals had to sort out options, listen to all the prophets, and arrive at decisions of their own in the best manner they could. Inevitably the results were mixed. Some fared better than others; some stayed in America and others returned home. Immigrants existed who became radicals and others worshiped the ethic of entrepreneurship. Some did not even care either way. In many cases decisions were incomplete and imprecise. These were after all neither heroes nor villains but ordinary people. Life for them as for us was never clear cut. What was ultimately important amidst the political and economic currents of their times was not only how they adapted to it all but what if anything endured in their lives and brought it order and stability. What follows is not only an attempt to uncover the nature of their involvement with capitalism, what they abandoned and what they retained, but it is also an effort to learn if they simply accepted one ideology or life style or whether they valued other things not as evident to those who look only at the obvious arguments and debates of their times.

The Transplanted

1 /

The Homeland and

Capitalism

The Structure of Emigration

Most of the immigrants transplanted to America in the century of industrial growth after 1830 were in reality the children of capitalism. They were products of an economic system and, indeed, a way of life which penetrated their disparate homelands in particular parts of the world at various stages throughout the nineteenth century. While the new order of capitalism may have represented an opportunity for surplus and abundance to those possessing the resources to take advantage of its promise, to ordinary farmers and laborers throughout the pre-industrial lands of the world it represented a new dimension to the ongoing challenge of finding a way to sustain the welfare of family, kin, or the small group which formed the boundaries of everyday life. Before promising them opportunity and enhanced material well-being, capitalism presented them with a choice of options. Some would decide to retain traditional, pre-modern modes of life, others would attempt to adjust to the new realities presented by capitalism in the homelands, and still other would formulate plans to confront changing economic and social demands in industrial regions such as the United States. The circumstances under which these decisions were made and the specific individuals who made them form a crucial dimension for understanding American immigration and the relationship of these transient people to capitalism itself. Without an appreciation of the lands and the times from which the immigrants came, the ultimate story of their experience in America cannot be understood.

Traditionally the impetus for American immigration has been

linked to the disparity between an improving standard of living in America and impoverishment of premodern societies throughout the world. Stimulated by improvements in transportation which lowered the real cost of moving freight and passengers and which facilitated the expansion of both domestic and foreign markets, American economic growth accelerated during the half-century after 1870 with marked productivity increases in both manufacturing and agriculture. Not surprisingly, by the 1920s, scholars were interpreting immigration as a product of American business cycles. Good times led to increased demands for labor, which in turn pulled workers from areas of labor surplus; lean years led to rapid curtailment of the flow. This belief received a rather sophisticated support in the writings of Brinley Thomas. Interested in the connection between migration and economic activity, Thomas went beyond short-term business cycles and concentrated on long swings in the rates of economic growth and capital formation. When investment was high in Britain he argued, the rate of growth slackened in America and the westward movement of men and money fell off. When capital flowed into the United States, economic activity expanded and migrants quickly followed. Thomas began the tradition of emphasizing the pull of American economic activity as the prime motive underlying immigration. He concluded that by the late nineteenth century American industrial growth became the dominant attraction of money and men in the Atlantic economy.[1]

Evidence exists to support much of the Thomas view. Richard Easterlin found increases in immigration coming after rises in the American demand for labor. A moderation in emigration to the United States did take place during the 1850s from Germany, Ireland, England, and Scandinavia when American unemployment rose. American growth in the 1870s saw a concurrent expansion in emigration from Germany. During the Panic of 1907–08 a marked decrease in arriving immigrants was evident among nearly every group. Croatian emigration to America, which measured over 22,000 in 1907, dropped to 2,800 during the following year. And few can deny that as American industrial wages climbed they proved attractive to those abroad.[2] American wages were about five times those of Hungary by 1900. Logically, increases in wages abroad could deter many from coming to America. Such a situation, for instance, occurred in Germany after 1900 and caused Poles in Prussia to remain at home.[3]

The essential problem with the scholarship which has emphasized the attractiveness of the American economy to the less fortunate of the world, however, is that it badly obscures the complexity of social and economic forces which were affecting emigrants in their homeland. If immigration was caused largely by the lure of America, then we would expect that struggling people everywhere would come here in relatively equal numbers with common intentions and, for that matter, backgrounds. But historical reality suggests a different explanation to this process. Rates of emigration were not the same everywhere. Ultimately, it is impossible to understand even the nature of American immigrant communities without appreciating the nature of the world these newcomers left.

If immigrants were simply being drawn to America without any compelling reasons for leaving except impoverishment or relative economic disadvantage, then we would expect to see a certain similarity between countries. Available figures, however, indicate that the intensity of the flow varied by country and by decade. Moreover, in nearly every case, emigration patterns experienced a small beginning, a peak in the middle, and a decline at the end which was often unrelated to the American economy. For instance, the rate from Germany in the period 1830–34 was 2.2 per thousand population. It peaked at 9.0 per thousand in the first half of the 1850s but declined to only 3.8 between 1880 and 1884 and to less than 1.0 per thousand in the early 1900s, a period of relatively high economic growth in the United States. Furthermore, within Hungary in 1905, the rate among Magyars was 4.0 per thousand while at the same time it was 19.2 among Slovaks and 15.1 among Ruthenians despite the fact that all knew equally as much about American opportunities.[4]

The pattern was prevalent wherever emigration took place. During the 1870s the rate of emigration was twice as heavy from Norway as it was from nearby Sweden. The rate per 100,000 population from England and Scotland was 470, but it was over twice that from Ireland and less than half that from Germany. Northwestern Europe, the heart of the "old emigration" was certainly not acting in concert with American economic patterns. Everywhere emigrant tides rose and fell in a manner unrelated to capital flow and American economic expansion. From 1870 to 1920 American industry steadily expanded and attracted more immigrants. But during the same period emigration began to decline in Denmark, Sweden, Norway, England, Ireland, and Germany. Even where it increased, it did not do so evenly among various groups. In 1912 in Austria-Hungary, an area with an expanding emigrant tide, Poles were leaving at a rate of 711 per 100,000 and South Slavs at a rate of 604, but the rate for Czechs and Magyars was about one-half the figure for Poles.[5]

Most accounts of American immigrants have tended to describe newcomers as emigrating from particular countries like Italy, Germany, or Poland. Yet, tremendous variations existed within national boundaries with some regions and districts experiencing intense bursts of emigration and other almost none at all. If the social and economic context of emigrant origins is to be fully understood, close attention must be paid to specific geographical locations, for emigrants came not so much from a particular country as they did from a specific region.

In Scotland, for instance, regional variations distinguished emigration patterns. Areas of severe economic depression such as the Highlands did not participate in the exodus as much as the Lowlands which were not only experiencing a widespread commercialization of agriculture, but which were closer to industrial areas. Generally, Lowland emigration exceeded the Highland exodus by a proportion of 17 to 1. In the "old order" Scottish Lowlands, most settlements were small in size usually containing a huddled group of cottages and farm buildings with a mix of tenements, cottagers, servants, and tradesmen who plied their trades of weaving, tailoring, shoemaking, and carpeting. By 1800 this structure was undergoing rapid change, however, as small holdings were thrown together and commercialization and vast agricultural improvements entered the Lowland regions. In the north where commercialization of agriculture progressed more slowly, smaller farms and thus a wider distribution of ownership was retained much longer.[6]

Movement from nearby England and Wales, while significant, was not nearly as intense as that from Scotland. From 1881 to 1931 Wales lost an average of 7 inhabitants per thousand and England lost 14 per thousand. In Scotland the figure was more than double that of England—35 per thousand. In England, agricultural counties near London sent relatively few emigrants as did similarly located counties near cities such as Stockholm and Budapest. Areas farther away such as Sussex and Cornwall had the highest rates prior to the 1850s. After the 1850s those departing often came from the ranks of industrial workers. This was especially true in Wales. Stimulated by industrial disputes, low wages, and unemployment, many iron workers and miners left South Wales and moved to specific occupations in the United States.[7]

Ireland, of course, differed from the rest of western Europe and was always an exceptionally rich source of emigrants. It, more than any other country, weakens the argument that American opportunity by itself was a sufficient force to sustain emigration. During the five decades after 1830, the rate of people leaving Ireland was more than

Counties of Ireland, 1850s

Ulster

Londonderry

Donegal

Derry

Antrim

Tyrone

Belfast

Connaught

Leitrim

Fermanagh

Armagh

Down

Monaghan

Sligo

Cavan

Louth

Mayo

Roscommon

Longford

Meath

Galway

Westmeath

Galway

King's

Dublin

Dublin

Kildare

Queen's

Wicklow

Clare

Carlow

Munster

Leinster

Limerick

Kilkenny

Limerick

Tipperary

Wexford

Waterford

Kerry

Cork

Cork

0   50 Mi.

CLL

twice that of Scotland. It was even higher in the late 1840s and early 1850s. Since persons ravaged by extreme famine and repression made up the Irish emigration of the late 1840s, it clearly possessed many of the characteristics of a flight from poverty, although heavy Irish emigration later in the century had a considerably different cast and consisted of individuals with specific industrial skills. But even in Ireland the poorest were not the first to leave and regional variations were evident. The exodus from the most backward and densely populated regions in the west lagged behind that from the wealthier counties of Ulster and Leinster until long after the famine.[8]

By 1800 Ireland's east and central sections were also showing characteristics of agricultural regions slowly commercializing, since they were producing for the English markets. Traditional kin-based farms were giving way to the improvements and consolidations of larger landlords. In the west of Ireland, traditional Irish culture and clans predominated much longer, although economic conditions remained more depressed.[9] It was from the "dynamic" regions of the Irish economy that emigrants tended to come, especially from Connaught and Leinster. In the west the tie between the peasantry and the land remained unbroken. Even during the 1846–54 famine emigration, the heaviest flows were from the central and eastern counties. Movement from areas of either negligible or extremely high poverty was always least. Only one-third to one-half as many people left counties containing the highest proportion of landless, such as Cork, Tipperary, Waterford, and Kilkenny, as left Leinster.[10]

German emigration also displayed some of the regional variation characteristic of other lands. In its early phases it centered in the southwest and northwest especially during the heavy years of the 1850s. Twenty years later it emanated primarily from the eastern and northeastern regions. The early dominance of the southwest took place especially in Baden and Württemberg, where the family plot decreased in size as land was continually divided and small businessmen and artisans suffered from an increase in manufactured goods comig into the region. Between 1840 and 1847 about one-sixth of the weavers of Württemberg went bankrupt and the subdivision of land was carried almost to an extreme. From areas like Upper Swabia, however, where large estates predominated, almost no emigration took place.[11]

As emigration shifted to northeast Germany after 1865, a change in the composition of the emigrant flow was discernible. The small landowner of the southwest was replaced, as modern historical scholars have demonstrated, by lower orders of peasants, their landless

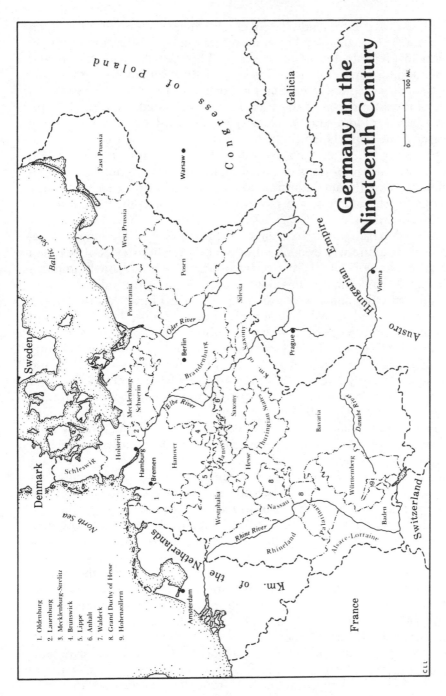

Germany in the Nineteenth Century

1. Oldenburg
2. Lauenburg
3. Mecklenburg-Strelitz
4. Brunswick
5. Lippe
6. Anhalt
7. Waldeck
8. Grand Duchy of Hesse
9. Hohenzollern

children, and farmhands. Even nearby areas such as Prussia which were industrializing, could not absorb enough of the region's population to prevent movement overseas. This alteration by region and composition in German emigration led to fewer numbers of family units in the migrant stream and a growing number of individuals. As departures from east of the Elbe River accelerated, individuals actually began to dominate. While 55 percent of the farmers and 50 percent of the workers leaving the port of Hamburg between 1871 and 1884 were family members, only 28.4 percent from industrial and commercial occupations departed in family units. Thus, as emigration increased from industrial towns, which were often temporary stops for the landless, the movements came to consist primarily of individuals.[12]

Sweden demonstrated characteristics similar to Germany. A regional structure was evident with direct correlations evident between high emigration rates, distance from large cities, and small amounts or arable land suitable for plowing. As in Germany, migrants from industrial cities and towns also comprised a significant portion of the movement and revealed that emigration was only largely but not entirely a movement from agriculture. Southern Sweden was strongly represented as was the city of Stockholm. Rural Jonkoping County supplied large amounts of newcomers to Chicago between 1860 and 1880. But nearly one in every four migrants from 1850 to 1920 came from a town. Low levels of emigrants, however, left regions surrounding Stockholm, Uppsala, and Gothenburg. Large cities tended to dissuade nearby residents from crossing the Atlantic, though many rural residents eventually moved across the ocean after temporary stays in expanding urban areas. Finally, parishes with much land suitable for plowing saw few leave; those who owned land in these regions remained fixed to the soil. Those with marginal land or no land at all in the flat lands of Sweden began to look to cities.[13]

Neighboring Finland did not differ greatly. As the nineteenth century drew to an end, the proportion of landless people increased and large population losses from emigration were evident in rural provinces such as Kuopio, Turku, and Pori. Kuopio had the highest proportion of landless, while Turku and Pori were centers of crofters farming rented land. Although crofters could be rather independent despite their status as renters, they clearly formed a bottom layer of the agricultural social order.[14]

Denmark was another country which displayed regional variations even if it was not the origin of large numbers of American immigrants. Those leaving came largely from the southern portion especially the island of Bornholm. In a massive study of several hundred thousand Danish emigrants, Kristian Hvidt found the emigrant stream comprising a continual mix of rural and town dwellers. Rural dwellers held a slight majority from 1868 to 1900, but this was reversed after 1900 as more came from Copenhagen or regional market towns. This alteration should be understood in its proper context. Most of those leaving the towns were originally rural dwellers who fled to towns because of economic difficulties in agriculture and then decided to move again. This was as true in Denmark as it was throughout Scandinavia, Poland, and other regions. The underlying impetus for departure continued to be problems in rural economies. While a city such as Copenhagen did experience industrial expansion and to an extent could absorb many newcomers, regional towns often could not. Indeed, in 1882 twelve of every 1,000 inhabitants of Danish provincial towns left the nation. Hvidt further discovered that most of those leaving provincial towns had moved previously from rural areas, an indication that at least for Danes the decision to move abroad was often made in stages, especially in "idyllic little towns" without new factories and workshops.[15] The rural areas losing the most people were regions where large estates were consolidating their holdings. The increased demand for land drove up prices, making it difficult for ordinary workers to buy sufficient land to sustain themselves in farming. Their experience contrasted to that in areas in Italy and Sweden, where emigration emanated more from regions of widespread land ownership.[16]

While the emigration of the Dutch was of a comparatively low intensity, regional differences were no less marked. Prior to 1880 emigrants tended to originate from agricultural areas of grain cultivation rather than dairy farming or mixed farming areas. It was in these areas that commercialization of farming was most advanced and ties to outside markets strongest as cash crops were grown for export. Commercialization not only made it more difficult for the landless to start farms of their own, but connections to distant markets brought goods into these regions which undercut local craftsmen. A leading historian of this movement, Robert Swierenga, not surprisingly found that 66 percent of the Dutch emigrants were craftsmen and day or farm laborers. While farmers predominated in the early period of Dutch emigration prior to 1860, ultimately they represented only about 22 percent of the nineteenth-century total, an indication that as Dutch emigration continued it began to encompass a wider segment of the social structure as it had in Germany and elsewhere.[17]

The dual monarchy of Austria and Hungary was a hardy producer of emigrants to America especially after 1880, but not all regions of the empire participated equally in the movement. In general, regions which had larger proportions of agricultural estates employing a landless proletariat and fewer artisans who could be displaced sent very few emigrants. These regions included Lower and Upper Austria and Salzburg. In Galicia and Bukovina, where much greater numbers of small landowners—usually from 2 to 5 hectares—and artisans lived, emigration was considerably more intense. Emigration to America could be particularly heavy in regions where no nearby industrial areas existed to absorb the surplus agricultural population. Thus, the tendency to emigrate was greater in northeastern Hungary than in districts closer to Budapest. In fact, the beginnings of Magyar emigration were in counties north of the Tisza River, many of which now lie in Slovakia or in the Ukraine. Zemplin County was the area of heaviest emigration during the peak years from 1899 to 1913. There was not a village in the county, according to the Hungarian scholar Istvan Racz, from which someone did not emigrate. Racz attributed the phenomenon to the region's system of entailment which limited inheritance of property to specific heirs in such a way that property could be transferred only with great difficulty. This made the acquisition of additional land especially hard and served to encourage the persistence of smaller holdings.[18]

Galicia and Bukovina were major centers of departure from the empire. Although Galicia had the highest rate of emigration, the distribution of land ownership was widespread in both areas, with Bukovina actually exceeding Galicia. Ninety percent of the owners in Bukovina possessed less than five hectares, a generally recognized minimum for self-sufficiency. Galicia had the highest rate of people leaving in both relative and absolute terms. During the three decades after 1880 fully 10 percent of the population actually emigrated. Even in Galicia, however, a pattern could be detected in which the region with the lowest per capita income (Eastern Galicia) was not the region of heaviest emigration. Indeed, the western area saw more individuals emigrate than any other part of Galicia and yet its per capita income was among the highest. Throughout Galicia, however, "dwarf" farming was all too common with 81 percent of the enterprises below five hectares, a size necessary for minimum survival.[19]

South Slavs from Croatia and Carniola also contributed above average rates to the empire's emigrant total. Again agricultural regions with a broad distribution of land ownership and underdeveloped industry led the way. For instance, the rate from Lower Carniola was

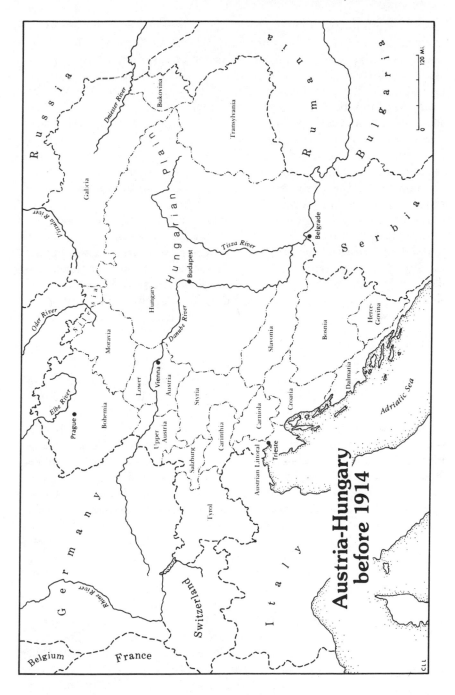

Austria-Hungary before 1914

twice the rate for the whole of Slovenia; emigration from more industrialized Upper Carniola was much lower.[20] Lika-Krbava, a district of
heavy Croatian emigration, was also predictably characterized by
small plots of land, low wages, and an absence of industry. Emigration also rose farther inland as railroads drove deeper into the interior
from the Dalmatian coast. Ironically, many who worked on the construction of railroads in Croatia put themselves out of work since
much of the income of inhabitants in the interior had been derived
from transporting cargo over the mountains.[21]

Serbs leaving the empire constituted a particularly good example
of the repeated theme of emigration as much more than a flight from
poverty. Most of the Serbs leaving for America came from Croatia,
especially from the region of Voivodina, and not Serbia proper. In
Croatia they had encountered better soil and superior access to the
markets of Budapest and Vienna. Because agriculture in Croatia was
more tied to commercial markets, these Serbs found it increasingly
difficult to survive on small plots. Since Budapest and Vienna were
not about to encourage industrial development in Croatia or even
much of Slovenia, thousands of South Slavs had to look elsewhere to
make ends meet.[22]

When the case of Slovakia is considered, a further understanding
of the type of region most likely to supply emigrants is possible. Like
Croatia, Slovenia, and Galicia the industrialization of Slovakia was
restricted severely by the government in Vienna. Indeed, all of Hungary was sometimes considered to be an agricultural supplier for industrializing Austria. Compounding the lack of industrial opportunity
was the declining number of landowners after 1869 throughout Hungary, especially in Slovakia, where nobles were increasing their holdings at the peasant's expense. The county of Zemplin witnessed the
departure of both small landowners and a growing landless labor
force after 1890. Activity was more intense among Slovaks and Rusins
than among Hungarians in the southern end of the county.[23]

Poles outside of Galicia also showed regional variations in their
emigration patterns. While the very earliest left Upper Silesia in the
1850s due to difficult agricultural conditions, they were quite able to
"afford" travel expenses to Texas. Prussian migration, while important before 1880, subsided, as industrial growth in Silesia absorbed
some of the surplus or marginal rural work force. The massive migrations after 1890 continued from all areas but mostly from Congress
Poland and, of course, Galicia. Evidence exists which suggests that
districts supplying the most emigrants had the highest density of villages. It was in these villages that former farmhands, servants, and

day laborers lived before leaving for abroad. Between 1893 and 1901 these three groups grew from 13 percent to 43.7 percent of village populations in areas of high emigration, such as Kalisz, Warsaw, Kielce, and Piotrkow.[24]

Italy proved to be no exception to the pattern of regional differences in emigration. During the 1880s the rate per 1,000 population was 0.6 percent for the entire country, but it was 2 percent from Lucca and 2.2 percent from Palermo. Coastal areas that were closely involved with trade, such as Genoa, tended to send emigrants abroad before inland regions.[25]

In a brilliant study of Italian migration to San Francisco, historian Dino Cinel found that only four provinces supplied most of the emigrants to that city: Genoa, Lucca, Cosenza, and Palermo. The two provinces in the north were more industrial than those in the south. About 10 percent of the people in Genoa worked in industry in 1890, whereas the figure for Palermo and Cosenza was less than 3 percent. Within regions, some villages were more likely to supply emigrants than others. Among nine cities and villages which sent their human cargoes to San Francisco, two were in mountainous areas which produced no cash crops, and two were in regions where wine and wheat were staples of the economy. One village consisted of 80 percent fishermen. Emigrants from larger cities such as Genoa and Palermo were familiar with trade, business, or industrial skills.[26]

If the lure of America was an overpowering magnet to the impoverished people of the world, emigration from any country or region would have been essentially a random process draining the lowest elements of society from nearly every geographic area. But emigrants clearly came from some regions and not other. Abundant evidence exists, moreover, to suggest that those departing were not coming from the depths of their respective society but occupied positions somewhere in the middle and lower-middle levels of their social structures. Those too poor could seldom afford to go, and the very wealthiest usually had too much of a stake in the homelands to depart. It was Frank Thistlethwaite who first alerted scholars to the fact that immigrants were not an undifferentiated mass but represented specific regional and occupational groups. Unfortunately his analysis did not go beyond the mere statement of the concept to detail the specific occupational or regional streams or to explore the exact structural origin of emigrants.[27]

Germany provided a good case of how emigrants tended to leave the middle levels of a society. The earliest stirrings of German emigration during the modern era occurred in the two decades after 1830.

Italy in the Nineteenth Century

A relaxation on emigration limits after the Napoleonic Wars and improved transportation links between coastal and inland areas facilitated such movement, but primary motives were found deeper in the German social structure. The persistent pattern of selectivity was already apparent in the 1830–45 period as emigrants tended to be almost entirely "middle class": small farmers and independent artisans. Centered in southwestern German provinces where populations were increasing and land holdings were being fragmented by 1830, those perched precariously in the middle were haunted by the threat of losing what they had; those below offered them a glimpse of what they might become if their holdings or crafts disappeared entirely. The lower orders of farmhands and apprentices were unable to muster sufficient resources to cross the Atlantic even if they wanted to do so. Great landowners, of course, enjoyed a measure of economic stability. The chief reason the middle-class Germans emigrated was to retain a secure economic existence. Because they owned property they could turn it into cash and muster the resources to travel abroad. An observer in Stuttgart commented in 1846 that those leaving were afraid even their modest property holdings would be lost should they decide to remain.[28]

After 1850 the spread of industrialization and commercialized agriculture let to further declines in the number of landholdings that could support families. This situation, as always in the nineteenth century, was exacerbated by continuing population growth. These forces inevitably and repeatedly led to a process, not only in Germany but in southern and eastern Europe as well, whereby the emigrant stream gradually encompassed a wider and wider segment of the social structure, from the craftsmen and farmers of the first waves toward apprentices, day laborers and farm workers.

Initially emigrants from Germany and elsewhere were likely to move in family units, but in later stages solitary individuals predominated who might reconstitute their family group at a later time or start one of their own when their resources were more abundant. As northeastern Germany replaced the southwest as a leading center of emigration by 1853, a greater proportion of those departing were individuals from lower social orders, especially those who were propertyless and unmarried.[29] After 1880 the composition of German emigrants, coming increasingly now from Pomerania, Mecklenberg, and East and West Prussia, was decidedly from the ranks of farm laborers. Family units as a portion of the emigrant stream peaked around 1881 at about 65 percent, and then individual males and females became more common. No longer possessing sufficient capital to initiate farming or small business in America, these migrants were more likely to move into accessible occupations such as domestic employment or industrial work. In the first decade of this century, less than 10 percent of the German emigrants were independent farmers.[30]

The structure of emigration from Great Britain exhibited remarkable similarities to the German pattern. During the two to three decades prior to the 1850s, the lower-middle-class landowners and artisans in rural regions composed the vast bulk of those leaving. Maldwyn Jones, a student of the subject, found that it was rare for really well-to-do farmers or the poor to leave. Industrial centers, usually growing at this time, supplied almost no migrants. Those who did leave despaired of their futures. They had not yet been engulfed by poverty but such a prospect seemed entirely possible.[31]

Throughout the rest of the British Isles, similar patterns existed. In Wales, few paupers were included in the emigration streams. Prior to 1850 small farmers and laborers who had not yet reached the "stage of destitution" were much more common. In early nineteenth-century Scotland those deepest in poverty, such as farm tenants, endured on the land and seldom moved. But those with modest capital who saw the potato crop fail in 1846 and cattle prices fall "resolved to emigrate before their means were exhausted."[32]

Just as the scope of German emigration widened as the nineteenth century progressed, British migrants began to come increasingly from poorer, landless ranks of rural dwellers and even industrial workers who now sought to use their acquired skills to either secure higher wages in America when times were good or replace jobs they lost when conditions worsened in Britain. No doubt improved means of transoceanic transportation facilitated the movement as did new railroad links connecting inland and coastal regions on the European continent, but root causes remained linked to structural conditions in the British economy. While some sought economic improvement and vaguely followed the "flow of capital," an equally significant number were simply dislocated from their jobs and resettled in similar American jobs by their unions. The movement was especially strong from South Wales where miners and iron workers moved with increasing frequency especially in times of depression or wage reductions at home. After the McKinley Tariff of 1890 destroyed the monopoly of tin-plating Wales had enjoyed, scores of tinplate workers were brought to the United States to work. Plants in St. Louis and Indianapolis specifically recruited them. When any area of Britain is examined after 1860, urban artisans figured prominently in the emigrant tide.[33]

Sweden, while not replicating the experience of Britain and Germany, showed strong similarities in the social characteristics of its departing citizens. Some early pioneers may have had an upper-class background but most of the nineteenth-century wave prior to 1860 consisted of small farmers, their children who had little prospect of launching agricultural enterprises of their own, and many skilled workers, especially lumbermen, who watched their forest holdings absorbed by timber companies. Not surprisingly, a study of Chicago Swedes in 1880 found over 64 percent in skilled jobs. Again, those too poor to leave, such as farmhands, were less visible in the early currents. In the case of married farmhands, they were not only of little means but often reluctant to abandon yearly contracts. Well-to-do farmers and their children were almost never found among those departing.[34]

The consistency of the patterns observed in Germany, Great Britain, and Sweden was broken, however, in Denmark. Kristian Hvidt found that a vast majority of the Danes came from the agricultural proletariat. Between 1868 and 1900 over 43 percent were rural laborers and 25 percent were urban domestic and industrial workers. Craftsmen (18.5%) comprised a significant portion as always but independent farmers, usually a significant portion in other countries during the early stages of emigration, represented less than 4 percent of the Danish total. Some qualifications might be made concerning Hvidt's conclusions, however, before Denmark is written off as simply an exception. By looking at figures entirely after 1860, Hvidt is inevitably concentrating on a period in which the lower agricultural orders were joining the migration stream in increasing numbers everywhere; his time-frame is inevitably biased against middle-class emigrants who tended to predominate before 1870. Even throughout the period he studied, Hvidt found a constant increase in the number of 15- to 19-year-olds leaving a rural area, indicating the possibility that his "rural laborers" were frequently the children of independent farmers who were unable to acquire farms of their own and who may have left in larger numbers prior to 1860.[35]

One nation that clearly stands as something of an exception to the trends observed in the rest of western Europe is Ireland. Populated more densely than any other European country by the late eighteenth century and possessing much larger proportions of landless laborers, Irish emigration was already intensifying by the 1830s even before the onset of the great potato famine of 1845–48. While a growing number of young adults were unable to inherit land throughout Europe, in Ireland the problem was more acute. Under such circumstances the number of landless and impoverished would inevitably constitute a great portion of the emigrant stream. Because so many were poor in Ireland, emigrants were less likely to be of the "lower middle class" trying to stave off further economic decline. Even among the small Irish landowners, a decline in living standards had already set in prior to the famine as diets came to rely increasingly on the potato. Frequently, pigs were not eaten, for instance, but fed on potatoes and sold to pay the rent.[36]

Despite the markedly poorer condition of the rural Irish, even here a structure of the emigrant mass was still discernible. While the Irish may have had large numbers of immigrants from the lower orders of society, some were inevitably better off than others. Before 1850 those with more resources crossed the Atlantic, while poorer "exiles of Erin" could afford transportation only to England. Not surprisingly, families with young children were more likely to travel to England than America. By the late nineteenth century the proportion of Irish born in London was higher than it was in Philadelphia.[37]

Irish emigration, moreover, not only predated the famine but its rate actually increased during the last half of the nineteenth century after the pressures of the famine had subsided. No doubt the famines years of the late 1840s intensified a trend, but high rents, lack of available industrial opportunities, and evictions, as well as population pressures, continued to plague the Irish. Emigration continued even though, as Robert Kennedy has demonstrated, Irish life expectancy rates were better in rural Ireland than in urban America. In a fashion similar to other regions of northwestern Europe, more single men and women filled the ranks of the emigrants from Ireland the longer the process continued. Although the number of single people was always high among the Irish, by the 1870s the proportion of married emigrants among the Irish coming to America was less than 16 percent. Single people proliferated in the country where marriages were usually postponed due to a severe inability to inherit sufficient amounts of land on which to start a family.[38]

At first glance the composition of the exodus from Austria-Hungary might appear to represent a departure from the profile of northwestern Europe with the possible exception of Ireland, since movement from the empire was broad based and included sizable proportions of agricultural workers and day laborers. These occupational groups represented 20.5 percent of the empire's population in 1910 but about one-half of the emigrant total in that year. Between 1902 and 1911 the largest category of emigrants among the Croatians, Poles (from Galicia), and Slovaks was agricultural day laborers. About 30 percent of the Slovaks, Magyars, and Croats were small independent farmers; their numbers were significant but did not dominate the rural emigrant total. Exceptions proved to be the Czechs and the Jews, whose largest emigrant clusters were to be found in the skilled trades—30 percent for the Jews and 25.5 percent for the Czechs.[39]

Unlike northwestern European countries where the crisis in agriculture struck in the earlier decades of the nineteenth century when unskilled jobs requiring almost no capital or experiences were relatively scarce in America, the forces of industrialization and commercialized agriculture impacted upon most of Austria-Hungary after 1880. Reduced transportation costs and direct links especially to the ports of Bremen and Hamburg combined with lowered entrance requirements in terms of capital and skills to entice emigrants from a broader spectrum of the empire's social structure. This did not mean that the rural crisis was any worse there; small independent farmers still constituted a significant portion and still feared a decline in status. But circumstances were such after 1880 that more could take advantage of emigration as an alternative to their economic status. Thus all emigrants to America in the late nineteenth century tended to move toward industrial jobs and wages, regardless of whether they came from Ireland, Germany, England, Galicia, or Croatia.[40]

Some historians still maintain that it was the "middle peasants" who left the rural regions of the empire first as they did from northwestern Europe. But intensive local studies of the rural regions of northern Hungary and Slovakia have shown that from the beginning cotters, day laborers, shepherds, and even miners were leaving. One study of Slovakia found the earliest stirrings of overseas migration depended not so much on social status as the proximity of villages to main transportation routes. In Hungary, moreover, by 1905 only 10 to 15 percent of those departing were independent farmers while over one-half were farmhands or day laborers. Subsequent evidence will suggest that these groups may have been the sons of landowners unable to inherit anything of consequence. Independent artisans and merchants combined for less than 4 percent of the emigrants in the 1899–1913 period. At the same time in Croatia independent farmers accounted for almost one-half of the departures while day laborers represented over one-third. As in other late nineteenth-century streams, moreover, skilled workers were much in evidence. They actually predominated in Bohemia, which was already industrializing, and like their English and German counterparts sought to translate their industrial skills into higher wages or stave off a decline. Their exodus was heavy enough in Prague to generate complaints about labor shortages by the 1890s.[41]

[19

Jews from Eastern Europe constituted nearly 98 percent of all Jews coming to America by 1903. Originating from unusual circumstances, many had fled poverty, persecution, and overcrowding in the Jewish Pale, a sprawling area to which Jews were restricted and which stretched from Lithuania through Congress Poland and the Ukraine. Jews from this area were unable to own land and tended to concentrate in urban skills and trades, thus their emigrant ranks seldom contained small landowners or agricultural laborers. Nevertheless, some structure did characterize their flight from Europe. Jews tended to leave more in family units, an indication of the permanency of their move. Skilled workers accounted for 64 percent of the Jews from 1899 to 1914 from the Pale. From Austria-Hungary, from 1902 to 1911, 38 percent were skilled tradesmen, while less than 1 percent were from professions and about 1 percent were independent farmers. Simon Kuznets discovered that the movement from commercial-agricultural pursuits was less because Jews in these professions had an intimate knowledge of cattle and grains in the Russian market which had little transferable value to America.[42] Even among Jews, however, evidence exists that among the very poor emigration was as difficult as it was for the lowest stratum of other groups. In Galicia many who could not make sufficient earnings from their trades took menial jobs to avoid hunger. In Turek County Jews who broke stones on road-building jobs, in some villages those who cut and transported wood from the forest to railway stations, and in the village of Limanowa those who engaged in tanning were unable to muster the resources to emigrate.[43]

The image of poor peasants fleeing to America has also dominated much of the scholarship on Italian emigrants but closer analysis reveals that the very poor seldom left. For instance, the average yearly wages in Abruzzi e Molise and Calabria were well above those in Tuscany and Lombardy, and yet emigration was heavier from the former provinces than the latter. Usually those who left were in the middle and lower-middle levels of the peasantry. Supplementing this stream was a characteristic segment of artisans, craftsmen, and others with skills which were increasingly difficult to implement in societies undergoing either a commercialization in agriculture or growing competition with manufactured goods.[44]

The pattern is confirmed in a spate of contemporary works. A study of Italians in three American cities—Rochester, Utica, and Kansas City—concluded that those most likely to emigrate were agriculturalists or townsmen who had a "stake in society" in the form of a skill or a parcel of land. Lower strata day laborers were among the least likely to leave. In fact, an analysis of Sicilian passports between 1901 and 1914 by historian John Briggs found 54 percent of the adult males leaving nonagricultural operations such as fishermen or skilled tradesmen.[45] Not surprisingly, areas in Italy characterized by wide distribution of landownership and, therefore, many small landowners were more likely to send emigrants than regions where large estates employed the poor and the landless, although this explanation was not always valid throughout Europe.[46]

The "agro-towns" which supplied small landowners also sent skilled Italians. Immigrants of artisanal or petty merchant background came to New York City, for instance, in above average numbers. In the village of Sambuca artisans and petty merchants were only one-sixth of the family heads but represented a quarter of the town's emigrants. From Abruzzi e Molise, a region of heavy Italian emigration, over one-half of those leaving were from construction and excavation trades. And the figure for these trades among departures from Sicily and Calabria was over 30 percent.[47]

Poles departed Europe not only from Galicia but from Congress Poland and Prussian Poland as well. Even from these areas the general pattern was consistent with the rest of the continent. Initial waves which originated in Prussia in the 1870s consisted of small landowners and artisans who moved in family units, although a number of farmhands did join this movement. Subsequent movement from Russian Poland and Galicia intensified after 1890 and continued strong until World War I. As with other waves at the turn of the century, the tendency of agricultural workers and day laborers to join the small farmers and craftsmen had become considerably more pronounced. By 1908, for instance, about two-thirds of all males leaving Galicia were agricultural laborers and about 7 percent were trained craftsmen. By 1912 about one-half of all emigrants from Congress Poland were landless, about 20 percent had factory skills, and 27 percent were peasant landowners. As in Austria-Hungary, a much greater segment of the Polish and other European groups of emigrants, in contrast to northwestern Europe, had yet to own land of their own.[48]

Generalizations about Polish emigration are difficult because, of course, the land was divided by Germany, Russia, and Austria-Hungary. Conditions differed especially between regions such as Silesia, which was experiencing rapid industrialization, and Galicia, which was heavily rural and suffering from growing parcelization of land. By 1900 dislocated Poles in Prussia could move into nearby industrial cities while those in Galicia were more inclined to migrate abroad. Despite countless individual variations, however, enough evidence does exist to suggest that regardless of region, Poles of the upper class failed to emigrate because little was available for them in any other place, and they preferred not to decline into manual labor. As elsewhere, the very poor seldom left as well. Franciszek Bujak's valuable studies of Polish villages showed clearly that rural villages could be highly stratified with many in "good" or "marginal" economic conditions willing to migrate. Those at the bottom in abject poverty, however, remained fixed to their homes.[49]

Although Europe supplied the vast majority of American immigrants prior to World War II, significant other sources had begun to emerge which would provide the foundation for much larger movements in the period after World War I. Turn-of-the-century Mexico, a major source of emigrant labor prior to 1920, reflected many of the characteristics of European agricultural regions. The origins of emigration were located in central Mexico where the vast portion of the population, perhaps as much as 80 percent, lived in small, communally owned villages called *ejidos*, which provided enough food for self-sufficiency. As railroad connections with the north appeared in the 1890s, however, pressure on communal lands mounted from eager owners of large estates, or haciendas. These politically powerful individuals began to see the potential in commercial agriculture for export. They were particularly excited by the commercial possibilities of coffee and sugar and began to acquire more of the arable land, sometimes creating estates of over 40,000 acres and driving peasants from their *ejidos*. Many peasants declined into debt peonage on large estates or migrated to Mexican cities. The government of Porfirio Diaz, influenced by large owners, deprived the *ejidatarios* of their land. European immigrants were enticed with offers of "public" land in hopes of stimulating more capitalistic agriculture even while native peasants were increasingly dispossessed and impoverished. By 1910, in many central Mexican states, an average of 98 percent of the families held no land at all.[50]

Like areas undergoing the commercialization of agriculture in Europe, a migration stream began to emerge in Mexico. At first, it consisted mostly of small peasant proprietors or their sons who sought extra earnings to buy more land, the key ingredient to becoming a commercial farmer. The dispossessed who could not earn enough to pay food prices, which had been rising as many staples were in shorter supply due to a concentration on cash crops for export, moved elsewhere. They moved first to central Mexican cities, such as Monterey or Mexico City. But more and more began to move to northern Mexican areas, such as Sonora and Chihuahua, when mining operations were opened and rail lines extended southward. In these northern regions, migrants from central Mexico first learned of American wages and employment opportunities and began to expand their migration routes north of the border.[51]

By the late nineteenth century commercial agriculture also began to influence rural Asia. Wealthy landowners in Japan began consolidating their holdings and consequently expropriating the land of the less fortunate, a process which accentuated social stratification in many villages. By the later Tokugawa period many peasants were forced to sell their land and become servants or tenants on large estates, although there, as elsewhere, the very poorest tended not to emigrate. At this time the percentage of rented land to total arable land increased from 29 percent in 1872 to 46 percent by 1930. Instances of infanticide were recorded as children became insupportable. Emigration also increased from rural villages even as early as the 1850s, especially among sons unable to succeed their fathers on the land.[52]

A final point concerning the nature of the emigrant wave to America needs to be emphasized. Those departing not only tended to be concentrated in the middle and lower-middle ranks of society but scattered findings indicate that individuals who made the longest moves tended to be more literate than those who moved only short distances or who did not move at all. Among Swedes the greater the illiteracy the shorter the distance the migrant moved. In Hungary 41 percent of the entire population was illiterate and yet among Slovaks who emigrated the rate was only 22 percent and only 11.4 percent among departing Magyars. Studies of Irish newcomers to Canada confirm the trend. While about 54 percent of the inhabitants of Ireland could neither read nor write in the 1840s, the figure was only 20 percent in a Canadian sample of 1861.[53]

The Spread of Commercial Agriculture

It was no accident that emigrants tended to come from specific regions and sectors of the social structure. Throughout the nineteenth century the same forces of industrial expansion and urban growth which were transforming America were also affecting the emigrants' homelands. Even in rural lands, where social and economic change was less apparent, the nature of agriculture could be rapidly transformed from an emphasis on subsistence to one on production for export to distant urban markets. Indeed, wherever ag-

[23

riculture tended to become commercial and affect existing patterns of landownership, the beginnings of mass emigration became visible.

After the late eighteenth century, in much of central and eastern Europe, the old order of nobles and peasants rapidly gave way. Pushed aside aggressively by the rising power of the state, nobles could no longer count on the loyalty or subservience of the peasantry, who now looked more kindly upon the government and monarch responsible for granting them emancipation from their servile conditions and the first opportunity many ever had to own land of their own. Emancipation moved relentlessly eastward from Denmark in 1788 to Bavaria in 1808, to Hungary in 1848, to Russia and Poland in 1861. It is true that peasants, in order to gain their newly won freedom, were sometimes forced to pay indemnifications to their former superiors in the form of dues, labor, or land and these payments added to the peasants' tax burden. In Prussia peasants redeemed some thirty million days of service between the decree of 1807 and the end of the century, while in places like Hungary there was no indemnity at all. And emancipation did not always lead directly to landholding. In fact, except in Poland and Romania, emancipation measures made no provisions for cotters and landless workers.[54]

Even after emancipation was an accomplished fact, landowning was not always an inevitability, although the possibility was certainly more real. For years after emancipation, peasants paid a full land tax, while nobles were assessed at a lower rate or no rate at all in Denmark, Prussia, Russia, and Romania. In order to achieve fiscal stability, new leaders of the Meiji Regime in Japan transformed the traditional feudal tenure in land into private property rights. Taxes had to be paid, however, on the newly owned land and for many the burden became great enough to force them to sell or even to migrate. In some areas of Poland and Romania peasants were limited in the extent they could subdivide their holdings, a move designed to hinder excessive fragmentation or concentration of land. Such measures, however, could further inhibit younger peasants from acquiring land of their own.[55]

Emancipation did not always stem from a simple rise of the state. As industrialization proceeded over Europe, internal pressures increased in rural areas to maximize the efficiency of agricultural production in order to meet the demands of growing urban markets. It soon became quite clear that the old peasant-noble order was something of an obstacle to improved agriculture, however, with its array of rights and obligations. Indeed, in central Europe it was the slow pace of agricultural production in the 1830s and 1840s which led to growing support for the abolishment of serfdom from large owners themselves. Thus it was not surprising to discover that emancipation was carried out without destroying large estates and, ironically, often fostered their proliferation in subsequent years for they were indispensable for efficient, large-scale commercial agriculture. In Hungary, consequently, 53 percent of the land remained in the hands of big landowners. In Austria and Bohemia, where industrialization was accelerating by the end of the eighteenth century, large estates moved even faster toward commercialization making it more difficult for the small landowner to acquire sufficient property. The Hungarian scholar, Julianna Puskás, has estimated that by 1900 only 30 percent of the Hungarian peasantry owned enough land to assure an independent existence.[56]

The movement toward commercial agriculture in Austria-Hungary as elsewhere rested on an expanding knowledge of agricultural improvements. In 1863 only 194 steam engines could be found on Hungarian farms. Eight years later the number had climbed to nearly 3,000. More crop rotation was used on large farms, and plowing was improved by the introduction of steam plows and methods of deeper plowing. Crops were being restricted to cash staples such as corn and wheat, and by the late nineteenth century the time required to complete the harvest declined from about 40–60 days to 14–21 days. Small landowners who had less access to credit and knowledge of agricultural improvements found it difficult to compete in this process.[57] The fact that east central Europe provided a full 20 percent of all Eurpoean wheat products by 1914 was an indication that its economies were steadily concentrating on staples for export. In regions such as Galicia, where landholdings had proliferated drastically, even large owners found it difficult to gain additional holdings because demand had driven land prices so high. Many were forced to sell off parts of their holdings to larger peasant landowners in order to stave off ruin and eschew their plans for commercial expansion. In his valuable study of the village of Liminowa, Franciszek Bujak found that the price of one *morg* (6,578 square yards) climbed steadily from 400 crowns in 1870 to 1,200 crowns in 1900. So strong was the desire for ownership that peasants from neighboring villages were even establishing farms within Liminowa itself. Townsmen with no land leased it from peasant-owners and cultivated and harvested it. After 1885 even peasant holders were learning about the use of fertilizers and increasing the amount of arable land. Indeed, the number of real estate transactions was considerable, doubling between 1880 and 1900 and amounting to over 300,000 crowns in Liminowa alone. Families with small holdings had particular difficulty in passing land on to off-spring because excessive divisions lowered the value too greatly. If a property had debts and inheritors were unable to pay them off, the house was usually bought by a Jew in Liminowa and the land by a Christian. The heir was usually forced to leave the village.[58]

In some cases in Austria-Hungary peasants resisted agricultural improvements due to entrenched conservatism. This was true especially in Bosnia-Hercegovina after 1886. But generally smaller landholders attempted to adopt the improvements used by the large estates, though they seldom had the resources in land or cash to compete economically. In Slovenia, pushed by large holders, provincial agricultural societies took an active role in fostering modern farming methods on smaller holdings. The government of Carniola pursued vigorous efforts to improve the quality of livestock through breeding control programs and when the capital outlay required for new machinery was too large, machine cooperatives were established, such as the Farm Society of Carniola.[59]

In Prussia emancipation also stimulated land fever among the lower and higher orders of societies. Again it was large owners who were most successful in acquiring estates sufficient for commercial production. By 1880 they were so successful that fully 80 percent of the agricultural population of Prussia were wage earners working for large estates or migrating to industrial areas of Silesia. In fact, the monopolizing of the land by a few made intergenerational transfer of land very difficult in Prussia and caused entire families, Germans and Poles, to emigrate. In Congress Poland and Galicia the parceling of land proceeded much further than in Prussia, in part because fewer restrictions existed against the division of holdings by parents among their children.[60]

Where large estate owners emerged and predominated as in Poznań, the products of small farmers were usually displaced in local produce markets since they tended to be more expensive. Large producers were not only preempting the export trade and most of the good land, but their excess was even undermining the local markets of small producers. Invariably the small owner was forced to look elsewhere either to supplement his income or to support himself entirely. Fifty-eight percent of the owners in Poznań with less than five hectares were forced to seek outside income and, consequently, they created the major source of "labor for industry" in the region. Between 1871 and 1905 over 300,000 persons emigrated from the Poznań area to other regions of Prussia, especially Brandenburg and Berlin.[61]

26]

Throughout the whole of Germany the movement toward large estates proceeded inexorably. Sometimes entire villages burdened by debts sold their communal lands to large landholders and departed with the profits. An expanding population here as elsewhere was squeezed out by "snowballing estates" of large owners, and many formerly independent peasants became wage laborers. In 1846, for instance, 40 percent of the Hesse-Darmstadt emigrants were wage laborers and only 20 percent were independent peasants. This process was especially acute in vast grain producing regions such as East Elbia where pressure mounted on smaller landholding peasants to maintain their holdings and compete. Some, of course, resisted the loss of land by turning to nonagricultural sidelines in regional craft industries or nearby factories in Silesia. In these fertile districts peasants cultivated little or no cash crops because they could afford neither the seeds, the necessary agricultural improvements, or additional land.[62]

In Italy and Mexico peasants fared little better as agriculture became increasingly commercial throughout the nineteenth century. In the Mexican state of Jalisco, which probably produced more immigrants to Los Angeles than any other, much land was turned over to the growth of corn for export and private entrepreneurs expropriated massive amounts of communal land. An 1806 Italian law encouraged the division of public lands among serfs, but it was rarely enforced. In a pattern which was now quite familiar, groups of large estate owners, possessing more leverage with the state, were able to expand, while small independent owners and the *contadini* obtained inferior land because they lacked capital or sold out to wealthier owners all together. By the late nineteenth century, large estates *(latifondi)* were increasingly important in the economy. In Sicily, which was a source of large numbers of emigrants, a long history of exporting grain had existed prior to the nineteenth century and close ties had been nurtured with the economy of the industrial world. But as population grew and industrialization expanded, elite agriculturalists fell back on their traditional role of exporting. Unlike those in many other regions, most of the Sicilian landed-elite resisted modern agriculture and other modern institutions, such as a strong central government. Prisoners of their past, they continued to harvest without fertilizers or machinery and to transport goods from the interior to the coast by mule train. Sicilian wheat consequently became less competitive, and the importation of cheap manufactured goods eventually displaced local crafts. At the same time her domestic agriculture was failing to modernize,

[27

Sicily was feeling the effects of agricultural commercialization elsewhere and was soon exporting less wheat and more people. Between 1876 and 1925, 1.5 million individuals left Sicily, although about one-third actually returned and tried to use new agricultural methods, despite worsening conditions.[63]

In some respects Ireland's agricultural history would appear to stand as an exception to the rest of Europe. Due to political domination by England, Irish agriculture was not entirely free to modernize. Large amounts of land were in the hands of middlemen, who subdivided their plots and rented or sold for short-term gains. By the 1840s about one-half the holdings in Ireland were below the minimum needed to maintain a sufficient income—usually about five acres. Even the process of agricultural improvement and consolidation, which occurred in Germany and Austria-Hungary, was generally retarded in Ireland. Some commercialization did take place but on a smaller scale than in other countries. In fact, the British corn laws in the 1840s, which ended preferential treatment for Irish grain in British markets, resulted in a decrease in the amount of tilled land in Ireland. A consequence of less land in tillage was a drop in the demand for rural labor. When this decline combined with the over-division of Irish holdings, a lack of domestic coal and iron, and the fact that domestic industrial development was severely arrested by Britain, the rural Irish were ready for emigration. The potato famine only accelerated a process which would have taken place anyhow.[64]

In nearby Great Britain, agricultural development was much closer to that of the rest of Europe than to Ireland with a steady movement taking place toward holdings large enough to make scientific farming practicable. New techniques improved agricultural efficiency to the point where the demand for agricultural labor decreased. In Cornwall, landed gentry after the Napoleonic Wars began to see that larger profits could accumulate if tenancy agreements were made with a few large farmers rather than hundreds of small renters. In the Lowlands of Scotland the process was particularly pronounced. Improvements were introduced into Scottish agriculture almost continuously after 1775. The acreage under plow was always being extended and the yield per acre doubled during the nineteenth century. Livestock yielded a much larger proportion of farm income. Whereas small families had viewed 5 to 15 acres as a desirable minimum for survival, profit-oriented commercial farmers now sought at least seventy acres and some who reached 600 acres did not hesitate to evict tenants to attain it. On these larger tracts gradually appeared multiple plow teams and even threshing machines.[65]

In some areas the commercialization of agriculture did not proceed very quickly at all and emigration was either retarded or stimulated at a later date when land became hopelessly subdivided. Austrian trade barriers in Galicia frustrated extensive commercialization in that region by extensive subdivision. Galician Poles, for instance, emigrated but only after their brothers from Prussia and Russian Poland had. In the Ukrainian province of Kharkov, peasants showed little inclination to work more than was needed for their subsistence needs, since export crops were not yet possible. In areas of the Balkans such as Serbia proper and Bulgaria, governments emphasized military preparedness and even national expansion rather than agricultural developments, and thus relatively little emigration took place.[66]

The commercialization of agriculture in Scotland and elsewhere did lead to some opportunities for a few rural workers, but it generally lowered the levels of agricultural employment. The use of more plow teams meant that the job of plowmen became highly prized and insured a lifetime of employment. But the use of the thresher and improved roads led ultimately to lower labor requirements during harvests and reduced costs in the transportation of goods to market.[67]

Ironically, despite the lowered demand for farm labor in the lands undergoing commercialization, they were nearly always characterized by a labor shortage. The fact that agricultural wages rose in nineteenth-century Scotland was not an indication that conditions for rural workers were improving, but rather it was evidence that agricultural labor was in short supply and large owners had to bid higher to fill the fewer jobs still available. This situation sometimes led to the importation of agricultural labor into areas which were sending emigrants to America at the same time. Large farms in Scotland imported Irish laborers for the summer and harvest periods.[68] Admittedly, available jobs were more often seasonal tasks on the estates rather than permanent sources of income, but they were proliferating at a time when the young work force best suited to perform them was leaving.

The combination of labor shortages, rising wages, and emigration existed throughout Europe. Because of these shortages many governments, influenced by agricultural and mercantile interests, both of which had an interest in keeping wages down by keeping population levels high, pursued expansionist population policies. In Elbia large landowners lobbied for measures which would lead to a large supply of cheap labor. In Austria-Hungary large landowners were continually complaining about a dearth of labor, even though their own practices of bringing in more machinery and devoting more land to commercial crops were driving away the native supply of toilers. One great estate owner in Bukovina complained that all his peasants had emigrated and "we sit here completely without workers and must spend a lot of money to bring people from Russia and Rumania." Indeed, labor shortages prevailed in Bohemia, Moravia, and Upper and Lower Austria. The shift to capital-intensive land use was not accompanied by a movement to more labor-intensive agriculture.[69]

Those that could work, of course, often benefited from the wage increases. In Germany between 1850 and 1913 the wages of agricultural labor rose 127 percent even as thousands emigrated. In Kalisz, Suwalki, and Plock, three centers of Polish emigration to America, wage scales rose continuously for men and women. In Kalisz the scale for a day's wage was double that for the rest of the country. Bujak found that in the village of Maszkienice the day's wage for a field worker increased 80 percent and that of threshers 125 percent between 1899 and 1911.[70] In Limanowa he discovered that the cost of farm labor had risen considerably after 1885. This rise was due not only to the shortages created by emigration but to a newfound desire on the part of town dwellers to avoid field labor if they could and hire someone else to do it. "No townsfolk will work with a scythe and sickle in the field," he observed.[71]

Capitalism and Craftsmen

While the development of commercial agriculture was a clear sign that world capitalism was creeping into rural and less developed regions, it was usually not the first. Commercial agriculture ultimately affected the greatest number of individuals and forced millions to consider emigration. But the very first emigrants from Germany, Italy, Poland, Hungary, and elsewhere were often displaced craftsmen and artisans who were smaller in numbers but significant in establishing patterns of movement that many of their rural countrymen would follow. In the transition from feudalism to capitalism, craftsmen in small towns and even rural dwellers who manufactured crafts by hand for supplemental income faced increasing competition from cheaper goods produced in factories. The transportation which linked cities to rural regions not only took emigrants out but also began to bring in mass-produced goods. By the early 1800s a spectacular increase in cottage production was evident throughout Europe as peasants tried to supply expanding urban markets and recover lost income from their declining ability to sell crops.

What they could not know, of course, was that the process of industrial and factory production which promised to give them new markets was simultaneously undermining their craft endeavors by mass-producing goods more cheaply.[72]

The displacement of rural or village craftsman was usually a first sign that links with industrial-capital markets—a prerequisite for the commercialization of agriculture—were beginning. By the 1830s the Black Forest clock industry in southern Germany was destroyed, causing many impoverished craftsmen to consider moving elsewhere. By 1825 industrialization was forcing skilled British artisans to move internally and even overseas. Crowds of English miners arrived in eastern Pennsylvania coalfields in the 1820s. Several decades later skilled British textile workers left Britain for America because they were either displaced or recruited by American industry. English and Scottish weavers, bricklayers, carpenters, painters, and stonecutters even began a seasonal migration to the United States to help make ends meet. Tailors, pottery makers, and metalworkers in Sweden began to move in greater numbers by the 1860s.[73]

Early German emigration prior to 1860 originated not only in the southwest but in northwestern regions as well. Common to all northwestern areas of heavy emigration was a well-developed cottage linen industry carried on by the rural lower class on a part-time basis which was now being weakened by machine competition. In the district of Munster, emigrants tended to come from the ranks of the lower class and agricultural labor which had been subsisting on a combination of small agriculture and small cottage production. This population movement had few, if any, ties to the changing agricultural or landholding patterns; it was related almost directly to fluctuations in the market for linen goods.[74]

Among East European Jews, of course, a huge concentration of craftsmen existed because Jews were seldom able to own property and enter agriculture. Since Jewish cobblers, tailors, blacksmiths, carpenters, and bakers depended on the economic well-being of villages and towns, a decline in the agricultural fortunes of others threatened Jewish craftsmen as well. Combined with the inroads of factory production, Jews were desperate by the 1880s. In Lodz, cotton factories emerged which mass-produced woolens and in Czestochowa even toys were produced in factories. Jewish craftsmen could either flock to these Polish cities to work, which many did, or emigrate abroad. Historian Moses Rischin has written that the introduction of the Singer Sewing Machine was forcing many Jewish women to work as seamstresses even in Europe. By 1890 Jews were 28 percent of all factory hands in Poland. In Russian Poland, the government became so anxious to promote industrialization that it encouraged the inmigration of skilled Germans. Bujak found declines in Galician villages in the number of shoemakers, tailors, printers, and butchers between 1880 and 1900 among Christians and Jews. Rural traders and shopkeepers were also in difficulty and being forced to travel more and more into the countryside to compete with larger shops in towns, which carried more mass-produced goods and sold them cheaply. Not surprisingly the first to emigrate from Hungary were well-to-do German merchants from southern and western regions. They were soon joined by tanners, weavers, and blacksmiths. Destitute day laborers were also in difficulty but many lacked the means to pay for intended travel. Even in distant Japan, imports after 1860 began to displace rural women who had supplemented their families' income.[75]

An implication of pinpointing specific segments of the old world social structure which were likely to supply emigrants should not go unnoticed. Emigrants left societies which were not composed of undifferentiated masses of impoverished people but were carefully structured along layers of ranks and hierarchies based on wealth and skill. The world the emigrants left was neither monolithic nor homogeneous, with rank usually determined by the size of landholdings. After emancipation, landholdings were increasingly subdivided and peasants were cast into an almost infinite hierarchy of holdings from full, to three-quarters, one-half, and even one-quarter parcels. Cotters who had a house and a yard and landless laborers who worked on larger estates held positions below all landowners, and at the bottom, servants and hired hands toiled for those more prosperous.[76]

This general structure of preindustrial society throughout much of Europe often was more complex from region to region. In Ukrainian villages, peasants were often differentiated by the amount of work animals they owned. The structure in Italy was just as intricate. For southern Italy the *signori*, or large landowners, stood atop society. Just below them were found a professional class consisting mostly of merchants. Afterwards in descending order came small shopkeepers and artisans, and peasants or *contadini*, who were further stratified into countless levels according to landownership and family reputation. One electoral list from Sicily categorized merchants and artisans by the products they sold or made and peasants by their contractual relation to the land or the type of farm work they did. A sample of occupations from the passports of emigrating Sicilians further reinforces the image of an intricate social structure. While *contadini* represented the largest percentage of those emigrating (36%), also to be

A View of Zabludów, Poland, 1916
Rural villages such as this one in Poland slowly became
connected to a world economy through transportation
routes, trade, and commercial agriculture. *YIVO Institute
for Jewish Research*

found were *bracciani* or farm laborers, fishermen, and skilled tradesmen.[77] An equally complex structure was found in Austrian society
with rankings progressing upward from an "agrarian proletariat" at
the bottom of society consisting of servants, laborers, and the landless
to an "agricultural administrative body" at the top which managed
large farming operations. In some villages various social strata frequently used different streets to conduct their daily travel. In
Limanowa, Bujak asked the town's residents themselves to identify
the local system of stratification. He was informed that the groups
included the "rich, wealthy, middle-class, lower-class, and paupers."
The chief criteria for sorting out the population was yearly income
with paupers earning almost nothing and the wealthiest earning as
much as 2,400 crowns a year. By 1900 only 10 percent of Limanowa's
inhabitants lived above the middle-class level and 58 percent found

themselves in the lower-middle class, the group most likely to emigrate.[78]

An Expanding Population

While the transformation of agriculture and the dislocation of crafts were crucial in explaining the movement of people from rural regions to industrial ones, a simultaneous process usually characterized emigrant homelands whose origins and links to immigration are less clear. Historians have not fully explained why during the century after 1750, throughout Europe especially, population levels were growing very rapidly. They were growing at the same time that large estates expanded to create an unprecedented demand for land which was best suited for agriculture. Some exceptions existed, to be sure. France stagnated somewhat, and Ireland experienced an actual population decline during the nineteenth century.[79] The Irish decline, it should be noted, was attributable not only to the potato famine but also to a system of primogeniture which restricted the number of children who could eventually hope to inherit land of their own. Many children delayed marriages waiting for their inheritance, a move which constricted the length of female fertility. Others, with no hope of receiving land, simply left or remained celibate.[80]

While the causes of the European population rise are complex, most likely the factors varied somewhat from region to region. Some have argued that agricultural changes improved diets, and the population consequently became more resistant to infectious diseases, the main cause of death at the time. Mortality rates did decline everywhere and improved transportation helped distribute food more widely and stave off famine during years of poor harvest. Population growth rates had increased before, in the thirteenth and sixteenth centuries, for instance, but now the growth was sustained over a much longer period of time.[81]

Population expansion, of course, had distinct implications for peasant families and farms throughout Europe. Such farms relied mainly on family labor to work the land. Even in preindustrial peasant families, however, recent evidence has made it clear that some birth control was practiced within marriages and families frequently sought to control their numbers. Many did this by remaining unmarried for a longer while. In fact, apparently a higher proportion of the population of western Europe remained unmarried in the eighteenth and nineteenth centuries than in the eastern sectors of the continent.[82]

Where the population grew and no commensurate increase took place in arable land, farms, of course, would get smaller. If partible inheritance was practiced with land passing to all the sons or children, individual holdings became smaller and inadequate to sustain agriculture. Where primogeniture was prevelant and only the oldest son inherited the land, less subdivision occurred but the future prospects for younger children in agriculture still remained precarious especially if they could not obtain larger plots in the era of agricultural commercialization. Failure to gain sufficient land in the midst of this population growth forced individuals either to work as tenants or to emigrate. Population increases further complicated the futures of younger farmers; more people seeking land invariably escalated its price. Thus, in nineteenth-century England the agricultural population began to sort itself into three broad categories: those who owned land but did not farm it themselves, tenant farmers who rented the land from the owners, and agricultural laborers who were paid wages but lacked much land themselves. Almost unrepresented in this structure was the small landowning, self-sufficient farmer who was becoming an endangered species in much of nineteenth-century rural Europe. Indeed, overpopulation could often be detected through such signs as rises in tenancy, pauperism, and especially seasonal and permanent migration.[83]

A microscopic examination of four English villages offers a more precise view of the impact of capitalism in the form of manufactured goods and commercialized agricultural production upon rural societies, the societies most emigrants left, and its potential relationship with the advance in population. Some evidence exists to believe that during the transition from feudalism to capitalism long-established constraints on family formation, which had helped to maintain something of a demographic equilibrium, were weakened. Fewer reasons to postpone marriages existed because inheritances were becoming less likely all together. As the number of tenants, laborers, and migrant workers grew, individuals simply had no incentive for delaying marriages and thus childbearing was initiated at an earlier age and over a longer period of time, a phenomenon which inevitably produced higher fertility rates. Even children of craftsmen were now more likely to be cast adrift on their own. As more individuals became proletarian in either industry or agriculture, they became economically independent at an earlier age, if not more economically stable. Communal restraints were weakened, although as subsequent evidence will suggest, they could be reimposed in industrial society.[84]

An easy temptation exists to attribute emigration's underlying

[35

causes to this demographic revolution but this would obscure the complexity of the relationship between an emerging capitalism and its links to rural societies. Indeed, it is quite possible, as indicated above, that demographic growth was another component to this process. What is certain is the extent of the population growth. In Great Britain in just over a century, from 1801 to 1911, the population quadrupled. From 34 million inhabitants in 1843, the population of Germany practically doubled by 1913 and life expectancy at birth rose a full 24 years in the six decades after 1870, primarily because of lower infant mortality rates. Yet rural overcrowding in itself seldom led directly to mass emigration, as Ireland in the 1830s, Hungary in the 1880s, and Greece in the 1890s illustrates.[85]

It is worth noting that in some areas of western Europe, such as Germany, fertility rates did begin to moderate and actually decline during the last two decades of the nineteenth century, through populations kept increasing because of the earlier growth and the even greater declines in infant mortality. Although the decline in fertility rates began initially in urban areas, it spread to rural areas as well. Individuals in urban occupations led the decline and those in mining and agriculture lagged behind. Fertility was also correspondingly declining in upper social strata as compared to lower classes. This trend, however, did not immediately alleviate the problems in rural areas, such as eastern Germany in the 1870s, which were likely to send emigrants to urban places. These areas were usually the last to experience fertility declines, a hint that fertility rises, like emigrants themselves, may have originated in rural areas undergoing transition. These regions were much slower to accept fertility limitations and were still embracing the newfound ability to initiate families earlier. John Knodel found that fertility consistently declined in Germany in areas where primary industries and agriculture declined and manufacturing enterprises rose. Employment of women outside of agriculture invariably increased in such areas and, thus, an inverse relationship was established between the level of fertility and rise of "secondary or tertiary" industries. In Italy, fertility declines were noticed first in late-nineteenth-century cities of Lombardy and Tuscany, where prolonged periods of breast feeding were initiated among the wealthier classes to hinder additional conceptions.[86]

Prior to the decline in Germany, and we can suggest elsewhere, strong reasons exist to believe that the process of emancipation, which stimulated more family formations as long as the supply of land held out, and agricultural commercialization moved fertility to higher levels. In Prussia after emancipation many new family holdings were created. Many peasant children were forced to live as independent laborers or work as farmhands but even here family formation was possible, for their labor was in demand either on large estates or in expanding industrial towns.[87]

In eastern Europe population growth also began to accelerate but usually later in the nineteenth century. Between 1800 and 1910 Austria-Hungary and Russia more than doubled their population. Russian Poland increased its inhabitants by 179 percent in the four decades prior to 1900, especially in the villages. Of course, industrialization and commercial agriculture reached this region later than western Europe. Not surprisingly population growth (and emigration) was found to be more pronounced in regions of cereal production where grains could be grown for export rather than in hill districts where commercial agriculture was difficult. In Romania, between 1859 and 1879, for instance, population climbed by 42 percent in hill counties, while it increased by 77 percent in counties on the plains. The newly established links to capitalist markets stimulated expansion of farms, thus making it more difficult for sons of small landholders to remain in farming by starting enterprises of their own. New employment possibilities appeared on the large estates or in industrial areas and regional towns. The upshot was that families could be started at an earlier age, since means of support (jobs) were easily accessible; a delay in marriage plans for an eventual inheritance became unnecessary.[88]

Again local studies are instructive. In the Galician village of Limanowa, the population was fairly stagnant between 1800 and 1860 but rose considerably during the next four decades. Local records indicated that the Christian population increased 53 percent during the six decades after 1840, while the Jewish population grew by a staggering 663 percent. From a population of 787 in 1841, Limanowa inhabitants numbered 1,790 by 1900. This growth stemmed not only from a rising Jewish birth rate but in-migration from the surrounding rural regions. Bujak attributed the higher Jewish birth rate in part to their pattern of earlier marriages, a phenomenon which would be partially explained by the fact that few owned land and thus children were not forced to delay marriages for the sake of inheritances. Not surprisingly Christians, who usually married later, had higher rates of illegitimacy (6 percent of all births). As expected, Bujak was able to prove that the emigration rate of Jews, with higher fertility rates, exceeded those of Christians from the village.[89]

[37

The Adaptive Household

In the specific regions of high emigration and among the social categories which were inclined to move, landholding changes and increases in population brought tremendous pressures upon individuals to seek either alternative places to live or at least to obtain a temporary means of supplemental income. But this should not be construed as a suggestion that emigrants were simply being forced off the land and prevented from selecting any options. In fact, they proved to be calculating people, quite able to make realistic decisions about their present and future. At times they could be reactionary and defiantly reconstruct an imaginary peasant world of colorful costumes and gay music in the face of sweeping social change. But more often their behavior was rational and pragmatic. They frequently organized voluntary associations and credit cooperatives. Emigration itself was a rational act often done in spite of official opposition from the government. And they remained pragmatic because one context of their world did not entirely change despite the economic transformation they were experiencing. Individuals still lived within the orbit of family responsibilities.

As individuals faced the new demands created by changes in landholding patterns, work opportunities, and population pressures, they usually did not make decisions alone but in the context of a family or household. If emigration was tied to specific regions and social categories, it was also linked to the goals of household groups who sought to adjust to shifting social and economic realities. If an understanding of the emigrant world is to be reached, the pull of familial obligation must be defined.

Families were not only the center of economic production in most preindustrial lands, they were the focus of life itself. In religion, in love, in work, and in all of life, perceptions existed and decisions were made primarily in family terms. As one study of Italian villages concluded, "Le Famiglia" was at the center of Italian life. Families were not only biological arrangements facilitating procreation and socialization but society's basic mode of economic organization in the preindustrial land.[90]

While the actual structure of family life often differed in the premigration lands, nearly all family forms pursued economic well-being under a particular system of order and authority. In Hungary, power resided, for instance, in the male head. No one was permitted to contradict him. He guarded and managed the money even in households of extended kin and his wife could direct the work of a daughter-in-law. Property, moreover, was nearly always identified with a family unit rather than an individual, and in many regions prohibitions existed against its division not only to insure sufficient land for agriculture but to preserve the integrity of the family production unit. Because of economic conditions, families had to organize hierarchical structures and assign roles and duties on a systematic basis in order to insure the family's existence. Consequently, children were used on family farms whenever possible. In different economic circumstances, such as in the households of cottagers or herdsmen who owned almost no land, children were sent away as servants or laborers; parents invariably exerted less leverage and control over their children's lives if they lacked even modest property.[91]

Because family structures differed from region to region, often in response to specific economic conditions, it did not follow that families were only incidental to economic survival. Invariably the family was a locus of economic as well as emotional attention which helped to shape goals, aspirations, and individual obligations throughout the emigrant homelands. Family farms could change over time; families could be the central institution for maximizing resources or of providing the barest subsistence but always it structured attitudes and behavior.[92]

Scholars continue to debate family structures in the European past. The strongest arguments seem to reside with those who have demonstrated that the nuclear family has dominated household arrangements even in preindustrial times and that industrialization did not fragment an assumed world of extended family structures and produce the nuclear home. Households almost always consisted primarily of parents and their progeny.[93]

Exceptions to the dominant nuclear household forms, of course, existed. In southern France some regions suffered so much economic recession or depopulation from plagues that large, complex family structures were pervasive. In the Czech-Austrian border regions in the eighteenth century, adult sons nominated as successors to their fathers stayed in their home in part because they could remain exempt from military service. For a while in the nineteenth century in parts of Croatia and Serbia, large *zadrugas*, or stem families, with several conjugal units cohabiting were commonplace. Normally, though, from England to Romania the conjugal family unit was identical with the household.[94]

An easy assumption that extended families were only of minor importance, however, cannot be made. If the focus of attention moves from western to eastern Europe, the role of extended family

[39

relations and even the stem family became more important. Historian Lutz Berkner has demonstrated the central role of stem families in eighteenth-century Austria in which married children remained at home to inherit the family property. The transmission of an inheritance was not always harmonious and frequently a father had to insist upon a contract to insure sufficient support from his son. In Poland, evidence existed of children actually taking steps to hasten a parent's death in order to acquire an inheritance faster. But in most cases such a system, where it prevailed, worked effectively to support parents and one of their offspring, usually, but not always, the eldest son. Most important, the wealthier the peasant the greater the likelihood that he could retire early and pass the farm to his eldest son. Stem family structures, in other words, were linked to social status with 15 percent of the poorer Austrian sample consisting of stem families and about 40 percent of "richer farms." Stem structures also tended to predominate in early marital stages when parents were still alive or in older stages when children marry. When families owned no land at all, the extended family was rarely found, a point which underscores the pervasive and vital link between property ownership, age structures, and patterns of familial life.[95]

The general impression emerging from central and eastern Europe was definitely that families were living in more complicated households, although nuclear families were still predominant. In Latvia over 50 percent of the households were extended or multiple in 1787. In Russia certain families had two household heads and often two brothers occupied a home with their respective families. As in Austria, Russian family structures could change throughout the lifecycle with extended forms largely absent in middle years but common when heads were very young or retired. In east-central Europe widespread examples of stem families and joint families were found. In contrast to stem families where only one son remained with his parents (other children usually received a settlement and moved away), in joint families several sons remained in the original homestead with families of their own. The classic example of married sons remaining together even after the death of their father was the zadruga of the Balkans. Although zadrugas probably represented less than one-half of the population at any one time, they were widespread and persisted into the twentieth century. They rested on an assumption that households could strengthen their economic power by having an abundance of manpower, thus the cooperation of several conjugal units. During the nineteenth century in central Serbia this notion was particularly strong as economic conditions worsened.[96] Extended family forms were also found to be widespread in Hungary, especially among Serbs and Croats in the south and Slovaks and Russians in the northeast.[97]

Everywhere in the immigrant homelands survival and economic well-being were intimately linked to the land. Succession in family lines of authority were crucial not only for maintaining a system of order in the family but for insuring that the family's economic stake was in the best possible hands. Even if emancipation offered new opportunities for individuals to strike out on their own, they still married and formed families. On expanding estates landlords even encouraged marriages in the hope that more producing units would lead to higher incomes. Individuals were told to marry earlier in Russia, since life expectancy of family heads was not all that great. In the Baltic regions examples of servants and farmhands being brought into the family core existed as a means of increasing productive capacities and thus insuring the security of the family and household. But whatever the family form, the function remained the same: Kin responded to existing economic systems in any way they could to insure family survival.[98]

While a tendency toward earlier family formations characterized the initial years of emancipation and agricultural commercialization in nearly every country, the pattern eventually reversed itself. Patterns of earlier nuptials and higher fertility rates almost always gave way to postponed marriages or declining rates of child-bearing as resources needed for starting households became scarce or more people moved to urban areas. The classic case was Ireland, where economic conditions deteriorated to the point that marriages and, therefore, family formation had to be delayed. This stood in marked contrast to earlier periods of commercialization when marriages were actually encouraged whenever possible. In late nineteenth-century Hungary, Poland, and elsewhere internal disputes mounted within families. Sons grew apprehensive about waiting any longer for inheritances, which might prove insufficient. A move to an industrial region jeopardized the support parents expected during old age. Actual fights became more frequent in fields and at home. The spectacle of married sons' families cooking only for themselves instead of the entire household grew more common. In craftsmen's families the young had occupied a position similar in some respects to that which they occupied in farm families. Increasingly, children of craftsmen, by the late nineteenth century, went farther away to study under masters as they had a more difficult time in assuming their father's trades at home. For instance, by the 1890s Czech and other Slavic children predominated among apprentices in Vienna. In Austria-Hungary, as in Ireland, a pattern of fewer and later marriages was appearing by 1900. In one district, for instance, only 19 percent of the male and female workers were married as fewer individuals were able to inherit sufficient property to start families of their own.[99]

In late-nineteenth-century Italy, families continued to provide each of their children with assistance but only one with land. Other sons, who were paid the initial costs of emigration by the fathers, relinquished claims to family property. If the emigrating son sent any money back it went to his own personal account in a bank and not always for family support. In one village the process was so advanced that of 125 families sampled only 14 had no emigrating sons. Moreover, land pressure was greatest among smallholders. Farm-wage laborers and town workers who had no land to protect from excessive subdivision showed a lower tendency to emigrate. Also, as in Ireland, Germany, and Hungary, nuptial ages began to rise near the end of the nineteenth century.[100]

In certain circumstances and times, the transfer of property between generations could affect rates of migration, and existing patterns of inheritance could influence the initiation of migrant streams, although they counted for less as time passed and emigrant tides began to swell from the ranks of those without skills or property. The existence of an undivided inheritance pattern in northwestern Germany prior to 1860 partially accounted for its rate of emigration being heavier than that from the southwest. Usually only one heir, designated by the father, received land in nineteenth-century Ireland, thus stimulating emigration even further. Germans left southern Hungary before Magyars because, unlike Magyars, they practiced an undivided system of inheritance. Most of Hungary practiced a partible system, but eventually emigration grew from these areas as well. Equal division among the children was prevelant in Romania, Serbia, and Bulgaria; emigrant streams in these areas remained underdeveloped, and so did commercial agriculture on the whole.[101]

Rural Japan, like many areas of Europe, also had a one-son-succession rule which precluded the formation of many households with more than one married couple during the nineteenth century. Frequently a very wealthy family with sufficient resources to distribute to several sons would choose to transfer property to only one in order to avoid a decline in social status. Extended or joint households in which the families of married brothers lived was rare. Exceptions, of course, did exist. Underscoring the close relationship between economic structure and family form, extended families were found in certain hill districts where the soil was poor or where resources were exceptionally limited. In Takayama, a large town in central Japan, newly married couples not in the line of succession lived in an annex attached to the house of one of the spouses. Together, the attached families formed an economic unit. In the Shirakawa-Mura district in the middle of the nineteenth century, land was in such short supply that no new households could be formed. Second and third sons began to stay in the same households with parents and the oldest son's family. For the time "visiting marriages" appeared where men and women lived in different households and visited each other only at night. It was eventually from houses such as these and in villages where one-son rules of succession predominated that individuals began moving away.[102]

Whatever the particular form of the Japanese peasant family, the household was the chief unit of production, especially in the production of rice. Households held varying amounts of land which surrounded each village and were responsible for production of food. Family-productive units were considered so important to the national economy that they ranked just behind the intellectual elite of administrators, military men, and scholars in the nation's social structure. Merchants who engaged in rice exchange and craftsmen actually stood below them.[103]

Familiarity with Transiency

If family units were central to organizing social and economic life for individuals in immigrant homelands, families were also quite familiar with the potential benefits of migration for supplementing household income or even enhancing a household's resources. Traditional views of static and isolated peasant villages in the preindustrial world simply were inaccurate and most rural and town dwellers knew long before they ever heard of America that people frequently had to migrate to meet economic realities. Patterns of temporary and permanent migration had characterized Europe and other lands throughout the eighteenth and nineteenth centuries. The growing connection between industrial and agricultural economies did little to temper this widespread transiency and usually served to intensify it.

In northeastern Europe internal migration was often more important than emigration. In England greater numbers circulated within the country than actually left. Emerging industrial centers, such as Lancashire, Yorkshire, and London, all recruited regional populations. Similarly, in Scotland migration within the country predated emigration and always affected more people than did movement to other lands. By 1851 at least one in every three Scots had moved internally, though peak emigration rates were less than 1 percent of the population per year. Prior to 1800 Welsh farmers had moved at harvest time to English border counties and Welsh women traveled to eastern England to pick fruit. By the 1880s people moved routinely from rural Wales to industrial Wales, and once there they decided to remain, return to their farms, or move overseas. The Irish, of course, were the most transient of all. By the 1830s Irish farm workers were moving seasonally to England and Scotland and by 1861 over 18,000 at least temporarily to the iron-making districts of South Wales. Internally, eastern Ireland with its greater concentration of large estates attracted seasonal harvest workers from the western counties. Migrants, not unexpectedly, came from counties such as Connaught, where people either held small scraps of land or no land at all. Temporary harvest migrations were common in southern France, where differences in elevation produced varying harvest seasons in the region of the Alps and the lowlands and allowed workers movement from one harvest to another.[104]

Throughout the vast stretches of Austria-Hungary the patterns were much the same. By 1900, for instance, over 44,000 migrants from Galicia were living in Bukovina, 50,000 in Silesia, 23,000 in Bohemia, and 31,000 in Moravia. Large clusters appeared among the mining crews and coke plants of Silesia and Moravia. In Romanian villages in the Carpathian foothills entire families of shepherds migrated seasonally. Jews were leaving Galician villages for Bavaria and Brandenburg. From the Galician town of Maszkienice men were migrating in the 1860s, long before movement to America, to work on railroad lines or on construction gangs in Congress Poland. By 1907 over 350,000 people from Galicia and Russian Poland were working throughout Germany, especially in industrial Silesia. They were joined by an additional 20,000 Hungarians. Russians were moving into Riga in the 1890s because the city's expanding economy had already absorbed most of the surrounding Latvians. Throughout the nineteenth century large property holders in Lower Austria depended upon the annual migrations of thousands of Czechs, Slovaks, and Croatians. In Wallachia peasants came down from the hills to harvest in fertile plains. Slovenes by the 1860s were working in nearby industrial cities such as Graz. Serbs had been moving steadily into Croatia and Russia. Ivan Čizmić found over 43,000 "foreigners" working in Croatia and Slovenia in the first decade of this century.[105] A study of a group of Szeklers found they would move seasonally to Romania, Galicia, and even Russia for "there was no work they would not accept."[106] In Budapest by 1875, 35 percent of the iron and machine workers were foreign-born. Between 1850 and 1900, in fact, Budapest received over 100,000 Slovaks. Of course, Slovak tinkers had temporarily migrated out of the county of Spis to Romania, Bulgaria, Serbia, Turkey, Russia, and Poland for decades.[107]

Italy and Mexico also became familiar with transiency and migration prior to large-scale movement overseas. Mexicans began to move from the central plateau to the four northern states in the late nineteenth century because mines and factories were opening there which paid wages higher than one could earn in agriculture. In Cosenza during the 1880s several hundred men had been leaving every spring to work in either Sicily or the Italian South. In one sample of four Italian villages, from 16 to 37 percent of the twenty-year-old males were certified as "away from home" in the decades between 1820 and 1900. From one village 300 people left every November to work in Lombardy until the spring. When they returned, another group left to work until Christmas in the Piedmont. Seasonal migrations were also common in Lucca province as early as the eighteenth century. More adult males from the households of small landowners than laborers would migrate each year to large estates in Sardinia, Corsica, and France. To save as much money as possible these seasonal migrants lived in large common huts where meals were taken together and life was very frugal. While the evidence is inconclusive, there is reason to believe that at least in Italy and Austria-Hungary regions which were familiar with seasonal migrations were more likely to send emigrants overseas. For instance, in Italy the rate of emigration for the entire nation was 0.6 per 1,000 population during the 1880s, but it was 2.0 from Lucca and 2.2 from Palermo, provinces with a long history of temporary population moves.[108]

The Pragmatic Context of Emigration

Emigrants then were not simply isolated people who had been shaped by long-standing traditions and cultures. They were products of particular social categories, households, and regions who had adjusted their goals and behavior throughout the nineteenth century to meet the changing economic realities induced by factory production, commercial agriculture, and landholding patterns. While these categories were the chief shapers of emigrant consciousness,

[45

another force influenced the calculations and loyalties of the rural dweller. In nearly every instance the emigrant was attached in some way to a particular nation or state. Often, as was the case in England and Sweden, national identity was subject to little dispute. Across the great agricultural regions of central and eastern Europe, the concept of nationhood was somewhat less developed. Nationalism in Germany, Italy, Poland, and Austria-Hungary was emergent during the beginnings of nineteenth-century emigration from these lands and its attachment to those who left was tenuous.

Nationalism in its nineteenth-century form seemed to be linked to the rise of industrialization, commercial agriculture, and emigration itself. It was the middle-class business and agricultural elements which benefited from the rise of the state and emancipation. Emancipation not only helped to tie peasant loyalty to the state but assisted business interests, such as commercial farmers, to expand and grow especially through international trade. Nationalism as an ideology began to flourish as a justification for the emerging, middle-class state. In the search for legitimacy and meaning, the state and its supporters looked to the past and to the traditions of the peasants who faced new realities in economics and society. To be sure, the most significant component in the nationalist movements were usually intelligentsia,[109] but even among peasants in the emigrant lands a new awareness of their past and themselves as a people began to take hold precisely when their world seemed in the midst of unprecedented transitions.

As peasant society produced more and more for a national economy, it became more intimately aware not only of alternative economic futures but the outlines of its unique past and "national" culture. While emigration itself was an example of peasants acknowledging a new economic order and attempting to adjust to its realities, peasant society also began to recreate a past worthy of preservation. Ultimately the reaction of ordinary people to the intrusion of capitalism in the form of urbanization, industrialization, and commercial agriculture was complex. Some acquired new concepts of individual gain. Most sought to secure a modest existence on the land through inheritances or temporary migrations to nearby cities or overseas. Some, of course, resisted change all together. Recent historians have overemphasized, in fact, the extent to which peasants incorporated modern notions such as upward mobility. They were just as likely to rivet their attention upon the presumed glories of a past and a cultural heritage that they even sought to enrich.[110]

In Hungarian villages the complexity of the peasant response to the urban-industrial system can be seen most clearly. Growing trade contacts brought new goods to villages, for instance, and peasants began to decorate their homes with greater variety. Interest in decorative arts intensified. Despite growing differences in economic functions, the desire to retain a "peasant way of life" was widespread. Costumes continued to be made in a peasant fashion, ignoring differences in social rank and strata. In fact, more "peasant styles" of dress as they are known in the twentieth century appeared precisely when peasants began to interact increasingly with urban people. Peasants—and the nationalist leaders who discovered them by the late nineteenth century—began to drift away from an earlier trend of adopting the music and language of the upper classes and initiated a quest for a more authentic, peasant-based culture. In everyday life trends toward patterns of the gentry now gave way to a "peasant" look.[111]

The pattern was repeated elsewhere in Europe. In Vierlanden near Hamburg rural folk art began to grow more "rustic" and manifest an anti-urban bias.[112] In Moravia and Slovakia folk costumes became more elaborate and colorful in a defiant gesture toward urban functionalism. This self-awareness was especially marked in towns near expanding cities such as Bratislava and Brno. Ornamentation on costumes increased. Hunting costumes contained so many decorations that men could no longer hunt in them. Specific occupational groups began to embellish their traditional costume design. Millers in Moravia, for instance, wore close-fitting blue breeches. Even religious and ethnic attachments were expressed more strongly in dress, especially among minorities such as Germans in Czech-dominated villages or Slovaks in Magyar towns. In areas of less diversity and nationalization, such as Russia, the entire process was less pronounced. In Italian villages peasants sought a mythical past without exploitive landlords and hungry mouths to feed. In the village of Nissoria a movement was begun to change the patron saint of eight centuries from one who had been identified with petty nobility to St. Joseph, who was seen as a special protector of laborers. Elsewhere, revolts against church authorities who sought to switch festivals from traditional dates of celebration took place. In Ireland religious attachments were being reinvigorated among the peasants on the eve of emigration.[113]

In many instances the flourishing of peasant art, culture, and costume by the late nineteenth century was not simply an expression of growing peasant self-awareness but also represented a growing integration into the national state, especially in Germany, Italy, and

[47

Hungary. Rising elites, whose fortunes were tied to the state, sought to revive "traditional" peasant cultures in order to strengthen their particular conception of nationalism. Dance masters and composers in Budapest, for instance, sought peasant dance and musical forms as a basis for mobilizing nationalist sentiment and in the process hoped to draw peasants into their movement. In fact, nationalist sentiment was becoming so strong in Hungary that the government did not become concerned about emigration until Magyars—who took longer to move away from their psychological moorings than other groups—began to leave.[114]

Minorities found themselves in disfavor wherever nationalist currents arose. Slovak schools were eroded by Magyarization. In Prussia, Bismarck worked openly against Poles, banished Polish priests, and outlawed the teaching of Polish in areas such as Poznania by 1887.[115] A year earlier Prussia had attempted to establish a Colonization Commission to buy lands from Polish gentry and sell them to German colonists. As a result, Poles of various social classes were drawn together much more than normally would be the case, and countered with agricultural "circles" of their own to disseminate information on improved farming methods and create a land bank to facilitate the establishment of Polish farmsteads.[116]

The attack upon minority identity was even carried abroad. Many Slovak clergymen were prohibited from going to America and taking over congregations, for fear they would spread anti-Magyar sentiment. Prussian police watched emigrants in America and reported on the activities of Polish nationalist and socialist movements. Such agents were actually planted among emigrants to America. Indeed, the existence of these reports have established direct and continuous links between nationalist and socialist movements in Europe and America.[117]

It would be a mistake, however, to view peasant behavior as simply reactionary. Rural people were more likely to be quite realistic about facing widespread social and economic change. In many areas large numbers of agricultural workers and other toilers formed organizations to further the aims of workers and provide for a modest amount of economic security. In Bosnia-Hercegovina the Association of Skilled Workers and Day Laborers was formed. Mutual aid societies proliferated in the premigration world. After emancipation, peasants were often forced to make redemptive payments, improve their farms, and buy or rent land. Drawn increasingly into a cash economy, peasants lacked the qualifications and connections to acquire much capital on their own and thus founded credit unions and cooperatives. By 1914 in Denmark most of the rural population belonged to one of these associations. Germany had over 1,000 credit groups by 1883 and over 23,000 by 1910. Hungary had 2,830 credit associations in 1903. In Slovenia peasant loan cooperatives had 165,000 members by 1910 and attempted to generate not only funds for capitalist development but consciously sought to prevent the acquisition of Slovenian real estate by non-Slovene capital as well.[118]

In Slovakia, Hungary, Croatia, and elsewhere increased drinking, wifebeating, and sexual offenses were reported everywhere as older institutions and mores were challenged. But such "breakdown" was not the norm. Among the South Slavs, for instance, a peasant movement led by Anton and Stephan Radic sought to restore the interdependence of the rapidly dissappearing zadruga with newly established cooperatives. Because they also sought to preserve peasant architecture, folk dance, and costumes did not mean they were totally unaware of new economic demands.[119] In Russian Poland loans from the Peasant Bank were responsible for 5 percent of the entire amount of land owned by the peasant class. In Romania even shepherds formed mutual benefit societies, which offered loans and death benefits by the 1890s.[120] Upper Silesia, not surprisingly, was not only the oldest industrialized region of Poland but the first to experiment with mutual aid societies and the first to send migrants to America.[121]

Jews in eastern Europe, increasingly restricted in their economic activities and prevented from attending many universities, realistically sought learning and economic equality with non-Jews. Some Jewish leaders called for adaptation through a modernization of Jewish customs. Young Jews were attracted to cities such as Vilna, where they studied religion less and the gospel of socialism more in an attempt to improve the lot of the working classes. The tensions between a growing secular pragmatism and a longing for a romanticized but rapidly disappearing past could partially be witnessed in the culture of *Yiddishkeit*, which emerged among late-nineteenth-century eastern Jews. I.L. Peretz and other writers in Warsaw wrestled with the themes of hope and fear for the future, raised concerns about the promise of secular progress, and turning lovingly back to a Jewish past, discovered a treasure of legend in folk and Hasidic sources.[122]

Government leaders had reasons other than loyalty for instilling a new sense of nationalism among citizens. Emigration itself was frequently viewed as a serious loss of productive citizens which would seriously harm economic growth. National governments hoped that those leaving would not only retain their national loyalties but that

[49

they would ultimately return. In Great Britain mercantilists strongly opposed emigrant departures, because they felt emigration was a drain upon national strength. Italian Catholic publications publicly censored those who left for neglecting their duties to their families and their land. The conservative gentry in Russian Poland were unreservedly opposed to peasants leaving, since they wanted to retain a surplus labor supply in rural areas. In Galicia the Austrian government supported the gentry's opposition to emigration. In 1868 the Galician *Sejm* abolished restraints on the free disposition of land, in part to prevent peasants from sinking into a landless proletariat which might be more inclined to leave. The minority which correctly argued that parcelization would actually encourage emigration was ignored. In 1888 residents near Kosice, Slovakia, complained that few people were left in local villages to perform the needed agricultural work and those remaining would have to bear a large share of the tax burden.[123]

But homeland governments did not persist in attempting to prohibit something as uncontrollable as massive population movements. They often saw benefits to be derived from the emigration of their citizens and sometimes moved to encourage it. As the nineteenth century progressed in Great Britain mercantilists gradually dropped their earlier opposition and began to see emigration as an outlet for overpopulation, a means of reducing the burden of caring for the poor (even though the poorest seldom emigrated), and a safety valve for popular discontent. Emigration was also viewed as a safety valve by some in Austria and Denmark and as a means to help liquidate debts and tax liabilities, since migrants sent money home. Despite opposition from the landed gentry and even the military establishment who feared a loss of manpower, commercial transportation interests often stood to profit from migration streams. Social liberals even argued on behalf of the peasants' right to emigrate to improve their standard of living.[124] Understandably, when governments realized they could not totally control the exodus and that they were often caught between opposite political factions, they moved to regulate the process in order to avoid a loss of influence altogether. Thus, the Croatian government established a foundation to which all emigrants paid a fee before they left. The funds collected were used to assist penniless Croats in American to return home. Various emigrant aid societies were established by concerned governments and citizens. The Polish Emigration Society, headquartered in Cracow in 1909, sought to assist all Poles in need beyond the borders of the Austro-Hungarian Empire. Hungary sought to profit from the emigrant

Hebrew Immigrant Aid Society, Warsaw, 1921
Immigrants could use a number of organizations to acquire
information on travel, jobs, relatives, and possible
destinations. *YIVO Institute for Jewish Research*

traffic by contracting with the Cunard shipping lines to pick up emigrants at the port of Fiume. The advantage for Hungary would be
that her emigrants would avoid German ports and keep expenditures
within the economy of the empire.[125]

Explanations for emigration from rural societies often range from
a flight from poverty thesis to a newer view which stresses the raised
expectations of newcomers and their determination to acquire the
riches offered by industrial and urban societies. A classic study of
economic and social change in nineteenth-century rural Europe, indeed, stressed a kind of modernization theory with peasant expectations moving from traditional priorities of group survival to modern
ones of individual self-interest. Jerome Blum argued that the phenomenon of the rural exodus told of a new freedom villagers had to
"pursue their own self-interest." Other scholars have rallied to this
general view. Studies of Italians in America have stressed that these

newcomers had high expectations of individual advancement and proprietorship in America. Hungarian county administrators at the turn of the century noted a widespread desire among emigrants for riches and linked the goal of individual advancement to the emancipation of peasants, which caused everyone to want to be an independent farmer and to go heavily into debt, if need be, to gain sufficient land.[126]

Although the abundant literature which proved emigrants were not originating from the poorest sectors of society has discredited the flight from poverty thesis and recent accounts have shown there was an increase in individual expectations, an easy assumption should not be made that the question of motivation has been satisfactorily answered. Several points still must be considered. First, most emigration took place in village and family networks and not on an individual basis. Second, many who left farms could only go if others agreed to remain behind and perform necessary tasks. Third, sizable amounts of money were sent back to homelands and large percentages of people remained in America only for several years.[127] These points do not support an image of self-interest but one of individuals closely tied to family responsibilities and homeland priorities.

Rather than being bound to tradition or modern notions of achievement, much evidence exists to suggest that immigrants were pragmatic and weighed carefully the original decision to emigrate in the face of contemporary economic and social conditions. They were already formulating ways to confront industrial capitalism prior to moving to urban America. The first to leave were usually artisans and independent farmers who were truly dislocated but not impoverished. They certainly desired to avoid impoverishment, however. Among the mass of landless and marginal owners who eventually formed the bulk of each migration stream, the decision to move usually meant a temporary quest to earn higher wages which alleviated economic pressures at home and often provided additional resources to acquire more land and become self-sufficient in agriculture. Since they were not tied to a distant past or future, their goal was adjustment to the present realities of capitalism as manifested in their homelands. Among Italians, for instance, emigration was not random but tied closely to assessments of economic conditions. Italian emigration was heaviest in years in which harvests were poor. A warm spring which boded well for the winter wheat crop kept many in their villages. They knew an abundant harvest could lead to greater farm employment at home. In the 1880s the residents of one village learned that Pennsylvania coal miners were getting nearly two dollars a day and quickly estimated that in two years they could save enough to return to Italy and purchase sufficient land to support a family. Even among those who stayed in America the dream of returning home to establish independent farms persisted.[128] Some sociologists have described peasants as inhabitants of a culture of poverty which favored immediate gratification over forced savings. But no such culture characterized most emigrants to America who were making realistic decisions about familial and individual survival.[129]

No phenomenon is more central to understanding the motives of those moving from agricultural to industrial regions nor more revealing about the predisposition to use industrial wages to improve or maintain status in the rural world than the process of return migration. Because everyone did not or was unable to return should not obscure the fact that a return was usually every emigrant's goal. The only major exceptions seem to have been those who had worked as craftsmen or those who ventured to America before 1860 with sufficient capital to initiate farming or commercial enterprises in the new world and groups such as East European Jews who faced severe political restrictions in the homeland. While estimates vary, return rates usually ranged from 25 to 60 percent, although most records on immigration are somewhat imprecise. Hvidt found about 30 percent of the Danes returning, and the German figure was between 35 and 40 percent. About four of every ten Greeks returned, and the Polish figure was only slightly below that. The most likely of all to return were those from central and southern Italy (56 percent) and northeast Hungary. Magyar rates have been estimated at 64 percent and those of Slovaks at 59 percent.[130]

Like emigration itself, however, the return movement was diverse and composed of various sectors of immigrant society and stimulated by several motives. Finnish farmers with wives, and presumably with more of a chance to sustain themselves in farming were considerably more likely to return than landless laborers. A sample of returning Finns listed homesickness and family obligations, such as farm responsibilities, as the leading factors. Unemployment was always a significant cause of return and a sharp upturn in the return of Finns and others was noticed after 1929. Welfare agencies actually initiated repatriation efforts of Mexicans even though their own government admonished Mexican consuls to keep as many as possible in the United States.[131] Conversely, the Hungarian government supported an extensive program of "American Action," which used financial inducements to gain control over immigrant churches and newspapers in America in order to maintain a desire on the part of emigrants to return with their American earnings and to blunt disaffection from the cause of Hungarian nationalism. Their efforts were rewarded, as one study of a Hungarian village found more than 50 percent of those who had gone to America to have returned within three to five years. Even among those who stayed, many continued to buy land in Hungary. "We'll only stay in America and work hard until we have (enough money for) twenty acres, and then we'll go home," one Hungarian recalled.[132] In Italy remigration was less frequent in the north than in the south. While southerners tended to return to their villages seasonally or within three to five years, those from the north often stayed away longer and did not necessarily return to the villages they left. In part, this can be attributed to the fact that more land was available for sale in the south than in the north. For emigrants who left regions of large holdings where parcelization was not as extensive, return migration rates were generally lower. This was not only true for northern Italy but for similar regions such as Austria and Prussia.[133]

Conclusion

The movement to America of millions of immigrants in the century after the 1820s was not simply a flight of impoverished peasants abandoning underdeveloped, backward regions for the riches and unlimited opportunities offered by the American economy. This tremendous population shift depended not only on the growth of American industrial capitalism but on transformations occurring in immigrant homelands as well. People did not move randomly to America but emanated from very specific regions at specific times in the nineteenth and twentieth centuries. Economic changes in the immigrant homeland rather than America industrial growth accounted for the cycle of each immigrant stream with its inevitable beginning, middle, and end.

Homeland transitions were so integral to explaining emigration because the same capitalism which altered the shape of the United States in the nineteenth century influenced social and economic developments in rural regions of the homeland as well. The immigrant did not encounter capitalism for the first time in American cities; he had already encountered some of its manifestations prior to departing and had arrived at certain decisions of how it should be confronted. Essentially capitalism intruded upon the immigrant homelands in two ways. First, as transportation networks expanded from industrial cities, cheaper manufactured goods flooded rural

Norwegians leaving for Europe, 1902–03
A very large number of immigrants eventually returned to
their homelands, especially during periods of economic
distress. *Chicago Historical Society*

markets undercutting the economic base of independent artisans and
household producers who engaged in weaving or other forms of production to supplement their agricultural income. Second, the rise of
industrial cities created a huge new market for agricultural produce.
Agriculture conducted on a large scale could generate a substantial
income if it moved from a subsistence to a surplus base and if a concentrated effort were made to specialize in cash crops.

These two manifestations of capitalism—manufactured goods and
commercial agriculture—served as the agents which precipitated
emigration from some regions and not others. Where transportation
lines did not bring factory goods or where land was not particularly
suitable for large-scale agriculture, such as in the mountainous areas
of the Balkans, emigration streams were unlikely to occur. Furthermore, these particular forms of capitalist intrusion meant that invariably each emigrant stream would have two major components. The

first to leave, although they usually constituted a minority of the emigrant population, were the craftsmen, artisans, and small, independent farmers who were threatened by cheap goods and by the drive to acquire large estates suitable for the production of cash crops. They wished to avoid any further declines in status, usually possessed a modest amount of financial resources, left in family units, and were less likely to ever return. This was the pioneer wave which would exercise considerable leadership and influence in American ethnic communities. The second major group to depart for American cities was usually the largest in each stream. This contingent originated in the social categories just below the level of respectable artisans and independent owners. It consisted of marginal owners who hoped to earn enough to return and increase their holdings, the children of modest and marginal owners, who even though they faced bleak prospects of becoming owners of any kind at home often emigrated as a means to enhance those prospects, and those who owned no land at all. This later group in a migrant stream consisted more of individuals than family units, individuals who initially, at least, still hoped to acquire the resources necessary to achieve a more respectable status as self-sufficient owners or even craftsmen in their homeland.

Because immigration was structured and selective, notions and myths about immigrants being tradition-bound, provincial peasants or excited and eager men on the make can no longer be sustained. These people did not leave preindustrial worlds but worlds which were already encountering capitalism and experimenting with ways to deal with its realities. Credit cooperatives, mutual aid societies, agricultural improvement societies, and forms of political agitation such as peasant protests and Jewish socialism, all demonstrated that these people were struggling for ways to cope with new and present economic realities and not captured by future hopes or even past glories. It is true that strong, romantic reactions to modernity ignited episodes of peasant revivalism in many of the immigrant homelands, but they were outweighed by an enduring sense of pragmatism, which continued to be rooted in the same institution even after feudalism's demise: the family-household. As long as individuals were concerned about insuring familial and household survival they would continue to be realistic. They would do whatever had to be done to meet changing economic realities, including a move to America.

2 /

Families Enter America

Networks of Migration

Throughout the immigrants' homelands families were forced to select emigration as one possible option in confronting the new order of capitalism. But a multitude of practical problems remained once the decision to move was made. How would information of specific jobs be found? Where could living accommodations be located? How in general did individuals enter sprawling new factories and expanding cities? The answers to these pressing issues emerged not from any long and tedious thought process but largely from familiar patterns cultivated over years of dealing with the vagaries of economic systems, social relationships, and human desires. Work, shelter, and order would be secured in industrial America—as they had been in the pre-industrial and proto-industrial homeland— through an intricate web of kin and communal associations. The immigrant would not enter America alone. The intrusion of capitalism in the premigration lands may have raised the alternative of emigration, but it had not destroyed the essential relationship between family and work that most emigrants, regardless of ethnic background, had nurtured. It was a relationship which would enjoy a rejuvenation in the mills and neighborhoods of American industrial cities.

Because families and friends were in close contact even when separated by wide oceans, immigrants seldom left their homelands without knowing exactly where they wanted to go and how to get there. Relatives and friends constantly sent information back regarding locations to live and potential places of employment. Thousands of Poles were brought from Gdansk to Polish Hill in Pittsburgh by aunts, uncles, brothers, and sisters who sent them passage money and instructions of what to bring and where to make steamship and railroad

[57

connections. By 1915, as a result of such patterns, investigators could find heavy clusters of families in city neighborhoods. About three-fourths of the Italians and one-half of the Jews who owned property in Providence, Rhode Island, lived in a building with kin at the same address. One Jewish immigrant explained that her father had bought a three-family house with his cousins. Her family lived downstairs, one cousin on the second floor, and another cousin on the top floor. An Italian working for the Scovill Company in Connecticut brought friends who were "big and strong" from Italy. Women brought their sisters or friends into domestic jobs or gave them references of where to go. Chicanos followed each other along railroad lines into Los Angeles and from there throughout southern California. In the early 1920s Chicanos like José Anquiano were arriving in the Chicago area after hearing about openings at the Inland Steel Company and then sending for friends and kin in Texas and in their home villages in Mexico. In fact, relatives and friends were often responsible for movement to second and third locations in America when employment became slack in areas of first settlement. Thus, Italians from southern Illinois moved to the Italian "hill" in St. Louis when coal mining operations were reduced in the 1920s, and Slavs from mines in western Pennsylvania and northern Michigan moved to Detroit's expanding car industry in the same decade.[1]

It was not unheard of for "middlemen" or labor agents to direct large flows of immigrant workers to particular industries or cities in return for modest fees. Such individuals usually shared a common ancestry and language with newcomers and could effectively gather them for shipment to a waiting industry. Oriental workers were channeled in such a fashion into western railroads for a time. Greeks were brought to firms such as the Utah Copper Company and the Western Pacific Railway by "labor czars," such as Leonidas Khliris; Italian "padrones" funneled their fellow countrymen to railroads and public works projects and into labor turmoil as strike-breakers. Ethnic "bankers," such as Luigi Spizziri, advanced passage to individuals in Italy and then found them work in Chicago. Hungarians were able to get contracts from the agents of Pennsylvania mine owners in the 1880s, which they could break only if they got someone to replace them. In nearly all instances, however, intermediaries functioned only in the early stages of a migration stream. Inevitably the continual and enduring movement of all groups into industrial America would rest on ties and links established in the old world.[2]

Immigrants did not need middlemen in the long run because they received a steady stream of information on labor market conditions

Immigrant Family, Ellis Island, New York
Most immigrants came to urban America in networks of
families and friends. *International Museum of Photography,
George Eastman House*

[59

and wages from friends and relatives, which allowed them to make reasonably well-informed decisions about where to go and what types of work they could expect to find. Immigrant letters were frequently filled with information on employment prospects, wages, and even the manner in which workers were treated. One Welshman wrote home in 1895 to describe the situation in anthracite mining and informed his readers that the coal trade was "extremely dull," labor was plentiful, and operators can consequently do just what they please. A Polish steelworker in Pittsburgh wrote to his family in Poland not to keep his younger brother in school much longer; an extended education would be unnecessary for the toil required in the Pittsburgh mills.[3]

Comparative analysis of Italians migrating to Argentina and New York City further revealed the specificity of the information immigrants used to make their decisions to move. In Argentina Italians formed a sizable portion of the economic structure and had access to numerous opportunities to own business and industrial establishments. At the turn of the century 57 percent of the owners of industrial establishments in Buenos Aires were Italian. The New York labor market offered considerably different opportunities for Italians. In the American metropolis they formed a much smaller percentage of the population and were unable to dominate any important economic sector. Because Italians were generally knowledgeable about the divergent opportunity structures in the two cities, different groups selected different destinations. Those from northern Italy, usually more literate, who intended to remain abroad permanently, went to Buenos Aires. Southern Italians, less literate and with less capital, who hoped to return to Italy, tended to move to New York, where they could easily find unskilled, temporary jobs. Indeed, some indications exist that over time, Italians in Argentina when compared to their American counterparts, invested more in business and their children's education than in housing, because they saw a greater chance for success in the future.[4]

It is highly possible that the wage differentials between American and British industrial cities were well known by British and other immigrants and caused them to favor the United States. Even though the cost of living was higher in Pittsburgh than Birmingham or Sheffield, an English bricklayer could make only about 30 percent of his counterpart in Pennsylvania in 1905; "public laborers" in England earned only 55 percent of those in America. Skilled American workers in Pittsburgh were especially better off in terms of hours and wages than in an English city, a fact which may explain as much as labor disputes and recruitment the steady flow of British workers westward after 1860. Even an ordinary steel laborer earned a weekly wage in Pittsburgh which was twice that in Sheffield, although he did have to work somewhat longer. Thus, even potential emigrants from areas outside England, especially if they did not plan to stay away from home long, may have had a relatively easy decision as to where they should go. In another part of the world the same situation prevailed. Mexican farmworkers by 1910 were fully aware that their wage of 12 cents a day on great "haciendas" was only about one-fourth of what they could earn clearing land in Texas or one-eighth of what they could expect on American railroads.[5]

Wages alone, however, did not attract immigrants to specific locations. They were frequently concerned about the type of work they would encounter. Italians often sought outdoor employment and were heavily represented in railroad and other forms of outdoor construction in many American cities. In Chicago they shunned meat-packing because they had heard of the intense cold of refrigerated compartments and the sweltering heat and offensive odors of the killing floors. Irish and other immigrants with older children preferred to locate in textile towns where their offspring could find employment. St. Paul, Minnesota, proved attractive to Irish and German women as a second stop in America because of numerous opportunities for domestic work awaiting them. In Wisconsin many Poles preferred to work on street railway construction or as dockhands because it was seasonal. East European Jews moved into garment trades run by German Jews because they found them easier to work with than Gentile employers.[6]

While immigrants clearly had preferences for work and some advance knowledge of wages and opportunities, however, they were not completely free to move into the industrial economy on an individual basis. Throughout the first century of American industrial expansion both workers and employers experimented with techniques of recruitment and job placement, and no method appeared to be as pervasive or as effective as that of informal familial and ethnic networks. The workplace of early industrial capitalism was a relatively accessible place especially during the six or seven decades after 1850, and kinship ties functioned effectively to provide labor, train new members, and effectively offer status and consolation. Poles, relying on relatives and friends, established occupational beachheads in Pittsburgh at the Jones and Laughlin steel plant, the Pennsylvania Railroad yards in the Lawrenceville section of the city, Armstrong Cork, and H.J. Heinz. As one newcomer recalled, "The only way you got a job was through somebody at work who got you in." Italians from the village of Ateleta brought *paesanos* to the pipe construction department of the Pittsburgh Equitable Gas Company. When one job was closed, relatives could even provide access to a second and third position. One Italian who lost his first job in America on the railroad relied on a brother-in-law to get him into a glass factory. Frequently fathers and uncles taught sons and nephews the operation of industrial equipment. At the Amoskeag textile mills in New Hampshire, French-Canadians brought relatives to work, assisted in their placement in the mills, taught them specific work tasks, substituted for them when they were ill, and informally established production quotas. Some newcomers left Amoskeag rather quickly because of the pace, noise, and dirt, but for those who stayed, the ability to rely on kin and friends was indispensable. In Boston's North End, Italian women congregated in candy and tailoring factories. Supervisors noted that Italian females similarly relied on one another at work to such an extent that it was not uncommon for all to stay at home if even one became ill. In one New England textile plant nepotism became so widespread in securing employment that workers with familial connections within the plant were actually held in higher esteem than "unattached" employees who were presumed to be more transient.[7]

Kinship not only facilitated the entry of immigrant males into the industrial economy but females as well. A 1930 study of 2,000 foreign-born women revealed that most had secured their initial jobs through relatives and friends. All had worked in either cigar or textile factories, and less than 10 percent had acquired relevant skills for those jobs prior to migrating. Surveys of full-fashioned, hosiery loopers discovered that the majority obtained their positions through acquaintances. One study of hosiery loopers concluded that during the period from 1900 to 1930 younger girls followed relatives into the mills as a "general practice," an indication that kinship ties to the workplace continued to influence the second generation as well. A 1924 investigation of Italian females in New York City reported that 75 percent acquired their first jobs through friends or relatives and that these women were "ashamed" to seek employment alone and would quit a job if friends or kin left as well. In Buffalo, Italian women assisted each other in obtaining work in canneries, while in nearly all cities immigrant women shared information on the availability of domestic work.[8]

The central dynamic, which gradually allowed the industrial workplace to be filled informally by clusters of unskilled immigrants who were usually related, was the quest for greater production. Capitalism in its steady drive toward larger profits and lower costs demanded that goods be produced as quickly and as efficiently as possible. Invariably this imperative required that newer forms of production and technology replace skilled workers. This would not only allow for a faster pace of production but would diminish the influence that skilled workers had exerted over a particular workplace and put more control in the hands of managers and owners. This is not to say that skilled workers never attracted kin to the workplace. Nineteenth-century German mechanics and cigarmakers were examples of some who did. But the process was accelerated wherever the ranks of the unskilled replaced craftsmen and it occurred in nearly every American industry at one time or another after the 1840s.

The most striking result of the decline in skilled jobs was the growing number of immigrant clusters in the nineteenth and twentieth centuries. Nearly one-half of the Philadelphia Irish in 1850 were in unskilled labor, for instance, while 67 percent of the Germans were artisans. In Buffalo, Germans dominated crafts such as masonry, cooperage, and shoemaking while the Irish worked largely as unskilled laborers, domestics, ship carpenters, and teamsters. This early bunching resulted directly from the possession or lack of premigration skills, and newer immigrants after 1880, generally with less skills than the Germans, intensified the pattern of clustering. By 1911 a study of seven urban areas revealed that nearly one-third of all South Italians were categorized as "general laborers" in contrast to only 9 percent of the Poles and 7 percent of the Germans. Fully 65 percent of the Poles were in manufacturing and mechanical pursuits compared to only 28.8 percent of the South Italians. Greeks were highly congregated in personal service endeavors, while over one-half of all Serbs were in general labor. Groups such as the Swedes, Jews, and Germans were considerably underrepresented in "unspecified labor" positions.[9]

Contemporary scholarship has substantiated the earlier suggestions of initial occupational concentrations. Stephan Thernstrom's massive study of Boston found significant differences in the distribution of immigrants. In 1890, for instance, 65 percent of Boston's Irish labored in low manual callings while about one-half of those from Canada and Germany obtained skilled employment. Studies of individual immigrant waves in various locations sustain the impression of limited dispersion into the occupational structure. In Indiana oil refineries, Croatians held jobs in only three categories: stillman helper, firemen, and still cleaners. In the ready-made clothing industry, Jews predominated in small firms with minimal mechanization and segmentation of labor while Italians concentrated in large factories which tended to require less individual skills. Serbs and Croats in New York City were heavily involved in freighthandling. Italians dominated construction gangs and barber shops in Buffalo, Philadelphia, and Pittsburgh. By 1918, Italians represented 75 percent of the women in the men's and boys' clothing industry and 93 percent of the females doing hand embroidery in New York City. Nearly all of the 3,000 employees in the Peninsular Car Company in Detroit by 1900 were Polish. Polish women dominated restaurant and kitchen jobs in Chicago by 1909, which they preferred to domestic employment. By 1920, one study found an incredible 69 percent of Slovak males in coal mining and about one-half of all Mexicans working as blastfurnace laborers.[10]

Much of this bunching of immigrant workers could be attributed directly to the alteration of skill levels of American workers. As early as the 1840s textile mills in Lowell, Massachusetts, were attempting to improve their productive capacity by switching to spinning mules which could perform more than twice as much work as the older throstle spinners and implement the stretch-out on the assigning of additional looms or spindles to each worker at reduced piece rates. These changes eliminated the homogeneity of the workforce, which was largely native-born, and led directly to an increase in the proportion of immigrants. At one mill, for instance, the foreign-born proportion of the labor force rose from 3.7 percent in 1836 to 61.8 percent by 1860. Thousands of Irish immigrants entered the mills including many women and children who needed the wages and were willing to accept speed-ups and stretch-outs, in part because they were not familiar with an earlier, slower pace. It was also true that some companies reserved the highest paying jobs for the Yankee women in order to reduce their turnover. Thus, the Irish in Lowell concentrated in the spinning departments.[11]

Historian Daniel Nelson has described the factory of the 1880s as a "congeries of craftsmen's shops." Yet a 1906 study by the United States Department of Labor noted an increase in the division of labor with more operations being subdivided into minute operations. The report explained that hand trades were rapidly becoming obsolete and labor processes were requiring less overall proficiency. The substitution of unskilled for skilled labor proceeded rapidly during the final quarter of the nineteenth century. Employers intensified the drive to establish more efficient worker training programs by reducing skill requirements for incoming laborers. Expansion of child, female, and unskilled, foreign-born labor and the decline of apprenticeship programs and of highly skilled operatives underscored the trend.[12] During the early decades of the twentieth century, the number of blacksmiths, machinists, and glassblowers declined substantially. Apprenticeships among brick and stone machinists fell from 39,463 in 1920 to 13,606 a decade later. The number of dressmakers and seamstresses was cut by over 300,000 during the period, while that of iron molders and casters was halved by 1930. Simultaneously the number of laborers in blast furnaces and rolling mills, shirt factories, glassworks, electrical manufacturing plants, and in the automobile industry increased markedly.[13]

The diminution of crafts and skills accelerated after 1900 and had a negative impact upon the older immigrant stocks from northern and western Europe. Germans in nineteenth-century Philadelphia predominated in skilled butchering, tailoring, and shoemaking positions. As these occupations declined, Germans were frequently dislocated and found it more difficult to transfer jobs to their sons. A similar pattern among skilled Germans in Poughkeepsie, New York, resulted in a greater number of second generation Germans becoming factory operatives than their parents or concentrating in low-paying trades such as barbering or coopering. Indeed, both in Philadelphia and Poughkeepsie less than 9 percent of second generation Germans were lodged in skilled categories; they began to appear in "lower" trades such as cigarmaking, which according to Clyde and Sally Griffen, offered "limited futures."[14]

The blurring of skill distinctions among workers and the implementation of new efficiency schemes were accelerated during the period of the "new immigration." With proletarian protest growing in the late nineteenth century and larger concentrations of workers emerging in urban areas, industrial managers began to impose a bureaucratic structure upon the work force with hierarchical gradations of unskilled and semiskilled operations. This restructuring of work itself resulted in something of a segmentation of the labor market, as some theorists have contended, which created an infinite number of "entry-level" jobs and intensified the process of clustering, while making it extremely unlikely that newcomers could implement any previously acquired skills.[15] The promise of industrial America to immigrant workers was not so much that one could rise as that one could gain access at any number of points of entry. Opportunity was not vertical but horizontal, a fact which tended to blunt any rhetoric of social mobility immediately upon arrival.

[65

If skills were no longer crucial to obtaining work in the expanding sectors of the economy, something else would have to take their place. The alternative would be a random entry of thousands of immigrant workers into the industrial complex. But the widespread existence of clusters suggests that a sense of order in joining newcomers and occupations was operative. In even the most cursory survey of immigrant job acquisition, kinship and ethnic ties invariably emerge as the vital link. But the infusion of familial and ethnic ties could not solely explain the pattern. To be sure immigrants carried strong kinship bonds to America, although ethnic ties were often nurtured *after* their arrival. Without the diminution of skills, however, these associations could not have been implemented on such a vast scale. Those who could explain immigrant adaptation as a function of premigration culture[16] or argue that immigrants entered occupations which allowed them to implement premigration skills[17] have neglected the structural transformation which characterized expanding industries and the extent to which a match took place between previously acquired behavior and available opportunities in America.

Clearly, the opportunity to directly transfer a skill into the American economy was greater for newcomers prior to the 1880s, although kin networks always played a predominant role. But in the early development of many American industries many workers with crucial skills were recruited directly into the workplace. In Newark, New Jersey, in the period before the Civil War when skilled tradesmen had not been widely assaulted by transformations in the workplace, it was no disadvantage to be foreign-born. In 1860, 57 percent of the city's craftsmen were born abroad despite the fact that the immigrants composed only 55 percent of the population. Most of Newark's leathermakers were Irish-born, for example. During the decade after 1850 all crafts in Newark experienced an increase in the number of practitioners who were foreign-born, an indication that immigrants could make penetration into even skilled jobs as the demand was expanding.[18] During the 1830s American textile mills even welcomed handloom weavers from England and Northern Ireland whose jobs had been displaced by power looms. It was this migration that established the fine-cotton-goods trade of Philadelphia. With unemployment and wage cuts widespread throughout Lancashire in 1869, trade unions helped hundreds of their members emigrate to New England, especially to towns such as Fall River. The British Cotton Spinners Society gave an emigration benefit to "members who were blacklisted after strike action." Nearly the entire English silk industry migrated to

America after the Civil War when high American tariffs allowed the industry to prosper on this side of the Atlantic; operatives swarmed here from England and Scotland. After 1860 foreign competition closed British copper mines and Cornish men with deep mining experience set out for North American lead, iron, silver, and gold, as well as copper, mines. Southern Illinois coal mines received many skilled miners from Scotland and the north of England who had been locked out by their employers during labor strikes. Similarly, British immigrants were indispensable in the early furnaces, foundries, and shops of the American iron and steel industry; English, Welsh, and Scottish puddlers could be found nearly everywhere.[19]

Skilled immigrants were a common occurence throughout the nineteenth century wherever the workplace had not yet been transformed. Irishmen who entered the iron industry in Troy, New York, in the 1860s had previously worked in English factories. The number of American-born heaters and rollers declined by two-thirds in the two decades after 1860 and the total of Irish-born almost doubled, indicating that even skilled workers were not immune to forming clusters of friends and kin. Germans and Canadians began to predominate among Troy's cigarmakers. In Milwaukee, Germans comprised 74 percent of all shoemakers and 70 percent of all tailors by 1860. The Milwaukee Iron Company recruited skilled workers from Staffordshire who were on strike in 1868, and in 1872 industrialist E.P. Allis obtained expert pipe casters from Scotland. Elsewhere, Belgian glassmakers and German brewers moved in groups into skilled trades. Continual importation of glassmakers was especially important because they were reluctant to impart their skills to others. By 1863 the Winslow Glass Company in New Jersey had obtained its entire work force form abroad with the employer paying all traveling expenses for newcomers. Tinplate manufacturers recruited thousand of Welsh and English workers with experience in tinplate production. English engineers were brought to American to run English-built locomotives. These engineers were noted for their secretiveness, having been instructed not to tell Americans about the intricacies of their engines. The brass industry around Waterbury, Connecticut, began in the 1830s to import skilled rollers, casters, and burnishers from Birmingham, England. Again, English newcomers refused to let apprentices approach their machines in order to safeguard their skills.[20]

Even among the "new immigrants" who arrived primarily after the transition to unskilled labor production, a few instances of direct skill transfer occurred. Italians from Genoa continued to display the same

[67

passion for trade in the United States that they had in the old country. This was confirmed in separate studies of Genoese in Chicago and San Francisco which showed their proclivity to establish careers as saloonkeepers, restaurateurs, and fruit vendors. By 1871 in Chicago, although they constituted less than one-half of one percent of the foreign-born population, they owned 25 percent of the city's candy and fruit stores. At home they had been known as the "Jews of Italy." In San Francisco, Genoese launched enterprises which evolved into the Del Monte Corporation and the Bank of America. Skilled Italians also found work as granite cutters in Vermont and silk workers in New Jersey.[21] A South Slavic group from the Dalmatian high country, skilled in butchering and boning, acquired jobs in the meat-packing industry. A number of Slovenes in soft coal mining had spent their early years in Austrian mines. Barrel factories in Bayonne, New Jersey, employed Slovak coopers as early as the 1880s. Skilled Czechs were making pearl buttons in America a decade later. And the match between Jewish tailoring skills and the expanding garment industry in New York City is well known.[22]

Whether immigrants were recruited directly for their abilities or followed existing networks into unskilled jobs, they inevitably moved within groups of friends and relatives and worked and lived in clusters. Friends and relatives functioned so effectively, in fact, that they invariably superseded labor agents and "middlemen" in influencing the entry of newcomers into the industrial economy and were usually able to create occupational beachheads for those that followed. Scholars who have accepted the "split-labor market" theory and its assumption that "middlemen" affected the placement of migrants in streams possessing a "sojourning orientation" have overlooked the more important role of networks which influenced both permanent and temporary arrivals.[23]

While most newcomers arrived in friendly groups, they were not allowed to function as independently as they might have thought. The industrial economy was certainly accessible but not at every particular point. Frequently, networks of families and relatives could function only where prospective employers allowed them to do so. Owners and managers had distinct inpressions regarding the abilities of particular groups, a fact which encouraged group rather than individual movement, and took steps to encourage the hiring of one group at the expense of another. A long-standing argument exists that American industry in the nineteenth century was quick to adopt forms of labor-saving technology because labor was relatively scarce.[24] But abundant instances exist of labor being quite plentiful

**Mexican Immigrants at Pacific Electric
Railroad Laborers Camp, Los Angeles**
Mexican and other immigrants often followed established
transportation networks in dispersing throughout the
industrial economy. *Henry E. Huntington Library and Art
Gallery, San Marino, California*

throughout the first century of capitalist expansion and employers
even being able to choose the groups they thought best suited to their
needs. On the Boston and Lowell Railroad in the mid-nineteenth
century, only Irishmen were hired as firemen, since it was believed,
unlike Yankees, they would not want further promotions. In early
Milwaukee, Germans were considered "thrifty, frugal, and industrious" by employers and Poles more industrious than Italians and
Greeks. Patrick Cudahy refused to hire Greeks in his meat-packing
company after a small group became involved in a fight with other
workers and drew knives. Jewish garment owners sometimes hired
only Italians because they were felt to be less amenable to unionization than Jews. On other occasions the owners hired only fellow Jews,
hoping that "fraternal instincts" with employers might keep them
from unionizing. At the Pullman Company in Illinois, executives
considered Germans, Englishmen, and Scandinavians as intelligent

[69

and industrious, although inferior to native-born Americans in "executive ability." Irishmen were considered undesirable and inclined to politics rather than "honest work." In Buffalo, Poles were considered more suitable for indoor work in mills than Italians who congregated in outdoor endeavors. At the Central Tube Company in Pittsburgh, ethnic groups were actually rated from poor to good for their ability to perform specific jobs. For instance, as hod carriers, Hungarians were rated "poor" while Irish and Italians were considered "good." Scandinavian women were strongly preferred in American homes as domestics, in part because they were Protestants while Irish girls were Catholic. This view caused Finnish women to be in heavy demand in large cities such as New York. The overall preference for western rather than eastern Europeans for better-paying jobs, it has been estimated, cost the "new immigrants" on the average of $1.07 per week in wages.[25]

In the case of Chicanos, employer recruitment and attitude were almost solely responsible for determining where their kinship networks would function. The first significant movement of Mexican workers into the southwest was due to the agitation of agricultural, mining, and railroad companies in the southwest. Restrictions of the 1917 Immigration Law were even waived during World War I. Chicanos could not move into Santa Barbara until the 1880s after inexpensive Chinese labor had been curtailed, and even then they were confined to work in laundries, domestic work, and railroad section gangs. In 1880, in Santa Barbara over 80 percent of the Chicanos filled unskilled jobs compared to only 11 percent of the Anglos. Mexicans, like other groups, were perceived as having peculiar characteristics. A general assumption existed in the southwest that they were interested in working only a short while and then returning to Mexico, although increasing numbers were settling permanently north of the border after 1880. At El Paso, railroad recruiters considered them "docile, patient, orderly in camp, fairly intelligent under competent supervision, obedient and cheap." They were also looked upon as "safer" than Orientals. Railroads such as the Southern Pacific were particularly active in recruiting Chicanos from El Paso and northern Mexico and spreading them throughout the West where they were able to establish themselves more permanently in railroad centers such as Los Angeles, the cotton fields of California's Imperial Valley, and the coal and copper mines of southern Colorado. Railroads, wishing to attract Mexican workers, lobbied continuously for the removal of any obstacles to their importation. Railroad employment also served as a first stage for Mexicans moving into Chicago. A 1928 survey showed nearly 40 percent of the Chicanos in the Wisconsin Steel Works listed their last previous occupation with a railroad. Some western companies were so anxious to attract Mexicans after 1924 when new restrictions curtailed European immigration that they made building materials available to them at little or no cost so they could build homes of their own.[26]

The Rise of a Family Economy

While it is apparent that immigrants were not free to move into the industrial economy wherever they desired, they were able to remain within the confines of small groups and networks, which assisted them tremendously. Such groups could mass around links of friends, villages, or regions but were mostly held together by ties of blood. Kinship formed the stable core of immigrant groups as they flowed into the openings available to them in particular times and places. Ironically, no concept so thoroughly pervaded the older interpretations of the American immigrant experience than the one which linked the growing movement of industrial-urban society to a pattern of family breakdown. This view originated with the belief that the modern capitalist system, especially in its manifestation of the factory system which removed production functions from the traditional family-household unit, simply destroyed the foundation of familial cooperation. Production became compartmentalized in factories and mills and workers began to function as individual components of a factory system and not as integral members of a household. This entire argument rested upon an assumption that families not only became less important in urban-industrial society but that families themselves operated in isolation from the larger economy of industrial capitalism which surrounded them.

The startling discovery of modern historical scholarship, however, has made it quite clear that immigrant families did not wither in their encounter with American capitalism. Immigrant kinship associations not only continued to perform indispensable functions in the industrial city, such as helping to organize the movement of workers into the economy, but actually flourished. At times the relationship between the industrial economy and immigrant families could almost be described as symbiotic, as kinship groups proved very responsive to demands of the workplace, the city, and the individual.[27]

The world the immigrant left had exhibited numerous examples of family, in one form or another, as a central focus of organizing life itself. Families were responsible for socialization patterns, the distribution of land and other resources, and even served as a forum to resolve the question of who should emigrate and why. Because they also performed valuable functions in industrial America meant they were not as much cultural baggage as they were institutions which continued to find a relevant role to play in both societies. Family economies were as much a product of industrial capitalism as they were of subsistence agriculture, for in both systems a mediating institution was necessary to stand between economy and society in order to reconcile individual and group demands.

The manner in which the immigrant family remained functional in two economies was its central and enduring attachment to the value of cooperation. Family members were continually instructed in the necessity of sharing and notions of reciprocity were constantly reinforced. Parents, children, boarders, and others who shared particular households were all assigned a series of duties and obligations. By working together, pooling limited resources, and muting individual inclinations, families attempted to assemble the resources sufficient for economic survival and, occasionally, for an improvement in their standard of living. But the first goal was always the most immediate: cooperate and survive. It was not until the era of postindustrialism after 1940, when kinship ties to the workplace were gradually weakened and success was equated with an individual quest, that the underlying system of familial cooperation would be threatened.

The immigrant family economy with its essential ingredients of sharing and reciprocity was found wherever immigrants settled and inevitably shaped their entry into the American economy and society. While not every ethnic group or family behaved in identical terms or pursued exactly the same objectives, an overwhelming majority lived their lives and pursued their goals through familial and household arrangements which often functioned in a similar manner. French-Canadian children in New England recalled how all contributed their savings to their parents. One who was raised in a large family claimed that it stood to reason that everyone was "gonna start working and pitch in." Similarly, Italian children in Pittsburgh asserted that "you never left your mother and father."[28] The ligaments of responsibility among kin were underscored by one child:

> I turned most of (my earnings) over to my mother. That's what I was working for. . . . I was raised with the idea that my mother was my mother and my family and they kept me. When I wasn't saving she would give me whatever she could. I was family; she was my mother.[29]

Another immigrant elaborated on the reciprocal nature of immigrant life. He recalled:

When you work, you understand, you used to bring your pay home and give it to your parents. And whatever they feel they want to give you, they decide. There was no disagreement. That was their style. And don't you dare talk about paying board, especially in dad's house. If you want to pay board you have to go somewhere else. "This is no boardinghouse. This is a family," my father would say. He said to us to bring our pay home and whatever it was, we would make do.[30]

Essentially, family goals came to supersede individual goals, and parents and children both worked vigorously to contribute to familial welfare. Immigrant parents were often able to direct the career paths of their progeny because of the leverage they derived from being able to provide access to industrial jobs or housing in crowded cities. Boys and girls were frequently asked to leave school early and start work either in a mill or in a family business. Girls were often kept at home caring for younger brothers and sisters or performing household chores. Females who wanted to study music were told it was more practical to stay at home and learn cooking, canning, and sewing. One girl wept when forced by her father to leave school after the sixth grade because he felt a woman did not need schooling "to change diapers."[31] Boys were urged to learn a job skill or a business rather than pursue a formal education, as families responded to the nature of the economy during the first century of American capitalism. Often they received such training on the job from fathers of other kin. Interviews with Poles in the Lawrenceville section of Pittsburgh revealed that during the 1920s and 1930s boys worked alongside their fathers in neighborhood foundries and meat-packing plants.[32]

The family economy was not a product of natural evolution, and the effort to insure that children participated directly in the mustering of resources for familial survival was not accomplished without turmoil and tension. Drinking was widespread among adult Irish females. Siblings often complained bitterly if one were allowed to stay in school longer than another. And a few resisted parental attempts to send them to work early. Individual plans and dreams were often formulated but reluctantly put aside for family need. Interviews with immigrant children found careers in electrical engineering, bookkeeping, the priesthood, and business relinquished at the insistence of

[73

parents. Studies conducted among Polish immigrant girls in the Chicago stockyard areas revealed that many complained if enough of their wages were not "returned" to them by their parents. Social worker Jane Addams actually criticized immigrant parents for being too repressive toward their children. Not surprisingly, some immigrant children left home, for they saw their parents as obstacles to happiness.[33]

But parents endured difficult tensions as well. In one study of northern New England textile mills, Steven Dubnoff found that Irish fathers lost some influence in the household as their children began to earn more of their own income. He also discovered that parents were considerably less likely to be absent from work than children and even boarders who were inclined to miss work when they felt like it. Parents may have had authority but they carried larger burdens of responsibility.[34]

It is not entirely surprising that the cooperative ideal pervaded most immigrant families. These newcomers were not coming from widely disparate sectors of their homeland social structures but from the ranks of middle-class farm owners and tradesmen and the mass of marginal farmers and landless laborers just below them. A sense of hierarchy existed within the total group but all resided somewhere in the middle of society and experienced neither the hopelessness of extreme poverty nor the self-assurance of power and wealth. Surviving together was a constant preoccupation. Moreover, differences in regional backgrounds were counteracted somewhat by a relative similarity in education and age structure. Most immigrants had something less than a secondary school education. Japanese arrivals at the turn of the century, for instance, had between four to six years of education and almost all came from agricultural provinces such as Hiroshima, Kumamoto, and Yamaguchi. The majority of the first-generation Japanese spent their formative years in the Meiji Era of Japan (1867–1912), in which the household unit, the most important force of early socialization, nurtured a sense of mutual responsibility, as households throughout agricultural regions did. Such households in Japan, Mexico, Germany, or Hungary were models of cooperative group management at their best and certainly examples of minimal cooperation at the very least. Invariably, children and other members who remained fixed to them were able to exert more influence than those who drifted away or were forced to leave and few members received an education extensive enough to allow for the formulation of individual pursuits separate from household interests.[35]

Most immigrants, moreover, regardless of their class standing in the Old World or regional background were relatively young. They were at an age when they were more inclined to think about forming households of their own or sustaining ones which had recently been initiated. Such a bunching of ages in the period of family formation could not but help the overall thrust toward familial and household organization. Early German newcomers in the 1850s in Milwaukee were mostly in their twenties or thirties, as were the Irish. About 70 percent of male German and Irish household heads were under age 40. Among Danes moving to America in the three decades after 1868, 68 percent were between the ages of 15 and 39. A sample of Poles born in the 1850s found that they were usually around age 31 when they emigrated. Similarly, Italian males and females were mostly in their mid-thirties in samples taken in 1893 and 1905 in New York State.[36]

Steeped heavily in a tradition of household and familial cooperation as a vehicle for achieving economic stability and finding an economic system in America which frequently encouraged a good deal of group assistance, immigrants who wished to remain found it relatively easy to establish households of their own. Indeed, the decision to do so represented not only a major commitment to remain in industrial society but suggested the means by which economic and emotional stability would be achieved in new circumstances. The creation of a new family often eased the pain of severing familial ties in the premigration society, especially for women who saw motherhood as a means of adjusting to a new life. Financial considerations also prompted many men to seek a companion who would cook, clean, and care for them for no wages at all. Many immigrants were anxious to reunite with wives and children out of fear that continued separation would ultimately lead to complete family disintegration. One scholar has found that southern Italians were quicker to send for their wives than northern Italians because they were sexually jealous and less culturally prepared to establish strong social relations outside the nuclear family.

If no wife existed in the homeland, immigrant males quickly took whatever steps were necessary to find women of similar linguistic and cultural backgrounds with whom they could establish a household. Marriage patterns remained largely within the ethnic group during the first and much of the second generation. Japanese men sought "picture brides" from Japan and initiated unions which stressed the importance of duty and obligation over love and romance. About one of every four Italians who moved to San Francisco actually returned to their native village just for a marriage. Whether they returned to the homeland or found a wife in America the chances were great she would be from the same region or village, a fact which reinforced notions about the manner in which families and households should function. Thus, it is not surprising to learn that among Germans in Wisconsin 86 percent of the first generation and 80 percent of the second married other Germans. Similar high rates were exhibited by Poles and Russians in the state. Additional studies found a general absence of widespread immigrant intermarriage in various locations with some exceptions for newcomers of middle-class backgrounds.[37]

But it would be erroneous to assume that the cooperative family economy grew inevitably out of premigration traditions of collective enterprise or the regional and cultural homogeneity of immigrant streams. Both of these factors contributed significantly to the shape of family and household life but would have been insufficient factors in themselves without the accompanying reality of an industrial workplace which encouraged mutual aid and especially the widespread existence of wages insufficient for even modest standards of living. American industrial wages may have looked attractive to the residents of rural regions undergoing transition, but the available information suggests that the families of most immigrants in this country could not survive on the income of one wage earner. Among Irish millhands in Lowell, Massachusetts, in the 1860s, most fathers could earn only about 54 percent of what was needed to support a family at a minimum level of subsistence. Among packinghouse workers in Chicago in the decade after 1910, the average individual wage earner could earn 38 percent of the minimum needed for a family of four; he could still earn only 48 percent in 1922. Among Buffalo's Italians in the early twentieth century, a family of five needed about $650 to $772 a year on which to subsist, but the average Italian laborer (1890–1916) could earn about $364 to $624. Clearly, family income had to be supplemented in some way.[38]

The economic margin of an immigrant family did not usually improve until children reached working age, about fourteen, and began to contribute to family income. In Philadelphia, to illustrate a case, the children of immigrant Irish and German families entered the labor market to a greater degree than did the children from native-born households. Child labor clearly reduced the disparities of income between immigrant and native families with Irish children contributing between 38 and 46 percent of total family labor. At the Amoskeag mills in the early 1900's, historian Tamara Hareven found evidence that the most solvent families were those in which a husband, wife, and at least one child worked. The most "vulnerable" economically were those with small children who could not work and who prevented a mother from working. At Amoskeag about 38 percent of all households had members working other than the head or the wife, but for immigrant households the figure was 50 percent. In fact, textile towns, because they offered employment to teenagers, tended to attract families with children of employment age. The percentage of family income generated by children in 1911 in eastern Pennsylvania was 46 percent among unskilled Poles and 65 percent among unskilled Irish workers. The respective percentages declined to 35 and 40 percent for families of skilled workers, further indicating that a direct relationship existed between the income of the head and the reliance on child labor. Families in Chicago's packinghouse district even sent wives and daughters into the packinghouses, a move which ironically helped to keep overall wages low. A report of Packingtown mothers in 1918 revealed the predominant motive for entering the local labor market was "insufficient income." In Detroit in unskilled, native-born white households only 43 percent of the boys and 16 percent of girls worked, but among unskilled Germans the figures were 66 percent for young males and 43 percent for adolescent females.[39]

Obviously, the presence of children was crucial to the smooth functioning of the immigrant family economy. Immigrant parents could have chosen to restrict the number of children but this was not always a viable option because methods of birth control were imprecise and child mortality rates were relatively high; most parents could expect to lose a young child to illness. In 1900 about one-third of the Italian and Polish women saw a child die before the age of one. Besides offering economic benefits in the long run, children could care for immigrants during their old age and serve as a source of honor and pride in communities which had traditionally valued close kinship ties. In gross terms, American women were having about half as many children at the end of the nineteenth century as they were at the beginning and even the total level of live births among foreign-born mothers fell in the earliest decades of this century. Some scholars believe that industrialization and urbanization, which drew people from farms, largely accounted for smaller families and the fall of fertility rates. But it appears doubtful that the simple act of immigration from a rural to urban area caused a fertility decline alone. In nearly every instance where comparisons were made, immigrants, who were almost always paid less, tended to produce more children than native-born Americans, even when controlling for social class. The Irish and Germans of Buffalo in the nineteenth century had higher fertility rates than natives. Italian women in Buffalo over age 45 in 1900 had produced an average of eleven children, outstripping even Polish females who had given birth an average of 7.8 times. Increased urbanization and literacy were making some inroads in moderating fertility. Rural Germans in Erie County, New York, had more children than urban Germans, and professional Italians in California tended to have smaller families than Italian fishermen. But for most immigrant families, who never achieved higher levels of status and literacy, the incentive in America remained the same as it had at home: produce children as essential components of a household economy.[40]

Additionally, where employment for women was minimal and access to unskilled work requiring little training was plentiful for adolescents, fertility could be quite high, an indication of how responsive immigrant families could be to particular economic structures and a suggestion that the simple movement from a rural to an industrial milieu, without significant changes in status, did not dictate a fertility decline. Thus, scholars such as Michael Haines have found that fertility rates for coal miners and iron workers exceeded other occupational groups. In Pennsylvania's hard coal region from 1896 to 1900 the fertility rates among foreign-born women were 45 percent higher than for native-born females. Haines also found that the region's foreign-born had higher fertility rates in the periods 1846–50, 1866–70, 1876–80, and in other periods as well. He also discovered that families with young boys immigrated to this region and others like it because of available work opportunities much like Irish and French-Canadian families had moved to textile towns. The structure of the labor market affected not only fertility decisions but locational choices.[41] Immigrants were far from ignorant about the new world of industrial capitalism.

While opportunities were sought for adolescent employment, immigrant women, like other women, usually terminated toil outside the household with marriage and focused attention on the roles of wife, mother, and homemaker. By 1920 in urban America, married women accounted for only 21 percent of the female work force. It is true that the percentage of wage earners among foreign-born adult females over the age of sixteen was one-third higher than the percentage for all white women, but this could be attributed to the heavier reliance of the immigrant family on the earnings of their unmarried daughters. Even for immigrant wives the general plan was not to leave home for work after marriage. Samples taken in Providence, Rhode Island, found 59 percent of the Italian wives and 69

78]

percent of the Jewish wives not working outside the home, although nearly one-third of the Italians cared for boarders. In Chicago in 1900 less than 2 percent of a sample of Polish, Italian, Jewish, German, and Irish wives left the household to toil, while between 52 and 74 percent of the unmarried females over the age of fifteen in these groups left each day for work.[42]

Strong imperatives existed in many immigrant families to prevent unmarried women to leave their homes in search of employment. Traditional perspectives on the domestic roles of mothers and wives persisted but were insufficient to account for the pattern by themselves, especially when it was not uncommon for married women to work in the fields of the rural world. Married women also had to raise children, manage the household, and care for boarders because they really had fewer employment opportunities than adult men and adolescents. Restricted opportunity in this case was continually supported by a myriad of cultural preferences. Irish immigrants strongly believed that married women should not work at all. This view was rooted not only in the model family of Irish Catholicism but in a social belief that a working married woman diminished the status of her husband. In Ireland female subservience had reached the point in the 1840s that married women had a shorter life expectancy than fathers and sons because the males were to receive the most nutritious food.[43] The "picture brides" of immigrant Japanese were expected not only to cook, wash, and care for their husbands but to work alongside them in fields or shops. In this instance work outside the home was allowed but strictly controlled. Italian males strongly opposed the employment of spouses outside the home. To the average southern Italian, somewhat powerless in the larger society, the conquest and possession of a woman offered a sense of control and authority. Greek families actually considered it a disgrace for a wife, and sometimes a sister, to work outside the house. Whatever the reason for keeping married women at home, the pattern of working-class domesticity was established prior to its celebration by middle-class reformers in urban America. Culture did not simply flow downward from social superiors.[44]

But the immigrant family was never totally insensitive to economic reality, and even married immigrant women could be forced into the labor market. Often their tenure was of short duration or they sought only part-time employment, but nearly always they worked only for familial rather than individual needs as part of a cooperative household. They even found ingenious ways to combine their dual roles as mother and worker. Not all could do as one

French-Canadian at Amoskeag who stayed at home and sold sand-
wiches to girls in the mill who did not bring lunches. Many mothers
relied on their skills by entering domestic work, which offered flexible
hours. Irish, German, and Scandinavian women were highly prized
by American employers for these tasks. By 1900 over 60 percent of the
Irish and Scandinavian women worked as domestics, while the figures
for Jews, Poles, and Italians was 20 percent or less. Jews and Slavs
were more likely to enter factories, because they often had skills in
needlework or rolling cigars. Italian women avoided domestic work
because they would be without the protection of their men or the
companionship of their friends while working. Thus, the Italian
female concentration in New York's artificial flower industry seems to
have been the result of a desire to work with kin. Some factory owners recruited married women because they thought they met production quotas better than single girls who did not need a particular job
as strongly. When unemployment became severe in the 1880s in
Santa Barbara among Mexican men, the "chicana" entered domestic
service and agricultural labor to keep families going. Chicano women
and children began to join the walnut harvest for several weeks each
year. Married Italian females in Buffalo would work, mostly in canneries on the Niagara Frontier because it was seasonal and they could
take their children along with them.[45]

Although familial need and economic necessity forced some married women outside the household, traces of individual goals and aspirations were found in their motivation and consciousness. Irish
women often delayed marriage to pursue individual jobs of their own.
At Amoskeag a few women who started working in their teens continued to do so after marriage because of the social ties they had
come to enjoy in the mills. Sometimes the skills women possessed,
such as Italian seamstresses or Jewish jewelry makers, caused certain
women to be in high demand. Jewish women in several communities
loosened traditional ties to the home and organized voluntary associations such as the First Hebrew Ladies Benevolent Society, which
met many communal welfare needs. Small numbers of mothers organized fraternal insurance organizations among Slovaks and Poles.
And mothers frequently organized and administered female auxiliary
groups to male union locals.[46]

Not only did a few women move outside to assist their families but
most of those who remained at home were able to exert considerable
influence and power. Too often women have been portrayed as help-
less before the demands of household obligations. One representative
conclusion by a scholar claimed that because occupational opportu-

Immigrant Women in Hat Factory
The work of immigrant females outside the home could be
indispensable for the maintenance of the family economy.
Immigration History Research Center,
University of Minnesota

nities for women were comparatively limited, females were prevented
from broadening their power within the family and thus the "traditional" role segregation of men and women was reinforced.[47] This
view is a distortion, however, on several counts. First, a considerable
body of evidence exists to suggest that immigrant and other women
actually entered into marriage as an act of independence from the
original obligations of their household economies. No matter what
new responsibilities they were incurring, they viewed the creation of a
family of their own as a positive, purposeful act which offered intrin-
sic rewards rather than simply burdensome obligations. Women often
viewed the birth of their own progeny as an additional, albeit psychological, contribution to their own parents who reveled in the joy of
grandchildren.[48] To an immigrant husband who left his parents at a
young age, his wife was more than a sex-partner or a co-worker, she
could be an adviser and a confidante as well. After all, in nearly every
immigrant-household economy, the central manager of financial resources, children's socialization, and the entire operation was the

[81

married female. Most immigrant children could share the recollection of one Irish woman that "mother always handled the money; my father never even opened his pay envelope." Because they had such an intimate knowledge of family finances and need, women to a remarkable extent usually made the decision to initiate small, immigrant family business concerns. Among Hungarian newcomers in East Chicago, Indiana, and New Brunswick, New Jersey, it was discovered that the idea of buying a farm or opening a saloon originated with women who had more "energy and ideas." In Connecticut's "Brass Valley," men had to consult with their wives over major financial decisions. Italian mothers may have been restricted in their employment opportunities but they were in charge of daily and long-range expenditures. Females in Chinese households strengthened their power at home in America and even determined their children's mate selection at times as men became more tied to workplace concerns. The evidence as to whether this influence on the part of wives in immigrant households was a departure or a remnant of premigration traditions is varied. For some, such as Sicilians, it appears to be a traditional trait. For others, like Syrians, it represented a departure from tradition. But in almost all cases women played highly influential roles in their homes.[49]

The immigrant household dominated by female managers usually consisted of only parents and children. To an overwhelming extent, the immigrant family was a nuclear family, although on occasion the household could expand to embrace other kin, boarders, or friends on a temporary basis. The predominance of the nuclear form, however, was clear cut throughout the nineteenth and twentieth centuries in both the premigration lands and in urban America. More complex family forms did tend to exist in eastern than western Europe, but it is now clear that nuclearity was not simply a product of the industrial economy, as it was long held. In fact, economic need might dictate that households could use all the wage earners they could get. The pervasive commitment to the nuclear structure, and the tendency to keep boarders only until children could work, suggests that something more than economic pressures explained family structure.

Even a brief survey of household structures among immigrant settlements attests to the hold of the nuclear model. Among Jews and Italians in New York City in 1905 about 95 percent of all households had a nuclear core. Among Germans in the same city in 1850, nine of every ten immigrants lived with kin. In Manchester, New Hampshire, the percentages were 88 percent for French-Canadians and 87.5 percent for the Irish. In Milwaukee, in 1860, 71 percent of the British households, 86 percent of the Irish, and 85 percent of the Germans consisted only of family members. Twenty years later in Detroit, 84.8 percent of the Germans and 88.1 percent of the Polish households were composed of simple nuclear families.[50]

Admittedly, there were stages in the course of familial development which could alter the composition of the household. Boarding was widespread in immigrant homes, as it offered a source of income. But boarders invariably appeared during stages of family life when children were too young to contribute to the household economy or had left to launch households of their own. Seldom were boarders found in the home when a nuclear family could support itself. The immigrant household could be flexible or "malleable" and take in boarders or other relatives who were in need of assistance, but it would inevitably snap back to the nuclear ideal when it was able. In Pittsburgh, for instance, the mean number of boarders in Italian and Polish households declined from the "young family" stage when children were too young to work to the "mid-stage" of family life when children entered the work force. Similar patterns were found among Lithuanian families in Chicago who had few other ways to make ends meet. Boarders could join the nuclear family in its private space but only for a time.[51]

When most working-class families had their choice, they preferred a private household consisting of parents and children. At times in the life cycle when children were able to work and contribute to finances, they were usually able to obtain their wish. The middle class was not alone in valuing the private household. But economic circumstances, primarily in the form of insufficient wages, forced parents to expand their households at specific times to embrace boarders and others in order to secure additional income.

Conclusion

The predisposition toward doing whatever was necessary to sustain a family-based household was nothing new. It had pervaded the immigrant homelands and received additional support ironically from the new system of industrial capitalism which restructured its labor market in a manner which facilitated the entry of groups of untrained toilers who were often related or at least acquainted with each other. Kin and friends were free to assist each other in entering America by providing access to jobs and homes and supplying important information of labor market conditions. New arrivals were adept at determining where they might enter a very large economy. The immigrant family economy survived and flourished among most new-comers in industrial America because new economic structures ac-tually reinforced traditional ways of ordering life and, consequently, contributed to a supportive "external environment" for capitalism to proceed. In this system, individual inclinations were muted and the household, managed effectively by immigrant females, superseded all other goals and objectives. In the face of a sprawling and complex urban industrial structure, newcomers forged a relatively simple de-vice for establishing order and purpose in their lives. This system would remain predominant among working-class families until the labor market was reshaped again after World War II and credentials and skills regained importance in entering new professional sectors of work. It was a system which would be challenged by outside institu-tions and values as the stay in America became more permanent.

Finally, it could be argued that not all immigrant families functioned alike and that significant differences existed in religion, cultural background, and particular family strategies. Certainly, this was true. But it was also true that such differences coexisted with a fundamental similarity. Families and households were the predomi-nant form in which all immigrants entered the industrial-urban econ-omy and ordered their lives. Members of nearly all groups received indoctrination in the need to remain loyal to the familial and house-hold unit. The goals of individual households could differ as a result of cultural background or positioning within the economy, and these divergences would come into play over time as separate paths of edu-cation, occupation, and mobility were taken. But in the movement to a capitalist world and in the initial decades of settlement, familial and communal networks abounded.

3 /

Workers, Unions, and

Radicals

Imported Traditions of Work and Protest

While the creation of household economies and family networks facilitated the immigrant's entry into new economic and social structures, families could not confront all issues faced by newly arrived immigrant workers. More sophisticated forms of organization were frequently required to contend with the workplace, the other important arena in which newcomers encountered capitalism on a personal level. At this point of contact the issues would revolve around wages, conditions, and control. Decisions would have to be made whether the needs and objectives of immigrant families could best be pursued alone, in conjunction with native workers, or by adopting one of a number of political ideologies which pervaded the world of the immigrant worker and awaited selection. Families and friends may have assisted newcomers in entering the workplace and heavily influenced an immigrant worker's basic obligations but they were not necessarily able to offer guidance in how worker goals such as wages, improved conditions, and fair treatment were best achieved. For behavior in the workplace immigrants had either to rely on any similar experience they may have had in the premigration lands or to choose from several models already available in the United States.

Skilled immigrants, who arrived in large numbers prior to 1890, had already encountered industrial capitalism in their homelands and had accumulated a useful residue of experience in dealing with workplace matters. They were usually able to bring that experience with them and use it effectively in their strike and protest activity in America throughout much of the nineteenth century. In Fall River, Massachusetts, for instance, strikes throughout the 1870s could be

[85

linked directly to the organization and activity of English mill operatives from Lancashire. In the vanguard of this strike activity were spinners and weavers who had emigrated from England in the 1850s and formed organizations such as the Fall River Mule Spinners Association. One cooperative association formed by mill hands became so large by 1881 that its store covered an entire city block. Mule spinners even started a store of their own where each member contributed a monthly sum for his family food, and one person bought wholesale for all. Since British unions had grown more rapidly and steadily in the 1840s and 1850s, thousands who fled economic difficulties and union upheaval in the 1850s brought well-developed notions of labor organizations with them. Some who moved into American textile mills after they had been blacklisted in England even had their moving expenses paid for them by their unions.[1]

Skilled newcomers were not only familiar with methods of textile production but were adept in dealing with owners, managers, and workplace issues. Many had been prominent in union organizations at home. Leaders such as Thomas Webb, George Gunton, and Henry Souvey moved from Lancashire to New England well-versed in English trade-union tactics, such as the use of cooperatives to reduce living costs, selective strikes against corporations considered to be financially unstable, and levies on the wages of union members who continued to work. Two crafts actually transplanted their old country unions to the United States: the Amalgamated Society of Engineers and the Amalgamated Society of Carpenters and Joiners. Even though textile workers had no strong national union prior to World War I, links were maintained between colonies of English and Scottish weavers through the use of "walking delegates."[2]

In nineteenth-century Chicago most German immigrant leaders who were influential in organizing fellow Germans into trade unions had been heavily involved in the labor movement at home, which was heavily socialistic. Hartmut Keil, a historian who has studied German-American workers, found that the impact of those leaders was so significant that the trade-union movement proved more enduring among Chicago Germans than ethnic political organizations. Thus, Paul Grottkau, the son of a Prussian noble, became president of the German Bricklayers and Stonecutters Union, escaped arrest for labor activities, and came to Chicago to edit *Chicagoer Arbeiter-Zeitung*. George A. Schilling, a cooper and railroad worker in Germany, became a leading Socialist in Chicago. Such men became effective organizers among Germans not only because of their previous experience but because of their language skills and the role they frequently played as editors of

Italian Silk Workers, Paterson, New Jersey
Immigrant workers were both courted and ignored by a
variety of American labor organizations. *Immigration
History Research Center, University of Minnesota*

immigrant newspapers. Few picnics or other social activities were held
among Chicago Germans without an invitation being extended to these
editor-labor leaders.[3]

Familiarity with trade-union practices, however, was not limited
to intellectuals and craftsmen of the "old immigration," who had
lived in societies already influenced by industrial capitalism. Some
members of the "new immigration," long thought to be entirely peasant in origin, were quite aware of advanced forms of labor activity.
The earliest organization of some East European Jews and Italians
were greatly facilitated by traditions they brought with them. The
trade-union orientation of Jewish artisans' *chevroth* and of Italian
workers' mutual aid societies provided useful models of organizational
response to capitalism. A case study of Providence, Rhode Island,
found Jews directly relying on their experience in eastern Europe
with the *Bund*, a major socialist movement, and Italians exploiting
their familiarity with agricultural workers' unions in southern Italy.[4]

An outstanding example of immigrants bringing their own agenda
for labor organization and activity was the movement for coal mine

[87

safety legislation in Illinois. In 1872 the Illinois General Assembly enacted a mine safety statute that established a precedent in American coal mining legislation, for no other state had yet provided for the regulation of all its mines. Previously, mine safety legislation was usually passed in direct response to a tragic accident. But the Illinois law of 1872 was prompted not by a particular disaster but was the result of a campaign by immigrant British coal miners who began arriving in the state during the 1860s. Among the immigrant leaders were Daniel and Thomas Weaver, Thomas Lloyd, and Ralph Green who had moved from the mining areas of Staffordshire to St. Clair County, Illinois, and helped form the American Miners' Association, the first union of miners in the United States which was national in scope. They maintained close contact with union leaders in Britain, some of whom visited American coalfields. In fact, English miners were prominent in the formation of the United Mine Workers of America in the 1890s, an organization initially led by John Mitchell, who came from the English and Scottish mining village of Braidwood, Illinois. When the time arrived to press their safety demands, these miners unhesitatingly borrowed legislation enacted earlier by Parliament and supported a miners' lobby at the state capital.[5]

While only a few immigrants could rely on particular forms of labor activity with which they were familiar prior to moving, nearly all the new arrivals were familiar with communal and collective responses to survival and need. The same pattern of group activity which formed the foundation of the immigrant household was still available to structure the earliest forms of immigrant labor activity and protest during the first encounters with American industrial capitalism.

Prior to the imposition of bureaucratic rules and organization by large-scale unions, immigrant workers relied on work traditions and concepts of group survival they had brought with them to deal with workplace issues. Long before leaders such as Sidney Hillman of the Amalgamated Clothing Workers were able to impose order and weaken the shop-floor independence of the Italians, Jews, Lithuanians, and others who constituted their ranks in the 1930s, immigrant clothing workers usually produced "flash floods of rebellion" in the form of unauthorized work stoppages. Effective and sophisticated forms of union activity would still have to be imposed upon immigrants as they became more accustomed to the realities of the capitalistic economy. Some skilled Jews and Lithuanians from the tailoring centers of Byelorussia and Lithuania had organized strikes in Europe under the auspices of labor organizations, such as the *Bund*, which spread ideals of revolutionary politics and secular learning. But

large numbers of Italians in the industry, lacking such artisanal traditions, entered the industry without tailoring skills and an underdeveloped working-class heritage. They clustered in larger factories where
previous abilities mattered little and even relied on women to produce
work at home. They were much more likely to remain unorganized
and ineffective in their labor activity. Thus, Italians were still unorganized by the American Clothing Workers even in leading centers
such as Rochester for a much longer time than Jews.[6]

Communal associations were central to the early labor activity of
most immigrants but such ties did not produce anything approaching
uniformity in terms of worker protest or thought. Some degree of
communal structure had to be created before immigrant militancy
could occur but not all communities possessed the same traditions or
existed in similar surroundings. A highly fruitful comparison of two
nineteenth-century industrial towns by Daniel Walkowitz serves to
illustrate the point nicely.

Cohoes and Troy, New York, were towns which depended heavily
on the labor of newcomers. The former was a mill town engaged
primarily in textile production which attracted large numbers of unskilled French-Canadians. The latter was a large, more diverse industrial
city with higher concentrations of skilled workers, many with Irish backgrounds. Not surprisingly the more complicated community structure
was forged in Troy, where networks of voluntary associations, ethnic
organizations such as the Fenians, and even a workingmen's political
party were created. While Troy developed a well-organized labor
movement, Cohoes, with its abundant supply of female textile operatives, had a movement characterized by powerlessness.[7]

Prior to 1866 the labor histories of Troy and Cohoes had not been
very different. Female cotton workers and male ironworkers had organized unions and waged strikes of short duration for limited objectives such as the restoration of reduced wage levels. It was a classic
example of immigrants with underdeveloped skills and notions of
working-class activity conducting deeply felt but loosely organized
protest. Eventually, the Irish in Troy, veteran industrial workers, had
moved upward in the local social structure, gained control over crucial skilled positions, and begun to construct extensive ethnic and
political organizations as well as laboring ones. The very complexity
of their community and the enhancement of their status led to an
expansion of their horizons and objectives. Their protest as workers
began to reflect their newly achieved status. By the late 1860s, Troy
iron molders used the rather sophisticated technique of a lockout to
strike not only for better wages but for a new vision of a "worker city"

which included greater Irish political control and even the establishment of a cooperative foundry of their own. In Cohoes, where
cotton-mill families lived nearer the level of subsistence and were unable to create a more complex set of institutions and expectations,
labor protest during the 1870s and 1880s remained rather limited and
tied to wage rates.[8] In Troy, labor conflict and protest became more
intense with beatings and street violence occurring during the 1870s.
The point was that the traditions of newcomers, which often explained working-class behavior, were not always alike and were subject to particular town and labor structures encountered in America.

In situations where immigrant communities consisted of fewer
skilled workers and were able to exert less influence within a city or
town, immigrant communal traditions better explained the nature of
worker protest. During the 1880s, for instance, Irish dock workers in
New York City and northern New Jersey resorted to the "boycott" as
a tool to pressure employers to accept labor demands. The term
"boycott" itself was adopted by the Irish National Land League to
describe an identical tactic used against landlords and uncooperative
peasants in rural Ireland. The implementation of the term, in other
words, revealed a strong association between ethnic communal values
and labor protest.[9]

For many Irish immigrant workers in the nineteenth century, a
link was established between the problems that affected workers in
America and peasants in Ireland. Both the industrial monopoly of
American capitalists and the land monopoly of the English in Ireland
were looked upon as an unfair "aggrandizement" of natural resources
which God had intended to be shared by all. Many Irish workers in
America, therefore, were not bent upon the attainment of middle-
class respectability but on the creation of a society which was unclut-
tered by institutional controls of the wealthy; American capitalists like
English nobility threatened to turn America into another Ireland. A
crusade of Irish-American nationalism rising in the late nineteenth
century became not only a movement for the liberation of Ireland
but simultaneously a strike for a democratic idealogy and working-
class rights on the part of ordinary, immigrant toilers.[10]

By the 1880s in New York City, leading labor organizations such
as the Central Labor Union and the Knights of Labor could only
hope to attract worker support if they also promoted Irish independence from England. Irish-American longshoremen collected money
for organizations working for the abolishment of landlordism in Ireland. Actually the funds which supported the Irish Land League
came mostly from day laborers and servants in America. Irish-

American editors, such as Patrick Ford, encouraged Irish workers to adopt techniques such as the boycott which were rooted in "Ireland's just cause." It was no wonder that the 1882 freight handlers strike on the New York and New Jersey waterfronts against the monopolistic practices of the railroads evoked widespread support from the immigrant working-class community. Land League branches throughout the United States aided the strikers by contributing money and supportive resolutions. While they were limiting to an extent, communal and traditional values continued to shape much of the nature of the immigrant worker's protest.[11]

Communal solidarity was characteristic of much immigrant labor activity in both the nineteenth and twentieth centuries and usually resulted in protest and violence which involved all family and community members. Communal strikes inevitably involved women and children as well as male workers. At Ludlow, Colorado, in 1913 female Greeks fought scabs with clubs studded with spikes while their husbands faced militiamen. At Lattimer, Pennsylvania, in 1897 similar episodes characterized several days of protest resulting in the shooting of over 35 immigrant miners.[12]

A vivid example of the interaction of communal values and labor protest surfaced in the coal towns of eastern Pennsylvania during the first third of the twentieth century. Immigrant miners and their American-born sons, mostly from southern and eastern Europe, began to support the United Anthracite Miners (UAM), an organization formed to compete with the older American Mine Workers of America. While the personal rivalries of labor leaders were involved, the UAM essentially fought for job equalization. In brief, the concept called for the even distribution of mining and processing of hard coal among the various collieries owned by a company, rather than restricting production to a few where coal was closer to the surface and, therefore, cheaper to get from the ground. In part, of course, miners were challenging the company's right to control the production process, but more importantly they were asserting the value of sharing scarce resources which was central to their immigrant families and communities. Spreading the work among all collieries would allow all workers to earn some wages and even prolong the mining of a limited resource.[13]

Perhaps one of the most salient features of the UAM protest was its collective nature. Supporters of the UAM attempted to curtail operations at various collieries by prohibiting men from going to work through the intervention of all family members. Women formed an auxiliary to the UAM and groups which beat men thought to be scabs. At local high schools, students boycotted their classrooms because several teachers had relatives working at collieries which were on strike. Men would pick coal for neighbors who were unemployed. And every family whether located in mining village, mill town, or urban neighborhood relied on the cooperative spirit of the local storekeeper who allowed immigrants to "buy on the book" and pay once the strike was completed. During violence in 1935, anthracite-area women were arrested for beating scabs. One miner was wrestled to the ground by ten women. In other cases women were found "defying" state police who had been sent to the region to restore order. Communal protest reached a peak when mining families stoned the funeral procession of a miner who was killed while working during the 1935 strike and filled the victim's open grave with tin cans. Eventually the police had to be called to prevent the protesters from removing the body from the grave.[14] Some scholars may assume that such behavior stemmed from pre-industrial traits of peasants, but familial and communal solidarity was fostered as much by the marginal nature of life in the industrial working class as it was in premigration worlds.

Ethnic Diversity and American Unions

Many scholars would conclude from the discussion of immigrant communal activity that immigrant communities inhibited the growth of a strong trade-union movement prior to the 1930s and that the "informal" stage of peasant-worker protest had to be eradicated before peasants became industrial workers in the truest sense and exhibited classic forms of organization and worker militancy. But several points must be made to qualify that assertion. First, immigrant workers were willing to protest against capital regardless of the stage in which they were located. Second, no easy transfer was made between the world of family and community and that of the industrial worker. They remained inextricably linked for a very long period of time, perhaps throughout the entire industrial era. Finally, instead of being inhibited by traditions and communal ties, immigrants were actually motivated by them. They were worth preserving. It was often American unions which neglected them and failed to exploit their inherent inclination to fight for what they valued most in life, a failure which helped sustain communal solidarity wherever it occurred.

Despite some strong evidence that immigrants could be good union members, historians and others still discuss the ways in which they arrested the development of labor solidarity and trade unionism. They have been described as indifferent to labor organizations or a source of divisiveness due to the ethnic antagonism they created, their strikebreaking activity, and their tendency to depress overall wage levels. Gerald Rosenblum concluded that the potential of the Knights of Labor to organize "one big union" in the late nineteenth century was undermined by the strikebreaking activities of immigrants, for instance, and the immigrants' predilection to labor for less. After 1887 the Knights, in fact, did begin to lose much of their support in cities with large concentrations of the foreign-born.[15]

Numerous instances do exist to confirm the fact that the plentiful supply of unskilled, immigrant workers facilitated tremendously the ability of American manufacturers throughout the industrial age to break up the work process, diminish the influence of skilled workers over production, and accelerate the process of employing unskilled operatives in their stead. Thus, Detroit's cigar industry changed dramatically in the decade after 1900. Most cigars had been made by handworkers who brought relevant skills from Belgium and Germany and who, incidentally, had eagerly joined the Knights of Labor. By 1915 most of the city's cigars were made by unskilled Polish-born women; over 7,000 were employed by Detroit's ten largest cigar factories. Indeed, it was the presence of many immigrant females in Detroit that caused factories of skilled workers in Kalamazoo to close and move to the "Motor City." Cigar trade journals complained that a person "must wear skirts" to work in a large factory but employers felt that immigrant women would work for lower wages and were less subject to labor agitation. In Newark it was Hungarian women who began to dominate the cigar industry, and in Philadelphia it was Russian Jews. As skilled cigar makers attempted to stem the tide of unskilled newcomers, skilled glassblowers resisted immigration by trying to limit production and thus stretch out available work. Similar reactions took place elsewhere. Tin millworkers in Elwood, Indiana, gave immigrants a "cold reception" when they arrived and told them to move on.[17]

Clearly, from the early decades of the nineteenth century skill and cultural differences widened and frustrated labor solidarity, although the process was ultimately linked to changes in the structure of the workplace and the policies of capital which encouraged immigration and not the immigrants themselves. In Newark what appeared to be a semblance of working-class unity was weakened by 1850 as Protestant workers began to abhor many of the customs of Irish and German newcomers, particularly the consumption of alcohol. As Susan Hirsch has ably demonstrated, Catholics retaliated against Protestant social codes enacted into laws forbidding tippling on the Sabbath.

[93

During an 1854 parade in Newark of the American Protective Association, an organization opposed to immigration, Irish Catholic workers heckled the marchers and full-scale violence ensued culminating in the ransacking of a German Catholic Church. Skilled workers, reacting to the assault of industrialization upon their traditional, lofty status began to vent their frustrations in political movements which defended not only their control of the work process but their traditional Protestant culture, including adherence to temperance. Unskilled newcomers, who were largely German and Irish Catholics, were viewed as threats not only to their status at work but to their religious and cultural values as well. Unskilled workers were not the only ones subject to communal and cultural ties.

Skilled workers could overcome ethnic differences in the formation of narrow craft unions, but larger working-class unity with most unskilled newcomers proved impossible. Thus in Newark in the 1850s the Whig Party was floundering on the "rock of ethnic conflict." Immigrant workers were thought to be subject to the authoritarianism of Rome, and many skilled immigrants could not make up their minds whether to side with those who shared their work status or those who shared their cultural backgrounds. Political and labor movements were both in disarray.[18]

In Philadelphia, prior to the Cival War immigration, revivalism and nativism were also linked and tended to undermine working-class solidarity. These forces "balkanized" wage earners into opposing sides and even fostered links between native-born skilled journeymen and small producers which would ultimately push American Republicans toward an anti-foreign party and Democrats toward a party more responsive to the needs of the foreign-born. Hard times in the 1830s promoted pervasive revivalism which focused on issues such as temperance and immigration. Revivalist preachers encouraged anti-foreign feeling by depicting immigrants as competitors in the labor market and persons who would lower the moral level of society because of their backwardness (and Catholicism). Revivalist workers were usually Protestant, militant defenders of faith and culture but deferential at work because of the common links they shared with their Protestant employers; both believed strongly in self-denial, diligence, and individual responsibility for one's station in life. As the arrival of the Irish, fleeing famine at home, drove Philadelphia's immigrant population upward by 1850, a Catholic world emerged not only to threaten a traditional Protestant one but to intensify working-class divisions. Irish Catholics and Irish Protestants established separate neighborhoods and separate fire companies, gangs, and voting blocks. Separate Irish gangs even served as surrogate unions, thus arresting working-class solidarity even more. They controlled access to work, negotiated with employers, and enforced unity during strikes.[19]

As in Newark, ethnic and cultural divisions in the labor force spilled over into the political arena. Opposing cultural spheres generated competing sets of leaders. Revivalist ministers in Philadelphia began to agitate for a moral component to public education as a means of preserving social order. This ideological stance usually meant the introduction of the King James Version of the Bible into the classroom. To Catholic clergy, however, such a move would endanger the souls of their flock. Agitation over the use of the Bible in the schools, like the furor over drinking, further divided Catholic and Protestant workingmen and contributed to the rise of Irish-Democratic political leaders in cities which were tied closely to Irish newcomers and to the rise of the American Republican Party, which sought to exclude immigrants from the suffrage and defend the use of the King James Bible in the schools. Immigration was certainly not facilitating the unification of industrial workers.[20]

After the Civil War, potential unity was again hindered by the increased immigration of unskilled, culturally different workers. Ultimately, this flow of strangers was generated by the continuing imperative of capital to reduce labor costs, minimize the control of skilled workers, and maximize productivity. In the textile town of Fall River, Massachusetts, a semblance of working-class unity had existed between English, Irish, and the few French-Canadian operatives. But by 1900, due to increased competition from Southern textile centers with lower wages and more modern machinery, New England mills were forced to increase the labor intensity of their work force to compete. Cheap immigrant labor in the form of Polish and Portuguese toilers was attracted, and existing labor organizations retreated into narrow craft protectionism rather than embracing the newcomers. Workers lost continuity with their traditions of solidarity.[21] Similarly, at the Cleveland Rolling Mill Company in Ohio in the 1880s skilled workers replaced by technological changes blamed their loss of jobs on immigrant Poles and Bohemians, who filled their positions. The introduction of Bessemer converters and open-hearth furnaces had severely reduced the need for skilled workers and increased the demand for low paid, unskilled laborers throughout America to feed iron ore into furnaces, pour molten metal, and keep fires going. As immigrant English, Scottish, and Welsh skilled workers reacted angrily to the transformations wrought by the capitalism they had once

[95

embraced, unskilled newcomers eagerly replaced them. The craft-dominated Amalgamated Association of Iron and Steel Workers could never really bring itself to extend a cooperative hand to the mass of unskilled strangers. In 1885, when Bohemians and Poles rejected repeated wage cuts and, armed with guns and clubs, forced their way into the mills and closed them, skilled workers offered them little sympathy. Recent immigrants continued their strike for days despite threats from their clergy that they would not receive the rites of their church, but their skilled comrades held back and refused even to attend rallies and meetings in a local, empty lot.[22]

Instances of ethnic and skill disharmony continued to punctuate industrial America throughout the industrial age. Cornish miners in California, immensely proud of their traditional mining skills, bitterly resisted the importation of inexpensive, Chinese labor. In a 1910 garment strike in New York, Italians and Jews argued over the number of Italian representatives in the garment union. Jews in the same strike wanted to reach an agreement earlier than Italians because they would need money for an upcoming religious holiday. During the national steel strike of 1919, skilled men and their unions failed to adequately support the militancy of immigrant strikers in the Pittsburgh area. And in the early twentieth century, the general union movement in southern California shunned Mexican and Japanese workers and forced them to form their own associations to negotiate contracts for sugar beet workers. In 1903 Chicanos had to proceed alone in their strike at the Johnston Fruit Company packinghouse and formulate their own tactics, which included work stoppages at the height of the packing season.[23]

Immigrants not only had difficulty getting along with American workers and other newcomers, but they frequently had problems with the pace of industrial production lines and did not always conform easily to new routines of labor. While a few historians have suggested that immigrants actually facilitated the transition to industrial society because they failed to resist technological innovations at work and adopt American traditions of protest, repeated instances exist of newcomers being at odds with the goals of industrial managers. At the sprawling Amoskeag textile factory in Manchester, New Hampshire, French-Canadian immigrants would react negatively to company attempts to speed-up production and stretch work out. When "winders" at Amoskeag were slowed down by frequent breakages in the yarn and unacceptable raw materials, they took matters into their own hands, removed boxes of yarn that were unsuitable, and insisted on the right to determine their own speed. In Pennsylvania, immigrant coal min-

English Class at Industrial Plant in Chicago, 1919
Industrial firms such as the Ford Motor Company and the
Barrett Company, pictured here, often took steps to
Americanize and socialize workers to facilitate their
adjustment and make them more efficient.
Chicago Historical Society

ers effectively restricted the number of cars a man could load each
day so work would last longer and the supply of coal would not be
depleted too quickly. In mills and factories throughout American
cities, immigrants would seldom work on their particular religious
holidays. And when industrial work proved too demanding or burdensome, immigrant laborers left their jobs for another or returned
home. Absenteeism, especially from Sunday merrymaking or labor
turnover, was particularly widespread. Evidence exists that newer
immigrant workers either learned how to resist unfair managers from
American workers or reacted instinctively to modern pressures by restricting output when faced with speedups or criticizing fellow toilers
who failed to participate in slowdowns. Cornish miners in California
resisted the introduction of dynamite which would reduce the
number of men needed to drill. Filipino workers in railroad cars even

[97

manipulated passenger checks in the 1920s to increase their own income and immigrant women shortened their workday so they could leave for home early to care for their children.[24]

The intractability of many immigrant workers forced American industries to devise special programs and modify their personnel policies. Immigrants did not simply feed the engines of capitalism but forced capitalists to adjust as well. At the Ford Motor Company after 1910, for instance, the skills necessary for factory operatives were drastically diluted and thousands of unskilled immigrants swarmed into the factory in Highland Park, Michigan, especially Poles, Russians, Romanians, Italians, and Sicilians. But many newcomers had personal agendas which differed from Ford's and planned to work only a short while. Others found the pace and the noise of the plant bothersome and soon left. Rates of absenteeism were so large by 1913 that 52,000 workers had to be hired to maintain a work force of 13,600. Obviously, immigrants were not advocates of capitalistic values at all costs.[25]

The response of the Ford Motor Company to the widespread labor turnover, a problem which existed whenever immigrants filled industrial jobs, was not only direct and dramatic but symptomatic of a much broader effort to transform the values and behavior of immigrant newcomers. To improve efficiency, eliminate worker transiency, and mold new behavioral forms which were better suited to the needs of mechanized production, Ford instituted the "Five Dollar Day." But the money was not there for the taking. In order for a worker to qualify for the wage, the Ford Sociological department had to certify that he was thrifty and sober, and it sent investigators into immigrant homes to ascertain the extent newcomers conformed to Ford's values there. A savings and loan association was even formed to encourage thrift and compete with immigrant bankers who sold steamship tickets and, thus, facilitated transiency. As historian Stephen Meyer has insightfully concluded, the Ford program, which did reduce labor turnover significantly, was an instrument of social control which sought to restructure working-class culture around middle-cass industrial values of sobriety, thrift, and diligence.[26]

The program at the Ford Motor Company was only one of many initiated by American industries after the late nineteenth century to reform the behavior of industrial workers, strengthen their ties to a particular manufacturer, and regulate more closely the entire scope of labor-management relations. Some companies resorted to corporate welfare schemes which relied on paternalistic measures to alter worker attitudes much as Ford did. Other firms professionalized their personnel management operations and recruited trained personnel managers rather than shop-floor foremen to handle grievances and recruitment problems. Scientific management represented an additional weapon in management's arsenal which aimed at a tighter organization of production and even incentive pay to keep labor loyal. Everywhere one or a combination of these approaches was used. John D. Rockefeller established a sociological department a decade before Ford. At the Goodyear Tire and Rubber Company an employee representative plan was organized but voting privileges could not be obtained unless a worker first became an American citizen. Cambria Steel and other companies opened libraries and Americanization classes to foster an acceptance of American ways. Company dentists taught immigrants to brush their teeth and physicians instructed them in good medical habits. Visiting company nurses entered immigrant homes to instruct women in child care, finances, and hygiene. Some firms actually attempted to regulate the amount of alcohol newcomers could consume. At the New Jersey Zinc Company immigrant children were organized into a "penny provident bank" to learn thrift, and at the Colorado Fuel and Iron Company kindergartens were established so that Americanization programs could ultimately reach parents through their children.[27]

It would be misleading, however, to suggest that the immigrant worker was continually at odds with employers or American toilers and their unions. Contention from unions which sought to exclude them, hostility from employees with different religious backgrounds, and factory owners who wanted them to transform their lifestyles were all pervasive themes. But another theme runs through the experience of immigrant labor which has been insufficiently stressed in the past. In numerous industrial cities and plants, American workers and their organizations frequently launched serious efforts to embrace newcomers in order to widen the base of working-class solidarity. Often this solidarity was facilitated by work structures which forced immigrants and natives, skilled and unskilled, to toil in close proximity such as coal mining, carpentry, or the floor of slaughterhouses. Separation seemed more evident in large mills where departments were kept farther apart.

American historians have long debated the issue of whether immigrants were receptive to union organizations. Scholars such as Edwin Fenton and David Brody suggested that immigrants generally resisted joining unions while others, such as Victor Greene in his study of Slavic coal miners and Leslie Hough in an analysis of Bohemian coopers in Cleveland, found immigrants more eager to

[99

join unions than native-born workers. The situation appears even more complicated if events such as the Great Steel Strike of 1919 are examined. In areas such as Pittsburgh, immigrants played a central role in leading strike action. In steel towns farther east, such as Bethlehem, however, immigrants remained outside the main body of strikers and played a considerably more passive role.[28]

The issue remains a standoff if examples of immigrants joining unions are simply placed alongside contrasting examples of their lack of participation. Some immigrants did arrive in industrial America with previous experience in unionization and labor activity. They composed a relatively small portion of the total immigrant stream, however, were usually skilled, and concentrated in the period prior to the 1880s when skills were easily transferable into the American economy. The massive numbers of new arrivals, while being familiar with some form of collective response to the exigencies of life, were not particularly predisposed one way or another toward labor unions. This left the ultimate burden of immigrant participation to the unions themselves and the degree to which the labor organizations were willing to overlook differences in skill, culture, and ethnic background, as Robert Asher has incisively suggested.[29] To return to an earlier example, immigrants in Pittsburgh during the 1919 steel strike were effectively organized by men of similar backgrounds employed by the American Federation of Labor. In Bethlehem and Steelton no such organizational efforts were made. If immigrants were approached by individuals they trusted and could understand, they could be mobilized quite effectively. Asher was even able to demonstrate that if the number of foreign-born grew large enough in any trade or occupation resentment toward newcomers on the part of unions quickly subsided. Thus, marble workers rejected Jews and Italians at first but then decided to organize them. Similarly, carpenters rejected immigrant members in their organizations in 1880 but realized the need to incorporate the foreign-born by 1887 and in Chicago actually perfected a system of local ethnic organizations which embraced Germans, Czechs, and Poles. In Milwaukee in 1886 the Knights of Labor drew increased Polish support after they hired the editor of a local Polish newspaper to organize for them. Coal miners learned the lessons of ethnic solidarity in the Illinois coalfields early and extended those lessons to other states to make the United Mine Workers an organization open to immigrant workers.[30]

In a surprising number of cases, efforts were made to incorporate immigrants into unions. Militant organizations such as the Industrial Workers of the World actively sought to recruit immigrant and migrant labor. Even the American Federation of Labor, a stronghold of skilled craftsmen, made a few efforts to incorporate newcomers. Among Mexican female laundry workers in San Antonio, the A.F. of L. did attempt to organize those who became citizens. In 1920 unskilled brass workers in Waterbury, Connecticut, formed ethnic locals of the A.F. of L. for Poles, Russians, Portuguese, French, Italians, and Lithuanians who worked there. In New York City, Jews found receptive labor leaders as they entered the city's industries for many shared their religious and cultural traditions. These labor leaders understood the need to weave Biblical references into their recruitment speeches to attract a sympathetic ear. Strikes broke out in the garment, cigar-making, bakery, and hat-making industries which depended upon the leadership of Jewish Socialists and labor spokesmen such as Abraham Cahan or Joseph Barondess. The Amalgamated Clothing Workers of America even underwrote the construction of cooperative apartments in New York City for Jewish workers.[31]

In Chicago successful attempts were made to involve immigrant toilers in organized labor. In the packinghouse district skilled butchers and other workers, faced with a transformation of their craft and the expansion of the pool of immigrant, unskilled workers in their industry, did not hesitate to incorporate newcomers into their organization. Pioneer butcher unions actually had a long tradition of immigrant participation, for butchering was a skill directly transferable from rural homelands. Consequently, Germans, Jews, and Bohemians had all formed their own butcher unions during their earliest days in America. Faced with low wages, chronic unemployment, insecurity, irregular hours, and high accident rates, Chicago's skilled butchers by 1900 were quite willing to teach newcomers the value of organization and rational responses, such as strikes, to workplace conditions. On Chicago's South Side unionization became a process of Americanization. By 1900 craft control and close personal ties among Irish butchers were no longer a viable basis for working-class organization; the colorful parades fo Irish butchers with their bloodied aprons marching behind banners proclaiming "Workingmen's Rights" were no longer sufficient to influence an industry rapidly dividing its work force by skill, task, and ethnicity. Thus, older skilled butchers moved quickly to embrace Slavs, Lithuanians, and even immigrant women and to transmit their ideas of organization and protest. Organizers were now recruited from the ranks of immigrant newcomers after 1900. John Kikulski, for one, was paid and appointed by the A.F. of L. to organize among Poles and Lithuanians. He was closely tied to the immigrant community, having been

[101

active in the Polish Alliance and the Polish Falcons. During the organization drive preceding a 1904 strike, he started his own paper which attracted thousands of newcomers to the union.[32]

Even as early as the 1870s, cases existed where ethnic antagonisms were insufficient to divide workers in certain industries. In Fall River, Massachusetts, as skill differentials were muted somewhat and economic conditions worsened, a spirit of unionism was ignited between 1879 and 1884. Led by a large number of spinners from England with previous union experience, the emphasis was placed not on separatism but on "pan-craft" unionism, as English, Irish, and French-Canadians sought to work together. As one union leader explained, "Unity of thought and action in industrial warfare is the stepping stone to victory." Steeped in the tradition of craft unions, many spinners did have difficulty in accepting unskilled immigrants, especially French-Canadians, who had earlier entered the mills as strikebreakers. But the effort was made to transcend internal divisions and all groups participated in three major strikes in the decade after 1884. Ranks were kept solid and the union hall came to function as a social center despite the fact that immigrant priests and shopkeepers, usually encouraged by local capitalists, as they were in most mill towns, led an attack on unions by denying strikers credit and even the means to salvation. Often union detractors had more influence with older immigrants who were tied more closely to ethnic institutions than younger workers who appeared more eager to embrace unions.[33]

The International Ladies Garment Workers Union (ILGWU) was another illustration of a labor organization extending an invitation to newly arrived workers from abroad. Union officials saw the growth of unskilled, foreign-born women in the industry and responded to this change in the structure of work by approaching the newcomers. After a 1909 strike, the union's newspaper began to publish editions in Italian as well as in Yiddish and English. The tragic Triangle Factory fire in New York, which took the lives of 145 females, gave further impetus to the movement to incorporate women and upgrade their conditions. The ILGWU moved to launch a massive garment strike in 1913 in New York of all "women's trades." As elsewhere, ethnic organizers played a central role. August Bellanca and his brother, Frank, spread pro-union propaganda among Italians. Throughout the strike, Italian women displayed militancy and strong union support. In the Ridgewood section of Brooklyn, 6,000 workers, many of whom were Italian women who had never before been reached by unions, asked to be organized.[34]

One union that made several attempts to unionize immigrant

workers was the Industrial Workers of the World. In 1909 at McKees Rocks, Pennsylvania, immigrant workers at the Pressed Steel Company initiated a strike over what was perceived to be an unfair method of calculating wages. The company had apparently devised a labor-pool system of production in which all members of a pool were penalized for time and production lost by a slow worker and men who worked feverishly on an assembly line knew what their weekly earnings would be. While unskilled immigrants initiated the strike, skilled American-born employees, unable to accomplish much with most of the work force out, joined the effort for a time but quickly reached an agreement with management and returned to work. Immigrants, influenced by several men who had experience in European labor and radical movements remained more defiant. They formed a committee of their own and, after the killing of a Hungarian striker, vowed to take the life of one of those fighting against them.[35]

At this juncture the strikers apparently invited the I.W.W. to come to McKees Rocks. While the movement presented the radical labor organization with an opportunity to capture the loyalty of the town's unskilled toilers, the spectre of an immigrant-I.W.W. alliance evoked bitter opposition from the company, local public officials, and skilled workers. While the strike eventually produced severe violence, the killing of six strikers, and a state police search of every home in McKees Rocks, the company eventually capitulated to immigrant militancy and made concessions which not only ended the strike but undermined any potential immigrant support for the I.W.W.[36] Immigrants could be as militant as any industrial worker, even with only a minimum of union encouragement.

In the textile mill town of Lawrence, Massachusetts, the I.W.W. had an even better opportunity to make inroads among the immigrant ranks and worked persistently to do so after its formation in 1905. Certainly conditions were ripe in Lawrence. Wages were low, immigrant tenements were overcrowded, and infant mortality rates were shockingly high. Little wonder that by 1911 the Lawrence local of the National Industrial Union of Textile Workers adopted the I.W.W. statement of principles which included the abolishment of the wage system, a stand quite a bit more radical than any taken by other locals of the textile workers' union.[37]

When a strike broke out in Lawrence in 1912, the radical immigrant organizers and spokesmen sent by the I.W.W. quickly brought unity among diverse groups of Italian, Irish, French-Canadian, and other immigrant workers. In addition to "Wobblie" leader, Bill Haywood, Italian-born leaders such as Joseph Ettor and Arturo

Giovannitti magnetized the towns' millhands. Local men also rose to leadership roles during the strike: Angelo Rocco among the Italians and Samuel Lipson among the Jews and Luis Picavet among the French-Canadians. All quickly embraced Haywood's advice when he exclaimed, "There is no foreigner here except the capitalist."[38]

Immigrants unfamiliar with union tactics quickly learned the I.W.W. methods of industrial warfare in their quest for higher wages. Mass picket squads formed near mill gates to keep out nonstrikers. And intimidation was used against unsympathetic workers by hurling insults or organizing mass parades. Newcomers also relied on communal ties as they had elsewhere. Women struck with the men, attacked policemen in groups, and threw one of them into an icy river.[39] As usual, companies attempted to retaliate through ethnic institutions, especially local Catholic priests, believing that newcomers were influenced more by their institutional leaders than the demands of their households or the rhetoric of radicals. But the effort of the strikers continued and assistance came from workers in other cities; the Italian Socialist Federation sent Italian children to the homes of Italian families in New York City to remove them from the scene of violence. When local officials attempted to stop the exodus of children from Lawrence with force, they evoked a national outpouring of protest and investigation which attracted support and contributions for the strikers from all over the country and led to wage increases and an eventual resolution of the conflict.[40]

Once the strike ended immigrants, pressured by the need to live and survive within the mills and sustain their familial and communal arrangements, drifted from their support of the I.W.W. in Lawrence, just as they had done in McKees Rocks and just as they would do in the famous strike of 1913 at Paterson, New Jersey. Immigrants could be effective strikers and militant workers especially when encouraged by existing labor organizations, but they could not jeopardize the marginal foundations of their familial and communal networks for too long a period by remaining away from work.

Immigrants and Socialism

Immigrant workers experienced an uneven relationship with American labor organizations and, as a result, exhibited both conservative and militant behavior at the workplace. They were also exposed to the tenets and influences of the Socialist Party in America but again found serious obstacles to integrating themselves with an organization ostensibly interested in the plight of working people. Ultimately, the relationship between the Socialist Party in America and immigrants was a weak one which never really established a firm foundation for supporting or directing the activity of immigrant workers. American Socialist leaders never did a good job of attracting the mass of unskilled toilers and remained fixed to groups of middle-class reformers, skilled Germans, English-speaking workers in declining crafts, and a substantial number of Jews. The party concentrated much of its energies on local issues such as the municipal ownership of utilities and, in the opinion of historian Milton Cantor, never really developed a strong theoretical posture which could attract diverse segments of the industrial work force.[41]

The failure to attract widespread immigrant participation is curious, since it was not at all unusual for immigrant groups to bring some strain of socialist tradition to the United States after the middle of the nineteenth century. Despite the image of immigrants as conservative refugees, the premigration encounter with capitalism had already raised the political consciousness of many newcomers and had resulted in cells of socialist consciousness being established in immigrant settlements throughout America, from Milwaukee and Chicago to smaller towns such as McKees Rocks and Lawrence. Some immigrants even adopted socialism once in the United States. Finns in the lumber and mining camps of Minnesota and Michigan were influenced by American models of cooperative associations. At a 1904 meeting in Cleveland, Finnish Socialists argued for the establishments of cooperatives in order to provide training in commerce and business for the future managers of the "socialist commonwealth."[42]

A heightened sense of class consciousness was usually brought to America by newcomers themselves, however. German revolutionaries from the uprisings of 1848 fled to the United States with detailed programs of economic and social change. English immigrants before the Civil War such as William Heighton, a Philadelphia cordwainer, and George Henry Evans, who edited the *Working Man's Advocate* in New York City, thought that workers should act as a class and seek equality with capitalists through the acquisition of free land and free access to education. Marxism itself arrived in New York in 1851 through the immigration of one of Marx's disciples, Joseph Weydemeyer, a young Westphalian who called on German immigrants to join unions and political organizations and who helped organize the German Workers League in 1853. Adolph Germer, another German immigrant, helped organize Illinois miners and spread radical labor doctrines. Daniel De-Leon, who was born in Curaçao, assumed control of the Socialist Labor Party in 1889 and gave it his Marxist views. And Jewish Socialists brought their views to cities such as Milwaukee, New York, and elsewhere.[43] It is true that most of these immigrants had not come from rural hamlets but from small industrial towns in England, Germany, Poland, and Russia, had worked in factories, and had experienced industrial relations and inequality.[44]

Germans especially played a central role in the importation of Socialist thought to nineteenth-century America. In Milwaukee the powerful Social Democrats resembled more the party in Germany than any American political organization by the 1880s. It was no accident that the city's Central Labor Union campaigned vigorously for the eight-hour day in 1886 and advocated ethnic solidarity. German Socialists in the city even had their own multipublishing empire headed by Victor Berger, which eventually included German, English, and Polish weeklies. The party sponsored carnivals, bazaars, and socials and, in general, followed the patterns of the German Social Democrats, considered at the time to be the most successful Socialist party in the world. By 1910 in the Milwaukee municipal elections the Socialists won the largest victory they ever registered in a major American city and carried not only the German wards but some Polish neighborhoods as well.[45]

The nature of New York's garment industry appeared to suggest that organizing Jewish workers and spreading labor and socialist doctrine would be difficult. Many workers were women who were tied more to familial rather than labor concerns, and many did piecework in their homes and tenements rather than in a large factory. But Jews arrived not only with tailoring skills but a well-developed socialist tradition and social consciousness. Women like Theresa Serber Malkiel, who was born in Kiev, toiled in sweatshops and organized a Woman's Infant Cloak Makers Union. She told her fellow immigrants that economic solidarity was insufficient to achieve labor's goals and urged the formation of political organizations. She eventually joined the socialist United Hebrew Trades and then helped align it with the Socialist Labor Party of America.[46] The efforts of Jewish intellectuals like Abraham Cahan further identified socialism with labor causes. While frequently motivated more by a concern for the poor and oppressed than by formulating a dogmatic socialism, Cahan, as editor of *Forward*, reported on labor violence throughout America and turned the paper into a workingman's organ. Immigrant Jewish idealism and socialism created the environment which produced early labor organizations such as the United Labor Party and labor leaders such as Samuel Gompers and Adolph Strasser, who in their younger idealistic years, steered the cigar-makers section of the International Workingmen's Association into "social idealism" by recruiting women, tenement workers, and even establishing a cooperative store.[47]

While the number of Italian Socialists was never extensive, small groups did exist in many cities, mill towns, and mining regions. Among Italian cigar workers in Tampa, Florida, radical clubs were formed by newcomers from several villages in Sicily, especially Santo Stefano. Tampa's Italians also received socialist literature distributed by fellow cigar makers from Cuba who read radical literature to the immigrants as they worked much as Jews did in New York City.[48] In small mining towns where other immigrant institutions did not exist to compete with radical initiatives, Italian socialism could also be quite strong.[49] In 1902 at Hoboken, New Jersey, an Italian Socialist Federation was formed with its own newspaper, *Il Proletario*. But even where socialism flourished, division existed over objectives. Some wanted to form mutual-aid societies while others, like Carlo Tresca, argued for direct political action through organizations such as the I.W.W. American unions, such as the garment workers, were also recruiting Italian organizers, however, thus siphoning off much potential leadership from the socialist cause.[50]

Slavs and Hungarians proved no exception to the trend of establishing cells of socialism in various immigrant settlements. A Magyar section of the Socialist Labor Party was in operation in 1892 consisting most of skilled workers, artisans, and craftsmen. By 1896 small groups also existed in Cleveland, Newark, and Bridgeport. In each of these communities, Socialists stressed self-education among workers, internationalism, and the "ideals of socialism." The Socialist Hungarian Workers Benefit Association actually rose to the level of a national organization and consisted mostly of skilled rather than peasant Magyars. Hungarian Socialists also developed a rich cultural heritage especially with the plays of Sandor Kalassay on topics such as "The Real Victory" and "Strike."[51]

A similar pattern existed among South Slavs such as Slovenes, Serbs, and Croats. Like the Italians, Yugoslav immigrant socialism was stronger in smaller towns, especially mining settlements, than in larger cities. It was in the smaller centers that competing leaders such as the clergy could exert less influence in combating radical ideologies. Thus, the first Socialist newspaper among the Yugoslavs, *Glas Svobode*, was published in Pueblo, Colorado. In fact, the Pueblo area produced some of the key figures of South Slav socialism in America such as Charles Pogorelec, a Slovene, who led Colorado Slavs in the Mine, Mill, and Smelter Workers. By 1910 Croats, Serbs, and Slovenes had created a tenuous alliance to form the Yugoslav

Socialist Federation. The organization, however, continually suffered from ethnic divisions, publishing newspapers in three languages: *Proletaec* for the Slovenes, *Radnica Straza* for the Croats, and *Narodni Glas* for Serbian members.[52]

Among Finnish immigrants, socialism actually made considerable inroads. Although the Suomi Synod exerted a tremendous religious influence among American Finns, socialist organizations competed strongly for immigrant loyalties. Historians have estimated that about one-quarter of Finnish newcomers supported the socialist-labor cause, a relatively high figure for any immigrant group. In 1906 the Finnish Socialist Federation even joined the Socialist Party of America. It should be stressed, however, that Finnish immigrants were essentially "hall socialists." That is to say, they were primarily loyal to their local organizations and the social, cultural, and economic programs emanating from their communal halls rather than to a larger political movement or consciousness. Finnish Socialist leaders continually had a difficult time in persuading the rank and file to become involved in larger American working-class movements. During the 1920s when Communist organizers tried to push Finns to Americanize in order to mute ethnic divisions among American Socialists, Finnish Communists actually left the party because they did not want to relinquish the rich social and cultural contacts and activities which existed in their respective settlements.[53]

Clearly, centers of Socialist activity could be found to varying degrees in nearly every immigrant concentration. Yet, seldom were Socialist organizers able to capture more than a fraction of the immigrant working class. No single reason can explain the arrested development of socialism among newcomers who frequently brought socialist traditions with them, but several important factors certainly played roles. Central to any explanation was the chasm which existed between American skilled and unskilled workers. Peter Shergold, in a comparison of wage structures between Pittsburgh and Birmingham, England, demonstrated that prior to World War I wage differentials between skilled and unskilled workers were considerably wider in the United States than in England. The result was that English workers were tied together more closely, for instance, in their greater reliance on cooperatives. The skill differentials of American industrial workers were exacerbated by greater wage disparity, a fact which combined with ethnic and cultural variations to impede American labor solidarity.[54]

The cause of socialist solidarity was not helped, moreover, by the fact that leaders in each immigrant community frequently competed with radical organizers and placed alternative agendas before the immigrant working class. Immigrant religious leaders and businessmen constantly attacked socialism or preached gospels of self-improvement, thrift, and industry which captured much worker attention. Even within the same group, fragmentation of immigrant-worker thought was widespread. German "revivalists," as contrasted with German Catholics, resisted confrontation with their employers out of respect for individualism and entrepreneurship which emanated from their evangelical Protestantism. Some immigrants followed the various political leaders and lost interest in a purely class struggle.[55] Because much of the labor protest of the nineteenth century was not simply a response to working conditions but an effort to prevent the collapse of American republican ideals and institutions, many skilled newcomers were engulfed in narrow, artisanal political crusades for Jeffersonian ideals of "independence" and the freedom to ply their own trades without external restraints. In fact, both labor and capital in the early nineteenth century worked to maintain the ideals of independence and virtue; all men, they argued, should be judged by the worth of their labor and not reduced to a dependent class.[56] Even later immigrants after 1890 could demonstrate some degree of commitment to traditional republican virtues of "personal development" and individual initiative. New York Jews frequently endured degradation as mere workmen to eventually attain educational and personal advancement. Italian cigar makers in Tampa and construction workers in Pittsburgh frequently invested savings in small businesses such as fruit and vegetable dealerships to pursue entrepreneurial gain. Rank-and-file Finnish Socialists even complained that their leaders were too interested in political activities and insufficiently attentive to everyday concerns of managing cooperatives or entertainment events.[57]

Religious leaders invariably represented a powerful deterrent against Socialism. To the extent an individual's fate was in the hands of God and religious figures who represented Him, class warfare seemed somewhat unnecessary. Catholicism especially favored ritualistic devotion and muted overt attempts at individual betterment on earth. German Catholic leaders in mid-nineteenth-century New York passed resolutions against revolutionary agitation. The German Catholic Central Verein warned German immigrant workers to take no part in "agitation" or for that matter in the Republican Party, which was not radical but in the hands of "fanatical Republican Protestants." Clerics also stressed that radicals and Socialists opposed family life as well as religion. During a 1910 building workers' strike in Buffalo, Italian priests at St. Anthony's Church urged women in their congregation to persuade their husbands to return to work. Such appeals to refrain from strike or radical activity frequently were effective because employers acted upon the recommendations of local priests in hiring job applicants, thus supporting their leadership role.[58]

Textile unions found it difficult to organize workers in Woonsocket, Rhode Island, prior to the 1920s because French-Canadian pastors had so much influence over the workers. It is true that an element of anticlericalism existed among most Catholic groups; priests were often identified with the gentry or the state in both the old world and the new and criticized for their failure to perform much manual labor. Clerics were often courted by industrialists in American cities and towns. During 1919 many foreign-born strikers clearly disregarded clerical appeals to remain at work. But anticlericalism was usually a viewpoint of a vocal minority and generally clerics had at least as many supporters as detractors. Thus, a Socialist monthly for American Slovaks folded nine months after it was founded in 1894 because of strong clerical opposition.[59]

Immigrant socialism was further restricted by the inability of some Socialist leaders to understand the mentality of potential followers or to focus on work-place issues alone. Leaders well-grounded in socialist ideals were often insensitive to the everday needs and realities of ordinary workers. Radical spokesmen like Daniel DeLeon attempted to gain followers by relying heavily on ideals, while neglecting immediate reforms and compromises. On the other hand, unions and leaders tied to local needs were considerably more effective. Young Jewish intellectuals such as Abraham Cahan understood Jewish workers, to cite a case, and knew they could be more effectively reached through a Yiddish newspaper such as the *Jewish Daily Forward*, which he started in 1897. Printing his journal in simple Yiddish, Cahan, while nominally a Socialist, drifted from the party discipline of DeLeon and informed his readers about life beyond the work place. He identified the occupations Jews were finding in the city, the residential areas they were occupying, and the information they would need to survive.[60]

Socialist newspapers also existed in most immigrant communities but were invariably short-lived or crowded out by more powerful organs representing more conservative viewpoints. Financing was always tenuous for immigrant newspapers and subsidies from large religious or political organizations and advertisers were usually indispensable to survival. The Republican Party underwrote substantial portions of ethnic newspaper operations in large cities such as Pittsburgh. Often a homeland government subsidized a paper in order to support a particular political stance or frustrate ideologies such as ethnic separatism, which threatened national unity at home. Indeed, ethnic nationalism dominated the hearts of many intellectuals and editors and, therefore, the political agendas of much of the immigrant press. Between 1886 and 1921 at least 20 Italian-language newspapers appeared in Chicago. While some were strong socialistic publications opposing Italian patriotism and nationalism, most were bourgeois organizations which gloried in the supposed diplomatic and military success of Italy. *L'Italia* told its readers how to acquire American citizenship, attend schools, and enter politics. It censured adult Italian males who married teenage girls and parents who kept their children out of school so they could work.[61]

One of the strongest and most successful attempts to cement the relationship between ethnic nationalism and the mind of an immigrant working class, a move which would weaken worker commitment to exclusively work-place issues, was carried out through an immigrant newspaper by Patrick Ford. Ford turned the *Irish World* into the voice of the Irish-American working class by concentrating on those issues which were dear to Irish newcomers and their children: nationalism and Catholicism. Ford was able to combine those issues ingeniously and effectively into a general critique of the position of Irish workers within American society. The *Irish World* continually linked the land struggle in Ireland against the British with American social issues by establishing the Land League, which agitated not only for the abolishment of the landlord system in Ireland but the end of slavery and other forms of inequality in America. If the monopoly of land in Ireland was wrong, so was the monopoly of capital in America. It was this association which prompted thousands of Irish workers to make financial contributions to the Land League and eventually to support organizations such as the Knights of Labor. Unlike the explanation of historian Thomas Brown, Irish-American nationalism was more than a defensive reaction to nativism but a step in the assimilation of immigrant laborers into American working-class traditions of anti-monopoly and labor organizations such as the Knights. Prosperous Irish businessmen tended to complain about nationalist endeavors and the clergy frequently condemned calls for violence and even reproached as Socialism proposals for land distribution. The Irish-American leader of the Knights, Terence Powderly, was actually threatened by papal authority for secret aspects of his union which appeared to have "quasi-masonic" elements. Yet, much of the immigrant working class did retain their ties to Ford and his newspaper, although it should be emphasized this allegiance was a form of working-class consciousness with loyalties divided between work-place issues and international politics.[62]

The spread of Socialism was not only impeded by forces within immigrant communities but from the actions of American Socialist leaders themselves. Unfortunately for the cause of Socialism many of its leaders in the United States held a strong bias in favor of skilled workers, despite the urgings of some organizers who pleaded the cause of the unskilled. Victor Berger and other old-line Socialists were comfortable with the A.F. of L.'s orientation toward skilled workers and considered them the backbone of the industrial work force. Some leaders such as Morris Hillquit even took strong stands against the immigrant of groups like the Chinese and Japanese. Immigrants were seldom allowed to participate in the formulation of party policy. Hungarian Socialists were particularly upset with the American Socialist Party for devoting so much attention to political campaigns. Since most Magyars were not citizens, they felt much of the party's effort was misplaced and resented what they perceived to be attempts to "Americanize" them. Many immigrants, of course, divided with the party—when it opposed American participation in World War I—in order to escape charges of being unpatriotic, something to which immigrants were always very sensitive, and to more effectively pursue goals of national liberation for their homelands which they thoroughly cherished. Yugoslav Socialists, for instance, were especially vehement over the party's anti-war stand and the failure to support wars for national liberation. Among Poles in Milwaukee, the Socialist vote declined precipitously between 1916 and 1918.[63]

The Immigrant Working Class and the 1930s

By the late 1920s and 1930s when economic difficulties reached unprecedented levels, immigrants and their working children had to decide again on an appropriate response to secure their families, jobs, and communities. By 1930 this mass of first- and second-generation newcomers numbered close to 40 million and was concentrated largely in the industrial, working-class population.[64] In whatever manner they chose to respond to hard times, they would play a significant role in determining the history and politics of the 1930s and the short-term direction of American capitalism. Direct, radical action and an attempt to restructure the entire system of capitalist-labor relations was one alternative. Complete passivity and resignation was another. But as even a general survey of the depression decade makes clear, industrial workers were ultimately neither passive nor radical but moved vigorously to establish large, industrial unions in order to safeguard their jobs, improve their condition, and rationalize but not destroy the basic nature of their relationship with capital. They did this because by the 1930s they had already been severed from radical parties and programs and integrated more fully into the process of unionization than previously realized. Even if unions were somewhat quiet in the 1920s, they clearly had strong links to immigrant communities which would be expanded during the Depression.

Much of the analysis of the rise of unions during the thirties has focused on the workplace, especially the shop-floor experience. Emphasizing the pace and process of production and internal activities such as the grievance system, some historians have suggested that the impetus toward unionization involved, above all, power and its redistribution, with workers seeking to resist further incursions of managers into the workplace and to expand their control over the basic system of production. This view has been supplemented by indications that men in the shop represented a new breed, often second-generation Americans, who were rational, less intimidated by foremen, calculating, aggressive, and "possessed of an impulse for self-improvement." Michael Piore, an economist, felt the labor upheaval of the 1930s resulted partly from the efforts of second-generation immigrants to move from the unskilled or secondary labor market upward to the skilled section. There is no question that individual workmen were angered by management's abuses of power but several qualifications must be made when evaluating control of the workplace as a primary objective. Struggles in the workplace, like working-class behavior in general, were often more complex than a simple contest between workers and owners. Workers themselves were divided over internal struggles for power and position and shared-work experiences did not inevitably obliterate personal ambitions as some men sought to gain favors from foremen and owners. Those who view the twentieth-century surge for labor unions as a quest for power in response to the growing rationalization of work and loss of control may have overlooked other motives which were equally strong.[65]

Indeed, the focus by many historians on skilled workers as the catalyst of industrial protest of the 1930s has obscured the role of the less-skilled ranks where immigrants and their children were concentrated. Yet, the available evidence suggests that many semiskilled and unskilled workers were also generating support for unionization on their own, in part because they had been exposed to union activities earlier and in part because many recalled the experiences of their parents in textiles, mining, and in steel to gain union recognition. In the Pennsylvania steel towns of Braddock and Aliquippa, for instance, less-skilled rail straighteners, drillers, chippers, and pilers in the finishing department became dissatisfied with existing unions of skilled workers, such as the Amalgamated, and attempted to pressure John L. Lewis to organize steelworkers even before Lewis established the Steel Workers Organizing Committee. Unskilled aluminum workers at the Alcoa plant in New Kensington, Pennsylvania, organized in 1933 not because they were skilled workers seeking to stem the rush of scientific management but because their ranks were filled with former United Mine Workers of America members, a union which had traditionally welcomed immigrants and their children, and who had fled the coalfields after the violence of the 1920s. Former U.M.W. members in the twenties had also fled the mines of southern Illinois for factories in St. Louis, and miners from several states had flooded the expanding auto plants of Detroit. When hard times struck, they were ready to implement familiar organizational responses to the mounting challenges of unemployment and insecurity.[66]

If immigrants and their children in the 1930s had a legacy of organizing activity and union battles, they also had one of strong obligations to familial and communal networks and household economies which also had a great deal to do with the nature of their motivations and the eventual objectives they sought. Some scholars have suggested that these workers were inherently militant but were eventually co-opted by conservative union leaders and the programs of the New Deal. It is true that most union leaders were either native-born or skilled[67] and that New Deal legislation tended to induce rationalization into labor-management relations and mute direct political action, but it is revealing that most unions ultimately sought not just work rules and regulations but seniority and job security. It was a secure, steady job which stood at the foundation of the familial networks and household economies and which ordered the lives of not only much of the first generation but their American-born progeny as well. Substantial discontinuity between the early generation of industrial workers would not occur until public institutions and culture made broader inroads into the private lives of American workers. Certainly, some workers toiled outside the confines of an ethnic, communal, or familial network but nearly all were bound to a household economy of some kind or another. The depression really did not dash their hopes of social mobility since they had not had a great deal of that before; little happened in the 1920s to drastically raise their expectations. But the enduring attachment between the family-household and the workplace continued and was now severely threatened. Security and compensation for their families and their children were as important as working conditions themselves.

114]

The links between family, community, and work were still present throughout depressed cities in the 1930s. Auto workers participating in pervasive sit-down strikes protested increased work paces not only for the strain it created at the plant but also because it left them too tired when they came home to spend time with their families; auto workers' wives even complained about husbands too fatigued to perform sexual roles. At Flint, Michigan, in 1937 the sit-down became a family and communal affair, as strikes frequently were throughout the period prior to 1940. At strike headquarters in Flint, wives and children, many of whom were first- and second-generation Americans, helped print bulletins and arrange for relief. Women formed an auxiliary and the Women's Emergency Brigade which actually participated in strike action. When strikers at the Bethlehem Steel plant in Lebanon, Pennsylvania, discussed their strike plans in 1937, they decided not to destroy company machinery. They realized that such actions would eventually delay the attainment of their ultimate goal: to return to work. When the drive for improved conditions and treatment at work was combined with a quest for household stability, the labor movement was suddenly riveted to powerful goals which could temporarily transcend ethnic and skill differentials.[68]

Conclusion

A final legacy helped shape the response of the immigrant working class to the Great Depression. In addition to a familiarity with unions that may had acquired in America and an attachment to familial and household needs, immigrants had already acknowledged in their homeland that they were basically willing to accept the wage economy. Even among many who stayed behind, attempts were made to join the movement toward commercial agriculture. Those who moved implied in their act of migration that they were attempting to deal with capitalism and survive within its realm rather than retreat into an imaginary peasant past which was an available alternative. This did not mean they suddenly embraced all values associated with bourgeois capitalism, such as individual achievement or the constant drift toward a material and secular world. Their acceptance involved a decision to do what had to be done in order to keep family and community together. The decision about values and ideologies would take generations and much discussion. This decision, moreover, represented neither submission nor acquiescence, although it clearly enabled the capitalist class to retain control and avoid confrontation with a radical labor force. But for now the decision on the part of immi-

[115

grants and their children was real and clear. Survival, order, and family had to be protected in a world which appeared beyond their control. Oscar Handlin and numerous other writers who have attributed the lack of radical behavior to a persistent strain of peasant conservatism on the part of newcomers, including a tendency to defer to authority, have completely failed to recognize that these people were bound to the present not the past. They made a basic assessment of what was possible when capitalism first confronted them. They refined that assessment with their recent experiences with unions and capitalist power in America and formulated a limited response which included union organizations, concessions, and gains, but in their own minds, they did not relinquish crucial attachments to households and kin. Historians who lament the missed opportunities for radicalism in the 1930s and even organizers who were working among these people have never realized that the decision to deal with capitalism, albeit on their own terms, and to do whatever was necessary to survive was made *before* coming to America, and was the decision of people neither locked to a present nor counting too heavily on vague promises of a better life in some distant future.

Immigrant workers, then, could be both militant and passive supporters of unions and members of provincial ethnic and communal aggregations. To a great extent it depended upon their premigration backgrounds. But even more than their backgrounds, the level of their class consciousness was tied closely to the way they were treated at the workplace and by labor leaders and organizers. Before 1940 the American labor market may have been more homogenized and dominated by blue-collar workers than it would be in the period after the war when "salaried professionals" and marginal or "secondary" workers would rival factory workers in a more segmented structure. But greater homogenization did not inevitably lead to a more militant class-consciousness. Militancy and loyalty to the political and economic goals of workers were not givens. Those who extended themselves often found immigrant workers willing adherents to labor organizations and ideals. This is a point which seems to have been lost on a large portion of the Socialist leadership in the United States. Ethnic and religious leaders, furthermore, did all they could to evoke a different sort of loyalty and inevitably undercut working-class solidarity. During the Great Depression immigrants and their children flocked to unions more than they did to radicalism because they had a legacy in many union organizations in the United States and had only weak and generally underdeveloped ties to the most militant forms of ideologies and organizations.[69]

4 /

The Rise of an Immigrant

Middle Class

Divided Communities

If the immigrant homelands provided newcomers with a legacy of mutual assistance which heavily shaped the manner of their entry into the American economy, it did not necessarily follow that immigrant communities were harmonious and united in purpose, orientation, and direction. The homelands themselves were stratified and immigrant streams consisted of groups with unequal resources, skills, and divergent orientations. Those usually in the vanguard of the movement were familiar with a higher status than most new arrivals and were considerably more inclined to cast their fortunes with the new order of capitalism since their prospects for return were minimal. Limits, moreover, existed to mutual assistance and neither a shared ethnic heritage nor a lowly status was sufficient to insure cooperative behavior especially beyond the level of kinship. Fragmentation and contention co-existed with forms of cooperation and solidarity in urban-immigrant communities, as some newcomers sought and acquired more wealth, influence, and power than others. Competing leaders and prominent individuals emerged. And the pursuit of stability and security in a capitalistic economy through means of mutual assistance could sometimes lead to an intensification of entrepreneurial and profit goals rather than toil in mills and factories. While most immigrants remained ordinary workers, the world of the urban immigrant was not only a working-class world but one which included self-employed shopkeepers, fraternal officials, and other businessmen who fostered fragmentation by separating themselves from their humble moorings or mobilizing separate aggregations of newcomers to sustain their own power and prosperity. This immigrant middle class was characterized by a mentality of its own which celebrated individual status and gain to a greater degree than did the working class, although it was by no means devoid of cooperative and familial concerns. It was also tied closer to the business culture of urban American than the culture of immigrant workers. Ultimately, the immigrant communities in industrial towns and cities would become as stratified as the societies which had been left behind.

Older views of American ethnic communities suggested that they were simply "decompression chambers" or transition zones where newcomers temporarily stayed and acquired the necessary values and behavioral patterns to move inevitably into middle-class American society.[1] The difficulty in accepting this view was that assimilation was seen as a linear progression into a common American mass. The widespread divisiveness which pervaded immigrant communities was ignored as was the constant tension between rival ideals, leaders, and factions. And most significantly, class distinctions did not exist in this view in either immigrant communities or the larger American society.[2]

In nearly every immigrant settlement of any consequence in urban America, however, division based upon old world backgrounds, status distinctions, or class was widespread. The case of the Jews is an excellent example. During the years of large East-European Jewish migration, well-established German Jews were reluctant to be identified with downtrodden newcomers. Yiddish, a language understood only by Polish and Russian Jews was denounced as "piggish jargon." Russian newcomers were even forced to Germanize their names to get credit from wealthier German Jews. In a pattern which would be repeated throughout immigrant America, some leaders among the German Jews attempted to transform these new arrivals into middle-class citizens through educational programs such as the technical training and the English-language instruction of the Hebrew Institute in New York City. The earliest synagogues and *Landsmannschaften*, organizations in which Jews assisted each other in death and sickness, further reflected regional differences since they were usually organized along old village lines.[3]

In a similar manner, the backgrounds of Mexicans in California contributed to group factionalism. Those born in the United States adopted the prejudiced views of Anglo society and looked unfavorably upon newer arrivals from Mexico in the late nineteenth century. During the first decade of this century intermarriage between American-born and Mexican-born Chicanos was the exception rather than the rule. Church formation among early Poles also reflected regional origins with Kassubian Poles from Prussia establishing large churches in Chicago and Detroit, which often remained apart from Galician Poles who arrived later. By 1870 in New York City sizable portions of Germans were associating mostly with fellow immigrants from Prussia, Bavaria, or Württemberg. Genoese Italians who established a fishing industry in San Francisco fought with Sicilians who arrived later and were perceived to be intruders upon their monopoly. A Serbian church in Gary, Indiana, divided over conflict between Serbs from Lika and those from Montenegro when the latter group concluded that the priest favored the "Licani." At St. John's German Church in Cincinnati in the 1880s, Northern and Southern Germans openly detested each other. Most discord surfaced in Chicago when Greeks from Sparta wanted to tax newly arriving Arcadians who wanted to use their church. A worker in Connecticut's "brass valley" recalled that Irish from County Kerry were reluctant to marry Irish from Queens County. Indeed, Irishmen from different counties would even be buried from separate funeral homes.[4]

Regional factionalism was frequently supplemented in immigrant communities by differences over cultures. Ethnic and cultural homogeneity was not a given in urban immigrant settlements. Debates raged continuously over whether traditional ways should be retained or modern customs adopted. In the German district of nineteenth-century Cincinnati, schools taught German during one-half the day and English during the other half. During voting on a referendum to retain German-language instruction in the St. Louis schools in 1887, although many Germans came out in support of the measure, others simply remained indifferent and at home. Long before the shocks of World War I, the German community was far from united over the issue of cultural preservation. Germans, of course, were also divided ideologically among Jews, Protestants, Catholics, and Freethinkers. Liberal Germans were antagonistic toward German Lutherans because of the "ministerial domination" to which Lutherans were subjected. This factionalism in St. Louis caused the establishment of numerous *vereins* often reflecting different religious and economic backgrounds. Especially divisive was the gap between the mid-nineteenth-century wave of Germans which consisted of large numbers of political exiles and late nineteenth-century migrants who brought skills which allowed them to move into the machine and brewing industry.[5]

Perhaps the most frequently overlooked cause of fragmentation in immigrant communities was class. It is difficult to be specific on the extent the social structure of the homeland was duplicated in industrial America, although evidence does exist that differences in education, status, and skill did influence the experience of some newcomers in this country. More literate Prussian Poles or skilled Germans had advantages over unlettered Galician Poles or German peasants when it came to assuming leadership rules or starting businesses in American cities. But the fact that class antagonisms separated ethnic aggregations is indisputable.

Stratification, often nurtured in the premigration homelands, was ubiquitous. In Milwaukee, Kathleen Conzen found that much of the German associational life in the city prior to the 1860s was not the product of peasant culture or a defensive reaction to native hostility but the transfer of a rich, middle-class culture that had existed in German cities. These new arrivals had been urban artisans and shopkeepers and they simply replicated their churches, beer halls, and fraternal organizations in Wisconsin. In Cincinnati, between 1880 and 1910, an entire new wave of German societies different from those already in place, had been established by craftsmen who were moving to the city at that time and who differed in social standing from peasants and even intellectuals.[6] Complex internal status hierarchies have been found by sociologists in a number of immigrant communities. These gradations were found to be based upon many factors—including length of stay in America, ethnic organizational involvement, wealth, occupation, and education—much as it was in the old world and in the larger industrial society.[7] As early as 1900 an East-European Jewish middle class could be detected in New York, including Yiddish-speaking millionaires who moved beyond the East Side into Jewish neighborhoods in upper Manhattan and Brooklyn. Distinct associational lines were discovered among Swedes in Chicago and in Worcester, Massachusetts, between a broad lower-middle class largely emanating from agrarian origins and a smaller group with an urban, intellectual background. The *promenenti* were clearly visible in most Italian communities as an upper-class group. And by 1900 a business elite was emerging in most Polish-American communities.[8]

The Fraternal Movement and Early Enterprise

The very earliest leaders and entrepreneurs in immigrant communities frequently achieved recognition in the larger community through their role in the establishment and running of fraternal organizations. Ironically, through the institutionalization of traditional concepts of mutual assistance, modern notions of individual status and power began to emerge in the minds of a few immigrants. During the initial encounter between immigrants and urban-industrial economy, the path of adjustment and the leaders who would advocate particular forms of response to industrial capitalism remained unclear. Confined to networks of familial and communal assistance, immigrant resources were clearly limited. Since settlement houses, labor unions, and other institutions of the host society had achieved only a limited influence among the first generation and since widespread urban social service and government programs did not exist, particular strategies for meeting the exigencies of unemployment, widowhood, burial or even social activities would have to be generated internally. This caused immigrants to rely heavily on traditions of mutual assistance which were already well established to deal with nascent capitalism in their homelands and leaders, usually from the small clusters of skilled workers and intellectuals in all migration streams, who had been fortunate to receive forms of training and education inaccessible to most peasants prior to leaving.

The earliest secular fraternal organizations clearly had antecedents in the premigration homeland and involved leaders from the ranks of artisans and the educated in the old world. Among Hungarians, for instance, the earliest organizers in America were mostly craftsmen and artisans. They drew upon traditions of tradesmen associations and communal security. Not surprisingly a number of early Magyar fraternals had charters specifying that only those who had been "manual workers," as contrasted with peasants in Hungary, could be officers. These early fraternals, establishing a precedent which would last for decades, adopted the egret-feathered hat and braided coat of the Magyar landed gentry for their fraternal dress rather than the peasant mode of costuming. By 1911, Hungarians had formed 800 such organizations along.[9] Romanians as well saw their earliest fraternals in America formed by immigrants who had been independent craftsmen and somewhat ambitious in their homelands. Those men were removed from the mass of the peasantry, tied less to communal traditions, and often more interested in individual mobility and gain.[10]

Additional links between the early fraternals and the old world were evident and were based upon more than the aspirations and experience of the artisan class in each immigrant stream. The cooperative tradition, rooted deeply in the experience of most peasant households, also served newcomers well in deciding how to confront the unpredictability of the industrial economy. Recent evidence among Croatian immigrants suggested that the first fraternal lodges rested on the cooperative traditions of the Croatian *zadruga* or communal family structure. Even for those outside the confines of a joint-communal family, Croatians could rely on the *molba*, a tradition whereby 30 or 40 friends would gather to assist in the harvest in return for food and drink. Similarly, Slovak scholars have sought to establish a link between medieval guilds established by skilled workers in Bohemia and Slovakia among blacksmiths and boatmakers, for instance, and immigrant fraternals in America. In both the guilds and the fraternals the blessing of banners was a major event. Anton Ambrose, a fraternal leader in Pittsburgh, actually learned the history of guilds from his father and conducted the meetings of his lodge along the lines of guild rituals. The coastal areas of Dalmatia which supplied the first Yugoslavs to America, had *Bratoustine*, fraternal brotherhoods from the thirteenth century, which provided assistance to families in times of illness or death.[11]

Despite the availability of traditional models of mutual assistance, the classic study of the *Polish Peasant in Europe and America* preferred to explain the origins of fraternal societies within the context of a clash between traditional concerns of assistance and a rising tide of individualism in America. The *Polish Peasant* argued that in America mutual assistance was no longer connected with the very foundation of social life and individuals became increasingly concerned for their own well-being. Because individuals could no longer lay claim to assistance from kin (a dubious assumption), assistance had to be formalized and regulated through mutual-aid associations. Fraternals were never seen as extensions of ethnic and kinship networks or ultimately as affirmations of even a particular social standing.[12]

While the stress on the growing preoccupation with individual well-being in America is suggestive, mutual assistance organizations providing sickness and burial benefits and even credit were already being formed in the homelands in response to nascent capitalism before emigration. It does appear, however, that these early organizations were more likely to involve skilled workers and artisans than the mass of peasants, although that could be attributed to the fact that these groups were experiencing the intrusion of capitalism first. Certainly, peasants demonstrated they could organize for ends such as credit and agricultural improvements when it was necessary to do so. As the market economy made greater penetration into small communities, artisans and some peasants either expanded their kinship networks outside the household to secure more apprenticeships, cared for children so relatives could work, or formed voluntary associations to insure against illness and death, supervise education, foster agricultural improvements, or pursue political aims. Josef Barton found such activities flourishing especially after 1870 in Czech, Romanian, Slovakian, and Italian villages. Larger organizations now were likely to supplement households, but not replace them, in meeting particular social and economic needs.[13] Workers in Upper Silesia turned to mutual-aid societies in the 1850s for protection. It was from this region that most of the earliest Polish migration to American emanated, including many founders of the Polish Roman Catholic Union. Southern Italians formed over 6,000 voluntary associations before 1894. Artisans again had been the first to organize mutual-aid societies and labor-union cooperatives in Italy. Although most were formed in the north, they were not unknown among the southern Italian peasantry. In both regions they were often more of a social and psychological benefit than an economic one.[14]

Most early immigrant fraternal associations, not surprisingly, were based on village and regional ties as they had been in the premigration homeland. Thus, the number of early fraternals in most American settlements was usually equal to the number of village clusters which constituted particular streams. Even in urban areas like Chicago, this pattern held. Polish societies offering burial benefits were composed of individuals from the same villages. It has been estimated that between 1910 and 1920 about 160 Italian benefit groups came into existence in Chicago based mostly on village and regional associations.[15]

Usually, fraternal associations preceded even the formation of churches or labor organizations and aimed at fulfilling only limited functions. The Pennsylvania Slovak Catholic Union was formed in 1893 by miners who faced numerous injuries and wanted to assess members monthly fees which would cover burial expenses. The sophisticated use of accumulated reserves and the use of actuarial tables had not yet been learned. Similarly, the Ukrainian Workingmen's Association began in 1910 when newcomers started "chipping in" a few dollars a month for the families of men killed in the mines. A few fraternals were organized just to mute the influence of religious or secular leaders with workers. For instance, the Slovene National Benefit Society forbade the use of any religious names or symbols in its constitution and bylaws.[16] Finally, some functions not needed in the homeland were now included. Yugoslavs in New Orleans in the 1870s, influenced by the example of German, French, and Italian settlers in the city, organized the United Slavonian Benevolent Association, in part to preserve their "Slavic heritage" in a new land. Consequently, the Croatian language was to be used exclusively in conducting the association's affairs.[17]

The directors of the earliest fraternals provided additional examples of how independent men in the lower-middle class, but above the level of ordinary toilers, demonstrated organizational leadership. Over 60 percent of Czech fraternal heads in Chicago and 70 percent of their Italian counterparts had belonged to mutual-aid organizations in their homelands and were usually artisans or small businessmen. The core of organized German leadership in late nineteenth-century Cincinnati was lower-middle-class craftsmen and shopkeepers. The German Pioneer Society had officers consisting of a delicatessen owner, an insurance agent, a butcher, and an artisan. The president of the Bavarians, a mutual aid society, was a saloon-keeper. A wallpaper hanger, three machinists, an ironworker, a carpenter, and a cigar maker constituted the rest of the officers. Biographical descriptions of the pioneer leaders of the United Slavonian Beneficial Association indicated that businessmen predominated as leaders. The founder, Michael Drascovich, had developed a prosperous saloon business. The vice-president owned and operated a wholesale fruit company. Throughout the 1880s and 1890s the occupations of the association's officers remained remarkably similar: realtor, grocer, oyster dealer, restaurant or saloon owner, boardinghouse keeper or insurance salesman.[18] Early development among Polish fraternals also involved the efforts of men and women who came from a small, educated middle class born or reared in the homeland. John Smulski of the Polish National Alliance or Emily Napieralska of the Polish Women's Alliance were prime examples. The first president of the National Slovak Society had been trained as a skilled machinist in the homeland, and Michael Yuhasz, who headed a fraternal newspaper for Rusins, had received previous training in publishing.[19]

William Toll's study of Jews in Portland, Oregon, suggested that local Jewish fraternals were initially founded by skilled workers and eventually taken over by members of the professional classes. Skilled workers in the nineteenth century, such as tinners, harness makers, glaziers, and small merchants, formed the backbone of the early B'nai B'rith lodge in the city. The earliest lodge in Portland emphasized communal traditions and relied on community members for entertainment and social activities. As more middle-class professionals took control, however, a "higher" cultural level shaped social activities. Symphony orchestras, glee clubs, and learned lectures began to predominate and the older "working-class" began to withdraw.[20]

Among Italians small, regionally based mutual-aid lodges proliferated. Unlike the Italian experience in Argentina where Italians from higher social categories tended to emigrate and a strong middle class rapidly created large broad-scale fraternal organizations, Italians in the United States tended to be of lower social origins and tied largely to village or regional lodges, which retarded somewhat the development of national fraternals. In America, though, the regionally based societies did come under the influence of the *prominenti*, usually earlier arrivals who had learned English and established a business to serve the mass of immigrants, such as publishers, bankers, boardinghouse keepers, or even padrones. These leaders had an interest in maintaining regional differences. In 1892, in a recurring theme, the Czech Workingmen's Sokols were established in New York by an immigrant anthropoligist and educator.[21]

Finally, religious leaders played a major role in shaping early fraternals, especially on a larger territorial basis. While their influence will be dealt with at length in a subsequent chapter, it should be noted that they were crucial as early advocates of mutual-aid associations. In 1893 four priests founded the Ukrainian National Association. The Reverend Vincent Barzynski, the most prominent Polish clergyman in America before 1900, molded the Polish Roman Catholic Union. Peter Rovnianek, who had studied for the priesthood in Europe and acquired strong Slovak nationalist views, established the National Slovak Society in 1890.[22]

But to attribute the early activity of lodge building solely to immigrant "elites" would be misleading. While their influence was dominant, a few early organizers were ordinary, unskilled workers. The pioneering historian of Slovak-Americans, Konstantin Culen, described the founders of the St. Joseph's Society in Cleveland as an ironworker, a cabinetmaker, a grocer, three manual laborers, and a priest. Coal miners were responsible for the Ukrainian Workingmen's Association. The idea for the First Catholic Slovak Ladies Union came from the mind of a common, immigrant woman, Anna Hurban, who called a meeting in Cleveland in 1892.[23]

Inevitably, competition for members among local lodges intensified over time as various leaders sought to expand and sustain their base of influence and power. Since these associations represented one of the few institutions which could mobilize large segments of the immigrant community, they were used by ambitious newcomers to embellish their financial and social standing within the group and promote political agendas. Consequently, the history of fraternals closely paralleled the evolution of internecine strife within most immigrant settlements. Illustrative was the bitter rivalry between

Polonia's two largest fraternals, the Polish Roman Catholic Union (PRCU) and the Polish National Alliance (PNA). The PNA, through its organ, *Zgoda*, was led by politically minded emigrees, was open to all Poles regardless of their religious preferences and stood as a continual champion of Polish nationalism. The PRCU, on the other hand, was heavily influenced by the church and saw Catholicism as indispensable to all Poles.[24] A similar split existed between the First Catholic Slovak Union and the National Slovak Society, which felt organizations based solely on religion created division.

The role played by fraternal organizations in internal immigrant politics was usually pivotal. After years of tension between Ruthenian and Ukrainian factions within the Uniate Church in America, it was the Rusin-dominated Greek Catholic Union which organized and attacked the "Ukrainian menace" and caused a permanent split between the two groups in 1918. Much of the struggle between organized crime elements and law-abiding Italians in Chicago took place within the confines of the Sicilian Union; the reformers attempting to end the society's identification with crime in 1925 by changing the organization's name to the Italo-American National Union. Among Ukrainians, the proponents of Ukrainian nationalism largely carried on their struggle against pro-Russian elements through the Ukrainian National Association and its daily organ, *Svoboda*. The Croatian Catholic Union, in fact, was formed as a splinter organization from the national Croatian Society because of the Socialist leanings of several leaders of the parent organization.[25]

Because fraternals slowly came under the influence of ambitious leaders who sought to galvanize a portion of the immigrant community under their aegis, they invariably moved to achieve more than simply economic ends. Their founding concept of local mutual assistance was eclipsed by political and ideological goals pursued through nationally based organizations. The fact that the economic benefit offered by fraternals always remained minimal—a $1,000 death benefit was a norm—further underscored the fact that these organizations played wider, noneconomic roles.[26] Even a cursory glance at early fraternal charters underscored this point. In Cincinnati, the German-American Day Association and the German National Alliance both attempted to make the preservation of "Germaness" their primary goal. The Reverend Vincent Barzynski intended the PRCU to teach the Catholic faith and the culture of Poland as well as to facilitate the Americanization of the Poles. In fact, both the PRCU and the PNA began with ideological goals and added insurance programs at a later date. Similarly, the National Slovak Society embraced the concerns of its founder Peter Rovnianek: ethnic consciousness, the Slovak language and culture, and a commitment to formal education and Americanization.[27] The Greek Catholic Union endorsed several major goals in 1892, including a desire to aid the families of members materially at the time of death and to foster the ethnic and religious education of the Rusin people.[28] The meetings of lodges and national conventions became important social functions themselves with some annual meetings lasting eleven or twelve days and local lodge gatherings providing a basis for picnics, dances, and other forms of social interaction.[29]

In addition to cultural and social ends, fraternals also assisted newcomers in purchasing homes and even rendered support at the workplace. The largest area of Polish-American fraternal investment was real estate. Fraternals promoted the goal of home ownership by lending money directly to members or by purchasing mortgages from banks and building associations. By 1927 the Polish Women's Alliance had over 86 percent of its assets invested in mortgages and the Polish National Alliance had over 85 percent.[30] While national fraternal organizations seldom took strong stands on labor issues, such was not the case for local lodges, tied more intimately to the daily concerns of their members. The national fraternal, like some of the immigrant press in general, was partially subsidized by political parties, which could directly soften any stance on labor issues. Immigrant editors, struggling with finances most of the time, were often glad to accept contributions from political and business interests. The charge of Yugoslav Socialists in Chicago that some immigrant organizations were simply "arms of the Republican Party" reflected associations fraternal leaders often made.[31] On the other hand, local lodges became so involved with worker issues that some prevented strikebreaking explicitly in their charters and secured jobs for members who were unemployed.[32]

Gradually but persistently, however, local lodges came under the influence of national organizations and leaders and relinquished much of their autonomy. By 1929 all of the main Serbian fraternals in America had coalesced into the Serbian National Federation. As early as 1910 the Slovenian Catholic Union had completed most of its national organization. Almost all village and regional societies in Cleveland by 1920 had joined the sons of Italy. One of the earliest attempts at integrating regional and local lodges occurred in 1873 when Polish priests attempted to unite all Polish colonies in America. Although the attempt failed, the new organization was revived in the 1880s as the Polish Catholic Union. Similarly, the Croatian Catholic

Union merged 45 lodges by 1921 and four years afterwards joined with three other regional associations to form the Croatian Fraternal Union.[33]

While most local lodges had been formed by artisans and small merchants with limited goals of mutual assistance, the drive toward the national consolidation of fraternals was fueled by ambitious leaders who viewed these larger organizations as outlets for their entrepreneurial energies and drives for personal gain and status. Emanating largely from those with more formal education, these career-oriented fraternalists had strong idealogical positions and gradually adopted modern American business and investment procedures to increase the stability and efficiency of their growing ventures.[34]

Once the embryonic national organizations took shape, goals had to be established which would transcend the parochial interests of individual members and lodges and sustain a measure of national identity among newcomers from diverse regional and social backgrounds. It was precisely this need that moved national fraternals to become one of the chief forces for generating a strong attachment to the group's common ethnic origins, an attachment which was rather loose and underdeveloped at the time of immigration. The desire to accentuate an ethnic past did mark many of the nationalist and reactionary revival movements occurring during the periods of capitalist intrusion into their homelands. But it had not yet infused a widespread ethnic identity into the minds of people tied largely to region, village, social category, and household. National fraternals, ironically, also spearheaded a drive toward Americanization, concluding that the tendency of many newcomers to return would eventually undermine the financial base of their growing memberships. Consequently, English-language programs and especially American sports activities for children were established for most local lodges. National fraternals reached forward under the banner of Americanization and backward under the guise of ethnic identity in order to sustain the loyalty of large portions of immigrant communities.

Fraternals worked especially hard to sustain ethnic identity among the young in all groups. In 1913 the National Slovak Society opened a Young Folk's Circle in order to attract youth and stimulate an appreciation for the Slovak language and traditions. By the 1920s many organizations such as the Croatian Fraternal Union established English-speaking lodges as well as to accommodate growing numbers who did not speak the ethnic language anymore.[35]

During the Great Depression of the 1930s, fraternals assisted

Fraternal Gymnastic Club
Fraternal organizations sponsored numerous social and
athletic groups in an attempt to maintain the ethnic
solidarity upon which their economic survival often
depended. *Author's personal collection*

numerous cultural organizations which appeared to offer much needed relief from the daily reality of making a living. The organ of the Serbian National Federation, *American Srbobran*, specifically emphasized the value of ethnic activities as an antidote to the "fatalism" of the depression and called on all Serbs to "carry on" the traditions of their fathers. The list of activities initiated in response to appeals of this nature was endless. The Ukrainian Folk Ballet, the Croatian Singing Society, the Slovak Boys' Band, and numerous theatrical groups were all supported by fraternals and their lodges. In Chicago, the Serbian National Federation had its own Tamburitza Orchestra, weekly classes in the Serbian language and Serbian history, and numerous athletic teams.[36] Many fraternal newspapers began picking all-American football teams consisting of members of their particular ethnic background during the thirties. In 1938 *Jednota*, the organ of the First Catholic Slovak Union, compiled a list of Slovak-Americans prominent in wrestling, boxing, baseball, and football which served as a model of Americanization and ethnic pride for its readers.[37] In fact, fraternals linked sports with ethnic identity in order to retain ties to the second generation and demonstrate that ethnic solidarity, the foundation of fraternal support, and Americanization were not incompatible. As *Zajednicar*, the newspaper of the Croatian Fraternal Union, exclaimed: "And the better side of it (sports) all rests in the fact that we as a people—a so-called foreign-language group—stand to obtain much more recognition through the field of sports than through any other method."[38]

A final point must be raised about the fraternal organizations. Despite their attempts to cultivate the loyalty of the immigrant masses, they were only partially successful, a sign that newcomers had loyalties to other ideals and institutions. A study of Germans in Cincinnati determined that about 52 percent of adult German males joined ethnic fraternals and similar organizations. The majority of Romanians probably never affiliated with any cultural or beneficial group. Only about one-half of the potential members joined the United Slavonian Benefit Association in Louisiana. A survey of 3,000 families in Chicago in 1920 by the Illinois Health Insurance Commission found that only 57.8 percent of Italian families sampled had some form of life insurance, the basic economic benefit offered by fraternal membership. The figure of membership in Italian lodges was probably even lower because by 1920 some Italians surely had insurance with American companies, who were already recruiting salesmen in each ethnic settlement. Among Poles, statistics suggest that fraternal membership rates were below 50 to 60 percent.[39]

Immigrant Entrepreneurs

Fraternals were an important arena for a small portion of the immigrant community to develop and promote American business skills but other avenues leading away from the body of the immigrant working class existed as well. In every settlement a group emerged to pursue entrepreneurial ventures which depended upon the support of the immigrant community. The proportion of the immigrant business community varied from group to group and in some instances it moved beyond the confines of the ethnic community to serve outside interests. In nearly all cases immigrant entrepreneurs had some business experience in their premigration lives which facilitated the transition to such ventures in industrial America. The greater the premigration experience the more likely the newcomer would engage in entrepreneurial activity in this country. Even in the earliest years of settlement, moreover, these entrepreneurs began to act differently from the mass of immigrant workers. In one important way, however, these businessmen continued to behave much like other immigrants. Both workers and entrepreneurs closely linked their toil with concerns and welfare of their families and frequently encouraged kin to labor together much like the working class.

Immigrant businessmen, like immigrant workers, could only function in sectors of the economy open to them. In the early nineteenth century in Rochester, New York, for instance, native-born family businesses dominated trade with the surrounding rural, native population. Small grocery concerns and retail stores serving the city's working class were left largely to Irish newcomers who usually shared the immigrant's background and who could earn the immigrant's trust and good will. Irish businessmen avoided the rural trade and the Irish-Democratic newspaper found few readers in the countryside. Irish artisans such as coopers maintained business relations with larger mills but steadfastly retained their own customs and business traditions. They would work feverishly from Tuesday to Saturday to deliver their barrels but spent Sundays drinking and Mondays visiting friends and shopping.[40] By the 1880s in Troy, New York, Irish shopkeepers, grocers, and saloonkeepers were well established. They were even expanding their trade to a greater extent than native-born residents because of the large size of Troy's Irish contingent.[41] These types of small concerns proliferated in most immigrant settlements and were easier to start in an era when monopoly capital had not yet replaced the pattern of commercial capitalism. Exclusion from one economic sector simply directed activity into another. Thus, Michael Kelly became a successful moneylender in Poughkeepsie, New York, because Irish Catholics were kept from playing an active role in local banks dominated by the native-born.[42]

Entrepreneurship could even take a less constructive turn in immigrant settlements. It took very little capital to pursue income and influence through forms of petty crime which characterized most towns and neighborhoods. Prior to prohibition, Jewish gangsters in New York earned income by terrorizing strikers into returning to work or even picking pockets on crowded streets. Italians operated extortion rings in San Francisco as early as the 1890s and prostitution houses in South Chicago. Some immigrant entrepreneurs combined legitimate and illegitimate activities by running family-based food stores and loan-shark operations which preyed on the inability of immigrant workers to obtain credit or loans through normal channels.[43]

Many immigrants who struck out on their own and moved into openings where they could, possessed exceptional resources or experience. Some German families actually arrived in Milwaukee in the 1840s with over 20,000 dollars in gold. Conrad Poppenhusen, who became a leading manufacturer in New York City, had been a textile producer in Hamburg. Henry Ginz, a skilled cabinetmaker and politician in Hesse-Darmstadt, became prominent in social, economic, and political activities among Germans in South Bend, Indiana. John Bibza, a Protestant Slovak who had protested Hungarian repression, was a trained machinist in his native country and was promoted rapidly at a steel mill in Duquesne, Pennsylvania. By 1908, six years after his arrival, he had opened a grocery store, become an agent for several fire insurance companies, and sold foreign money orders for the American Express Company. He eventually obtained a banking license and became active in both Slovak and American business worlds. Similarly Vincente Garza was a businessman in Monterrey, Mexico, and El Paso, Texas, before establishing a small tailor shop in East Chicago, Indiana. He happened to marry the daughter of another immigrant entrepreneur who ran a real estate company and eventually established a Mexican clothing factory in nearby Indiana Harbor.[44] Anton Nemanich, a Slovene in Joliet, Illinois, provided a good example of how immigrant enterprise would flow in directions open to it. Nemanich created a prosperous career for himself by acting as an employment agent for the International Harvester Company, operating a meat market, a mortuary, a florist shop, and a brewery.[45]

**Grocery Store of Stanley P. Balzekas
(right), Chicago, circa 1914**
Most immigrant businessmen lacked access to large
amounts of capital, remained small, and served
neighborhood clienteles. *Chicago Historical Society*

But immigrant enterprise did not have to be solely an individual endeavor. Pervasive traditions of mutual assistance and household cooperation were not necessarily lost among entrepreneurs, although they often could be. A penetrating study of the formation of a native-born middle class in nineteenth-century New York State by historian Mary Ryan also established a link between entrepreneurial ventures and family solidarity. Emerging from the ranks of farmers, shopkeepers, and artisans who adopted strong notions of Protestantism—hard work, sobriety, thrift—these individuals confronted the growing realities and opportunities of a rising capitalism. These values were promulgated not only to influence the conduct of their employees but to insure that their own children would retain the fragile middle-class status they had acquired. Their early business activity, moreover, was not simply the result of individual quests but depended heavily on family associations. Partnerships of family members were formed; relatives were a common source of credit and capital. Mothers did their part by forming maternal associations and female reform societies to cultivate temperance and sexual restraint in their husbands and children. Such voluntary associations sought to shape family and individual values so children would be raised with a deep desire to retain their middle-class standing.[46]

Jews and other immigrants demonstrated that familial and kinship cooperation in the pursuit of business success and middle-class standing was not limited to native-born Protestants. German Jewish families moved into business ventures more rapidly than most immigrants because they entered New York City in the mid-nineteenth century with not only a good deal of business acumen but substantial amounts of capital which allowed them to open large department stores and even enter the field of banking. Jewish banking houses such as those of the Guggenheims, Wertheims, and Baches actually received financial and human resources from Jewish bankers in Europe. Businessmen such as Julius Rosenwald, who purchased Sears, Roebuck and Company, used the notion of a mail-order enterprise from Germany as well. Between 1860 and 1870, consequently, the number of German Jewish firms deemed worthy of commercial ratings rose considerably in the United States, insuring that capital could be attracted from even wider sources. For East European Jews their initial business ventures were considerably more modest and often symbolized by the pushcart. Religious laws concerning the preparation and handling of food drew many of these newcomers into opening meat and poultry establishments. A flourishing soda-water business among Jews early in the 1900s was attributed

**Bank and Bar of Liccione-Pittaro and Company, corner
of Hester and Mulberry streets, New York City**
Immigrant entrepreneurs could usually function only in
sectors of the economy from which they were not
excluded. *Immigration History Research Center,
University of Minnesota*

to nonalcoholic drinking habits of the immigrants. In cities such as
San Francisco, Jews often followed kin after spending time in eastern
cities where they gained valuable business experience. Still the key to
success and survival in business was credit. The ratings of Dun and
Company, for instance, did not make it easy for Jews. Invariably,
evaluators claimed Jews "failed the character test" and credit reports
actually called them "trashy." Indications even exist that the origins
of American anti-Semitism began in the early-nineteenth-century city
when Jews competed with Gentile merchants in economic life. Already by the 1840s and 1850s the credit reports of the R.G. Dun
Company were making it difficult for Jews to obtain credit and creating stereotypes. Jews circumvented these barriers, however, by obtaining credit and loans from relatives or business associates. Jewish
capital from the East Coast directly supported the establishment of
Jewish firms in San Francisco to such an extent that as early as 1852
Jews constituted 10 percent of the city's merchant population.

[135

Inevitably, many Jews and other immigrants rose from the ranks of petty merchants to the level of wholesaling and manufacturing activities. But their origins as entrepreneurs could be located ultimately in a web of old world experiences, kinship ties, and available opportunities.[47]

Italians had been familiar with credit cooperatives in the old world, especially skilled artisans in the north. In America they too shared resources to launch business ventures and, not surprisingly, men from artisan and "middle class families" in Italy predominated among the ranks of early entrepreneurs in the Italian colonies. For instance, in Utica, New York, where 27 Italian grocers and meat markets accounted for over 16 percent of the town's list of businesses in 1900, Vincenzo Marrone and Rocco Lofaro built a large wholesale food enterprise. Local Italian papers provided rich details on the backgrounds of such men chronicling their families' road to middle-class respectability on both sides of the Atlantic. Lofaro's father had been "self-made" man in the silk industry at home and Marrone was the son of a tradesman and had prosperous cousins in the Italian civil service.[48] A.P. Giannini, a native Californian of Genoese descent, built the Banca d'Italia by exploiting close, communal ties among Italians in San Francisco and providing them with loans and credit after the devastating 1906 earthquake. By spreading the bank's deposits as widely as possible, he cemented his ties to the colony and overcame peasant reluctance to leave savings in the hands of bankers. Kinship and ethnic ties also fed directly into small-scale business ventures in Boston. Subcontractors such as Louis Reppucci relied heavily on kinship and village ties to supply workers from his native Avellino. Italian fathers and sons also launched numerous barbershop ventures in nearly all American cities.[49]

In a similar fashion Greek immigrants moved into the restaurant and food business in Chicago. Initially, restaurants and food peddling were among the few business ventures open to them in the city's economy and in their colonies. Once they began to move beyond the boundaries of their own settlements they confronted other immigrants, such as Italians, whose entrepreneurs were also restricted to similar endeavors. By 1920, Greeks in Chicago had established themselves as restaurant operators, ice cream manufacturers, florists, and wholesale distributors of fruits and vegetables. In competing against Italians, they also relied on other members of families and groups especially for labor and capital. Greek bootblack ventures proliferated in Chicago when successful shoeshine parlor operators recruited inexpensive labor from the pool of kin and friends they left behind in Tripolis.[50]

136]

Business development always suffered, of course, when capital was restricted. Skilled Germans in Milwaukee remained butchers with small meat shops because they lacked access to capital sufficient to open large-scale meat-packing plants. Prior to the 1860s even German-American banks did not invest heavily in immigrant ventures. The shops of most craftsmen were built on capital brought over from Germany or accumulated slowly by working for others.[51]

An outstanding example of the confluence of kinship ties and available opportunities occurred among Japanese immigrants to America. Scholars have sometimes implied that ethnic bonds among newcomers were something primordial, an inevitable basis of association growing from common ancestral ties. The ability of the American industrial economy, however, to nurture and sustain kinship and ethnic ties has been demonstrated to underscore the point that ethnic and family solidarity certainly had an economic base, at least for the first generation of newcomers. Where openings existed in mines and mills the working-class family economy asserted itself and flourished. But not all groups encountered similar opportunity structures. Some were left with economic openings which called for collective, entrepreneurial effort to survive. In these instances, kin and ethnic attachments facilitated the recruitment of labor and provided sources of credit. In short, ethnic clusters became economic interest groups which directed the fortunes and goals of its members as long as it was to their economic advantage to do so. In these clusters, moreover, it must be stressed that only a few were in charge and the majority remained ordinary workers. Even tightly knit ethnic groups were not economically homogenous.[52]

The ventures of the early Japanese reflected the characteristics of most immigrant business. Credit was always in short supply and labor had to be secured as cheaply as possible. They tended to concentrate in small-trading activities or petit-bourgeois shops, such as fruits and vegetable distribution, markets, restaurants, laundries, and saloons, areas of the economy the larger society left open to them. Seldom did they resemble modern industrial enterprises. They were more likely to rely on kin and friends and foster ethnic or family solidarity as much as the accumulation of profits.[53]

Japanese-Americans created a niche for their business ventures on the West Coast, particularly in the market gardening of crops for sale in nearby urban markets such as Los Angeles. Despite the fact that most Japanese came with little money, vast amounts of capital were not needed to get started. Land was first acquired by renting and the rent paid from profits. Through strict adherence to thrift and mutual assistance these ventures would expand. Cheap, family labor cultivated every inch of ground. The traditional *tanomashi*, or credit association, a system by which members pooled money and provided loans to each member, in turn offered a source of credit. Japanese farm organizations were formed to further assist members in finding land, purchasing supplies, and in marketing crops. For those newcomers of less independent persuasion these "middlemen minority" concerns provided secure employment in a strange land and access to a complex economy. Eventually Japanese arrivals constructed a vertically integrated industry in Southern California with Japanese growers selling to Japanese wholesalers, who in turn sold to retailers of the same ethnic group.[54]

By 1940 the Japanese success in the area of food retailing was well established. For every ten or eleven adult male Japanese-Americans in Los Angeles, there was a fruit stand or grocery. About two-thirds of the Japanese-American labor force was dependent upon raising, gathering, preparing, distributing, and retailing food. It is true that Japanese economic development was allowed only along very narrow lines, as it was for most groups. But the Japanese, whose arrivals had been displaced by Mexicans from railroad employment, made the most of their limited opportunity.[55]

The New Middle Class

Some scholars have felt that immigrant entrepreneurs in each group served as effective agents of acculturation since they provided models of mobility and were often exponents of American business values.[56] But it is not clear at all to what extent the lives of these individuals influenced the perceptions of the massive foreign-born working class who contended with many union, political, and religious leaders as well as businessmen. In many cases, in fact, a social distance began to surface between foreign-born entrepreneurs and workers who were often responsible for their early success. Some successful immigrant businessmen began to disassociate themselves from the working-class communities in which they first lived. Leaders of immigrant fraternals or religious leaders, or course, had to maintain ties to ordinary individuals, but "self-made" men who were able to expand the economic base of their support became more independent of ethnic attachments and were among the first to make even further commitments to the new capitalist order than most of those who had already emigrated. Merchants and professionals among nineteenth-century British immigrants organized clubs with well-upholstered reading rooms to which they might have aspired at home. After 1900 such societies as the Victorian Club of Boston or the British Empire Association of Chicago contained men who probably could not have entered similar organizations in Great Britain. Upwardly mobile Irish Catholics began to move from central Philadelphia by the 1880s to ornate Victorian houses in west Philadelphia and Germantown and sent their daughters to convent schools. The growing Italian middle class in Utica, New York, constructed a theater to foster cultural events. Among Hungarians, wealthier immigrants began to hold balls like the Hungarian gentry had done as models for their own social evenings. It was usually immigrants from this new middle class which began moving from areas of original settlement into better neighborhoods and joining American political organizations in larger numbers. A sample of Irish shopowners in New York City in the period between 1880 and 1900 revealed that the group was more likely than any other to move their residence above 86th Street in Manhattan. It was from this same element, that Chicanos first moved from the impoverished neighborhoods of the southside of San Antonio to middle-class areas north of downtown. The first Republican and Democratic political clubs among Mexicans and Hungarians were organized by members of the middle class.[57]

As the social distance between the classes in each group widened, those moving into higher social categories did not simply abandon those left behind. Frequently they made vigorous attempts to preach the advantages of hard work and efficiency that they now believed explained their own success and the value of ethnic identity, an element which generated the cohesiveness necessary for many to succeed and attain positions of group leadership. Indeed, the celebration of ethnic solidarity generated by middle-class leaders not only served their needs by muting class and regional conflict within immigrant communities, but was quickly adopted by foreign-born workers to satiate their quest for meaning and ties to the past, a desire which was heightened during an era of rapid social change. During the latter half of the nineteenth century secular leaders worked hard among Swedes in Chicago to direct the scope of social and cultural activities, so that Swedes would retain their ethnic identity and their ties to those in position of prominence. Businessmen such as Charles John Sundell founded the Scandinavian Union in 1854 and the Svea Society several years later to promote libraries, lectures, physical fitness, and even theatrical performances. These associations attracted the most influential Swedes in Chicago and established models of culture and learning that Swedish workers could adopt if they were so inclined.[58] In San Francisco, middle-class Irish residents published the *Catholic Guardian* to instruct the rank and file. The paper took pains to layout its conception of familial roles. It stressed both rights and duties within the family. Wives were especially encouraged to praise their husbands in whatever enterprise they undertook from shoemaking to shipbuilding,[59] a point which suggests the recurring theme that familial solidarity transcended class standing and was not limited to the world of workers. Italian entrepreneurs in the same city, struggled to reduce the influence of regionalism among fellow immigrants, which hindered the plans to build efficient manufacturing and commercial enterprises. Marco Fontana needed a large, efficient work force to expand the productive capacity of the Del Monte Corporation. He hired Italians from diverse regions but worked to get them to overcome their differences in order to promote efficiency. Fellow Italian A.P. Giannini weaned immigrants away from regionally based mutual-aid societies so they would all save in his bank. In 1916 San Francisco Italian businessmen established an Italian Welfare Agency to meet the social problems of newcomers from all regions unlike the mutual-aid societies which were more parochial in their interest.[60] Japanese business leaders attempted to convey a need to act deferentially toward the dominant white society to the Japanese working class. They did not want to risk the gains made by the Japanese-American economy or the wealth they had accumulated by causing resentment among native-born whites. Consequently, Japanese-Americans in California frequently failed to protest their exclusion from particular neighborhoods, parks, and jobs. Yugoslav entrepreneurs, fearful that consumer cooperatives established by Socialists would undermine their own saloons and grocery stores, attempted to dominate local ethnic and community organizations. They even hired educated immigrants to run their newspapers, which would resist Socialism and promote American business values.[61] During labor disputes in the 1930s middle-class newspapers, such as *La Prensa* in San Antonio urged striking workers to cooperate, be good American citizens, and honor their national culture. Middle-class Mexicans in San Antonio even operated their own radio station to promote their interests.[62]

Germans in nineteenth-century New York offered a vivid example of newly emerging business elites attempting to sustain their dominance by shaping the consciousness of the rest of the immigrant community. German entrepreneurs frequently confronted the question of whether they should promote assimilation as a means of attaining equality with native Americans or establishing their own base of power. Successful leaders such as William Steinway ultimately decided German workers should reside primarily in German-American communities, a fact which hopefully would make them loyal to their employers. Conrad Poppenhusen, a rubber producer, and Steinway, a piano manufacturer, actually attempted to establish separate German-American towns on Long Island between 1860 and 1890. College Point, Long Island, for instance, attracted hundreds of German workers from New York City to its boardinghouses in the 1860s.

Long Island proved attractive for a number of other reasons. German leaders could claim that workers would feel more protected in "isolated" Queens County from the pressures of the temperance movement. German businessmen were quite aware that by promoting ethnic homogeneity away from the city they would diminish the influence of American labor organizations. Astoria became the escape route for the Steinway company where workers could remain loyal and be prevented from listening to communists and anarchists. With the assistance of the *Staats-Zeitung* and its editor, Oswald Ottendorfer, Steinway promoted attachment to American political parties as a goal for immigrant workers. Ultimately, College Point came to resemble an industrial town of the Ruhr with mansions of the rich located on hilltops and the attached homes of workers at the bottoms.[63]

In Harlem, an area of second-stage settlement as was German Long Island, Jewish businessmen worked closely with religious leaders to overcome divisions between German Jews and East European Jews by emphasizing a commitment to a form of acculturation which allowed the retention of the Jewish religious heritage. Wishing to promote adherence to a society and economic system in which they now held rewarding positions and status, Harlem Jewish leaders initiated a wide range of social and educational programs which taught immigrants the English language, found them jobs, and still allowed for attendance at the "talmud-torah," where immigrant children could receive intensive instruction in rabbinic texts. Creating a form of American Orthodoxy, the movement in Harlem sought simultaneously to promote Americanization and the essence of traditional Judaism, and found its most profound expression in the establishment of institutions such as Yeshiva University. Jewish settlement-house workers labored diligently, moreover, to provide more acceptable, middle-class models of behavior to ghetto youth.[64]

Conclusion

Much evidence exists to suggest that immigrant communities in industrial America were far from monolithic and that separate classes emerged within their confines. The immigrant community was not a transitional experience from a traditional past shared by all newcomers to a common future of well-being and contentment. More precisely these communities were arenas in which people sorted themselves out into workers and owners, leaders and followers, traditionalists and modernizers. Above all, in this arena a new middle class emerged which in many ways owed its status to premigration experiences and which was frequently ambivalent about its relationship to the mass of immigrant workers, alternating between separateness and involvement.

This middle-class status was, moreover, not generated specifically by social mobility in an industrial society or the adoption of American traits but ironically through reliance on familiar ways of doing things. Old world backgrounds as artisans or intellectuals actually facilitated the attainment of a higher status in the American ethnic community. Mutual assistance and kinship proved to be as compatible with middle-class behavior as with working-class behavior, especially in generating supplies of capital and inexpensive labor. To a large extent what you were in the homeland would play an important role in determining what you would become in the structure of industrial capitalism, a point which suggests that inequality within and among immigrant groups often originated not from a vague American system of social mobility or nebulous cultural variables but from an inherited status. Success depended less upon the fact that you were a Jew, an Italian, or a German and more upon where your structural origins were in the premigration homelands of Jews, Italians, or Germans.

Finally, the new immigrant middle class was divided in its relationship to the immigrant rank and file. Frequently they would abandon their brothers and sisters for better neighborhoods and new associates and friends. If their elevated status relied on the support of the larger immigrant community, however, they attempted not only to retain a close association to the mass of newcomers but influence their thinking as well. This was especially true of clerics and political leaders who fostered an adherence to religious, ethnic, and nationalist goals which would sustain a following for their own leadership or business venture. Because the immigrant middle class consisted of competing entrepreneurs and leaders, it articulated different agendas: religious, secular, traditional, and modern. But ultimately these were only differences in emphasis and most of the immigrant middle class became staunch advocates of the new order of capitalism and all that it involved. Thus, religious traditions and ethnic solidarity could be stressed but not to the exclusion of Americanization, hard work, thrift, and free enterprise. Middle-class immigrants presented the large foreign-born working class with models of modernity, personalized manifestations of a new economic order that they were free to accept or reject.

5 /

Church and Society

The Role of the Church

If workers, shopkeepers, artisans, and peasants had to adjust to the realities of a capitalist economy and society, it stood to reason that immigrant institutions could not remain insulated from contemporary realities as well. Curiously, however, the assumption that immigrant religious bodies were somehow resistant to alteration was extremely widespread. Unlike the malleable family and the emerging immigrant entrepreneur, both influenced by the new realities of a capitalist economy, the immigrant church was thought to be unaffected by the existence of urban society. Individuals who had adapted to commercial agriculture in Europe seized unskilled jobs in American factories, or identified openings for entrepreneurial ventures, but when it came to religion many scholars found those same individuals huddled together, as their ancestors before them, seeking solace in a strange, new land.

If the immigrant desire to huddle together in churches was unaninous, one might expect these church communities to be rather placid places, free of serious discord, and overflowing with harmony and contentment. At times, of course, they were placid and, especially from the outside, appeared to be islands of tranquility in the rough seas of industrial society. But just as the ethnic communities of which they were a part could not remain unchanged, church organizations could neither avoid swirling currents of discontent and disagreement nor remain unaffected by the larger societal struggles for power and status. The massive, beautifully constructed churches of the first generation which still dot the American urban landscape were often troubled places.

The belief in the immigrant church as an extension of a conservative peasant tradition pervaded nearly all the early literature on immigrants and needs little elaboration. Immigrants certainly continued religious traditions in a society which was growing more secular and found much comfort in doing so. As a scholar of Greek-Americans concluded, "the thought of never being able to return home to his ancestral origins and the fear of dying in a strange land caused the Greek to embrace his religion in America with a fervor unknown even in Greece."[1] Such sentimental attachments to established patterns of religious practice were real for many newcomers, but motives such as the "natural desire" to worship with those of common ancestry serve as insufficient reasons to explain the feverish level of religious affairs among newcomers.

The view of the immigrant church as an extension of tradition has certainly been challenged. Stephen Shaw has emphasized their "Americanization" role and described German churches in Chicago which actually taught "American business skills." In a powerful argument, Timothy Smith interpreted the pervasive attachment between ethnic identification and religion in immigrant America as a process by which ethnic groups mobilized to pursue political and economic agendas. Belief in a shared descent was seen as a "contrived" ideal by leaders in respective communities who wished to mobilize legions of immigrants to support their own particular political and economic goals. Smith rejected ethnic religious organizations as being something primordial and argued that immigrants were predisposed toward change and looked upon their pastors and rabbis, whether they were Greeks, Lithuanians, Magyars, Slovaks, or Swedes, as "agents of progress." By intensifying the "psychic" basis of religious commitment through association with an ethnic past, religious leaders provided an explanation for migration itself; immigrants could believe they were "pilgrim people" legitimately in search of education, upward mobility, and their share of American capitalism.[2]

Smith's argument, of course, presupposed that immigrant leaders themselves were in agreement, that these leaders all felt comfortable with the association between ethnic identity and religion and that the expressions of religious leaders, many of whom were members of the immigrant middle class, were identical to the private thought and feelings of immigrant workers and their families. All three assumptions, however, appear to be extremely tenuous when an investigation is made into the history and evolution of these ubiquitous church communities. On the contrary, indications exist that not only were religious leaders and their followers frequently incompatible but serious divisions existed between groups of leaders themselves and the ideals of religious devotion and ethnic identity.

[145

Much of the initial impetus toward immigrant church formation involved a desire to hold on to traditions, which appeared threatened, and was generated by aggressive religious leaders. But progress seemed to be furthest from their minds. Early nineteenth-century Germans in American cities revealed these characteristics in their church activity nicely. During the 1840s German Catholics in New York City were concerned that settlement in America threatened the faith and language they had known. In 1841 the Reverend Johann Raffeiner used his own money to purchase land and build Holy Trinity Catholic Church. When this early congregation was challenged by a Catholic bishop who opposed a separate German Church in a neighborhood of German and Irish arrivals, the Germans struck a compromise whereby church sermons would be in English and German. German-American leaders were so concerned in 1868, in fact, over the ability of newcomers to retain their religion that they appointed two agents in New York to meet incoming ships in New York and Baltimore to direct immigrants to German neighborhoods and churches. Between 1868 and 1890 over 16,000 German arrivals used this service.[3]

German Lutherans also demonstrated that religious attachments could be stronger than ethnic ones. They too established missions and aid associations to direct Protestant German arrivals to the proper church much as Catholics had done. Friedrich Steimle, from Württemberg, was so anxious to found his own Lutheran Church in Brooklyn Heights, New York, that he held Sunday services for a while in a beer hall. His motivations were clear. Americanization was to be opposed at all costs. He and his congregation moved in the late 1860s, inscribed the word *Deutsch* over the church doors, and established laws that all church administrative and religious activities would be conducted in the German language.[4]

If a particular immigrant stream possessed backgrounds different or unusual by the standards of religious leaders, they could be made to feel quite defensive. The Greek Catholic rite practiced by thousands of Rusin immigrants in America faced just such a challenge from Roman Catholic bishops who felt their rite was the only correct one for American Catholics. They were especially disturbed by newcomers like the Rusins, who brought unfamiliar practices to America including a tradition of allowing priests to marry. These priests, like Reverend Alexis Toth of St. Paul, Minnesota, were rejected and humiliated when they presented themselves to local bishops. Reverend Toth, another disaffected immigrant leader, and his congregation solved their dilemma by joining the Russian Orthodox Church, a move which required virtually no changes in Rusin religious practices.[5]

On a national level, the central force in carrying on the Rusin struggle was the Greek Catholic Union, a fraternal organization run largely by laymen. Because a lay board usually owned Rusin church property, laymen were also influential in Rusin affairs and frequently hired and dismissed their own pastors. It was Rusin laymen who adamantly defended their rite against the "threats" of American church leaders and even Hungarian and other non-Rusin forces in Europe and America. By 1908 priests who were considered to "represent the interests of the Hungarian government" were excluded from the Greek Catholic Union. By holding on to their property, they could defend their rite and identity. When they knew their rite was no longer threatened, they could be quite willing to sign over their property to church leaders and, in fact, those that converted to Russian Orthodoxy did so.[6]

Rusins in America even feuded with Ukrainians who shared similar religious backgrounds and were somewhat similar culturally. Ukrainians led by the "American Circle," a group of clergymen who had dedicated their lives to ethnic-national work in America, took over a fraternal insurance society, changed its name to the Ukrainian National Association in 1915, and embarked upon a publication program which urged ordinary Ukrainian immigrants to support Ukrainian cultural enterprises, join unions, and strike if necessary to improve their lot.

Leaders and followers could also create relatively harmonious communities among Protestant congregations as well. A good example of this pattern was found among German Lutherans. While a measure of independence characterized many American Protestant denominations during the nineteenth century, German Lutherans in the Missouri Synod tended to accord their pastors the same deference and respect they had in Germany. These immigrants were definitely influenced by the currents of Bismarckian nationalism and frequently merged symbols of religion and nationalism, but more importantly they huddled together in German congregations which provided what one scholar called "comforting assurance in a strange land." German-speaking pastors, usually more educated than most German newcomers, were indispensable in sustaining this image and earned much respect when they conducted rites of baptism, confirmation, communion, and marriage, which Lutherans held in high esteem.[7]

Immigrant church communities were also founded on premigration regional and kinship associations which served as powerful inducements to keep them intact on the part of the laity regardless of what leaders debated. In a sense, because they were an extension of communal ties, they continued to serve important social functions. In the minds of most immigrants, the church was not an abstract entity but a localized one based on region, family, neighborhood, and even social class. It was this social basis of religious organization which explained the proliferation of the immigrant church as much as notions about ethnic separatism or competing elites. East European Jews, for instance, repeatedly established orthodox congregations along regional lines. Between 1874 and 1914, for instance, twenty-four such communities were established in Providence, Rhode Island. Among Irish Catholics in antebellum New York, St. Paul's Church was in an area of squalor and makeshift shanties with a membership consisting of nearly all manual laborers. St. Ann's, on the other hand, was composed of wealthier Irish newcomers who tended to live in fine homes near Washington Square.[8] For Greeks, Slovaks, and Poles traditional regional and village ties formed the key associations which established churches in conjunction with mutual aid societies, coffee houses, and schools.[9]

Immigrants participated in church communities not simply because they were drawn to particular forms of belief or ideology but because these communities continued to provide forms of mutual assistance which were an integral part of working-class life. In a strange land it was especially satisfying to listen to the gossip and information of congregations where newcomers knew most everyone by sight. Family events such as births, deaths, and weddings attracted wide participation. The first communion of 59 children at St. Procopius Czech parish in Cleveland in 1880 began at nine in the morning with a parade for parents and neighbors and ended with a carnival and a huge feast. Immigrants annually perused the list of financial contributions to the church and discussed individual donations. Pastors admonished children to obey their parents and wives their husbands, thus reinforcing the family economy, the central institution in the adjustment to capitalism. Fellow church members could offer assistance during periods of unemployment or solace at times of death. Many churches actually institutionalized social services by setting up welfare organizations, hospitals, and orphanages. The Magdalen Asylum was founded by San Francisco Irish in 1864 under the charge of the Sisters of Mercy, and by 1880 it had cared for over 600 patients. An infant shelter established in the same city in 1874 cared for the young children of working women during each day. Immigrant churches such as St. Stanislaus Kostka in Chicago for Poles and St.

Going to Church, Pittsburgh, circa 1939
Immigrants not only found solace in their churches but
often competing ideologies and leaders. *Library of Congress*

Peter's in Milwaukee for Germans formed mutual-benefit associations, women's groups, and youth clubs. St. Stanislaus even established a parish bank where interest on workers' savings was often waived by depositors to make improvements on the parish church or school. German Catholics, through organizations such as the Central Verein, helped fellow immigrants find homes after arrival. Austrian Catholics formed the Austrian Society of New York in 1898 which housed thousands of Austrian newcomers during the first decade of its existence. Among the Greek Orthodox, membership in the *Koinotis* or community was limited to dues-paying members, thus offering a strong incentive for immigrants not to live unaffiliated outside the colony. Because they offered so many services in a hostile world, urban parishes tended to be quite large. While the degrees of individual participation in church affairs varied, many congregations reached membership levels of several thousand. St. Joachim in New York had 20,000 Italians by 1900 and St. Stanislaus Kostka counted over 50,000 Chicago Poles by 1900.[10]

Class, Culture, and the Church

But to end the analysis of the immigrant church on a note of cultural retention or smoothly functioning enclaves would be grossly shortsighted. In nearly every locale deep fissures and ferocious battles shook church communities as private and public agendas were forced together by the realities of a new social structure. Class and ideological tensions fully permeated immigrant institutions. While leaders were central to the actual rise of German ethnic churches, in most instances, such as that of New York's Most Holy Redeemer Church, the initial impulse for organization came from the laity. Here Germans from diverse regions in the Old World could meet to share what they held in common: their religious and ethnic ancestry. Indeed, German Catholics who arrived prior to the Civil War were often lax in their participation in religious affairs; attendance at Sunday Mass was frequently neglected. Due to the encouragement of their pastors, they began to increase their participation in mission services, communions, and baptisms. New York German laymen even established separate churches over quarrels with Irish bishops concerning the need for separate German cemeteries. In Philadelphia, Germans, unsettled by their minority status both within Protestant America and the Irish-dominated Catholic Church, argued that national parishes were the best means to protect the Catholic immigrants against the loss of their faith.[11]

In the 1890s a zealous Catholic in Germany, Peter Paul Cahensly, demonstrated the concern of many already in America that the faith of the immigrants was threatened by Protestants and unsympathetic Irish-American Church leaders. Cahensly not only organized a society to acquaint emigrants with the physical and spiritual hazards of their move but sparked a movement in Europe and America to establish more German-American bishops and influence within the Catholic Church. While this move would clearly benefit German Catholic clerics, it also represented a widespread grass roots feeling that German faith and culture required special action if they were to be safeguarded in a world populated increasingly by non-Germans. The German view was only reinforced by response of Irish-American leaders, such as Archbishop John Ireland, who actively opposed any effort to create a German-American "party" within the church and argued that disparate immigrant cultures could not be transferred directly to the American Church.[12]

Irish leaders, of course, faced few ethnic challenges within the church, but they could become quite anxious when looking at the widespread existence of Protestantism in America and sought mainly to sustain a traditional ideology against an old enemy. A long, bitter relationship with British Protestantism, of course, served as a backdrop to nineteenth-century Irish attitudes. In America the hostility simply continued. Nativists attached Irish Catholics in Philadelphia in the 1840s and excluded them from political office in Massachusetts. Protesant domination of American public schools only exacerbated general fears; by the 1870s the Baptist Home Mission Society was actually trying to convert Catholic newcomers. If Irish Catholicism was to survive and Irish Church leaders were to retain their positions of influence, stern measures had to be taken to intensify and sustain the faith of the masses.[13]

Irish leaders and religious zealots not only feared, however, the outside challenge of Protestantism but worried over the internal level of faith displayed by most Irish immigrants, especially before the 1860s. Most of the two million Irish who emigrated between 1847 and 1860, much like their German counterparts, were rather weak in the practice of their religion. Drinking and violence were excessive. But the impact of poverty and social distress during the famine actually produced a revival in religious feeling in Ireland, which was quickly exported to America to save immigrant souls. Large numbers of nuns and priests by 1860 had come to work among the newcomers and transform them into practicing Catholics. Mission preachers were sent in large numbers to immigrant settlements throughout America

[151

and their services were measured in the number of confessions and communions they generated. Church building, religious vocations, and devotional regularity expanded tremendously. Religious teaching and worship were standardized with the production and distribution of catechisms, preprinted sermons, and routinized parish functions. In some instances national or ethnic parishes were encouraged, if it would serve the larger goal of intensifying the practice of the faith. Even folk traditions which emphasized the use of holy water or the wearing or protective crosses were retained in support of an effort to revitalize religious practice.[14]

German Redemptionist priests in nineteenth-century New York City labored particularly hard to revive faith. The Redemptionist society had built the largest German Catholic parish in the city by 1851. In order to combat socialist and Protestant thought both within and outside the German Catholic community, the Redemptionists held periodic revival meetings designed to bring lapsed Catholics back into the church and promoted the cult of Mary which had been one of the bases of the order's popularity in Germany. Marianism proved especially effective in providing a sense of continuity and security for Catholic immigrant women in both the German and other ethnic groups as well.[15]

In their labor to intensify faith, consolidate their own power, and deal with a rising tide of ethnic diversity, Catholic leaders pushed the administration of the church to greater and greater levels of centralization. The push for central authority and ecclesiastical order not only intensified religious practice among newcomers but quelled potential stirrings of trusteeisms. Church officials, like their counterparts in the business community, began not only to think and act like the middle-class individuals they were becoming but attempted like immigrant businessmen to impart their views to the mass of immigrants. Bishops, such as William Henry O'Connell of Boston, by the 1890s identified with the cultural style of Rome rather than the working-class modes of the shanty Irish. O'Connell and others like him supported the movement toward the standardization of religious practices and opposed other leaders such as John Ireland who desired an American church somewhat autonomous from Rome. The process of centralization had to be carried to its logical conclusion. Consequently, O'Connell further centralized authority by turning the *Boston Pilot* into an official church organ, consolidated local parochial schools under a superintendent where possible, and opposed the power of local pastors. Similarly Archbishop John Hughes of New York attacked the entire notion of lay trustees exerting control in parish affairs and the calls for ethnic separatism. Hughes and others also realized the financial resources which could be generated by a consolidated rather than a divided administrative system. In Philadelphia Dennis Cardinal Dougherty pursued centralization to such an extent in the twentieth century that he created a land bank estimated to be worth over a billion dollars by 1965.[16]

While the fostering of religious ritual and administration preoccupied the leaders, the ordinary immigrants often moved toward religious institutions for other reasons. Many groups of newcomers had to share church facilities when they first arrived with individuals of different ancestry. Slovenes, for instance, shared a church with Germans in late nineteenth-century New York on Second Street, and grew to dislike the arrangement. Hungarians and Slovaks, emanating from neighboring regions in Europe worshipped in the same buildings but increasingly feuded. Slovaks especially disliked priests who preached in Hungarian and contributed money to causes such as building a statue for Louis Kossuth, a Hungarian. Letters from both Slovak and Magyar priests in America sent to Europe revealed the importance of maintaining ethnic pride as a foundation upon which immigrant churches rested; several claimed that national sentiment evoked more support than religious feeling itself. In numerous cities early Italian settlers were often poorer than the Irish they worshipped with and could not contribute as much to church affairs. At some churches, services for Italians were conducted in the basement, a fact which created much resentment. "Duplex parishes" of Irish and Italians in New York, Newark, St. Paul, and Boston eventually split over such antagonisms and the traditional Italian attachment to anticlericalism.[17]

Immigrants frequently felt that bishops and other religious leaders from different backgrounds failed to understand their needs and concerns. When a Detroit bishop dismissed a Polish priest at St. Albertus Church for refusing to submit his financial books to the bishop for audit in 1886, the Polish congregation violently protested. Immigrant women actually blocked the entrance of the church to a new pastor and some Poles actually severed their ties from the diocese and built a new church without the bishop's consent. The most extreme form of Polish protest over what was perceived to be insensitivity by Irish-American Catholic officials was the formation of Polish-National Churches in a number of American cities. Where these parishes were formed the impetus usually came from laymen, as well as several Polish leaders. And it was not uncommon for these splinter groups to abandon the use of Latin in their religious services and to institute the Polish language.[18]

The immigrant working class, furthermore, did not always acquiesce to the demands of leaders and were quite capable of mounting a defense of their interests and traditions. An Italian priest in White Plains, New York, was shot at for proposing to abolish the traditional festival procession of St. Rocco. In Boston, Italians, at St. Marco's Church remained without any priests or sacraments from 1885 to 1889 rather than yield to a bishop's demand to turn over their church property to the diocese. At St. Louis Church in Buffalo, German and Alsatian laymen fought with church leaders over the issue of trusteeism in order to preserve European communal traditions of lay management. In 1852 the male parishioners petitioned Pope Pius IX for support in their campaign to hold their church property. The trustees of St. Louis Church actually lobbied for the cooperation of anti-Catholic state legislators in New York in obtaining passage of a law making legal ownership and inheritance of church property by an episcopal hierarchy an impossibility.[19]

Ordinary Italians also had reason to feel defensive about their religious and cultural practices. Both Catholic and Protestant leaders attempted to intrude upon the private world of newcomers and expressed notions that Italians were "pagans" or at least bearers of "anti-christian beliefs." Both major denominations defined Italians as a goal of their mission work in need of their attention and care and established churches, schools, and settlement houses in a struggle to win their faith and reshape their everyday concerns. In San Francisco, Irish Catholic leaders especially disapproved of Italian parades in honor of various saints. They exhorted immigrants, often through Italian priests, to bring the statues of the saints to church, reduce the number of processions, and join church organizations like the Holy Name Society. But the immigrant working-class Italians, like the Poles, Germans, Rusins, and others, were not completely amenable to appeals for regimentation and organization from middle-class leaders and were quite willing to defend elements of their own cultural milieu. In San Francisco Italians simply stopped inviting members of the clergy to their processions. In other cities many seldom fulfilled their obligation to attend Sunday mass and preferred to participate in local festivals and cult rituals to the madonna and saints.[20] Italians, in fact, as historian Rudolph Vecoli has effectively argued, represented an outstanding example of the inability of the American Catholic Church to serve as simply an agent of Americanization. Sometimes, experience within the church produced just the opposite effect. Even Italian bishops in Europe feared for the survival of the faith among peasants in America and organized pastoral assistance for their countrymen overseas and sent zealous priests to America. In 1887 Bishop

Scalabrini of Piacenza began an intense campaign to retain and even revitalize the immigrant's faith by founding the Congregation of the Missionaries of St. Charles, which agitated among the American hierarchy for separate Italian parishes and chapels. As both Italian clerics and laymen built the ethnic church, however, this campaign did not call as much for loyal adherence to ecclesiastical precepts as for defense of the folk-cultural community and symbols in a New World increasingly filled with strangers.[21]

Differences between various groups and tensions between laymen and pastors existed among Protestant congregations as well. Consider the case of the Dutch Reformed Churches in nineteenth-century America. As early as 1857 a major schism could be attributed directly to differences in homeland origins. Dutch newcomers from small villages emphasized traditional values and styles and were rather resistant toward Americanization, preferring to maintain ties to leaders in the mother country. Those with more cosmopolitan origins resisted religious isolation and wanted a church oriented more toward American ways. Divisiveness among the Dutch even penetrated into smaller groups who shared many beliefs. By the 1870s, for instance, Dutch Neo-Calvinists argued among themselves over the extent they should be involved in the world around them. One group saw worldly cooperation between believers and non-believers as possible and urged immigrants to seek achievement in society and politics. An "Antithetical Party" emphasized the world as a corrupt place and called for separate Dutch Reformed organizations to protect members from contamination in secular America.[22] Germans, as much as any nineteenth-century ethnic group, divided bitterly over internal disputes and leaders. In the 1860s some German Lutherans broke from English co-religionists and formed the German Evangelical-Lutheran Synod, whose officers argued adamantly for using the German language as a basis for retaining that inner feeling of "Germanness." In New York City at the same time many German Protestants remained unaffiliated with various congregations in part because of the conservative political views of ministers who disapproved of the German revolutions. Ethnic nationalism, in other words, proved stronger for these newcomers than religious doctrine. Most preferred to spend their Sundays in large, elaborate German beer halls where families gathered to dance and drink rather than in churches or even the meeting halls of freethinkers.[23] By 1850 German Protestants in Milwaukee who did attend church were forming separate congregations.[24] A recent survey of early Pittsburgh discovered just how extensive immigrant religious factionalism was. At

[155

St. John's Lutheran Church in the 1840s intense friction characterized the relationship between conservative congregants who held to a form of old Lutheranism and reformers who attempted to adapt Lutheranism to America. A Lutheran church in the Smithfield section of the city attracted German members from a wide range of regional backgrounds because of its rationalist leanings and cosmopolitan outlook. Some congregations reflected class differences. St. John's had more members who owned property and were craftsmen while Trinity Lutheran was more conservative and had a greater number of members who were laborers. It was conservative congregations, like Trinity, which were shocked even by the degree of change that had affected German-American churches established in the eighteenth century and decided to join the conservative Missouri Synod. Other poor Germans, who were Catholics from southern Germany and worshipped at St. Mary's, married other Catholics from similar backgrounds and maintained regional and religious ties from their homeland. The debate over modernization and Americanization was not a debate, as has often been described, between generations but was an issue which consumed the migrating generation, both in their homelands and in American cities. In Pittsburgh, Germans ultimately constructed a variety of congregations and associations which differed one from another.[25]

Competing Leaders

Communal factionalism could reach intense proportions when differences emerged between rival leaders within concentrations of newcomers. In Brooklyn, the ambitions of rising young clergy seemed to generate considerable internal dispute in the 1890s. While it may be too strong to assert that the multiplication of ethnic parishes was attributable solely to "clerical careerism," ambitions of leaders or those who aspired to be leaders played a strong role in stimulating factionalism. Immigrant churches were far from being simple transplants of some homeland tradition. At St. Stanislaus Kostka Church in Brooklyn constant discord revolved around newly emerged Polish businessmen who wanted greater control in church and ethnic affairs and traditional leaders such as parish priests. These secular leaders championed the formation of separate churches from St. Stanislaus in order to challenge clerical authority and promote their own status and business relationships. Because they wanted churches in which they could exert more control, they helped found splinter congregations.[26]

Elsewhere lay leaders and workers found reason to oppose clerical authority within their own group. In Hazelton, Pennsylvania, the Reverend Matus Jankola, despite his strong identification with Slovak nationalism, could not protect his rectory from being bombed when he insisted that the church organist could no longer teach in the parochial school. Younger clergy, usually more closely identified with the peasant rather than the gentry class, frequently attacked older clerics who had arrived with stronger ties to old world leaders and "oppressor" governments. Thus young Polish clergy often resented older men who came from a more privileged background in German Poland and were among the first to arrive. Younger Slovak clergy such as Jankola and Jozef Murgas waged an aggressive campaign against older Slovak priests who were thought to be pro-Hungarian. Scholars know now what immigrants may have only suspected: The Hungarian government was supporting many priests and editors financially.[27]

In Milwaukee, Anthony J. Kuzniewski has described internal competition among Polish leaders so intense that it very nearly preempted all the attention the Polish rank and file could devote to any social or political agenda. In the 1870s, the earliest days of Milwaukee Polonia, cooperation characterized the relationship between secular and clerical authorities. *Kuyer Polski*, the leading newspaper, and Michael Kruszka, its editor, worked closely with church officials. Both sectors offered strong support for the Polish Roman Catholic Union, a fraternal institution which stressed religious values over all others, and ignored somewhat the nationalistic Polish National Alliance. Michael Kruszka even won election to the Wisconsin legislature in 1890 over his support for parochial schools, something all Poles at that time could support.[28]

The alliance, however, was not to last. From the beginning it rested on a tenuous ideological union of religious faith and ethnic nationalism which was shaken in 1896 by the issue of secular education. In that year the Polish Educational Society (PES) was founded in Milwaukee with the help of the Polish National Alliance. The new organization's chief aim was the "betterment of schools and other educational facilities for the children of Polish descent." Plans were laid to found a Polish library and to secure the introduction of the Polish language into the public schools.[29]

Polish religious leaders argued that the pleas of the PES should be disregarded because Polish parochial schools did a good job in meeting the instructional needs of Polish-Americans and it would be useless to burden Milwaukee with the cost of additional teachers. The clergy even accused the members of the PES with "using the situation to secure personal political advancement."[30]

[157

Polish religious leaders opposed the PES and indicated that matters of religion superseded matters of nationality and that the two could in fact be distinguished, one important Polish leader could not agree. Michael Kruszka startled many when he used *Kuyer* to support the PES. Kruszka claimed that it was a matter of conscience for parents to decide which school their children ought to attend. Since Polish parents were enrolling their children in public schools, the editor felt it was important for them to obtain language instruction to "preserve these children for the Polish nation."[31]

Kuzniewski makes clear that the emerging dispute between secular spokesmen and religious leaders was not merely a debate over the relative merits of two different school systems. It was, however, a clear argument over who was to exert leadership within the ethnic community and a sign that the new immigrant middle-class was badly divided over the degree a new secular order should be embraced.

Since Kruszka owned the leading newspaper, Polish priests had to articulate their position from the pulpit. Their sermons increasingly characterized the editor of *Kuyer* as a fool and an unbeliever who consorted with the devil. *Kuyer* was labeled a "horrible, atheistic, and lying paper" which had printed slanderous material on the educational issues. The PES was referred to as a group of "dogs, fools, rogues, and devils."[32] Eventually Kruszka's enemies formed an opposition paper. After several unsuccessful attempts, *Nowiny Polskie (Polish News)* emerged in 1906 under the editorship of Reverend Bolesclaus Goral.

The gulf between secular leaders and clerical traditionalists widened in the late 1890s when the pastor of Kruszka's church announced plans to build a hugh basilica in Milwaukee with a dome which would be the fifth largest in the world. Immediately, secular leaders including *Kuyer's* editor attacked the plan as being too expensive. Kruszka pointed out that construction would cost each family in the congregation over $200 or about seven months wages for the average worker. Even Michael Kruszka's brother, a priest in nearby Ripon, Wisconsin, joined the protest and wrote in *Kuyer* that the entire project was unjust for it burdened working-class Poles with debts.[33]

With the alliance between nationality and faith badly shaken, proponents of ethnic pride pursued other issues with renewed vigor, especially the appointment of a Polish-American bishop. The bishop issue was a crucial one for nationalists who longed for acknowledgement of their status as an important group within the Roman Catholic Church, which was ruled almost entirely by Irish and German clerics. Yet true believers within the Polish community and the Polish clergy itself still maintained the need above all else to obey the

Immigrant Priest in America
Religious leaders often felt threatened in industrial America
by others who also competed for the immigrant's mind and
soul. *International Museum of Photography,*
George Eastman House

church hierarchy. And the hierarchy was not prepared to admit that ethnicity was a valid basis for appointing a bishop.

Nevertheless, once out from under the influence of religious leaders, nationalists such as Michael Kruszka and his brother Wenceslaus pursued the appointment of an ethnic Pole as bishop with a deep sense of purpose. Wenceslaus Kruszka even traveled to Rome and secured an audience with the Pope to press his demands, thus blatantly circumventing ecclesiastical authority in Milwaukee. The trip resulted in a papal emissary being sent to Milwaukee to investigate the situation. Kruszka's entire trip to Rome was covered in detail in the pages of the *Kuyer* and followed with such intensity in the community that he received a hero's welcome upon his return. In fact, when the Pope's representative arrived shortly afterwards over 50,000 Polish-Americans came to greet him. [34]

It was at this point that most of the Polish clerical leadership declared that obedience to Roman Catholicism superseded ethnic identity and rallied to the defense of the German Archbishop of Milwaukee, Sebastian Messmer, who resisted challenges to his authority and the notion that religious appointments should be based on ethnicity. Kuzniewski explained that Polish priests formed an association and issued a letter condemning the Kruszka brothers for fomenting anarchy and rebellion. At the insistence of Polish clergy, Archbishop Messmer sent Wenceslaus Kruszka a private letter to stop writing on the Polish bishop question. Continued attacks in *Nowiny Polskie* eventually generated enough subscribers among the Polish rank and file to challenge *Kuyer*, as numerous Poles accepted the argument that it was more important to preserve ecclesiastical unity than pursue ethnic nationalism. And Polish clergy even increased their attacks from the pulpit and the classroom, calling Wenceslaus Kruszka a "good for nothing" and his brother a heretic for not sending his daughter to a Catholic school. [35]

The dissension within the community reached a temporary reconciliation in 1908 when a Polish-American was appointed an auxiliary bishop in Chicago. All Milwaukee Poles could rejoice in the symbol of ethnic achievement and representation. But shortly thereafter the rival forces of ethnic pride and religious authority resumed their struggle. Michael Kruszka began to raise the issue of lay ownership of church property. Numerous Poles shared his sentiment that the people who work to build and finance church organizations should own them, not the clerical authorities. The issue continued to be fought in the pages of *Kuyer* and *Nowiny* and each group sponsored rival picnics and programs to entice the Polish masses to their side. The struggle continued until America's entry into World War I when the proponents of ethnic pride were forced to temper their arguments considerably in the face of national pressures to be fully American and not disruptive in any way of national unity during the war effort.[36]

As in Milwaukee, ethnic nationalism and religion through their spokesmen competed for the loyalties of the immigrant masses in Chicago prior to 1920. Leaders from the communities also vied for dominance. On one hand the religious order of the Resurrectionists took control of most Polish churches in Chicago, including the largest and most influential, St. Stanislaus Kostka. Resurrectionist leaders were staunch supporters of religious authority and the belief that Roman Catholicism was the fundamental basis of Polish identity and life. Contesting the preeminence of the religious leaders were the nationalists who concentrated in Holy Trinity parish and who argued for lay rather than clerical control of churches and the preeminence of Polish ethnic identity over religious authority.[37]

The power of the Resurrectionist clergy in Chicago and their most notable leader, Reverend Vincent Barzynski, originated in 1871 when they negotiated an agreement with the Roman Catholic hierarchy in Chicago allowing them to administer all Polish parishes in the city in return for granting the deeds of those parishes over to the diocese, an illustration that ethnic barriers within the church were not insurmountable. This plan allowed the Resurrectionists to position themselves strategically as the only recognized link between the Catholic diocese officials in the city and the mass of Polish immigrants.[38]

Reverend Barzynski worked hard to expand the notion of religious supremacy in Polish life. In 1873 Barzynski allied himself with Reverend Theodore Gieryk in Detroit and launched the Polish Roman Catholic Union (PRCU), a fraternal organization which sought to preserve Catholicism among future generations of Poles and assist the maintenance of a Polish Catholic school system. A distinguishing feature of the new organization was that it was dominated by the clergy.

It was the formation of the PRCU that specifically prompted a segment of Poles at St. Stanislaus to consider separating themselves and forming a parish of their own outside the orbit of religious leaders and more concerned with issues of ethnic nationalism and lay authority. Under the leadership of a layman, Ladislaus Dyniewicz, Holy Trinity parish was organized in 1876 independently of Barzynski's control. The new group immediately affiliated with the more nationalistic Polish National Alliance (the group that sponsored Wenceslaus Kruszka's trip to Rome for a Polish bishop) and started a nationalist newspaper, *Zgoda*, to compete with the Catholic-dominated one, *Dziennik Chicagoski*. This new group felt that Poles should work above all else for a free and independent Poland and declared that the chief obstacle to generating international pressure to free Poland was Polonia's clergy who "for centuries have kept the people in blindness."[39]

The Trinitarians of Holy Trinity parish were especially hostile to Barzynski's control of the parish bank at St. Stanislaus. The priest had established the bank as a means to raise funds for church and school construction projects. He continually encouraged Poles who distrusted American bankers to place their savings for very small rates of interest. Sometimes interest was even waived on the assumption that Barzynski was maintaining the financial strength of the Polish community. Charges by nationalists that Barzynski had mismanaged the funds were so effective that in 1893 the Vatican ordered Resurrectionists to relinquish all control over or ties with Holy Trinity, and it ultimately passed into nationalistic control.

Before Barzynski was forced to let Holy Trinity slip from the Resurrectionist control, however, he conducted a massive campaign to subordinate the nationalists and their church. After the establishment of Holy Trinity, Barzynski charged that a true Catholic owed his allegiance to the Pope, the Bishop, and his pastor. This hierarchial order was not to be questioned, for its stability was a powerful weapon against not only Protestantism and secularism but against Socialism and Masonry, forces viewed as capable of tearing the fabric of the community-parish apart.

Barzynski then launched into an attack on Holy Trinity, demanding that they relinquish their church by allowing it to be renovated into a school or hall. When Trinitarians pleaded with the Chicago bishop that they be allowed to remain separate, Barzynski retaliated by attempting to assimilate the funds of a nationalist fraternal lodge into the St. Stanislaus treasury and used the Resurrectionist leverage with Catholic diocese officials to have Holy Trinity closed until further notice. When the Holy Trinity pastor, Adalbert Mielcuszny, and officials refused, the bishop prohibited him from hearing confessions. Shortly thereafter, street rioting broke out near Holy Trinity and Mielcuszny was physically assulted by supporters of Barzynski. An open meeting to resolve the conflict in 1884 resulted in complete chaos and the bishop finally closed the church for five years.[40]

Slovaks, who migrated from the northeastern counties of the Austro-Hungarian Empire, especially from Saris, Zemplin, and Spis, to American cities, also established congregations which were shaken by internal disputes and turmoil. One of their largest concentrations was in Pittsburgh where thousands settled after 1880. Like Poles, they debated the relative merits of nationalism and religion, the chief components of ethnic identity. Even more than the Poles, however, they had to struggle first with factionalism based on the varying regional identities they brought from Europe.

Regional or local identity proved to be a persistent obstacle to unity among early Slovaks. The "Zemplinksa," for instance, migrated with and felt close to those who emanated from Zemplin County, especially villages east and south of Kosice. Early fraternal societies reflected this regional diversity. Slovaks joined the same lodges as other immigrants from the same villages or regions. For instance, in St. Matthew's parish in Pittsburgh, Slovaks from the northern tip of Spis County joined only branch 159 of the First Catholic Slovak Union. Branch 50 attracted members from Zemplin County. Lodge 460 of the FCSU consisted entirely of immigrants from the village of Tepla. Often contributions to churches would be made on the basis of village groups, with those from one town contributing a cross and those from another a stained-glass window.[41]

Frequently, prominent Slovaks, promoting centralization like most leaders, criticized the persistence of regional differences. In her study of Pittsburgh, June Alexander shows that regionalism was criticized. All Slovaks were asked to adopt a more nationalistic stance and remember that they were "all sons of one Slovak mother." In 1912, an election of officers for the local branches of the FCSU created considerable infighting when a majority from one village attempted to impose its will over a minority with different village origins. Regional diversities, however, began to give way in Pittsburgh after two decades or so of settlement. While persisting in some form, they eventually became secondary to the major divisive and often competing issues of religious authority and ethnic nationalism. Because the church was often the most important and powerful institution in ethnic life, leaders on both sides debated its role. Nationalistic Slovaks saw the churches as vehicles for promoting political or cultural nationalism and ethnic consciousness among the city's immigrants. Religiously oriented leaders, not wanting to lose their status, felt churches should adhere strictly to their primary religious function. Divisions between the two sides became evident when the issue of expanding church structure to include Slovak schools surfaced.[42]

During the early years of the twentieth century, Slovak laymen were often urged by leaders to build schools. Fraternal organizations such as the First Catholic Slovak Union actually required its members to send children to Catholic schools, especially Slovak parochial institutions, if possible. Religious leaders, equating the importance of language maintenance and Catholicism, deemed Slovak schools essential. Reverend Stephen Furdek, founder of the First Catholic Slovak Union, feared that if Slovak children became "Americanized" they might shed their parents' Catholicism as well as their mother tongue. Even Pittsburgh diocese officials required the establishment of parochial schools where possible in nationality parishes.[43]

Despite these pressures, Alexander writes that most of Pittsburgh's Slovak Catholic workers demonstrated little interest during the pre-World War I era in establishing schools for their children. In 1902, some South Side Slovaks included a school in their initial plans for a church in their neighborhood. But building a school was only a passing consideration and church organizers quickly dropped it from their proposal. In 1907, an advocate of a Slovak church in Frankstown simply assumed that organizing a parish would include establishing a parochial school in the neighborhood as well. However, plans for a school were not subsequently pursued as part of the effort to found a Slovak church. Building a school was clearly a secondary consideration for most Frankstown Slovaks. Once St. Joachim's was established, it was difficult to arouse enthusiasm for a Slovak school in Frankstown. By 1914, only St. Gabriel's parish had an elementary school. This school was the result of intense efforts by the parish pastor, not an out growth of lay initiative.[44]

Nationalists and non-nationalists argued at St. Joachim's parish in 1911. Joseph Bohacek pleaded with St. Joachim's parishioners to build a school. Although parish children were receiving religious instructions in St. Joachim's church basement, this failed to satisfy Bohacek. He wanted a regular Slovak parochial school. Alexander explained that Bohacek succinctly summarized the views of a Slovak Catholic nationalist on education when he reasoned that "without a school our offspring will be raised for foreigners and not us, and our churches will vanish." Bohacek insisted there was a crucial link between ethnic survival and the preservation of religion but was unable to convince his fellow parishioners.[45]

The debate over parish schools was in part a debate about the function of the church in Slovak communities. Slovak nationalists saw churches as vehicles for promoting ethnic consciousness and cultural nationalism among both adults and children in the community. Their less nationalistic, more religiously oriented countrymen supported churches but, at least during the early part of the twentieth century, saw them as having the limited function of serving the religious needs of the community. This function did not include providing a Slovak education for children. Underlying, yet central to the issue of establishing Slovak schools, was the question of how extensively Pittsburgh Slovaks embraced the Slovak nationalism that was gaining force in the United States during the pre-World War I era. The lay initiative responsible for the formation of four Slovak Catholic churches in Pittsburgh demonstrates the deep religiosity of Slovak Catholic immigrants. The subsequent weak and divided lay support for parochial schools, despite pressure from Slovak Catholic leaders, suggests that many of the city's Slovaks ignored the arguments of articulate Slovak nationalists as well as clergymen who stressed that a crucial link existed between the preservation of ethnicity and religion. On the issue of Slovak schools, in Pittsburgh, there was a gap between the rhetoric of articulate nationalist and Catholic leaders and the actions of Slovak parishioners.[46]

It must also be pointed out that the large Slovak working class had little reason to insist that their children pursue formal education. While religion may have provided psychic relief from the routine of industrial work and the strangeness of a new culture, only income offered immediate relief from the daily economic pressure of making ends meet. Children were more valuable as generators of additional family finances than they were as scholars, whatever it was they studied. Besides, jobs were very accessible in industrial cities like Pittsburgh. Immigrants could easily bring sons and daughters into a factory, and opportunities to gain familial and ethnic strongholds within certain industries were not easily ignored.[47]

Lurking behind many of the arguments which characterized immigrant communities were forces not always apparent to those caught in the immediate swirl of contention and conflict. The governments of the homelands that immigrants left did not always relinquish all ties to those who left. The assumption always persisted that most would eventually return home and, of course, many did. Homeland governments were always concerned that returning immigrants not be contaminated with dangerous political and social ideas and continually sought to influence opinion makers and leaders among countrymen in America. Prussian authorities, for instance, had secret policemen watching Poles in America, who might have exhibited anti-Prussian attitudes, since Poles were often a contentious minority group in Prussia who could return with heightened attitudes of Polish separatism. The Japanese Consulate General in San Francisco in 1909 caused the founding of the Japanese Association of America. Consular officials were able to exert influence over Japanese immigrants by controlling the issuing of official documents immigrants needed, including certificates which allowed a newcomer to bring a wife from Japan. Officials made certain, therefore, that individuals who headed local chapters of the Japanese Association adhered to the standards of behavior promulgated by the homeland. Immigrants were urged to keep a low profile, dress in Western fashion, attend schools, and not to bring disgrace to the country of Japan.[48]

Homeland government activity was particularly influential when it attempted to control the affairs of immigrant churches. The Austro-Hungarian monarchy, concerned over the future loyalty of its numerous ethnic minorities living abroad, instituted an "America Action" program which was aimed at blunting ethnic-nationalism in America and inducing immigrants eventually to return. Such a scheme was necessary, as one Hungarian official wrote, "because we are unable to prevent the return of the Slavs and because it is to be feared that after the economic depression that is likely to occur in America, great numbers of Slovaks and Ruthenians will return and their hostility to the dynasty will cause much trouble."[49]

The Hungarian government knew no limits when it came to assisting church leaders who were favorably disposed toward the monarchy. Loyal churches, priests, schools, and newspapers all received direct subsidies whether they were Magyar, Croatian, Slovene, Slovak, Rusin, or Czech. Protestant Hungarian congregations not tied too closely to higher ecclesiastical authority in America were frequently quick to develop strong ties with the mother country. In 1904 the president of the Reformed Church of Hungary came to America and offered financial support to congregations uniting with his organization. Except where congregations were led by ministers who were not trained in Hungary and who, therefore, feared losing their jobs, most joined. The first diocese of the Reformed Church of Hungary was founded in New York City in 1904. When a government in the homeland took less interest in its departed citizens, private efforts were launched. Thus, the Committee for the Advancement of the Gospel among Danes in America was an unofficial attempt launched in Denmark to retain homeland influence in the Danish Church of America.[50]

Conclusion

No institution in immigrant America exhibited more discord and division than the church. Families encountered tensions but functioned effectively to meet economic realities, and voluntary associations expanded and moved rapidly toward modern notions and forms of organization. Usually the church and other religious organizations were the only immigrant institutions to contain an entrenched, premodern cadre of leaders. As more and more new-comers adopted the new order of capitalism and the ranks of the secular middle class expanded, the authority and influence of prominent clerics was weakened. Forces and leaders outside the group, such as American political figures or Socialist organizers, presented a further challenge to traditional religious authority. No group made serious attempts to dismantle the immigrant family; the industrial economy actually helped sustain it. The immigrant business class could grow without an established counterpart within the group to oppose it. But traditional church leaders were embattled on all sides. Ecclesiastical authority suddenly consisted of individuals with different ethnic backgrounds. Socialists were now more organized and their influence was reinforced by the widespread labor turmoil of the surrounding industrial society. Within the immigrant group itself secular leaders became simultaneously more threatening and more aggressive, as they now agitated for increased ethnic rather than religious awareness in order to foster homeland nationalism, which would sustain their newfound status in the face of internal challenges from traditional religious leaders. It was the peculiar plight of the immigrant church to possess a threatened leadership, which lay at the heart of pervasive church turmoil. Threatened leaders labored feverishly to centralize authority, revitalize faith, and maintain the loyalty of their flocks in a rapidly changing world. Newly emerging secular and business leaders saw church authorities as really the only obstacle they had in achieving hegemony within the group. In the flurry of this splintered leadership could be found the energy which mobilized and sometimes alienated vast legions of the immigrant masses, forced them to take sides, and disrupted the communal harmony and solace which many of them sought in the first place.

Given the nature of this factionalism and innumerable divisions between traditional leaders, secular leaders, activist laymen, quiet followers, and those alienated altogether, it is difficult to cling to notions of the church as extension of tradition which simply retarded adaptation to a modern, capitalistic, secular society or even as an agent which simply fostered modernization and Americanization. At the very least it was both of these. Additionally, immigrant church activity actually furthered other goals including communal solidarity, an ethnic consciousness with varying degrees of national and religious identity, an aversion to radical thought, and sometimes a revulsion from religion and clerical leaders themselves. In the final analysis, such fragmentation left immigrant attitudes divided and really insured that immigrant communities would not last. The future path of the plain folk would be decided in institutions such as families, unions, businesses, or even political parties where a greater consensus was obtainable.

6 /

Immigrants and the Promise

of American Life

Immigrants and Social Mobility

If the expanding economy of industrial capitalism offered immigrants anything in the century after the 1820s, many scholarly and popular writers presumed it to be the promise of opportunity. The entire movement of millions of individuals from preindustrial homes to America has invariably been linked with the search for better times and higher status in the United States. The bargain struck between industrial America and most newcomers was never made explicit but it was presumed to run something like this. Leave your impoverished homeland, modify your culture, work diligently, and the fruits of a new economic order will be within easy reach. A lowly status would be abandoned for a higher one, income would rise, material possessions would accumulate, and the hopelessness of the old world would be replaced by the boundless optimism of a new one. The extent this scenario was applicable to the immigrant experience has been more often assumed than demonstrated, however. The model immigrant supposedly moved into tightly knit ethnic neighborhoods, labored for a while, and then abandoned them for middle-class locations elsewhere in an urban area, leaving the working-class areas behind for subsequent waves of newcomers. Certainly the newly arrived were industrious and gathered in urban enclaves, but it remains to be seen if they were able simply to exchange their huddled settlements and lowly status for the lofty plateaus of the American mainstream.[1]

Not surprisingly, the idea of social mobility and the assumption that it preoccupied so many new arrivals has fostered much contemporary historical research on American immigrants despite the fact that newcomers had a multitude of objectives—from return migration to family sustenance. Scholars have constructed hierarchies of occupational categories and measured carefully the rate at which newcomers moved upward and downward from one level to another. While debates have ensued over the methodology used in these studies, they have produced something of a broad portrait of how much immigrants could expect to improve or retain their working status throughout their lifetimes. In nearly all instances, of course, occupational standing was considered to be a good indication of social status.

Clearly, most immigrants began their careers in the lower social and economic levels of the American economy. If they were to move at all in their occupational standing, it would have to be upward, for in nearly every city examined, immigrants in the nineteenth and early twentieth century tended to congregate much more heavily in lower jobs than native Americans. Among Irish newcomers in Milwaukee, St. Louis, and Detroit in 1850 at least one-half or more were working in unskilled positions. In San Francisco in 1880 the Irish had five times as many unskilled workers as their percentage of the city's population would lead one to believe. In the same year in Detroit only 22 percent of the native-born population was in semiskilled or skilled work, while 42 percent of the Germans, 59 percent of the Irish, and 50 percent of the Poles were so located. In Boston the ratio of immigrants to American-born in the middle class was 38 for every 100. By 1930 the ratio climbed only to 44 for every 100. In Pittsburgh at the turn of the century less than 10 percent of the Poles and 18 percent of the Italians moved into skilled posts. For Mexicans in Los Angeles in 1917 and 1918 the pattern was similar. Over 91 percent were toiling in unskilled and semiskilled jobs.[2]

Although most immigrants had no other direction to go but upward if they remained in the United States, the overall impression from historical mobility studies is that such movement was an unrealistic expectation in their lifetimes. Among Dutch arrivals in the middle decades of the nineteenth century (1841–1870) about 31 percent were able to improve their occupational level from their first to last job. In Poughkeepsie, New York, 74 percent of a sample of Irish unskilled workers remained unskilled throughout their careers during the last half of the nineteenth century. Overall in Poughkeepsie only 22 percent of the first generation made the transition from manual work at their first job to nonmanual work at the completion of their careers. In South Bend, Indiana, prospects appeared a little better for the foreign-born to move from manual to nonmanual occupations after 1860 but never more than 30 percent were able to do so. In a study of a much larger city, Boston, Stephan Thernstrom found only 13 percent of workers born in the 1850s were able to climb out of blue-collar positions in which they started. For another sample born in 1900–1909, only 14 percent went upwards. From a sample of Italians, Romanians, and Slovaks in Cleveland who were born between 1870 and 1890 only 14 of every 100 starting their careers in blue-collar jobs were able to move to a higher standing during their careers. In New York only 14 percent of unskilled Italians were able to enter white-collar positions and an additional 10 percent acquired the designation skilled worker. Among Mexicans in Santa Barbara less than 5 percent were upwardly mobile in the earliest decades of this century. In nearby Los Angeles 8 of every 10 Mexicans there in 1810 remained in the same job a decade later, if they were still in the city. Generally immigrants were likely to find mobility horizontal rather than vertical or no mobility at all.[3]

While significant occupational mobility was not normally part of the immigrant experience in industrial America, some individuals and groups did better than others, a point which suggests that opportunity could be influenced by several variables including premigration skills and experience or even local economic conditions in the United States. In much of the nineteenth century German arrivals were considerably more likely to work in skilled crafts than Irish newcomers. In Boston in 1909 about 45 percent of the Jews were in a business attempting to make a profit but only 22 percent of the Italians and 5 percent of the Irish were so engaged. In New York City by 1905 over 41 percent of the Italians were in unskilled trades while only a meagre 1.7 percent of the Jews performed such menial work. In Cleveland, Romanians were found to be more upwardly mobile than Slovaks, and in Pittsburgh, Italians tended to initiate small business ventures much more than Poles. The point is that even modest rates of mobility were not enjoyed equally by all.[4]

The causes of such differences, of course, were varied and complex and cannot always be precisely described by historical research. Nevertheless, several explanations receive strong support in the literature. Traditional sociological arguments that Protestantism fostered greater individual initiative and, therefore, social mobility than Catholicism does not seem to hold. Among Germans, who were likely to be either Protestant or Catholic, no significant difference in mobility appeared between the two groups. In Poughkeepsie, German Catholics established businesses as often as German Protestants. In

Boston, samples of upwardly mobile Catholics and Protestants born in the mid-nineteenth and early twentieth century revealed almost no difference based on religion. A Protestant cohort born in the 1840s and 1850s moved ahead slightly more than Catholics but the pattern was reversed in a sample born in the decade after 1900.[5]

Two factors which did play important roles in shaping group mobility patterns, however, were the structure of immigrant streams, which included familiarity with specific skills, and the nature of a city's economic structure and stage of development, which existed when immigrants entered. In Pittsburgh, Italians who were used to supplementing their farming income with seasonal commercial endeavors easily started small-scale business ventures in the city while Poles, less practiced in such arts, remained tied to their factory jobs. Jews, of course, were the classic case of implementing Old World skills, especially commercial ones, to launch business ventures which often proved successful in urban America. In New York City in 1905 over 30 percent of the Jews were in low, white-collar jobs as compared to only 17 percent of the Italians. In Los Angeles, Jews moving into small business ventures were actually more successful than even native-born residents; most Jews who moved to the city came only because they had personal and commercial connections which facilitated their adjustment tremendously. As early as 1879 the mean value of Jewish property in Los Angeles was five times greater than that of non-Jews.[6]

Nineteenth-century Germans made an especially strong case for the influence of local economic structures to a small extent but for cultural baggage to an even greater extent. Irish arrivals were always more concentrated in unskilled jobs than Germans and tended to congregate in eastern cities like Boston, New York, and Philadelphia, where social structures were considerably more established than in cities farther inland. Germans, however, moved in greater numbers to interior locations like Chicago, St. Louis, and Milwaukee, where social structures were still forming, where American-born elites were less entrenched, and, most importantly, where they could implement their higher level of premigration skills to their advantage. Germans in the Midwest during much of the nineteenth century left an impression of some success when contrasted to the patterns of newcomers in eastern communities. In South Bend, they accounted for higher mobility rates than in eastern textile towns like Newburyport, in part because of the skills they brought and the needs of expanding industries after 1850 such as Studebaker Brothers and the South Bend Iron Works. As early as 1850 some 29 percent of the Germans in

South Bend owned real estate compared to an overall rate for New-buryport of 9 percent. In Cincinnati, quite a few Germans with skills were able to initiate full-scale manufacturing concerns in the 1870s and the 1880s. Several established plants to manufacture carriages, fireproof safes, soap, and, of course, beer. In Poughkeepsie, native-born craftsmen actually found themselves at a disadvantage with the foreign-born skilled. While 49 percent of the Poughkeepsie's skilled Germans climbed into white-collar positions, less than 30 percent of the natives an only 18 percent of the Irish who began careers as craftsmen moved upward. In Chicago by 1850, nearly one-half of the German household heads were already in skilled crafts. By 1880 men of German birth or patronage accounted for one-sixth of the city's labor force but one-half of all workers in shoemaking outside of fac-tories, tailoring, banking, butchering, brewing, and cigar making. In nineteenth-century Milwaukee, the image of downtrodden immi-grants certainly did not apply to Germans. They continued to infil-trate skilled tasks in the decades before the rise of large plants and the decline of skilled workers. Between 1850 and 1860 the proportion of carpenters who were American-born dropped from 40 percent to 12 percent while the German share rose from 28 to 54 percent.[7]

Occasional success existed for some but generally continual toil in the strata they entered upon arrival in industrial America was the fate of most newcomers if they remained. But the possibility existed, to the extent that individuals lived their lives in the future, that sub-sequent generations would realize the promise of American society and surpass the social standing of their parents. While instances of immigrant children attaining occupational ranks above those held by their parents existed, however, progress was neither inevitable nor simply a function of time. Women, of course, usually had no long-lasting career outside the home to measure. But sons who could ex-pect a lifetime of toil in the industrial economy were more likely to repeat the occupational patterns of their fathers than to rise above them. More than culture or any other factor, the status of a father usually foretold the social positioning of a son. In Boston a foreign-born father was a handicap occupationally, because the sons of a foreign-born were more likely to enter the labor market at the manual level. In a sample of men born between 1860 and 1879, among sons of blue-collar fathers some 65 percent of the Irish and 55 percent of the British remained in manual jobs. On the other hand, 67 percent of the Irish and 80 percent of the British reared in white-collar homes retained white-collar status. In Cleveland, 9 percent of the second generation made such an improvement during the decade after 1910.

In Steelton, Pennsylvania, only 7 percent of the sons of Slavic and Italian immigrants moved from manual to nonmanual jobs. In Poughkeepsie, New York, a slightly better story unfolded. During the later nineteenth century about 32 percent of the sons of unskilled Germans moved into nonmanual callings. The rate for the Irish was 17 percent for sons born in Ireland and 16 percent for those born in America.[8]

When measurements were made of the extent immigrant sons continued to toil at the same levels as their fathers, the results were remarkably similar. In nineteenth-century Fall River, Massachusetts, about one-half the sons of skilled English and Irish fathers maintained the skilled levels they inherited. In Boston in the 1880s, 77 percent of the sons of unskilled immigrants remained unskilled themselves. Nine of every ten sons of skilled workers retained their father's status in the same decade. In Cleveland between 1910 and 1920, 70 percent of the sons of unskilled and skilled toilers repeated their fathers' pattern. In New York City, the continuity rate was 55 percent for sons of skilled Italian fathers and 47 percent for the male offspring of unskilled Italians. About one-half the sons of skilled, Jewish father remained skilled while over 65 percent of the sons of "low white-collar" Jews kept the status handed to them. In small mill towns such as Steelton, 70 percent of the sons of semiskilled immigrants and 80 percent of the sons of skilled laborers remained immobile during their careers. This pattern probably accounts for the persistence of ethnic clusters in the American occupational structure by the 1950s when it was found, for instance, that Italians were still over-represented in the apparel industry, Germans as toolmakers, and Yugoslavs as miners. If one moved upward or remained static it was often within a certain path.[9]

Of course, a father who acquired a higher status in industrial America could not guarantee the same level to his son. In nearly every city or town for which mobility data was generated substantial numbers of immigrant children were unable to retain the skilled or nonmanual status they inherited and ended their careers in jobs less desirable than those of their fathers. In Poughkeepsie, 10 percent of the Irish and 8 percent of the Germans whose first-generation fathers had been skilled workers ended their careers in semiskilled or unskilled work. In Boston, about 20 to 25 percent of the sons of white-collar fathers finished careers in lower categories. In Poughkeepsie, the expansion of the factory system especially in the clothing industry actually made it more difficult for second-generation Germans to match the success of their fathers in launching careers in the apparel trades. It had been easier for immigrant German tailors to open shops prior to 1870. The rise of cheaper, factory-produced goods actually resulted in downward mobility for their sons born in America. In both Poughkeepsie and Philadelphia after 1880 a pattern of second-generation Germans deserting the dying handicrafts of their fathers such as shoemaking and tailoring was evident. Similarly, in San Francisco among Jews and other newcomers the second-generation of merchant immigrants after the 1870s failed to move up the occupational scale and often encountered a drop in occupational status. Grocery stores and small shops were forced to compete with larger and more efficient retail stores. Among second-generation merchants, 30 percent of the petty shopkeepers faced declines, a rate twice that of first-generation merchants. Indeed, more sons of San Francisco merchants were forced into blue-collar jobs after 1870 than among the pioneer generation of the 1850s.[10]

Passing Through the Ghetto

If immobility rather than success was more characteristic of the occupational patterns of most newcomers, spatially they were constantly on the move as were most residents of urban-industrial America in the nineteenth and early twentieth centuries. Among unskilled workers generally in Newburyport, many of whom were Irish, only 32 percent remained in the town between 1850 and 1860 and some 41 percent persisted between 1880 and 1890. In New York City in the 1880s, less than 27 percent of the Italians and Jews stayed in their same residences. In South Bend, persistence rates for the 1870s were 30 percent for the English, 18 percent for the Germans, 17 percent for the Irish, and 11 percent for the Polish. In Milwaukee in the middle of the nineteenth century, residents were more stable but persistence rates still remained below 50 percent for the Irish, British, and Germans. In Steelton, 41 percent of the Italians and Slavs persisted between 1915 and 1925.[11]

As with the population at large, immigrant transiency was generally influenced by factors such as social status and property ownership. Among Swedes in Chicago, 40 percent of skilled immigrants and small businessmen remained in the city during the 1960s while only 16 percent of unskilled laborers did not move. In Boston during the decade prior to 1920, 58 percent of the "high white-collar" class persisted but only 35 percent of the "low blue-collar." For Los Angeles during the same decade the rates for these two groups was 72 percent and 29 percent respectively.[12]

While the motivation for widespread transiency is difficult to determine, it was clearly varied. Many immigrants, of course, worked temporarily in America and returned to their homeland, often making several round trips. Some could not stand the noise, dust, or pace of industrial jobs and returned home or looked for more agreeable work. Where relatives provided access to employment, movement in and out of the mills and factories was relatively easy. Often, movement among workplaces assumed a regional dimension, such as the pattern established by Irish families throughout New England textile towns prior to 1900. Sometimes individuals were denied jobs after strike actions and forced to look elsewhere. In Fall River, Massachusetts, in the 1870s, English newcomers enjoyed a higher occupational status than the unskilled Irish but were more transient because of their strike agitation. Many immigrants were displaced from their homes by changing patterns of land use in the cities where they lived. Initial zones of settlements for Poles and Italians near downtown Pittsburgh were eventually taken over by commercial interests and immigrants were forced to move where affordable housing could be found. In Los Angeles after 1910 expansion of business and financial districts displaced Mexicans from the historical central barrio to the eastern parts of the city. Occasionally, geographic mobility stemmed from a search for improved conditions. Most of the Irish, for instance, who moved to San Francisco did not come directly from Ireland but from the eastern United States where they had acquired skills or expertise which facilitated their adjustment to a new city. By 1880, 60 percent of the children in San Francisco's Irish community had been born in New York, Massachusetts, or Pennsylvania. Many of San Francisco's Jewish merchants had worked first in New York City and, like Levi Strauss, ordered goods through relatives back east. Similarly, Yugoslavs followed relatives from western Pennsylvania mining areas to auto plants in Detroit in the 1930s. But a simple equation could never be made between transiency and upward mobility. It never became a case of the most successful moving first from immigrant settlements into American society. All newcomers moved and for a variety of reasons.[13]

Chicago's Swede Town was a good example of immigrant transiency. The area contained 63 percent of all Swedes in 1850 but only 48 percent three decades later. The population decline did not stem from a mobility process which saw successful Swedes abandon their community but from industrial expansion into the residential area and a decline in Swedish immigration. Swedish businesses, lodging houses, churches, and newspapers remained in the neighborhood, but most Swedes began to move up Chicago Avenue and fewer new arrivals came. Eventually Italians were attracted to the area by its low-cost housing and formed one-fifth of the area by 1910.[14]

Because immigrants moved frequently even within cities, traditional images of tightly knit ethnic "ghettos" clustered around churches or mills, a dominant view of immigrant historiography, must be considerably modified. If the social structure of immigrant communities was not monolithic, neither was the geographical construction. Few urban neighborhoods were populated exclusively by one particular group and seldom did one group choose to live in one specific location. Newcomers were constantly moving into areas of first settlement, generally where supplies of inexpensive housing existed near places of employment. San Francisco's North Beach area had the lowest rents in the city, which appealed to newly arrived Italians. Irish arrivals in nineteenth-century coastal cities lived near terminal and warehouse facilities they helped to construct. Mexicans in Los Angeles settled in the Watts area because of its proximity to railroad jobs they occupied. But always workers from other backgrounds were joining them. Olivier Zunz's massive study of Detroit noted such ethnic concentrations as early as 1880 and formulated the concept of ethnic dominance whereby one group was large enough to give identity to an area but did not exclusively populate it. Such a view appears to be considerably more valid than older notions of urban neighborhoods as ethnic ghettos or "melting pots." Thus, "Swede Town" in Chicago or "Polish Hill" in Pittsburgh each had heavy concentrations of one group but were ethnically mixed. In New York City in the middle of the nineteenth century Germans resided in at least four separate concentrations and not in any one "ghetto." In Philadelphia the development of immigrant ghettos was arrested because of an absence of cheap, concentrated housing. By 1880 in the City of Brotherly Love five identifiable clusters of Irish and one of German stock were discernible. But only one Irishman in five and one German in eight lived in such clusters and each group composed only half of the population of their respective neighborhoods. Chicago's "Swede Town" in 1870 comprised only 43 percent of the city's Swedes with the rest scattered in clusters throughout the rest of the city.[16]

After the late nineteenth-century, changes in economic structure and industrial development did alter the pattern of immigrant settlement somewhat, although the transformation was not total. Immigrant clusters were more pronounced in the industrial rather than the smaller, mercantile city and were probably more heavily working class, but they still did not achieve ethnic homogeneity; dispersal always coexisted with clusters in both centuries. In Philadelphia, after the 1880s, the increasing availability of cheap, older housing near manufacturing plants resulted in greater segregation among Italians, Poles, and Russian Jews. Similarly, the expansion of the auto industry in Detroit around 1920 accentuated class divisions by drawing clusters of workers around sprawling factories. Improved transportation also resulted in a decline in population density with streetcar suburbs and urban neighborhoods housing middle-class immigrants and blacks who continued to live near their places of employment well into the twentieth century.[17] Thus immigrants and their children established kinship colonies throughout the city wherever their ethnic and family ties could be attached to a workplace. By 1921 in New York City over 74 Italian colonies could be identified, all speaking different regional dialects. Industrialization may have accentuated class dimensions but it did not dismantle the ligaments of family and friends which underlay all immigrant settlements.[18]

For some who did achieve mobility and wealth and whose fortunes were not tied closely to a particular neighborhood, movement to a better neighborhood and geographical segregation from the original group did take place. By 1870 German Jewish merchants had already begun to leave the Lower East Side and set up shops and homes in Harlem. By 1900 many Russian Jews followed them, prompted by downtown slum clearance projects as well as social attainment. The Harlem, Yorkville, and to some extent West Side neighborhoods served as major outlets for those Jewish, Irish, and German immigrants and their children who had the resources to escape working-class enclaves.[19]

Transiency and ethnic mixture may have characterized most immigrant neighborhoods but it did not occur at such a pace as to inhibit the emergence of strong communal ties and activities. Certainly social mobility was modest enough to keep some form of immigrant community intact. Neighborhoods could still be secure and friendly places. An immigrant woman in Connecticut remembered the Saturday night gatherings at a friend's house where everyone would sit, drink, and sing. Neighbors gathered in urban neighborhoods and mill towns anytime a friend became ill or died to offer comfort and pay their respects. Neighbors frequently baked bread, canned fruit and vegetables, and made sauerkraut together. Men gathered to make wine and sausage. In halls, such as those owned by the Polish Falcons in Pittsburgh, dances, weddings, musical events, plays, and lodge meetings were held almost continuously. Chicano *mutualistas*, or mutual-aid societies, sponsored social events and gatherings to defend the rights of Mexico as well as to participate in

178]

Immigrant Neighborhood in Chicago, circa 1915
Immigrant neighborhoods often served as important
centers of social interaction but were by no means places of
permanent residence for individuals, who were quite
mobile. *Chicago Historical Society*

athletic events, barbecues, and fiestas. German beer halls proliferated
in American cities and served neighborhood populations. Those in
Chicago served not just men but entire families and combined with
German businesses to lend an image of "Germanness" to particular
neighborhoods. Just by going about his mundane duties in a neighborhood a New York City Jew could feel "unthreatened." Neighborhoods such as Flatbush, the East Bronx, and Brownsville, acquired a
"persona" all their own. Friends and relatives were able to exchange
meals, child care services, and gossip. One newcomer in Providence
recalled great "family" picnics in Goddard Park with 20 to 40 people
bringing meatballs, sausage, salads, pies, bread, and cases of soda and
beer. The presence of churches and merchants of similar ancestry
further reinforced the idea of a neighborhood and suggested why they
appeared timeless in a society that was steadily changing.[20]

[179

Immigrants and Homeownership

While urban life was transient and social mobility an unrealistic expectation for most newcomers, long-term residence in cities and towns frequently led to a degree of stability through the process of homeownership. While it is not at all clear that homeownership was a surrogate for social mobility since perceptions about success and immediate objectives could vary, it was a fact of life that homeownership was not a particularly difficult goal to reach and that it contributed to some degree of stability and longevity in various neighborhoods. Of course, it is crucial to remember that ownership was more likely in some cities than in others and this certainly influenced immigrant settlement patterns. The availability of land, access to capital, and characteristics of the local housing stock all influenced the rate of ownership, even though most cities after 1880 built a housing supply to keep pace with rapid population growth. In 1890 and 1920, two sample years, homeownership was twice as attainable in Buffalo, Cleveland, Detroit, and Milwaukee as it was in Boston or Brooklyn. About 40 percent of all homes were in some coastal communities. By 1930 ownership rates in Philadelphia, Baltimore, and St. Paul doubled those in Boston and Brooklyn.[21]

Significantly, homeownership was not uniquely a middle-class, suburban phenomenon. In Newburyport between one-third and one-half of the working class reported some form of property holding after at least a decade of residence between 1850 and 1880. The Irish workers actually attained property to a greater extent than the native-born, despite their relative inability to move upward occupationally. In Milwaukee by 1860, Irish and British laborers were increasing their proportion of property owners, even though the overall rate of ownership for the city was declining. In Detroit by 1900, working-class immigrants owned their homes proportionately more than middle-class, native-white Americans, despite arguments by some scholars that homeownership was probably an investment inferior to most throughout much of the century after 1830. During the two decades after 1910 in Cleveland, ownership rates reached 69 and 80 percent respectively for Italians and Slovaks who were upwardly mobile from blue-collar origins and even 59 and 65 percent respectively for those remaining in the blue-collar class. Even though the federal government's Home Owners Loan Corporation restricted the number of mortgages granted in white and black working-class, urban neighborhoods after 1930, the trend established earlier continued. By 1950, about one-half the residents of Pittsburgh's Polish Hill and over

Waiting for the Bank to Open, Chicago, August 22, 1916
To purchase homes, immigrants often saved their resources
in ethnic financial institutions, such as the one pictured
here. *Chicago Historical Society*

60 percent of the Italian-Americans in the Bloomfield section of the city owned rather than rented.[22]

Explanations for the proclivity of immigrants to become homeowners abound. The most widely held views include arguments that homeowners simply represented an extension of the peasant's desire for land or a surrogate for limited occupational advancement. The fact that some groups who moved more rapidly into middle-class pursuits, such as the Jews, were less likely to become homeowners than unskilled Irish or Italians offers some support to the conventional wisdom. The impressive level of activity among newcomers in generating mortgage money was a further indication of the intensity with which homes were sought. In San Francisco by 1859 the Hibernia Savings and Loan already had over 10 million dollars on deposit, much of which went into home mortgages. In Pittsburgh and Chicago, Poles were quite adept at forming their own building and loan associations to provide mortgage money from worker savings.

These institutions kept interest rates low (6 to 7 percent in the 1890s) and allowed extended repayment schedules. At least 74 Polish savings and loan associations existed in Chicago by 1916 to finance home buying. In Detroit and in many Pennsylvania coal towns immigrants operated outside the formal, higher-priced housing market and actually built homes themselves, an investment of time and energy which helped root them to a particular neighborhood.[23]

Homeownership could have represented achievement in America or fulfilled old dreams of landholding, but no widespread evidence exists that newcomers were riveted to goals of social mobility. Certainly, property was important to immigrants in their homelands and no reason exists to conclude its significance diminished in urban America. Some scholars would even suggest that homeownership was pursued at the expense of educating working-class children. But such a conclusion is difficult to verify. Indeed, one recent analysis of native and foreign-born families in Providence demonstrated a positive relationship between homeownership and extended schooling among all ethnic groups. Insufficient wages rather than a drive for homeownership or ethnic culture better explained child labor.[24] And the acquisition of property, where possible, usually represented more than a simple strike for security. A home was also the material and emotional center of the family or household economy. Children were raised there, and even housed within its walls after marriage, while they saved for a place of their own. Parents saw it as a refuge in their retirement as well. Where the family economy was directed toward commercial rather than industrial ends, such as among the Jews and Japanese, a single home was less likely to be purchased. But this did not imply that homeownership was simply a preoccupation of the working class. Commercially oriented newcomers often purchased buildings with space for their shops as well as apartments for rent and for their own residence. This resulted in lower homeownership rates but in no less a desire to acquire a material and emotional center for the central endeavor of fortifying the welfare of kin in a complex and unpredictable economy. Finally, it cannot be overlooked that homeownership on the part of newcomers was partly a function of their life stage. Most entered the American city below the age of 35 and were interested in forming families. Young families tended to purchase homes more than older families whose children had left home, a point which would tend to place immigrant ownership rates above those for the native-born. A case study of Irish arrivals in St. Paul after 1860 suggests precisely such a possibility. In fact, economic historians have long been aware of the relationship between a decline of residential construction during the 1920s, a pattern which contributed to the Great Depression, and the imposition of immigrant restriction laws.[25] Sometimes individual housing even afforded a degree of privacy some immigrants could never achieve in their homelands. Italians in New York found that single dwellings and even tenements offered more privacy than the crowded agro-towns of southern Italy where domestic space was quite observable to every passerby.[26]

Conclusion

Did newcomers "hunger for opportunity" and did they find the level of success and reward for their toil that could vindicate those who simply link immigration and the American dream? Those that stayed were mobile, to be sure, but their movement was usually a function of their transiency rather than their achievement. Most would labor in routine, difficult jobs throughout their careers as would the majority of their children. Progress existed and increasing numbers were able to acquire property but dramatic gains of any kind were not the norm.

As they moved from one community to another within cities, they passed in and out of ethnic neighborhoods and settlements. Immigrant ghettos were neither impoverished slums nor huddled communities fostering adjustment to America. Adjustment began prior to residence in the ghetto. Here they did find needed services, reassuring contacts with others from the same background, and sometimes homes of their own. But ultimately their lives were not tied to spatial settlements and buildings but to jobs and families. And when job locations changed, income improved, or work was unobtainable, even the ethnic "ghetto" could not confine them as they picked up and moved again.

7 /

America on Immigrant Terms:

Folklife, Education, and Politics

Folklife and the Quest for Meaning

Even if patterns of social mobility were not conducive to rapid structural assimilation into the mainstream of American society, the possibility of rapid and widespread cultural attachment of newcomers to the thought and institutions of capitalist America was still possible. After all, immigrants were certainly disinclined to turn their backs on the imperatives of industrial capitalism, so no reason existed to conclude that they would not want to embrace its attendant cultural and institutional manifestations. Unless, of course, it was possible that ordinary people, at the level of personal and communal experience, could fashion a culture of their own. Such a culture could scarcely be expected to remain unaffected by large economic structures and even past traditions. Yet, to a large extent, it might still be innovative, functional, and real. If such a culture were to be created, regardless of whether it was labeled working class, ethnic, or popular, it would clearly have much to say about the way immigrant workers and families ordered their lives. Immigrants demonstrated a degree of independence in establishing kinship networks, labor organizations, and churches. But the process of forging a culture could indicate something of the way they attempted on their own to give meaning to their lives and experience in the midst of conflicting leaders and ideologies. This culture could manifest itself in both thought and action and embrace numerous values and ideas both old and new. In viewing their folklife, their educational views, and their political predilections, glimpses are possible of newcomers struggling with both past and present realities in order to make a life as acceptable as possible.

Almost no dimension of the traditional life immigrants knew remained unaffected by the new order which confronted them. At the
same time most newcomers did not hesitate to exploit or draw upon
past belief and practice if it in some way would facilitate and render
intelligible their new life and condition. Even though most newcomers were unskilled toilers, they were in a sense almost all craftsmen in
their ability to creatively fashion culture and meaning to suit their
daily social and psychological needs. Consider their use of the rich
repository of song, dance, and folktales, which nearly all groups
brought to the American city. This body of lore and culture had been
generated in traditional communities and served effectively as a de-
vice for rendering meaning and understanding in a world which was
beyond the powers of ordinary people to direct. While these traditions
had already begun to recede in the premigration lands in the face of
modern explanations of an individual's plight which were tied to
science, industry, and political ideology, much of the folklife and culture of immigrants proved surprisingly resilient and actually functional in their new lives in industrial cities. Indeed, folk culture could
serve to reinforce group identity in the face of meeting new groups,
inform outsiders about immigrants and who they were, and even
provide explanations of their lowly status which all newcomers could
understand. Folk culture was simultaneously transformed and revi-
talized in urban America, as immigrants sought to enter capitalist society on their own terms and formulate their own definition of their
status and condition. Historian Lawrence Levine has masterfully
demonstrated how Afro-American folk beliefs offered black slaves a
source of power, for it provided access to alternative knowledge
outside that existing in the world of the master class. For urban immigrants, folk culture not only offered an alternative source of
knowledge but also the ability to generate meaning and understanding, important considerations in a milieu where conflicting agendas
and ideologies proliferated.[1]

Functional folkways existed throughout immigrant America as
newcomers sought to adjust to a new environment with whatever resources they could muster; in both the homeland and the new world
they generally had less resources and power than their social
superiors but they used what they had effectively. From their reserve
of folk thought and behavior they continued to hold celebrations and
festivals. While such festivities appeared to resemble long-standing
practices, they were, in fact, uniquely adaptive and changing. Finns,
for instance, organized the Finnish National Temperance Brotherhood in 1899, which initiated festivals with poets reciting traditional
verse to enable immigrants to cope with present difficulties in mines,

lumber camps, and mills. Czech harvest festivals, which were wide-spread in the homeland, continued to be held in America, but with a subtle change. Instead of entire communities participating, newcomers now living in American towns and cities divided themselves into groups of actors and spectators. All knew that the plays, dances, and activities which unfolded before them were drama, not ritual. Entertainment and emotional solace now required by urban workers was gained rather than any lesson on the importance of agriculture or the cycle of seasons. Portuguese newcomers in New England held *festas* nearly every Sunday with a procession honoring a patron saint. But processions were now usually limited to churches rather than moving through city streets, and bread was bought from local bakers rather than made by immigrant women. One Portuguese festival in 1915 featured a drill team in United States Marine uniforms, as new arrivals blended old and new realities to fashion a culture of their own. In Worcester, Massachusetts, Swedes and other newcomers celebrated the Fourth of July in the framework of familiar ethnic institutions, such as a church picnic.

In fact, immigrants resisted attempts by community leaders to alter the way in which they spent much of their leisure activity outside the workplace. Gambling, a traditional Chinese village sport, was expanded in America to include poker. Some Chinese immigrants in California took shares in gambling companies as a profitable investment. Conveniently, the Chinese could also call "foreign" undertakers to care for their dead as a means of practicing a traditional custom of putting the dead outside the home as quickly as possible in order to avoid contamination. Chinese laborers in the West used whatever tools necessary to perform their work: unfamiliar sledges and shovels in railroad work and familiar nets on poles in the fishing industry. Chinese launderers used both traditional charcoal-heated open irons and American made "sad irons." Italians went to American physicians but still carried traditional amulets in their pockets to ward off evil. They did not hesitate to abandon the purchasing of candles for festivals when economics dictated they buy bread instead. With economic burdens widespread in American cities, godparents were no longer chosen spontaneously but only after they were cautiously sounded out about their willingness to bear the appropriate financial burdens of buying gifts. Traditional and present realities continually mixed.[2]

In song and dance, long favorite ways of passing time in the homeland, new experiences and encounters began to intervene almost imperceptibly as newcomers fashioned innovations of their own. Irish traditional music, practiced somewhat differently in Ireland's

Immigrant Musical Group, Glen Lyon, Pennsylvania
Immigrants often adapted music and other elements of
their folklife to assist them in understanding their status in
a new social order. *Author's personal collection*

various regions, began to fuse in America into a new blend which was
considerably less authentic with the addition now of pianos but no
less enjoyable to Irish newcomers. The American travails of Irish
workers even provided the basis for newly generated folk tunes. The
Molly Maguires, immigrant miners in Pennsylvania, were celebrated
in song and tunes which reinforced worker attitudes. Thus a tune
about Pat Mullaly who would work a "mule's work to get two men's
pay" was understood by all Irish miners as a signal to slow down the
pace of work. Romanians also saw regional variations in dance and
music give way to new creations in American cities emphasizing
simple rather than complex dance steps as a pattern which could be
adopted by Romanians in Detroit, Chicago, or Cleveland, regardless
of their district origins. Hungarians wrote tunes depicting the boardinghouse experience and stimulated the development of "living traditions." These songs, in fact, led to the creation of a completely new
folk hero, the *foburdos*, or star boarder. In urban neighborhoods
throughout America, Polish polka bands, playing at small saloons and
special events, developed a repertoire of Polish folk songs and Ameri-

can music. Traditional reliance on the violin gradually grew to embrace the use of accordions, clarinets, and trumpets, since it was necessary to produce louder music in bigger halls. Traditional polka bands which consisted usually of family members now grew more complex in membership. Finns wrote new songs portraying themselves as wanderers separated from home, and consequently, were able to offer consolation through shared experiences. In the garment shops of New York City, immigrant women such as Feigel Yudin used their knowledge of Yiddish folk songs to weave new melodies in English and Yiddish to soothe tensions at work and pass the time on picket lines. Mexicans actually generated entirely new ballads which told of border crossings and hardships at work and which found an eager audience among other toilers from south of the American border.[3]

In theaters throughout immigrant settlements culture was further generated and spread among newcomers. Hundreds of amateur and semiprofessional theaters flourished, often sponsored by fraternal organizations, athletic clubs, or labor organizations, and all represented further attempts by newcomers to give meaning and comfort in a new rapidly changing and unfolding society. German Turnvereins, Czech Sokols, and ethnic schools and churches all participated in the spread of the functional immigrant drama. The "Circuolo Italiano" used the theater to create better understanding between immigrants and their children. Working-class themes continued to be prevalent as Irish settlers attended plays about "shanty" Irish who set up housekeeping in Central Park or Jewish newcomers took delight in "formula plays" in which humble peddlers outsmarted their social superiors. As early as the 1870s the *Gmina Polska* (Polish Community Society) sponsored amateur theatricals in Chicago which elaborated on themes close to the heart of the immigrant experience: "Peasant Aristocrats" and "Peasant Emigration." One of the few actors to accompany the immigrant stream from Italy, Edward Migliaccio, actually devised a new type of presentation, the character sketch, in which he described the various types of Italian immigrants he met in America. The Yiddish theater in New York mirrored the experiences and emotions of East European Jews and offered glamor and comic relief after hours in a sweatshop. Plays such as the "Exile from Russia," which started in a Moscow tavern and ended with a parade of foreign citizens in New York City dressed in red, white, and blue, may have been unrealistic but attracted a loyal and appreciative audience.[4] Evidence exists to suggest that immigrants even preferred American silent films which spoke of tensions and contradictions in their urban-immigrant world.

Finally, in the intimate relationships of immigrant neighborhoods and households, the traditional tendency to relate folktales, proverbs, and stories continued but predominantly in a manner which informed the experience of immigrants and not that of peasants. Tales of superstition and magic persisted but found considerably less utility. Stories of struggling workers and families who needed encouragement, consolation, and explorations about their newfound status gained widespread popularity. Romanian newcomers, for instance, told tales of medieval robber barons called *hai ducs*, who fought a class struggle of their own by fighting the oppression of Greek invaders. At the Angel Island detention center in San Francisco, Chinese immigrants felt compelled to scrawl poetry on the walls which described their migration experience. Even personal sagas of recent immigrants crossing the ocean and finding work in America gave inspiration and a sense of honor to all who duplicated such an experience. Moral and religious tales offered comfort to those with less of this world's power and goods. Romanians listened to the story of "The Worms in the Rock," in which Jesus demonstrated his divine judgement by showing that he cared for even lowly worms. Hungarian boardinghouse tales were a further means of offering comfort by disseminating shared experiences. Finns, Greeks, and others constantly issued proverbs which reinforced discipline and marriage, crucial ingredients in maintaining the family household. Greeks admonished their children, "If you don't have an old man, buy one," a suggestion that parental wisdom should be followed. An Italian proverb stressed that "home yields no war," reinforcing the concept of the family-household as a peaceful shelter. Tales emphasizing the latent talents of the powerless and downtrodden always appealed to newcomers who generally lacked much of the means of production or influence in industrial society. The symbolic Matt or John in Finnish stories demonstrated that untutored immigrants could match wits with elites or bosses. A Greek tale told of a humble nail maker who was happy despite his poverty. When he is condemned to death by a king, it is eventually the king who dies, because the nail maker is indispensable to the making of the king's coffin.[5]

Selective Schooling

In areas outside folk culture immigrants continued to exhibit a tendency to fashion a culture of their own in the face of widespread social change generated by industrial capitalism. They accepted change but invariably sought to temper its thrust, to establish something of their own preferences even while adjusting to other

ways and organizations, and to resist any attempt at complete transformations. Educators and public school officials, for instance, would
learn this lesson well when they attempted to draw masses of newcomers into the classroom.

Public schools and educational officials, of course, were always
interested in using the classroom to inculcate American values and
beliefs in the foreign-born and having them abandon their former
traits and beliefs which were often perceived to be strange, often radical, and simply undesirable.[6] But Americanization was a need which
fluctuated in intensity and never elicited the constant attention of
educational reformers as did the concern for vocationalism. If social
harmony was to be achieved in the face of increasing labor unrest
and immigrants were to be eased into industrial jobs and made productive as well, they would have to become proficient at skills needed
by the workplaces of an expanding capitalism. From the beginnings
of the American industrial revolution in the early nineteenth century,
manufacturing elites and entrepreneurs actively called for schools
which would properly socialize the work force in manual, moral, and
ideological terms. As industrial and urban growth spread throughout
the country, educational reformers dutifully mounted their attacks on
the traditional forms of schooling which emphasized the classics and
sought to direct the learning process toward effecting desired changes
in individual behavior which would allow them to be orderly and productive for industrial capitalism. Gradually the ideals of this reform
impulse emerged and began to structure the curriculum immigrants
would encounter if they decided on public schooling. Vocational
training would make newcomers more efficient and better equipped
for the mill or factory. Training in the English language and American government would instill patriotism and loyalty and reduce inclinations toward radicalism. Instruction in personal health, grooming,
and obedience would contribute to assimilation and root out deviant
behavior. And all of this would be achieved by a steady succession of
legislation which extended compulsory education to more states and
slowly eliminated child labor, a practice which had frustrated the
socialization objectives of the public school.[7]

In their attempts to correct social problems, however, educational
reformers were posing a direct threat not only to traditional values of
many newcomers but to the core institution of immigrant, working-
class life. Childhood, which had been the private preserve of the
family and household, was now being transformed into a responsibility of the state. Whereas children had been viewed partially as
potential contributors to the family economy, they were now being

Finnish Immigrant Schoolchildren
Immigrant children usually left school before
graduation and entered the work force. *Immigrant History
Research Center, University of Minnesota*

described as indispensable to national destiny, economic prosperity, and a harmonious social order. Through the elimination of child labor, the introduction of compulsory attendance, and the intrusion of professional teachers and social workers into the family through schools and settlement houses, parents were gradually being asked to relinquish control over their progeny to agents of the state and the new order of industrial capitalism. Massive immigration only served to accentuate the need for this type of educational reform. When foreign-born children outnumbered native-born children in Boston primary schools by 1850, officials were concerned that these working-class families could no longer effectively socialize their children and moved to gain compulsory school attendance laws to do the job.[8]

The classic example of educational programming aimed at transforming immigrant children into good citizens and good workers was a plan formulated in Gary, Indiana, by William Wirt. A true believer in the potential of schools to serve as incubators of social and cultural conformity, Wirt hoped to restore traditional values in the urban en-

vironment by achieving social order through the teaching of obedience and self-discipline. Wirt stressed basic reading and writing skills
but he also provided for vocational training each day and even moral
instruction. He actually instituted a plan of released time for religious
instruction in 1914 in cooperation with the city's Protestant churches
which emphasized "Bible study." Immigrant children in these classes
were encouraged to take Bibles home, so they could properly instruct
their parents. An extensive program of night schools attempted to
reach the foreign-born adult who was forced to labor during the day-
time. The Gary plan so reflected the temper of the times that it was
adopted in cities throughout the United States, including New York
City. And even where it was not, similar directions were taken when
it came to immigrant and working-class schooling. Philadelphia, for
instance, significantly expanded its vocational training in the 1920s.
Public schools in El Paso consciously stressed vocational training for
Mexicans in order to complement local labor requirements. School
officials argued that Mexicans should receive manual and domestic
education, which best assisted them in finding jobs, and that academic training could best be emphasized in neighborhood schools
serving native Americans on the assumption that once an immigrant
worker always an immigrant worker. Early in this century the Car-
negie Foundation for the Advancement of Teaching actually went so
far as to offer pension funds for older professors as an inducement to
retirement. The hope was that younger, more reform-minded professors would be hired to replace them. Not surprisingly, denomina-
tional colleges could only accept the funds if they relinquished their
religious affiliations, a move aimed directly at undermining traditional lines of authority.[9]

The movement to standardize education and break down group
behavioral patterns in favor of a national norm was not pushed solely
by American elites or reformers. Just as in the case of political and
business leadership, individuals existed within each group who were
sympathetic to the efforts of reformers and who sought to eradicate
traditional patterns. It was a German-American archbishop who
sought to curtail the use of the German language in Cincinnati. The
German Turner movement of the late nineteenth century, as most
Socialist organizations, was a steadfast supporter of secular education
because they felt it would ultimately uplift the status of ordinary
workers, even if it meant the abandonment of traditional practices of
language, socialization, and especially religion. Archbishop George
Mundelein in Chicago, while favoring parochial over public schools,
still sought to undermine ethnic separateness and implement stand-

ardized forms of education, including the use of the English language. German Jewish leaders established the Bureau of Jewish Education in New York in part to preserve Judaism but also to foster Americanization. A Czech-American paper urged parents in 1915 to keep their children in school, for it would be a more lasting legacy than money which could be spent or a "fine residence" which could be destroyed.[10]

What advocates of extended education did not fully realize, however, was that the immigrant working class in the entire century of industrial growth after 1830 was invariably resistant to attempts which not only appeared to threaten their cultural and religious traditions but which also threatened the integrity of the family economy. A relatively marginal existence made it very difficult to contemplate sacrificing the income children generated. Besides the fact that much of the curriculum still seemed irrelevant to the requirements of the industrial workplace, new arrivals incurred frequent indignities and insults which made school an unpleast experience, and, for many Catholic, Orthodox, and Lutheran newcomers, public schools were still perceived as an anathema to religious faith.[11]

The claims of the family economy were so strong and economic need sufficiently high that immigrant children in nearly every group and in every city throughout the United States chose work when it was available over extended schooling prior to the 1930s. Industrialization in early nineteenth-century Massachusetts actually led to a short-term decline in annual enrollments because jobs were so plentiful for teenagers. Scholars who have recently argued that emigration itself actually intensified an interest in schooling are not cognizant of the overall statistical record.[12] The failure and dropout rate for immigrant children was abnormally high in the public schools prior to the 1920s, when child labor was slowly eliminated and educational requirements for occupations began to rise. In the early twentieth century in New York, 60 percent of the native-born white children began high school, but less than one-third of the Germans and less than one-quarter of the Italians did so. By 1910 less than 10 percent of Italians, Polish, and Slovak children were attending beyond the sixth grade in Chicago and Cleveland. Jews admittedly were doing better, although two-thirds of all students regardless of their backgrounds were not in school in these cities at the time. In Catholic elementary schools the situation was not much different. In Gary, for instance, less than 45 percent of all Polish, Croatian, German, and Irish Catholic children were in parochial schools.[13]

And where immigrant children did tend to remain in school

longer, an intriguing pattern emerged. Persistence in the classroom generally came from the immigrant middle class rather than from the homes of humble workers, a hint that social mobility might have preceded rather than stemmed from extended education prior to World War II. In antebellum Milwaukee the children of German laborers attended school less often than the children of Germans as a whole. The Italian working class in twentieth-century Philadelphia was very slow to accede to the demands for extended schooling. By the 1920s it was apparent that most Italian youth who completed high school were the children of the Italian *promineni* such as doctors, lawyers, bankers, and entrepreneurs. The actual rate of increase in high school graduates at South Philadelphia High School from 1918 to 1932 was lower for Italians than for the population as a whole in that section of the city. Not surprisingly an investigation in the neighborhoods adjacent to Chicago stockyards in 1913 discovered a belief among Polish parents that education beyond the compulsory age was appropriate only to the upper classes. And to many Polish, Italian, and Jewish mothers "excessive education" might render their daughters unfit for marriage. Chicanos in Texas initiated a drive for equal schooling only in 1929 when an "incipient" middle class formed the League of United Latin Americans.[14]

No greater manifestation of immigrant reluctance to embrace public education existed than the tremendous expansion of religious and even folk schools throughout immigrant America. This phenomonon was not simply an act of working-class intransigence but originated from a belief on the part of religious leaders and many of their followers that public schools threatened the very moral fiber of their offspring. Clerical leaders had little difficulty in convincing immigrants strongly attached to a traditional faith that outsiders were using the classroom to infiltrate the minds of the young with dangerous and false beliefs. After riots between Catholics and Protestants in the 1840s in Philadelphia, Irish Catholic leaders began to take a hard look at the existing pattern of Catholic attendance at public schools. In New York during the same decade Archbishop John Hughes had even made a bold attempt to secure public funds for the support of Catholic schools, a move which was widely supported in the local German and Irish press. When San Francisco passed its Free School Ordinance in 1851, it actually permitted public money to be used in support of both public and private schools, a measure which reflected Irish Catholic strength in the city, but which was eventually repealed by a California legislature considerably less influenced by Catholic interests.[15]

Catholic schools continued to multiply after the middle decades of the nineteenth century. By 1883 all but two Catholic parishes in Chicago had a parochial school despite the fact that the Catholic population as a whole was largely poor. Nearly one-half of all Polish children in the city were in parish schools by the early twentieth century, and Czech Catholics were even building schools before churches for fear their children would attend schools operated by "free thinkers." Eventually in Chicago and other cities these diverse ethnic schools were brought under a more powerful, central bureaucracy, ethnic localism diminished and curricula were standardized. Catholics even extended their activity to higher education and by the 1850s had already established 42 colleges.[16]

Religious leaders were continually supported in their efforts to advance the concept of Catholic education by leading Catholic laymen and newspapers which helped foster something of a consensus on the issue. To the extent the Catholic working class sent their children to schools they usually attended parochial schools where they were available. Some ethnic newspapers resented not only the Americanization aspects of the public schools but also their emphasis on secularism. One excerpt from a Slovak Catholic journal will serve to make the point. The newspaper exclaimed in 1936:

> With a public school education they (children) go forth into the world, lost completely to the Slovaks. Their idea of life is a breezy and snappy novel, a blood curdling movie and lots of money. But our duty to our people commands us to save youth from the moral catastrophe that is confronting it.[17]

Catholic newcomers were not the only ones to attempt to control the education of their young in the face of secular and external group forces. The Missouri Synod of the Lutheran Church demonstrated a passion for developing its own schools almost from the time of arrival in the states of Illinois, Indiana, Michigan, Missouri, and Ohio. By 1938 the synod maintained over 1,300 schools with an enrollment of 75,000 pupils. Concerned ultimately with the retention of doctrinal purity and good morals, nearly every synod convention in the century after 1840 took action regarding the school system. Lutheran leaders told parents no Christian with a good conscience could send his children to a public school. During the initial years of immigrant settlement, synod visitors were regularly sent to German settlements to identify children of school age and to examine their knowledge of catechism and hymns. One early synod leader proclaimed that the educational program would lead "dear youth" out of their prevalent wildness and bring them up as a generation in good morals, well bred, and well disciplined.[18]

Other groups followed variants of the Catholic and Missouri Synod models. Danes established folk high schools, in part to preserve Danish culture and religion in North America. Many Orthodox congregations among Greeks, Serbs, Romanians, Russians, Bulgarians, Ukrainians, and Ruthenians developed ethnic-folk schools, which children attended for a specified time each day after public schooling. These centers emphasized ethnic languages, religious traditions, and history.[19]

Even Jews, often thought to be the quintessential adherents of American public education, did not flock to the classroom upon arrival and often had to achieve a social level above the working class before extended schooling as an alternative would be considered. Scholars have argued that Jewish traditional culture contained a deep reverence for learning and fostered a commitment to secular education on the part of American Jews. But Jewish "shtetl" learning in Europe was after all "ritualistic" and "conservative" and not necessarily related to the needs of a modern, industrial economy. What served Jews particularly well was their previous mercantile and banking experience. Economic success and mobility actually preceded a commitment to education. Most of the sons of German Jews who owned family businesses in the nineteenth and early twentieth century remained in the business. Some actually discouraged their children from pursuing academic training, especially when the curriculum was oriented more toward classics than economics. It is true that the transformation of American education into more socially relevant instruction accompanied the arrival of the large East European Jewish migration and some of these newcomers began to remain longer in the public schools. For instance, the City College of New York was being appropriately modernized around 1900 and offered free tuition. But the numbers attending were small with only about 200 graduating in 1913. Most Jews were wage workers and like other working-class families saw their children drop out of school early. By 1905, 54 percent of Jewish households in New York were headed by manual laborers; less than three percent of household heads were professionals. On the Lower East Side, space for students was in short supply and rowdyism and truancy were widespread. Russian Jews did tend to quit school at a later age than some groups. In 1908 a survey of "retardation," the proportion of children who were two or more years older than the average age for their grade, found the Jewish rate of 42 percent better than the one for southern Italians (64 percent) but below the 16 percent rate for Swedes.[20]

Jews also continued to show reluctance to the idea of entirely relinquishing the education of their children to forces completely outside the group. The Kehillah experiment in New York City was a broad-based program initiated by Jews to encourage assimilation and education on the one hand and maintain the integrity of the Jewish community and traditions on the other. Kehillah's educational programs attempted to facilitate the entry of students into the economy while still retaining ties to Jewish religious principles and values. Kehillah even attempted to arbitrate labor disputes not only to ensure social harmony but to temper the appeal of Jewish Socialists who offered an alternative, more secular vision which placed working class above ethno-religious solidarity. Indeed, Catholic educators and leaders were no less mindful of stemming Socialist influences when they opened their own schools.[21]

Immigrant Politics

If immigrants went to great lengths to retain control over the education of their progeny, they also exhibited a good deal of caution in casting their ballots. Politics like folk life and education could not be conducted outside the realm of deep-seated communal feeling and need. If immigrant lives were ultimately tied to the concerns of family and community, it really would be unrealistic to expect that their politics could be indifferent to these concerns. Immigrants listened to leaders of different persuasions and frequently became excited about particular issues, especially when it affected their homelands where many friends and relatives still remained. But nearly always their politics was an extension of their most immediate concerns, and they tended to side with parties and leaders who came closest to reflecting their cultural and instinctual inclinations even if it meant abandoning ethnic or working-class solidarity.[22]

The religious attachment which was inculcated by their leaders in the face of heightened social change in both the homeland and new world and strongly associated with the cycles of their families and communities at birth, marriage, illness, and death proved to be the major force in shaping political sides in the century after 1830. From the moment Protestants and Irish Catholic workers fought bitterly in Philadelphia in the 1840s and Protestant leaders called for a moral component to public education and the regulation of drinking, ethnic-religious differences figured prominently in many political decisions. Catholics were not about to abandon their traditions of imbibing nor allow their children to be exposed to alien versions of Biblical readings in the schools. This was not simply a defense of one group against the threat posed by another but involved ways of life and the future status of the young.[23]

Fundamental to the division between Democrats and Republicans in nineteenth- and early twentieth-century America was a divergence between pietistic groups who placed a high value on individual salvation and the moral reform of society and ritualistic elements such as Irish Catholics or German Lutherans who tended to practice their religious life through hierarchies, rules, and complex organizations. Ritualists placed a great deal of emphasis on "personal liberty" and opposed any temperance or sabbatarian legislation.[24]

This demarcation could produce religious and cultural hostilities in American politics to such an extent that internal cleavages characteristic of all immigrant settlements might be temporarily overcome. The know-nothing movement with its anti-immigrant stance actually brought various factions in San Francisco's Irish community together temporarily in the 1850s.[25] During the same decade in Pittsburgh the Whig Party declined in the city when native-born voters abandoned it for its association with Catholic immigrants. To Pittsburgh Protestants the foreign-born filled the poorhouses, drank on Sundays, and increased the crime rate. Growing political involvement on the part of newcomers was especially resented. In the vote for governor of Pennsylvania in 1851 the count was split roughly along religious lines with some Protestants taking oaths to oppose any political party which gave nominations to Catholics.[26]

The pattern exhibited in San Francisco and Pittsburgh was much the same throughout the nineteenth century. Sometimes newcomers could be coerced into voting one way or another. In Moline, Illinois, more workers voted Democratic in the 1870s at the John Deere plant than at the Moline Plow Company because the former had a more liberal attitude toward the politics of its employees. But it was ethnic and religious affiliation rather than coercion which generally explained political party attachment, as pietistic and ritualistic groups moved respectively into the Republican and Democratic parties. Thus, in one Illinois county in the 1870s, 100 percent of the German Methodists preferred the Republican Party compared to only 25 percent of the German Catholics. Ritualists saw pietistic attempts to reform society as an intrusion upon traditional ways of life and belief. Conversely, pietists identified immigrants, whether they were German Lutheran or Irish Catholic, with the ills of the city: crime,

corruption, and decay. This was by no means simple economic competition but a perception that each threatened the other's culture and
community. Each had to prevent the other from capturing the government to implement one standard over another. In Wisconsin, for
instance, this disparity manifested itself in 1890 in a controversy over
the Bennett Law, a piece of legislation designed to force all schools to
teach the English language and American history. Some Catholics
and Lutherans objected because they saw the measure as a threat to
parochial schools and "parental rights and family life." As a result of
this particular dispute, Democrats gained German support throughout the state. Even the issue of the United States acquisition of a
colonial empire between 1898 and 1901 evoked ethno-religious over-
tones. Irish and Polish newcomers, quite sensitive about foreign domination of colonial lands, opposed such efforts strenuously. Mass
meetings of protest among Irish-Americans accompanied American
takeover of the Phillipines. The Central Labor Unions of Boston and
New York led such movements and indicated how sensitive the working class could be to cultural issues and how independent they could
be, since a few high-ranking Catholic clerics supported American ex-
pansionism.[28]

In the pivotal political battles of the 1890s between William
McKinley and William Jennings Bryan, immigrants placed cultural
values and some economic considerations before party loyalty. Although Bryan received the Democratic endorsement for president in
1896, many Catholic and Lutheran ritualists could not support a man
whom they identified with temperance and pietism, whatever his
party ties. Immigrants who could not support Bryan either voted for
McKinley, left the party all together, or simply declined to vote at
all.[29]

Even when a candidate appeared with strong credentials to attract
the support of immigrant workers, cultural issues could overcome
other forms of consciousness. In a classic case in 1886, Henry George
ran for mayor of New York City. Recruited by the city's Central
Labor Union as a candidate and possessing an impeccable record of
support for Ireland and the Irish Land League, especially when he
served as the *Irish World's* correspondent in Ireland, George and his
socialist philosophies seemed to offer a guarantee of unifying the city's
heavily Irish and German working class. But George was still unable
to outpoll the Democratic candidate, in part because of his socialist
leanings. It was after all Socialists who endorsed earlier plans to regulate saloons and promoted secular education, albeit as a means of
uplifting the worker rather than eradicating traditional belief. Such

stands, however, raised the suspicion of Catholic leaders and workers.[30]

As the twentieth century progressed and growing class distinctions drove a further wedge into ethnic and religious solidarity, economic issues promised to override ethnocultural ones, although no abrupt transformation took place in this regard prior to the 1930s. During the famous presidential election of 1928, religion continued to be the most significant line of division. Economic issues were real enough in the 1920s, but Democratic candidates such as Al Smith, unlike Franklin Roosevelt, failed to develop an effective ideology which could capture the discontent of the working class and expended more effort convincing Republicans that he was trustworthy and respectable. Poles supported Smith despite Herbert Hoover's record of support for Poland following World War I. But by 1932 even Catholics were essentially drifting back into traditional Republican machines until economic hard times in 1936 forced millions from the immigrant working class to coalesce into unified support for Franklin Roosevelt, although even in 1936 ethno-religious motivations were not abandoned completely. Among voters in high economic ranks Jews voted overwhelmingly for Roosevelt while native-born whites did so in considerably smaller numbers. *Dziennik Zwiazkowy*, a Republican organ for over forty years, even asked Poles in Chicago to support F.D.R.[31]

Perhaps no issue galvanized widespread support in immigrant America and revealed the deep attachments of newcomers to kin abroad than the recurring cause of the homeland. Resurrected periodically by "internal leaders" in nearly every group, homeland issues were always sure to elicit a broad and enthusiastic response on the part of the immigrant working class and temporarily ameliorate internal divisions. Just as assuredly, however, they tended to be issues which were short-lived. Occasional bursts of activity could be followed by relative indifference and a return to fundamental, everyday concerns of salvation, income, and family welfare when homeland issues were resolved despite the best efforts of elites to keep it alive.

Fatherland issues were especially important in overcoming internal group differences. German leaders continually sought to mitigate fragmentation between Catholics, Protestants, and Socialists as well as regional tensions. Germans in Cincinnati constantly wavered in their support of one American political party or another and German Socialists would have nothing to do with either one. Events in the fatherland could provide unity from time to time but could also produce an opposite result. In 1874 Cincinnati Germans expressed criticism toward Junkers in Prussia for hindering the emigration of labor simply to avoid declines in their level of military manpower. Many German Catholics in the city actually opposed Bismarck and held an elaborate ceremony upon the death of his most able adversary in 1891. By the turn of the century, however, attitudes toward Germany became increasingly uncritical as Cincinnati Germans coalesced behind anti-British feelings, which grew concurrently in Germany and among German-Americans in the United States.[32]

Jewish leaders continually exhibited a strong interest in their coreligionists at home and used political agitation in the United States to assist them. As early as the 1890s German Jews in New York took an active role in attempting to assist persecuted Jews in Russia. As with most homeland political causes, initial efforts at public education and mobilization of support emanated from elites, such as Jacob Schiff, an investment banker from Germany, and Oscar Straus, a businessman also born in Germany. These particular individuals began to exert pressure on the U.S. State Department. By 1906 they were leading efforts to allow Russian Jews to escape further persecution by emigrating to the United States.[33] Much later, of course, American Jews fought for the creation of an independent Jewish homeland after World War I and attempted to force the Roosevelt administration to look into reported but unbelievable atrocities against Jews in Nazi Germany in the 1930s.

The aftermath of World War I was an especially intense period of immigrant involvement in homeland politics. Many of America's largest immigrant concentrations had a deep interest in the political settlement that followed the war and attempted to influence the decisions of Woodrow Wilson and his administration at the Versailles Conference. Inevitably, however, it was prominent individuals identified with each group who exerted the most influence on Wilson. Ignace Paderewski effectively pleaded Poland's case, Louis Brandeis and Stephen Wise looked after Jewish interests, Italian leaders lobbied for Italy's right to Fiume, and Gregory Zatkovich worked for Rusin interests in Czechoslovakia. Some groups did not get all of what they wanted from Wilson but their efforts were no less intense. Irish-Americans were able to influence several state legislatures to pass resolutions in support of an independent Ireland but were still unable to influence Wilson, who remained unwilling to disrupt Anglo-American unity. In fact, disgruntled Irish, Germans and Italians who did not get all that they wanted from Wilson hurt the Democratic Party considerably in the presidential campaign of 1920.[34]

Old world issues continued to stir ethnic-immigrant politics in the United States during the 1930s. Fights between Mussolini supporters and opponents took place among Italians not only in Rome but in New York as well. Some Italian-American parents responded so positively to Mussolini that they sent their children to summer camps he sponsored in the homeland. The emergence of Nazism provided another explosive issue which threw New York's Jewish and German communities against each other. Some Germans refused to believe reports of atrocities in Germany and claimed they were exaggerated. Antagonisms between the two groups in New York reached such a point in 1933 that Jewish War Veterans began a boycott of German goods and a German-American Business League retaliated against Jewish merchants. An analysis of the vote for Roosevelt in 1940 indicated that ethno-religious currents had still not subsided on the eve of World War II. Groups such as the Irish, Germans, and Italians who had some concern for Roosevelt's increasing support for England voted for him in considerably less numbers than they had in 1936, with less than one-half the German and Italian vote in New York going to the incumbent President.[35]

While the periodic involvement in homeland causes excited immigrants and their children and generated much publicity, the ongoing, day-to-day attachment of newcomers to American politics took place on a quieter, more localized level. It was in the urban neighborhood or mill town that most new arrivals worked out their most enduring relationship to the American political system through the operation of the local machine and reigning political boss. While threats from outsiders and the fortunes of the homeland enabled leaders to mobilize large numbers of immigrants from time to time, the political boss promised to meet daily needs on a communal and individual basis. He could supply clothing, food, influence with city officials, playgrounds, and especially jobs. In effect, the boss was an extension of the family and communal economy and based his power on values most working-class immigrants had learned at home: reciprocity and mutual assistance. In the unpredictable swirl of capitalistic economies, unrelenting work routines, and competing ideologies, the mass of newcomers, able to secure little of the economic surplus which was produced, knew one thing for certain: people helped each other when they could. Because local political machines usually recruited most newcomers into the political system and because, in order to succeed, they were forced to emphasize communal values paramount to newcomers, they inevitably diminished the ability of immigrant voters to focus exclusively on workplace issues. Local machines filled the gap left by the general failure of unions and other labor organizations to effectively address the entire range of communal as well as workplace issues which concerned immigrant workers, although, of course, some labor organizations proved an exception to this point. Increasingly, because of the rise of these machines, a separation in American politics between workplace concerns and community issues took place which arrested the development of a more militant, class-based political movement. The separation, to be sure, was never complete. In reality, however, immigrants again had to deal with a variety of leaders and organizations in the larger society just as they had to do so within the confines of their own group. In the world of the immigrant voter both familial, communal and workplace issues, such as the control of the pace of production, were all potentially important but machines, thriving on their ability to deliver communal services, such as neighborhood parks and city jobs, emphasized the communal over the class dimension and often consigned labor concerns to unions alone.[36]

The earliest urban, political machines were dominated by the Irish who arrived first in the nineteenth-century city and brought a tradition of basing their politics on personal loyalty to friends and relatives in the absence of a strong central government structure. With occupational mobility limited in urban America, aggressive individuals in Irish communities often found it possible to enhance the welfare of their families and their own personal position by extending small immigrant-based business ventures into centers of political activity. Thus, much political activity centered around local saloons where information could be exchanged and newcomers could acquire contacts for jobs and even a free lunch. To a remarkable extent both these ventures and political organizations emerged out of the combined efforts of relatives and friends. Thus, Irish-born John McAvoy was blacksmith in New York City in 1880 who owned a stable, a smith, and at least one saloon. Two of his sons also became saloonkeepers, all helping each other to get started in business. Two other sons, assisted by the family's prominence in the twelfth ward, entered politics. One became an alderman and assemblyman and the other became a police captain and a district leader for Tammany Hall. In no small way the family's position facilitated the climb of one son to a judgeship. In a sense, the boss himself was often a product of a cooperative effort to find a niche in the urban economy.[37]

As additional groups of immigrants entered the industrial city, enterprising individuals emerged who established themselves as mediating agents between established machines and clusters of newcomers. For instance, William Steinway was able to fill numerous federal government positions with Germans after the election of his friend Grover Cleveland. When Carl Schurz was elected senator from the state of Missouri, Germans from throughout the United States, electrified by the news of a German-American senator, came to ask him for favors, support for political causes, and jobs. C.C.A. Baldi, a Philadelphia Italian, similarly functioned as an intermediary between the Republican machine of William Vare and newly arrived peasants. Vare delivered favors and jobs and Baldi responded by mobilizing Italian voters, an arrangement which advanced Baldi into a position of leadership in the community. It was almost impossible to secure street cleaning, clerical, or track-gang jobs for the city without Baldi's approval. Similarly when the question of an independent Poland was resolved after World War I, Poles in Chicago redirected their political attention to gaining city jobs and local recognition within Chicago society. Statues were erected to Polish heroes and street names were changed to appease ethnic sensibilities. Poles made even more substantial gains with the election of a Slavic-American mayor, Anton Cermak, in 1931. Cermak's city controller, Matt Szymczak, organized a Polish-American Democratic Organization to "screen" all Polish-Americans who wanted jobs and assisted many in obtaining them. In the "Hill" district of St. Louis, political leaders such as Lou Berra realized that the success of their organization depended partially on their ability to convince immigrants to become naturalized citizens. In 1926 the "Hill" machine hired a clerk from the U.S. Immigration Bureau to teach citizenship classes to Italians, and Berra and other leaders actually accompanied hundreds of foreign-born Lombards and Sicilians to the courthouse to assist them to acquire citizenship papers. The federal government eventually investigated Berra. Because his name was on so many citizenship papers, he was suspected of selling them. In fact, because citizenship was usually a prerequisite for voting, men like Steinway, Schurz, Baldi, and Berra were always strong advocates of Americanization and contributed to the middle-class chorus in all immigrant settlements which sought to foster adjustment and accommodation.[38] Sometimes the power and influence of such leaders was so strong that groups in certain cities continued to vote for their party even after they had faded from prominence.[39]

Conclusion

Institutions which wanted immigrant participation, such as public schools and political parties, could have it but only on a limited basis and on terms immigrants viewed as beneficial to themselves. Schooling was appropriate but its secular and transformative aspects would have to be muted to accommodate the desires of immigrant workers and traditionally grounded leaders to retain control over the socialization of the young. Rank-and-file newcomers were also unwilling and unable to abandon the capacity of the progeny to contribute to the household economy. Similarly, when immigrants voted, it was usually to further protect the values of the group, including religious traditions which usually reinforced existing patterns of parental-child relationships considered indispensable for economic well-being. While newcomers were always interested in the plight of their kin in the homeland, they functioned most effectively in local political machines which promised to meet immediate familial and communal needs by providing access to jobs, services, and even recognition. Immigrants ultimately would acquiesce in the new order of urban capitalism but on terms somewhat of their own making. They would creatively construct their own cultural world, which was filled with rich currents of folk thought and strong ties to familial and communal needs. But this did not mean that they were tied to the thought and behavior of some distant past. They were very much tied to the present, to their inferior status, and to the place they found themselves in—the hierarchy of power and resources in urban America. Their response to all this and the best way they could make sense of it all was to pursue folklife, education, and politics with an agenda of their own and not to follow blindly the dictates of any particular ideology or institution.

8 /

Conclusion:

The Culture of Everyday Life

> It is not the consciousness of men that
> determines their existence, but, on the
> contrary, their social existence deter-
> mines their consciousness.
>
> KARL MARX

Because capitalism attempted to regulate human resources as well as natural resources, it became the central force in
shaping individual lives in industrial regions and in agricultural areas
to which they were linked. In one manner or another populations in
these regions in the United States, Mexico, Asia, or Europe were
forced to make decisions about how they would confront the imperatives of this new economic and social order. Some embraced the
promise of the system wholeheartedly; some rejected it completely.
Most struggled the best they could somewhere in between. Since
these responses were shaped largely by the material condition and
social position in which individuals found themselves and their relationship to existing resources and the means of production, they
helped to divide society into divergent classes, cultures, and
ideologies. These social fissures produced a dialectic which explained
a good deal of the political, social, and economic tension of urban
America. In the American city and industrial town, workers protested
the level of pay and the pace of production.[1] Sometimes, culture
served as a basis for group life and the societal struggle for power,

control, and wealth turned on ethnic or cultural terms. This explanation has probably been used by scholars of immigration more than any other. Preindustrial cultures were thought to survive the transition to capitalism and determine the behavior and thought of immigrant workers and merchants.[2] Divergent cultures were even used to explain varying group patterns of behavior and attainment.[3]

The thrust of contemporary American social history has probed beyond the realm of group dynamics, however, and has exposed the private and personal dimension of individuals facing the historical currents of capitalism, industrialization, and urbanization alone. Thus, recent scholarly inquiry has inundated readers with thousands of pieces of information on household life, work routines, mobility, childhood, and even female fertility which have enriched the texture of the historical portrait. This direction, however, has rightfully disturbed some scholars who have lamented the abandonment of coherent theories which can somehow hold all of this disparate information together. Furthermore, the focus on private history has assuredly diminished the stress of Marxist scholars on power relationships and class division and of consensus historians on progress and uplift. Private history, the pursuit of the particular, has clearly deserved the charge of being history with the politics left out. The converse was also true: Marxist and Progressive history both paid insufficient attention to the struggle and perceptions of individuals.

This study of American immigrants in the century after 1830 certainly cannot reconcile all the problems of new ways of thinking about the dimensions of social and political history and of reconciling the long-standing debates between advocates of a class-based history and a past explained by cultural imperatives. Political history and private history, however, need not remain apart nor continue to launch critiques at one another. Beyond ethnic cultures, narrow conceptions of class, and group dynamics lies another level of explanation which can at least be partially glimpsed from an analysis of the relationship between immigration and capitalism.

Immigrant adjustment to capitalism in America was ultimately a product of a dynamic between the expanding economic and cultural imperatives of capitalism and the life strategies of ordinary people. Historian Gabriel Kolko wrote that millions of immigrants in industrial America had neither the desire nor the capacity to relate to the social order of capitalism. But, as the preceding discussion suggested, this observation was far from accurate. Immigrant people by definition related to capitalism and its attendant social order in complex and often ingenious ways which have often been misunderstood.

Generally, this process of understanding and adjusting was carried on in two broad categories. In reality two immigrant Americas existed. One consisted largely of workers with menial jobs. The other, a smaller component, held essentially positions which pursued personal gain and leadership. Immigrants did not enter a common mass called America but adapted to two separate but related worlds which might be termed broadly working class and middle class.

These two components were represented everywhere. Middle-class supporters of capitalism could be found among commercial farmers in Mexico, Sicily, or Hungary, entrepreneurs within immigrants groups, or industrialists in all American cities. They wielded relatively more power than most of their contemporaries, enjoyed extensive reinforcement from loyal supporters in political and public life including government officials, educators and even reformers and placed a high value on individual freedom, personal gain, political power, and an improved future. Below them, although far more numerous, stood millions of ordinary people whose perspective was considerably more circumscribed. They were not immune to the satisfaction to be derived from personal gain or political power but could not realistically indulge in such pursuits for too long a period of time. Their power to influence public affairs and their supporters in public institutions were minimal. Tied considerably more to the concerns of family and communal welfare, they focused daily activities, in the words of folklorist Henry Glassie, "in the place where people are in control of their own destinies."[4] These public and private spheres were not totally separate and, indeed, were part of a common system, but one was substantially more expansive, confident, and less circumscribed than the other.

Somewhere in time and space all individuals meet the larger structural realities of their existence and construct a relationship upon a system of ideas, values, and behavior which collectively gives meaning to their world and provides a foundation upon which they can act and survive. Collectively their thought and action are manifestations of a consciousness, a mentality, and ultimately a culture. Immigrants, who were after all common men and women, could not completely understand what was taking place as capitalism entered their world. They were not fully aware of the sweeping political and economic decisions and transitions which were altering the nineteenth and twentieth centuries. In lieu of a comprehensive understanding of social and historical change, they fashioned their own explanations for what they could feel and sense. To give meaning to the realities and structures which now impinged upon them, they forged a culture, a constellation of behavioral and thought patterns which would offer them explanations, order, and a prescription for how to proceed with their lives. This culture was not a simple extension of their past, an embracement of the new order of capitalism, or simply an affirmation of a desire to become an American. It was nurtured not by any one reality such as their new status as workers but was produced from whatever resources were at hand: kinship networks, folklife, religion, socialism, unions. It was a product of both men and women, believers and non-believers, workers and entrepreneurs, leaders and followers. It was creative yet limited by available options. It drew from both a past and a present and continually confronted "the limits of what was possible." The demands of economic forces, social structures, political leaders, kin, and community were real and could not be ignored. Life paths and strategies were informed by knowledge from the past and estimates about the future but largely from the specific options of the present. Immigrants were free to choose but barely.

It must be made clear, however, that this culture of everyday life, while generated at the nexus of societal structures and subjective experience, was ultimately the product of a distinct inequality in the distribution of power and resources within the system of capitalism. It would be convenient to call this a culture of the working class but it was not tied that simply to the means of production or the workplace and was not simply the prerogative of laborers. It was also tied to traditional culture, although it was certainly not entirely ethnic or premodern. Its core was a fixation upon the needs of the family-household for both laborers and entrepreneurs and the proximate community. The relative lack of resources and of a comprehensive knowledge of vast social economic change forced immigrants (and probably ordinary people in other places) to focus an inordinate amount of their lives in two areas. First, they had to devise explanations of their status in terms intelligible to themselves by drawing on folk thought, religion, ancestry, and similar devices close at hand. Second, they had to devote nearly all their attention to that portion of their world in which they actually could exert some power and influence: the family household, the workplace, and the local neighborhood or community. They sought, in other words, a degree of meaning and control. Like peasants in the Pyrenees studied by Pierre Bourdieu, they forged a world view that allowed for safeguarding what was considered "essential" at all times. The alternative would have been a life completely out of their hands, entirely bewildering and completely orchestrated by industrialists, public institutions, and economic forces.

The thrust of almost all previous scholarship seeking to interpret the immigrant experience in urban America around considerations of ethnic culture or class has been much too narrow and has failed to make a crucial distinction between the content and foundation of immigrant mentalities. The content which drew from ethnic traditions and present realities seemed as much cultural as it was class-based. That is to say, the newcomers acted as workers but also remained tied to selected ethnic symbols and institutions which appeared to mute solely class concerns. But the basis for this preoccupation with familiar ways, as well as with working-class realities, was to be found in the placement of these ordinary people in the larger social structure of capitalism. Even traditional family and ethnic communities were a preoccupation ultimately not because they were familiar but because they represented somewhat manageable and understandable systems to people who possessed little control or understanding of the larger society. Because they possessed relatively less material and social influence, they were preoccupied with understanding and constructing life at very immediate levels. They did this in part because they were relatively powerless to affect the sweeping currents of their times but, ironically, in doing so they actually generated a degree of power and social control of their own and transcended a status as simply victims.[5]

This pragmatic culture of everyday life accepted the world for what it was and what it was becoming and yet ceaselessly resisted the inevitable at numerous points of contact in the workplace, the classroom, the political hall, the church, and even at home. *Mentalité* for the immigrants was an amalgam of past and present, acceptance and resistance. Ordinary people could never live a life insulated from the actions of their social superiors, nor could they ever fully retreat from their present. Peasants responded to the whims of nobles, immigrants responded to the profit-seeking activities of commerical farmers or industrial capitalists. Since they could not control the direction of either elites or capital, they placed most of their priorities and focused most of their attention on the immediate, the attainable, the portion of their world in which they could exert some influence. This was true in "material life" and life under capitalism as well. By implication the culture of everyday life, shaped primarily by social status and unequal ownership of the means of production and informed by traditions and communal needs, always aspired to modest goals and was devoid of extremely radical or liberal impulses. The extent newcomers would go in either direction depended a great deal on the ability and impact of various leaders. And still ordinary people left their mark. Leaders constantly had to modify their ideology to effectively attract immigrant support. Peasants in the homelands could do little to dissuade the upper classes from promoting the spread of commercial agriculture. They did, however, force local elites to pay more for their farm labor by deciding to emigrate. Similarly, immigrants could not make decisions where to locate plants or invest large amounts of capital, but they could force industrialists to change personnel and wage policies by their transiency which stemmed from their private agendas. Some scholars might call this a form of class antagonism, but it also represented an effort to construct life strategies within available options.[6]

Ultimately, then, the mentality and culture of most immigrants to urban America was a blend of past and present and centered on the immediate and the attainable. Institutions from the past such as the family-household were modified but retained; the actions of landed elites at home and industrial capitalists abroad forced them to confront a new market and social order which they accepted but somewhat on their own terms. They would move, several times, if they had to, and become wage laborers or even small entrepreneurs. They did so not because they were victimized by capitalism or embraced it but because they pursued the immediate goal of family-household welfare and industrial jobs which were very accessible. If they had the skills or capital, which some did, even a small business was not out of the question. Those that moved had eschewed any retreat into a fictitious peasant past or becoming large, commercial farmers, although many still dreamed of living on the land. Overall, however, for people in the middle, immigration made a great deal of sense. Barrington Moore, who has written about German workers in the early twentieth century, has suggested that they were consumed by practical issues, such as the possible inability of the breadwinner to earn a living. Secondary concerns did include injustice and unfair treatment at the workplace but basically their fears and hopes revolved around everyday life: getting enough to eat and having a home of one's own. They expressed hopes for a better future but were usually too busy making ends meet to do much about it.[7] The pattern apparently transcended time and space.

Since capitalism was the central force which created these immigrants, it is still not possible to conclude they made an inevitable and smooth transition to a new way of life and a new culture. They were not one-dimensional beings rooted only to old ways of life or a new economy. They did not proceed simply from an ethnic world to a class world. Rather their consciousness and culture were continually grounded in several levels of status and culture prior to emigration and after arrival as well.[8] It was tied simultaneously to the lower levels of tradition, household, and community as well as to the higher levels of capitalism, industrialization, and urbanization. Between the microscopic forces of daily life, often centering around ethnic communal and kinship ties, and the macroscopic world of economic change and urban growth stood the culture of everyday life. This was a culture not based exclusively on ethnicity, tradition, class, or progress. More precisely, it was a mediating culture which confronted all these factors. It was simultaneously turbulent and comforting: It looked forward and backward, although not very far in either direction. It could not hope to exert the influence on history that industrial capitalism did, but it was far from being simply reflexive. Depending on premigration experience and leadership in America, it could prepare the way for a transition to a working-class or a middle-class America but seldom did it lead to a complete embracement of any new order.

If the culture of everyday life dominated the lives of most American immigrants, it did not mean that all newcomers were alike. Even within similar ethnic aggregations, a preoccupation with the practical and the attainable did not create identical life strategies. Some manifested a sojourning orientation and planned to return home fortified in their ability to live off the land. Others came to stay and effectively exploited their skills and resources to establish careers and businesses in urban America. Still others never really made up their minds and simply worked from day to day. Divergent resources and orientations in the homeland, moreover, often led to varying rates of attainment and participation in the culture of capitalism; those who settled in higher social stations and were already further removed from "material life" prior to emigration began to move more purposefully toward the new culture of acquisitiveness and personal gain. The origins of inequality in urban America were not located solely in the industrial workplace, or the city, or even ethnic cultures. They were also rooted in the social structure of the homeland and immigrant stream. Such divisions, in fact, would fragment immigrant communities and insure that urban-ethnic enclaves and settlements would only exist temporarily. But fragmentation at the group level should not obscure the ties that most of the first generation had to the culture of everyday life and the need to take what was available and secure the welfare of those closest to them. Immigrants were generally part of the masses and the culture of the masses in the nineteenth and much of the twentieth century was not solely traditional, modern, or working class. It was a dynamic culture, constantly responding to changing needs and opportunities and grounded in a deep sense of pragmatism and mutual assistance. Fernand Braudel spoke of three levels of historic time: political, which was rapid and episodic; social, which was modulated by the slower pace of everyday life; geographical, where change was nearly imperceptible. Immigrants were closely preoccupied with social time and the realities of the immediate and the present, although the levels of time and culture were never completely separated.[9]

The center of everyday life was to be found in the family-household and the proximate community. It was here that past values and present realities were reconciled, examined on an intelligible scale, evaluated, and mediated. No other institution rivaled the family-household in its ability to filter the macrocosm and microcosm of time and space. Kinship and the household, of course, are not necessarily identical concepts and family and work need not be inextricably linked. The truth of the matter, however, was that during the first century of American capitalism they inevitably were. The family-household mobilized resources and socialized people. Even though capitalism entered the peasant household in the homeland and caused a shift from subsistence to market production, the transition was essentially one of function and not form. The linking of individuals to a wage rather than a household economy did not inevitably lead to a decline of the family-household.[10] In the first century of industrial capitalism, the family-household continued to remain effective because supporting institutions of capitalism such as the state, public education, and even federally regulated unions had not yet become strong enough to fully penetrate the confines of private space.

Because of the continued viability of the family-household, the small community or urban neighborhood, usually built upon congeries of such units, continued to function and the culture of everyday life persisted. But this did not mean that private space was immune from public ritual and activity. Repeatedly, albeit episodically, the culture of everyday life was punctuated by "political time," by the rhetoric and ambitions of competing leaders. A new society and a new economy presented opportunities for newcomers with particular skills or resources to pursue power and middle-class status, to forsake the ambiguity of the culture of everyday life for the single-minded culture of power, wealth, and personal gain. Among all groups, not just among Japanese or Jewish entrepreneurs, this process of middle-class formation and pursuit of individual power took place to one extent or another.

While leaders emerged within all immigrant communities, they did not all advocate ideas and values consistent with the new order of capitalism or with each other. Many successful entrepreneurs advocated rapid Americanization and individual achievement. These leaders, such as Carl Schurz, A.P. Giannini, and Peter Rovnianek, were usually reinforced by the larger society which supported them and shared their faith. American political parties actually subsidized part of the ethnic press and further attempted to violate the boundaries of everyday life. Opposed to these accommodationists, however, were those who exhibited a stronger defense of tradition and communal values. They included clerics and fraternal leaders, were usually less tied to the new economy than politicians and entrepreneurs, and while not opposed to Americanization, were skeptical of rapid change, growing secularism, and the dangers inherent in a pluralistic society which threatened their elevated status. Irish Catholic prelates, for instance, could allow for Americanization but not accept public education in a society dominated by other cultures and religions. Advocates of religious authority and homeland causes, while often bitterly divided, were both ultimately defenders of the "everyday culture" in which they usually held prominent positions. Because they were tied closer to the culture of the masses, they generally exerted a stronger influence than leaders attached to external cultures such as trade unionists, socialists, educational reformers, or national political figures.

For leaders to be effective at any time and able to mobilize support for their activities they continually faced the need to establish their authority and bind the dominant and the subordinate through mutual obligations. In new circumstances the competition for this authority could be intense. The presence of vocal clerics, nationalists, fraternalists, socialists, trade unionists, and politicians underscored just how great the competition was. Since these potential leaders usually lacked resources for direct coercion, they inevitably generated ideologies revolving around words and symbols which were designed to appeal to the broadest possible numbers. It was the free market for leadership that produced the rich web of rhetoric which pervaded immigrant communities. Religion, socialism, ethnic nationalism, Americanization, unionism, and vocationalism were only a few of the ideological manifestations of competing leaders who sought followers and who offered prescriptions for living within the new order of industrial capitalism.

But not all leaders or elites were equally effective. Ideology cannot be reduced to simple strategies advanced by the prominent to further their own interests nor does it simply flow from the top to the bottom of society. The rhetoric and symbols of leaders were most effective when they reflected to some extent the feeling and thought of ordinary people themselves.[11] Educational reformers, socialists, some political figures, and even trade unionists often failed to realize this fully. Those that did, such as unionists who recruited ethnic organizers or editors who championed the cause of the homeland, were much more successful in mobilizing portions of the immigrant population. The Irish Land League, the rise of Catholic schools, the quest for German-language instruction, the rise of the United Mine Workers, and the cause of Russian Jews even in the 1890s illustrate how private issues could effectively enter public space. Religion, the homeland, and labor matters were probably the most debated issues. These matters concerned key elements of the past and present and of everyday culture; religion and labor especially had deep implications for a well-ordered family-household.

Immigrants not only influenced their leaders in an episodic fashion but resisted intervention into the only world they could control on an ongoing basis even while adjusting to a new economic order. They were not simply duped by a hegemonic culture.[12] Neither the prominent within their groups nor the owners of the means of production were beyond their influence. Immigrant laymen fought to maintain control of churches, Italians practiced rituals in defiance of clerical authority, religious and ethnic schools were established to resist the culture of outsiders, laborers controlled production, left jobs they did not like and struck spontaneously in colorful, communal fashion if it suited their purposes. They never tired of assisting friends and relatives to find jobs and probably had as much as managers to do with shaping the informal system of employment recruitment which dominated American industry during the century before World War II. Leaders who urged newcomers to support extended schooling or various political parties usually made little headway unless they addressed the issues relating to the family-household and community that newcomers felt strongest about: homeownership, jobs, neighborhood services, steady work, and traditional beliefs.

Immigrants lived in scattered urban-ethnic enclaves which were heavily working class. But these settlements were neither structurally nor ideologically monolithic. Newcomers were tied to no single reality. The workplace, the church, the host society, the neighborhood, the political boss, and even the homeland all competed for their minds and bodies. On a larger level, industrial capitalism could not be stopped. But on the level of everyday life, where ordinary people could inject themselves into the dynamic of history, immigrants acquiesced, resisted, hoped, despaired, and ultimately fashioned a life the best they could. Transplanted by forces beyond their control, they were indeed children of capitalism. But like children everywhere they were more than simply replicas of their parents; independence and stubborn resistance explained their lives as much as their lineage. Their lives were not entirely of their own making, but they made sure that they had something to say about it.

Appendix

IMMIGRATION TO AMERICA BY SELECTED
COUNTRIES AND SELECTED DECADES, 1820–1955

	1841–1850	1871–1880	1901–1910	TOTAL 1820–1955
All Countries	1,713,215	2,812,191	8,795,386	40,413,120
Europe	1,597,501	2,272,262	8,136,016	33,874,574
Austria-Hungary	5,074	72,969	2,145,266	4,212,959
Germany	434,626	718,182	341,498	6,530,543
England	32,092	437,706	388,017	2,823,144
Ireland	780,719	436,871	339,065	4,369,926
Italy	1,870	55,759	2,045,877	4,849,033
Asia	82	123,823	243,567	992,704
China	35	123,201	20,605	400,830
Japan	—	149	129,797	293,806
Americas	62,469	404,044	361,888	—
Mexico	3,271	5,162	49,642	—
Total Immigration, 1901–1955				21,289,514
Total Persons Naturalized, 1907–1955				7,082,166

Source: *Annual Report of the Immigration and Naturalization Service* (Washington, D.C.: Dept. of Justice, 1955), pp. 42–45, 118.

Notes

Introduction

1. See Oscar Handlin, *The Uprooted* (Boston: Little, Brown, 1951); Rudolph Vecoli, "The Contadini in Chicago: A Critique of the Uprooted," *Journal of American History*, 51 (Dec., 1964), 404–17. Timothy L. Smith, "Religion and Ethnicity in America," *American Historical Review*, 83 (Dec., 1978), 1155–85.

2. See Immanuel Wallerstein, *The Modern World System: Capitalist Agriculture and the Origins of the European World Economy in the Sixteenth Century* (New York: Academic Press, 1974). Michael B. Katz, Michael J. Doucet, and Mark J. Stern, *The Social Oranization of Early Industrial Capitalism* (Cambridge, Mass.: Harvard University Press, 1982), pp. 16–18.

3. See Garbiel Kolko, *Main Currents in Modern American History* (New York: Harper and Row, 1976), pp. 1–8; Eric Wolf, *Europe and the People Without History* (Berkeley and Los Angeles: University of California Press, 1983), pp. 22–32.

4. See Robert Higgs, *The Transformation of the American Economy, 1865–1914* (New York: John Wiley, 1971), pp. 48–72; Jeffrey G. Williamson, *Late Nineteenth Century American Development: A General Equilibrium History* (Cambridge, England: Cambridge University Press, 1974), pp. 211–16; Paul Uselding, *Studies in the Technological Development of the American Economy during the First Half of The Nineteenth Century* (New York: Arno Press, 1975); Oscar and Mary F. Handlin, *The Wealth of the American People* (New York: McGraw-Hill, 1975), p. 99; Louis M. Hacker, *The Course of American Economic Growth and Development* (New York: John Wiley, 1970), pp. 140–42.

5. Higgs, *The Transformation of the American Economy, 1865–1914*, pp. 23, 36–37; Williamson, *Late Nineteenth Century American Development*, pp. 245–47; H.J. Habakkuk, *American-British Technology in the Nineteenth Century* (Cambridge, England: Cambridge University Press, 1962); Richard Easterlin, "Influences in European Economic Development and Cultural Change," 9 (April, 1961), 331–51; Easterlin, *Population, Labor Force, and Long Sweeps in Economic Growth* (New York: National Bureau of Economic Research, 1968), p. 190; Jerome Blum,*The End of the Old Order in Rural Europe* (Princeton, N.J.: Princeton University Press, 1978); Handlin and Handlin, *The Wealth of the American People*, p. 98; Peter Temin, "Labor Scarcity in America," *Journal of Interdisciplinary History*, 1 (Winter, 1971), 251–64; Simon Kuznets, "The Contribution of Immigration to the Growth of the Labor Force," in *The Reinterpretation of American Economic History*, ed. by Robert Fogel and Stanley Engerman, (New York: Harper, 1971), pp. 369–99; Temin, "Labor Scarcity and the Problem of American Industrial Efficiency in the 1850s," *Journal of Economic History* xxvi (1966), 277–98.

6. See Fernand Braudel, *Capitalism and Material Life, 1400–1800* (New York: Harper and Row, 1973), pp. 220, 373, 443–45; see also Wallerstein, *The Modern World System*, passim.

CHAPTER 1

The Homeland and Capitalism

1. Brinley Thomas, *Migration and the Rhythm of Economic Growth, 1850–1913* (Cambridge, England: at the University Press, 1954); Maldwyn A. Jones, "The Background to Emigration from Great Britain in the Nineteenth Century," *Perspectives in American History*, (1973), VII, 29–32; Kristian Hvidt, *Flight to America: The Social Background of 300,000 Danish Emigrants* (New York: Academic Press, 1975), p. 34; Harry Jerome, *Migration and the Business Cycle* (New York: National Bureau of Economic Research, 1926). Jerome's views are supported by Dorothy Swaine Thomas, *Social and Economic Aspects of Swedish Population Movements, 1750–1933* New York: MacMillan, 1935); Frank Thistlethwaite, "Migration from Europe Overseas in the Nineteenth and Twentieth Century," in Herbert Moller, ed., *Population Movements in Modern European History* (New York, 1964), who stressed overpopulation and the lack of economic growth in the homeland; and J.G. Williamson, "Migration to the New World: Long Term Influences and Impact," *Explorations in Economic History*, (Summer, 1974).

2. Mack Walker, *Germany and the Emigration, 1816–1885* (Cambridge, Mass.: Harvard University Press, 1964), pp. 197–283; Josip Lakatoš, *Narodna Statistika* (Zagreb: Tiskon Hrvatskog Stamparskog Zavoda, 1914), p. 62; Richard Easterlin, *Population, Labor Force and Long Swings in Economic Growth* (New York: Columbia University Press, 1968), pp. 11–41, 204–09.

3. Julianna Puskás, *Kivándorlo Magyarok az Egyesült Allamokban, 1880–1940* (Budapest, Hungary: Akadémiai Kiadó, 1982), pp. 106–46; Benjamin P. Murdezek, *Emigration in Polish Social and Political Thought, 1870–1914* (New York: Columbia University Press, 1977), p. 146.

4. Maldwyn A. Jones, "The Background to Emigration from Great Britain in the Nineteenth Century," *Perspectives in American History*, VII (1973), 47, 60; Wolfgang Köllmann and Peter Marschalck, "German Emigration to the United States," ibid., 518; Simon Kuznets, "Immigration of Russian Jews to the United States: Background and Structure," ibid. (1975), IX, 50–51; Puskás, *Kivándorlo Magyarok az Egyesült Allamokban, 1880–1940*, pp. 120–46; Branko Mita Colakovic, *Yugoslav Migrations to America* (San Francisco: R & E, 1973), p. 47.

5. See Johann Chmelar, "The Austrian Emigration, 1900–1914," *Perspectives in American History* (1973), VII, 334–35.

6. Maldwyn Jones, "The Background to Emigration from Great Britain in the Nineteenth Century," 83; Malcolm Gray, "Scottish Emigration: The Social Impact of Agrarian Change in the Rural Lowlands, 1775–1875," *Perspectives in American History* (1973), VII, 97–173.

7. Jones, "The Background to Emigration from Great Britain in the Nineteenth Century," 47; Alan Conway, "The Welsh Emigration to the United States," *Perspectives in American History* (1973), VII, 178–93, 264; Howard L. Malchow, *Population Pressures: Emigration and Government in Late Ninteenth-Century Britain* (Palo Alto, Calif.: Sposs Inc., 1979).

8. Gino Germani, "Migration and Acculturation," in *Handbook for Social Research in Urban Areas*, ed. by Philip Hauser (Paris, 1964), pp.159–78; Lynn Hollen Lees, *Exiles of Erin: Irish Migrants in Victorian London*, (Ithaca,

N.Y.: Cornell University Press, 1979), pp.22–24; R.C. Taylor, "Migration and Motivation," in *Migration*, ed. by J.A. Jackson (Cambridge, England: at the University Press, 1969), p. 132.

9. See Barbara L. Solow, *The Land Question and the Irish Economy, 1870–1903* (Cambridge, Mass.: Harvard University Press, 1971).

10. Lees, *Exiles of Erin*, pp. 25–39. Of course, the very poor simply could not afford to emigrate. Oliver MacDonagh, "The Irish Famine Emigration to The United States," *Perspectives in American History* (1976), X, 418–30, shows that small farmers with 5 to 15 acres, were most likely of all Irish to possess the means to emigrate.

11. Walker, *Germany and the Emigration*, pp.47–77.

12. Köllmann and Marschalck, "German Emigration to the United States," pp. 531–39; J.J. Lee, "Labour in German Industrialization," in *The Cambridge Economic History of Europe*, ed. by Peter Mathias and M.M. Postan (7 vols; Cambridge, England: at the University Press, 1978), VII, 488; Charlotte Erickson, ed., *Emigration from Europe, 1815–1914: Select Documents* (London, England: Adam and Black, 1976), pp. 39–55.

13. See Struve Lindmark, *Swedish America, 1914–1932* (Uppsala, 1971), pp. 17–27; Ulf Beijbom, *Swedes in Chicago: A Demographic and Social Study of the 1846–1880 Immigration* (Stockholm: Laromedelsforlagen and the Chicago Historical Society, 1971), pp. 134–55; Harold Runblom and Hans Norman, *From Sweden to America: A History of the Migration* (Minneapolis: University of Minnesota Press and Acta Universitatis Upsaliensis, 1976), pp. 136–40. By 1910 over 60 percent of all Swedes in America, despite their rural image, were city dwellers; see Beijbom, *Swedes in Chicago*, p. 11.

14. Keijo Virtanen, *Settlement or Return: Finnish Emigrants, 1860–1930, in the International Overseas Return Migration Movement* (Helsinki: Finnish Historical Society, 1979), pp. 24–100; see also A. William Hoglund, *Finnish Immigrants in America* (Madison: University of Wisconsin Press, 1960).

15. Hvidt, *Flight to America*, pp. 40–69.

16. Ibid., pp. 128–35.

17. Yda Saveressig-Schreuder and Robert Swierenga, "Catholic Emigration from the Southern Provinces of the Netherlands in the Nineteenth Century," (Voorburg, The Netherlands: Interuniversity Demographic Institute, 1982), pp. 1–18; Swierenga, "Dutch Immigrant Demography, 1820–1880," *Journal of Family History*, 5 (Winter, 1980), pp. 390–405; Swierenga, "Dutch International Migration and Occupational Change: A Structural Analysis of Multinational Linked Files," paper delivered at the Social Science History Association Conference, Bloomington, Indiana, November, 1982. Little discussion is provided for France since its emigration was very low, due primarily to a rise in agricultural production that kept ahead of a more slowly growing population. See David Grigg, *Population Growth and Agrarian Change: A Historical Perspective* (Cambridge, England: at the University Press, 1980), p.201.

18. Tibor Kolossa, "The Social Structure of the Peasant Class in Austria-Hungary: Statistical Sources and Methods of Research," *East European Quarterly* (1979), III, 430–32. Paula Kaye Benkart, "Religion, Family, and Community among Hungarians Migrating to American Cities, 1880–1930" (Ph.D. dissertation, Johns Hopkins University, 1975), pp. 10–11; Puskaś, *Kivándorlo Magyarokaz Egyesült Allamokban, 1880–1940*, pp. 130–56; Istvan

Racz, *A Paraszti Migráció és Politikai Megítélése Magyarországon, 1849–1914* (Budapest, Hungary: Akademiai Kiadó, 1980), pp. 111–15 provides details on Zemplin County.

19. Johann Chmelar, "Austrian Emigration, 1900–1914," 318–30; Franciszek Bujak, *Galicya* (2 vols.; Lwów, Galicia: Nakladem Ksiegarni H. Altenberga, 1908–1910), II, 270, for a discussion of limited industrial employment within Galicia. For examples of extreme parcelization and even contractual obligations to the land in Romania, see Daniel Chirot, *Social Change in a Peripheral Society: The Creation of a Balkan Colony* (New York: Academic Press, 1976), pp. 136–47.

20. Chmelar, "The Austrian Emigration, 1900–1914," 333–34; Frances Kraljic, "Croatian Migration to and from the United States Between 1900 and 1914" (Ph.D. dissertation, New York University, 1975), pp. 19–23; Toussaint Hočevar, *The Structure of the Slovenian Economy, 1848–1963* (New York: Studia Slovenica, 1965), pp. 83–85.

21. Ivan Cizmić, *Iseljenistvo i Suvremena Ekonomska Emigracija a Prodruja Karlovca* (Zagreb, Yugoslavia: Matica Hrvatska, 1973), pp. 17–30; Kraljic, "Croatian Migration to and from the United States Between 1900 and 1914," pp. 26–31.

22. Branko Mita Colakovic, *Yugoslav Migration to America*, pp. 24–56; Cizmić, *Iseljenistvo i Suvremena Kdonomska Emigracija a Prodrucja Karlovca, pp. 25–30.

23. Mark Stolarik, "Immigration and Urbanization: The Slovak Experience, 1870–1918" (Ph.D. dissertation, University of Minnesota, 1974), pp. 3–30; Josef Polisensky, "Slovenska do USA a jeho pribeh az do roku 1918, jeho priciny a Nisledky," in Josef Polisenky, ed., *Začiatk Českej a Slovenskej emigrăcie do USA* (Bratislava, Czechoslovakia: Vydavatelstvo Slovenskej Akademie Vied, 1970), pp.54–55.

24. Celina Bobinska and Andrzej Pilch, eds., *Employment-Seeking Emigration of Poles World Wide, XIX and XX Centuries* (Kraków, Poland: Panstwowe Wydawni Naukowe, 1975), pp. 39–79; Witold Kula, Nine Assordobraj-Kula, and Marian Kula, eds., *Listy Emigrantow Brazylii i Stanów Zjednoczonych, 1890–91* (Warsaw: Ludowa Spedzielnia Wydawnicza, 1973), pp. 241–330; John Bodnar, Roger Simon, and Michael P. Weber, *Lives of Their Own: Blacks, Italians, and Poles in Pittsburgh* (Urbana: University of Illinois Press, 1982), p. 38; T. Lindsay Baker, *The First Polish Americans* (College Station: Texas A&M University Press, 1979), pp. 8–25. The growing literature on Polish emigration is summarized in Irena Paczynsak and Andrzej Pilch, eds., *Materialty do bibliograii emigracji Oraz Skupisk Polnocej w Ameryce Polnocej i Poledniowej w xix i xx weiku* (Kraków, Poland: Jagiellonskiego University, 1979).

25. Rudolph M. Bell, *Fate and Honor, Family and Village* (Chicago: University of Chicago Press, 1979), pp. 189–93; Dino Cinel, *From Italy to San Francisco* (Stanford, Calif.: Stanford University Press, 1982), pp. 13–43.

26. Cinel, *From Italy to San Francisco*, pp. 13–31.

27. Frank Thistlethwaite, "Migration from Europe Overseas in the Nineteenth and Twentieth Centuries," *Rapports: XIe Congress International des Congres International des Sciences Historiques,* (5 vols.; Stockholm, 1960), V, pp. 55–56.

28. Mack Walker, *Germany and the Emigration, 1816–1885*, pp. 42–69;

Köllmann and Marschalck, "German Emigration to the United States," 503–07. See Walter Struve, "Die Republik Texas, Bremen und das Hildesheimische. Ein Beitrag Zur Geschichte von Auswanderung, Handel und Gesellschaftllishem Wandel im 19." *Jahrhundert* (Aug. LAX, Hildescheim, vol. 96, Historischen Verein fur Niedersachsen, 1982). See also Kathleen Neils Conzen, *Immigrant Milwaukee: Accommodation and Community in a Frontier City* (Cambridge, Mass.: Harvard University Press, 1976), p.28.

29. Walker, *Germany and the Emigration, 1816–1885*, pp. 163–66.

30. Ibid., pp. 183–87; Kíollmann and Marschalck, "German Emigration to the United States," pp. 541–45.

31. Jones, "The Background to Emigration from Great Britain in the Nineteenth Century," pp. 39–49. For an older but excellent treatment see Rowland Berthoff, *British Immigrants in Industrial America* (Cambridge, Mass.: Harvard University Press, 1953), pp. 31–65.

32. Conway, "The Welsh Emigration to the United States," pp. 200–201; Jones, "The Background to Emigration from Great Britain in the Ninteenth Century," pp. 83–87.

33. Ibid.; Charlotte Erickson, *Invisible Immigrants: The Adaptation of English and Scottish Immigrants in Nineteenth-Century America* (Coral Gables, Fla.: University of Miami Press, 1972), pp. 24–34, 232–39; Berthoff, *British Immigrants in Industrial America*, pp. 11–19. See also J.H.M. Laslett, "The Independent Collier: Some Recent Studies of Nineteenth Century Coal Mining Communities in Britain and the United States," *International Labor and Working Class History* (Spring, 1982), No. 21, 18–27, who saw some Welsh miners emigrating partially to preserve an agrarian way of life; Grigg, *Population Growth and Agrarian Change: Historical Perspective* (Cambridge, England: at the University Press, 1980), p.187. See N.H. Carrier and J.R. Jeffrey, *External Migration: A Study of the Available Statistics, 1915–1950* (London, 1953).

34. Beijbom, *Swedes in Chicago: A Demographic and Social Study of the 1846–1880 Immigration*, pp. 39–167; Runblom and Norman, *From Sweden to America: A History of the Migration*, pp. 132–43.

35. Kristian Hvidt, *Flight to America: The Social Background of 300,000 Danish Emigrants*, pp. 76, 106–18.

36. Grigg, *Population Growth and Agrarian Change: A Historical Perspective*, pp. 121–27; Lees, *Exiles of Erin*, pp. 40–43.

37. Lees, *Exiles of Erin*, p.43; Lees and John Modell, "The Irish Countryman Urbanized: A Comparative Perspective on the Famine Migration," *Journal of Urban History*, 3 (Aug., 1977), 391–408.

38. Grigg, *Population Growth and Agrarian Change*, p.132; Robert E. Kennedy, *The Irish: Emigration, Marriage, and Fertility* (Berkeley: University of California Press, 1973), pp. 42–85; Jones, "The Background to Emigration from Great Britain in the Nineteenth Century," 79.

39. Chmelar, "The Austrian Emigration, 1900–1914," 341–44; Hočevar, *The Structure of the Slovenian Economy, 1848–1963*, p.51; Edward Zivich, "From Zadruga To Oil Refinery: Croatian Immigrants and Croatian-Americans in Whiting, Indiana, 1890–1950" (Ph.D. dissertation, SUNY at Binghamton, 1977), p. 7. Puerto Rican emigrants to New York prior to 1920 tended to come from the higher rather than the lower ranks of the work force; see Virginia E. Sanchez Korrol, *From Colonia to Community: The*

History of Puerto Ricans in New York City, 1917–1948 (Westport, Conn.: Greenwood Press, 1983), p.39.

40. Chmelar, "The Austrian Emigration, 1900–1914," 239–42.

41. Josef Barton, *Peasants and Strangers: Italians, Rumanians and Slovaks in an American City, 1890–1950* (Cambridge, Mass.: Harvard University Press, 1975), pp. 36–39; Stolarik, "Immigration and Urbanization," p.14; Frantisek Bielik and Elo Rákos, *Slovenské Vystahovalectvo: Dokumenty, I, do roku, 1918* (3 vols.; Bratislava, Czechoslovakia: Slovenska Akadémia vied, 1969) I, pp. 30–40; Puskás, *Kivándorlo Magyarok az Egyesült Allamokban, 1880–1940*, pp. 130–56; Benkart, "Religion, Family, and Community among Hungarians Migrating to and from the United States Between 1900 and 1914," p.34; Chmelar, "The Austrian Emigration, 1900–1914," p.337; Puskás, "The Conflicts of Adaptation of the Hungarian Emigrants in America," paper delivered at the United States-Hungarian Conference on Industrialization, Budapest, August 23–25, 1982, p. 7; A. Klima, "Agrarian Class Structure and Economic Development in Pre-Industrial Bohemia," *Past and Present*, 85 (1979), pp. 49–67. A fairly complete breakdown of the occupational status of Hungarian emigrants is found in Racz, A *Paraszti Migráció és Politikai Megítélése Magyarországon*, p.85.

42. Simon Kuznets, "Immigration of Russian Jews to the United States: Background and Structure," *Perspectives in American History* IX (1975), 35–105; Moses Rischen, *The Promised City: New York's Jews, 1870–1940* (New York: Harper and Row, 1962), p.20; Chmelar, "The Austrian Emigration, 1900–1914," 341.

43. Franciszek Bujak, *Limanowa: Miasteczko Powiatowe w Zachodniej Galicyi Stan Spolecnzy I Gospodarczy* (Kraków, Galicia: G. Gebethner I Spolka, 1902), pp.42–47.

44. Barton, *Peasants and Strangers*, p.30; Charlotte Erickson, ed., *Emigration from Europe, 1815–1914: Select Documents*, p. 93.

45. John W. Briggs, *An Italian Passage: Immigrants to Three American Cities, 1840–1930* (New Haven, Conn.: Yale University Press, 1978), pp. 2–12.

46. Ibid.; Barton, *Peasants and Strangers*, p.32; Judith Ellen Smith, "Remaking Their Lives: Italian and Jewish Immigrant Family and Work and Community in Providence, Rhode Island, 1900–1940" (Ph.D. dissertation, Brown University, 1980). Rudolph J. Vecoli, "Chicago's Italians Prior to World War I" (Ph.D. dissertation, University of Wisconsin, 1963), p.106; Cinel, *From Italy to San Francisco*, p. 11.

47. Donna R. Gabaccia, "Houses and People; Sicilians in Sicily and New York" (Ph.D. dissertation, University of Michigan, 1979), pp. 125–27; Briggs, *An Italian Passage*, pp.12–16.

48. Adam Galos and Kazimierz Wajda, "Migrations in the Polish Western Territories Annexed by Prussia, 1815–1914," in *Employment-Seeking Emigration of Poles World Wide*, ed. by Celina Bobinska and Andrzej Pilch, p.67; Bodnar, Simon, and Weber, *Lives of Their Own*, p. 40.

49. Wladyslaw Rusinski, "The Role of the Peasantry of Poznan in the Formation of the Non-Agricultural Labor Market," *East European Quarterly*, III (1970), pp. 138–41; Bujak, "Wychodztwo Zarobkoe W Galicyi, Z. Odleglej i blizkeig przeszlosce," *Studja historycznogospodarcze* (Lwowj, 1924), pp. 229ff.; Rusinski, *Rozwoj gospodarcy Ziem polskich* (Warszawa, 1969).

50. Lawrence A. Cardoso, *Mexican Emigration to the United States*,

1897–1931 (Tucson: University of Arizona Press, 1980), pp. 1–7; Albert Camarillo, *Chicanos in a Changing Society: From Mexican Pueblos to American Barrios in Santa Barbara and Southern California, 1848–1930* (Cambridge, Mass.: Harvard University Press, 1979); Jesus Silva Herzog, *El Agrarismo Mexicano y la Reforma Mexicano y la Reforma Agraria* (Mexico City, Mexico, 1959), pp. 120ff.

51. Cardoso, *Mexican Emigration to the United States*, pp. 10–44; Camarillo, *Chicanos in a Changing Society*, pp. 58–60.

52. Chie Nakane, *Kinship and Economic Organization in Rural Japan* (London, 1967), pp. 48–53; Yusi Ichioka, "Recent Japanese Scholarship on the Origins and Causes of Japanese Immigation," *Immigration History Newsletter*, XV (Nov., 1983), p. 3; Yasuo Wakatsuki, "Japanese Emigration to the United States," *Perspectives in American History*, XII (1979), pp. 387–516.

53. Barbara A. Anderson, "Internal Migration in Modernizing Society: The Case of Late Nineteenth Century European Russia" (Ph.D. dissertation, Princeton University, 1973), pp. 35–38. I would like to thank Professor Ben Eklof for this reference. Puskás, *Kivándorlo Magyarok az Egyesült Allamokban*, 1880–1940, pp. 59–87; Benkart, "Religion, Family, and Community among Hungarians Migrating to American Cities," p. 32; Sune Akerman, "Swedish Migration and Social Mobility: The Tale of Three Cities," *Social Science History*, I (Winter, 1977), pp. 178–209; Harvey J. Graff, *The Literary Myth: Literacy and Social Structure in the Nineteenth-Century City* (New York: Academic Press, 1979), p. 65; Cinel, *From Italy to San Francisco*, p. 23; Richard A. Easterlin et al., *Immigration* (Cambridge, Mass.: Harvard University Press, 1982), pp. 8–9.

54. Jerome Blum, *The End of the Old Order in Rural Europe* (Princeton, N.J.: Princeton University Press, 1978), pp. 113, 376–404; Grigg, *Population Growth and Agrarian Change: A Historical Perspective*, pp. 30–32.

55. See Alexander Gershenkrom," Agrarian Policies and Industrialization, Russia, 1861–1917," in *Cambridge Economic History* (6 vols.; Cambridge, England: at the University Press, 1965), VI, pp. 750–54; Stefan Kieniewicz, *The Emancipation of the Polish Peasantry* (Chicago: University of Chicago Press, 1969), pp. 180–81; Blum, *The End of the Old Order in Rural Europe*, pp. 410–18; Yoshida Yoshburo, "Sources and Causes of Japanese Emigration," *Annals of the American Academy of Political and Social Sciences*, 34 (Sept., 1909), 379–84.

56. Benkart, "Religion, Family, and Community among Hungarians Migrating to American Cities, 1880–1930," p. 28; Ivan T. Berend and Gyorgy Ranki, *Economic Development in East-Central Europe in the 19th and 20th Centuries* (New York: Columbia University Press, 1974), pp. 28–41; Joseph Held, *The Modernization of Agriculture: Rural Transformation in Hungary, 1848–1975* (New York: Columbia University Press, 1980), pp. 22–50; Blum, *The End of the Old Order in Rural Europe*, p. 103; Erickson, ed., *Emigration From Europe, 1815–1914*, pp. 80–81; Geoffrey Drage, *Austria-Hungary* (London: Murray, 1909), p. 314; Puskás, *Kivándorlo Magyarok az Egyesült Allamokban*, 1880–1940, pp. 30–60. I am also indebted to Professor Charles Jelavich for helping me to understand Austria-Hungary.

57. Berend and Ránki, *Economic Development in East-Central Europe*, pp. 47–57; Drage, *Austria-Hungary*, p. 321; Erickson, ed., *Emigration From Europe*, p. 88.

58. Bujak, *Limanowa: Miasteczko Powiatowe w Zachodniej Galicyi, Stan Spolecnzy I Gospodarczy*, pp. 67–74.

59. Hočevar, *The Structure of the Slovenian Economy*, pp. 51–55; Chmelar,"The Austrian Emigration," 335; Peter F. Sugar, *Industrialization of Bosnia-Hercegovina, 1878–1918* (Seattle: University of Washington Press, 1963), pp.189–90. Bogdan Stossjsavl Jevic, *Istorijski Prikaz Gospodarskih i društvenih Prilika u Jednom Zagorskom Selu Sociologiia Sela*, IX (1974), 212–31.

60. Kieniewicz, *The Emancipation of the Polish Peasantry*, pp. 190–94; Bodnar, Simon, and Weber, *Lives of Their Own*, p.38; Blum, *The End of the Old Order in Rural Europe*, p. 107.

61. Rusinski, "The Role of the Peasantry of Poznan in the Formation of the Non-Agricultural Labor Market," pp. 510–22; Bodnar, Simon, and Weber, *Lives of Their Own*, pp.38–39.

62. Köllman and Marschalck, "German Emigration to the United States," 526–27; Walker, *Germany and the Emigration*, pp. 76–78.

63. Jane Schneider and Peter Schneider, *Culture and Political Economy in Western Sicily* (New York: Academic Press, 1976), pp. 4–8, 115–25; Vecoli, "Chicago's Italians Prior to World War I," pp.102–06; Bodnar, Simon, and Weber, *Lives of Their Own*, pp. 43–45. Unlike Sicily which played a peripheral role in supplying the industrial world, Tokugawa Japan went into isolation and was able to diversify and industrialize; see Schneider and Schneider, *Culture and Political Economy in Western Sicily*, p.122; Ricardo Romo, *East Los Angeles: History of a Barrio* (Austin: University of Texas Press, 1983), pp. 37–38.

64. Oliver MacDonagh, "The Irish Famine Emigration to the United States," *Perspectives in American History*, X (1976), 358–78; Kennedy, *The Irish: Emigration, Marriage and Fertility*, pp. 88–93.

65. Jones, "The Background to Emigration from Great Britain in the Nineteenth Century," p. 8; Malcolm Gray, "Scottish Emigration: The Social Impact of Agrarian Change in the Rural Lowlands, 1775–1875," *Perspectives in American History*, VII (1973), 124–35.

66. Harriet Hall Bloch, "Household Economy and Entrepreneurial Activity in a Polish Peasant Village" (Ph.D. dissertation, Columbia University, 1973), p.7; Zack J. Deal, III, *Serf and State Peasant Agriculture: Kharkov Province, 1842–1861* (Salem, N.Y.: Ayer Co., 1981), p.379; Barbara Jelavich, *History of the Balkans* (2 vols.; Cambridge, England: Cambridge University Press, 1983), II, 15–17.

67. Gray, "Scottish Emigration: The Social Impact of Agrarian Change in the Rural Lowlands, 1775–1875," pp. 132–55. Agricultural changes were slower in coming to Wales, which had poor transportation connections to England and which had many nonresident landowners who cared more for their estates in England; see Conway, "The Welsh Emigration to the United States," pp. 195,239.

68. Blum, *The End of the Old Order in Rural Europe*, p.439; Gray, "Scottish Emigration: The Social Impact of Agrarian Change in the Rural Lowlands," pp. 153–57.

69. Drage, *Austria-Hungary*, p. 372; Chmelar, "The Austrian Emigration, 1900–1914," pp. 332–57; Hočevar, *The Structure of the Slovenian Economy*, pp. 54–83.

70. Blum, *The End of the Old Order in Rural Europe*, p.439; Murdzek, *Emigration in Polish Social and Political Thought, 1870–1914*, pp. 156–57; Bujak, *Polska Wspolczzesna: Geografja życie gospodarcze* (Lwów: Jakubowski, 1923), pp.310–35.

71. Bujak, *Limanowa: Miasteczko Powiatowe w Zachodniej Galicyi Stan Spolecnzy I Gospodarczy*, pp. 67–75.

72. Peter Kriedte et al., *Industrialization Before Industrialization* (New York: Cambridge University Press, 1981), pp. 317–42. See Catherine Lis and Hugo Soly, *Poverty and Capitalism in Pre-industrial Europe* (Brighton, England, 1979).

73. Walker, *Germany and the Emigration*, pp. 70–71; Berthoff, *British Immigrants in Industrial America, 1790–1950*, pp. 21–54; Jones, "The Background to Emigration From Great Britain in the Nineteenth Century," pp. 43–54; Kïollmann and Marschalck, "German Emigration to the United States," 528; Runblom and Norman, *From Sweden to America*, pp. 143–44.

74. Walter Kamphoefner, "Transplanted Westfalians: Persistence and Transformation of Socioeconomic and Cultural Patterns in the Northwest German Migration to Missouri" (Ph.D. dissertation, University of Missouri, 1978), pp. 32–84, 97.

75. Rischin, *The Promised City; New York's Jews*, pp. 25–27; Murdzek, *Emigration in Polish Social Thought*, pp. 36–37; Bujak, *Limanowa: Miawteczko Powiatowe w Zachodniej Galicyi, Stan Spoleczny I Gospodarczy*, pp. 55–56; Puskás, *Kivándorlo Magyarok az Egyesült Allamokban, 1880–1940*, 31–71; Berend and Ranki, *Economic Development in East-Central Europe in the 19th and 20th Centuries*, p.23; Wakatsuki, "Japanese Emigration to the United States," pp. 397–99. For a discussion of the decline of crafts in Galicia, see Bujak, *Galicya*, I, 383; II, 270.

76. Blum, *The End of the Old Order in Rural Europe*, pp. 95–97.

77. Vecoli, "Chicago's Italians Prior to World War I," pp. 117–18; Bell, *Fate and Honor, Family and Village*, p.81; Sydel F. Silverman, "An Ethnographic Approach to Social Stratification: Prestige in a Central Italian Community," *American Anthropologist*, 4 (1966), 899–922; Gabaccia, "Houses and People," 22.

78. Kolossa, "The Social Structure of the Peasant Class in Austria-Hungary," 429; Bujak, *Limanova: Miasteczko Powiatowe w Zachodniej Galicyi Stan Spolecnzy I Godpodarczy*, pp. 67–75.

79. Grigg, *Population Growth and Agrarian Change*, pp.59–60.

80. Ibid., pp.127–47; Kennedy, *The Irish: Emigration, Marriage, and Fertility*, pp. 1–13.

81. Grigg, *Population Growth and Agrarian Change*, pp.44–63. The average rate of increase per annum between 1800 and 1900 was: England 1.27%; Sweden .79%; Norway .79%; France .35%; Ireland −1.01%; Netherlands .86%.

82. Ibid., pp. 21–43.

83. Ibid., pp. 21–28.

84. David Levine, *Family Formation in an Age of Nascent Capitalism* (New York: Academic Press, 1977), pp.1–13; Hans Medick, "The Proto Industrial Family Economy: The Structural Function of Household and Family During the Transition from Peasant Society to Industrial Capitalism," *Social History* 3 (1976), pp. 291–315.

85. Hvidt, *Flight to America*, p.8; Thistlethwaite, "Migration from Europe

Overseas in the Nineteenth and Twentieth Centuries," 55; Jelavich, *History of the Balkans*, II, 15–16; Puskás, *Kivándorlo Magyarok az Egyesült Allamokban*, 1880–1940, p.47. Overpopulation in Galician villages is described by A. Pilch, "Migration of the Galician Populace at the Turn of the Nineteenth and Twentieth Century," in *Employment-Seeking Emigration of Poles World Wide*, ed. by C. Bobinska and A. Pilch.

86. Jones, "The Background to Emigration From Great Britain in the Nineteenth Century," 5; Conway, "The Welsh Emigration to the United States, 198–99; John E. Knodel, *The Decline of Fertility in Germany, 1871–1939* (Princeton, N.J.: Princeton University Press, 1974), pp.4, 246–49, 250–87.

87. Köllmann and Marschalck, "German Emigration to the United States," 534.

88. Michael Mitterauer and Reinhard Sieder, *The European Family: Patriarchy to Partnership, 1400 to the Present* (Chicago: University of Chicago Press, 1982), pp. 145–46; Daniel Chirot, *Social Change in a Peripheral Society: The Creation of a Balkan Colony* (New York: Academic Press, 1976), p.137; Berend and Ranki, *Economic Development in East-Central Europe in the 19th and 20th Century*, pp.16–26; See Hla Myint, "The Peasant Economies of Today's Underdeveloped Areas," in *Subsistence Agriculture and Economic Development*, ed. by Clifton R. Wharton (Chicago, 1969), pp.100ff; Schneider and Schneider, *Culture and Political Economy in Western Sicily*, pp. 89–91; Kieniewicz, *The Emancipation of the Polish Peasantry*, pp.56–65, 190–94. Emigration rates were always less in mountainous areas of the Balkans where commercial agriculture was less feasible. Among Greeks who came to America 60 percent were common laborers and only 17 percent were farm laborers. The entire Balkan stream was relatively small, including the Greek. See Theodore Saloutos, "Causes and Patterns of Greek Emigration to the United States," *Perspectives in American History*, VII (1973), 381–437. Even where the Balkans had fertile land, it was relatively uncultivated; see H. Hearder, *Europe in the Nineteenth Century* (London: Longman, 1976), pp. 92–93.

89. Bujak, *Limanowa: Miasteczko Powiatowe w Zachodniej Galicyi Stan Spolecny I Gospodarczy*, pp. 36–47. The higher population growth of Jews was in evidence throughout eastern Europe; see Rischin, *The Promised City: New York's Jews*, p. 24; Kuznets, "Immigration of Russian Jews to the United States," p. 63.

90. Rudolph M. Bell, *Fate and Honor, Family and Village*, pp. 3–4.

91. Michael Anderson, "Household Structure and the Industrial Revolution, Mid-Nineteenth Century Preston in Comparative Perspective," in *Household and Family in Past Time*, ed. by Peter Laslett (Cambridge, England: at the University Press, 1972), pp. 215–35; Michael Mitterauer and Alexander Kagan, "Russian and Central European Family Structure: A Comparative View," *Journal of Family History*, 7 (Spring, 1982), pp. 103–30; Bela Gunda, "The Ethno-Sociological Structure of the Hungarian Extended Family," *Journal of Family History*, 7 (Spring, 1982), pp. 40–51; Peter Laslett, ed., *Household and Family in Past Time* (Cambridge, England: at the University Press, 1972), 7–17; Dinko Tomašic, "Personality Development in the Zadruga Society," *Psychiatry*, 5 (May, 1972), 243–45.

92. See Joel M. Halpern, "Town and Countryside in Serbia in the

Nineteenth Century, Social and Household Structure as Reflected in the Census of 1863," in Laslett, ed., *Household and Family in Past Time*, pp. 401–27; Milovan Gavazzi, "The Extended Family in Southeastern Europe," *Journal of Family History*, 7 (Spring, 1982), pp. 89–102; Mitterauer and Kagan, "Russian and Central European Family Structure: A Comparative View," 103–31; Bell, *Fate and Honor, Family and Village*, p. 75.

93. Laslett, ed., *Household and Family in Past Time*, pp.7–20; Mitterauer and Kagan, "Russian and Central European Family Structure: A Comparative View," 110–25. Chie Nakane, "An Interpretation of the Size and Structure of the Hosehold in Japan Over Three Centuries," in *Household and Family in Past Time*, pp. 518–43, shows the nuclear family predominated in nineteenth-century Japan.

94. Laslett, ed., *Household and Family in Past Time*, pp.40–58; Andreas Plakans, "Ties of Kinship and Kinship Roles in an Historical Eastern European Peasant Community: A Synchronic Analysis," *Journal of Family History* (Spring, 1982), 52–75; Michael Anderson, *Family Structure in Nineteenth Century Lancashire* (Cambridge, England: Cambridge University Press, 1975); Gavazzi, "The Extended Family in Southeastern Europe," pp. 89–102.

95. Lutz K. Berkner, "The Stem Family and the Development Cycle of the Peasant Household: An Eighteenth Century Austrian Example," *American Historical Review*, 77 (April, 1972), 399–405. Berkner feels that his findings tend to support the view that small nuclear families have always been more common among the poor and the landless classes as the only practical means of existence. He even criticizes Laslett for ignoring his own figures that laborers are less likely to live in extended families than yeomen or higher status groups. Thus neclear family structure was not a biological and psychological inevitability but was in part explained by social and economic structures. Berkner's view is supported by Michael Drake, *Population and Society in Norway, 1725–1865* (Cambridge, England: at the University Press, 1969).

96. Plakans, "Ties of Kinship and Kinship Roles in an Historical Eastern European Peasant Community: A Synchronic Analysis," 62–64; Mitterauer and Kagan, "Russian and Central European Family Structures: A Comparative View," 112–13; A.V. Chayanov, *The Theory of the Peasant Economy* (Homewood, Ill.: Richard D. Irwin, 1966), pp. 55–49; Halpern, "Town and Countryside in Serbia in the Nineteenth Century, " 401–27; Mitterauer and Sieder, *The European Family: Patriarchy to Partnership, 1400 to the Present*, pp.1–7; E.A. Hammel, "The Zadruga as Process," in Household and Family in Past Time, ed. by Laslett, pp.335–73.

97. Gunda, "The Ethno-Sociological Structure of the Hungarian Extended Family," 50.

98. Peter Czap, "The Perennial Multiple Family Household, Mishino, Russia, 1782–1858," *Journal of Family History*, 7 (Spring, 1982), pp.5–7; Mitterauer and Kagan, "Russian and Central European Family Structures: A Comparative View," 112–13; Gunda, "The Ethno-Sociological Structures of the Hungarian Extended Family," 50–55; W. Kula, "The Seigneury and the Peasant Family in Poland," in R.R. Forster and O. Ranum, eds., *Family and Society* (Baltimore, Md.: Johns Hopkins University, 1976).

99. Levine, *Family Formation in an Age of Nascent Capitalism*, p.9; Mitterauer and Sieder, *The European Family: Patriarchy to Partnership, 1400 to the Present*, pp. 101–25; Kennedy, *The Irish: Emigration, Marriage and Fertil-*

ity, p.152; Mitterauer and Kagan, "Russian and Central European Family Structure: A Comparative View," 113; Gunda, "The Ethno-Sociological Structure of the Hungarian Extended Family," 47–48; Hammel, "The Zadruga as Process," 335–73.

100. Bell, *Fate and Honor, Family and Village*, pp. 183–97. Villages studies included Nissoria, Castel, San Giorgio, and Rogliano Albareto.

101. Kamphoefner, "Transplanted Westfalians," pp. 28–29; Reinhard Sieder and Michael Mitterauer, "The Reconstruction of the Family Life Course," in *Family Forms in Historic Europe*, ed. by Richard Wall (Cambridge, England: Cambridge University Press, 1983), p.281; Biddle, "The American Catholic Irish Family," in *Ethnic Families in America*, ed. by Charles Mindel and Robert W. Habenstein (New York: Elsevier, 1980), p.93; Jelavich, *History of the Balkans*, II, 17.

102. Nakane, "An Interpretation of the Size and Structure of the Household in Japan over Three Centuries," in *Household and Family in Past Time*, ed. by Peter Laslett (Cambridge, 1972), pp.518–13. In most of China, all sons had rights of inheritance.

103. Nakane, *Kinship and Economic Organization in Rural Japan*, pp. 41–96.

104. Jones,"The Background to Emigration from Great Britain in the Nineteenth Century," 48; Gray, "Scottish Emigration: The Social Impact of Agrarian Change in the Rural Lowlands, 1775–1875," 140–62; Conway, "The Welsh Emigration to the United States," 195, 226–32; Lees, *Exiles of Erin*, pp. 34–36; Grigg, *Population Growth and Agrarian Change*, p.39.

105. Puskás, *Kivándorlo Magyarok az Egyesült Allamokban*, pp. 27–47, says Hungary's internal migration was less important because that country's economic development was limited and relied mostly on imported skilled Czechs and Austrians. It could not use farm surplus. Andrzej Pilch, "Migration of the Galician Populace at the Turn of the Nineteenth and Twentieth Century," in *Employment-Seeking Emigration of Poles World Wide*, ed. by C. Bobinska and A. Pilch, pp. 97–98; Stephen Corrsin, "Urbanization and the Baltic Peoples: Riga and Tallinn Before the First World War," *East European Quarterly*, XII (Sept., 1978), 81; Barton, *Peasants and Strangers*, *p.43*; *Bujak, Limanowa: Miasteczko Powiatowe w Zachodniej Galicyi Stan Spolecnzy I Gospodarczy*, pp. 42–47; Rusinski, "The Role of the Peasantry of Poznan in the Formation of the Non-Agricultural Labor Market," 83–141; Tadeusz z Gasinski, "Polish Contact Labor in Hawaii, 1869–1899," *Polish-American Studies*, xxix (Spring, 1982), 14–27; Zbigniew Stankiewicz, "The Economic Emigration from the Kingdom of Poland Portrayed on the European Background," in *Employment-Seeking Emigration of Poles World Wide*, ed. by Bobinska and Pilch; Adam Galos and Kazimierz Wajda, "Migrations in the Polish Western Territories Annexed by Prussia," in ibid., pp.71–73; Chmelar, "The Austrian Emigration," 321; Blum, *The End of the Old Order*, pp. 111, 439; Hočevar, *The Structure of the Slovenian Economy*, p.84; Hvidt, *Flight to America*, p. 7; Bodnar, Simon, and Weber, *Lives of Their Own*, p. 38; Cizmic, *ziseljenistvo i Suvremena Ekonomska Emigracija a Prodrucja Karlovca*, p.289; Colakovic, *Yugoslav Migrations to America*, p.75.

106. Linda Dégh, *Folktales and Society: Story-Telling in a Hungarian Peasant Community* (Bloomington: Indiana University Press, 1969), p.19.

107. Jan Siracky, *Stahovanie Slovákov Na Dolnú Zem 18. a 19. Storoči*

(Bratislavia, Czechoslovakia, 1966), pp. 100–120; Stolarik, "Immigration and Urbanization," pp. 1–16; Barton, *Peasants and Strangers*, p.41.

108. Romo, *East Los Angeles*, p.36; Cinel, *From Italy to San Francisco*, pp.3–33; Bell, *Fate and Honor, Family and Village*, p.196. In Mexico, another large area of emigration to the United States, a migratory labor class was well established in the central plateau by the 1890s for seasonal farm work or for labor in cities such as Mexico City and Monterey; see Arthur F. Corwin, "Causes of Mexican Emigration to the United States: A Summary View," *Perspectives in American History*, VII (1973), 559.

109. See, for instance, M. Dobos, "The Croatian Peasant Uprising of 1883," Ph.D. dissertation, Columbia University, 1974).

110. Benkart, "Religion, Family, and Community among Hungarians Migrating to American Cities," pp. 9–10; Karoly Voros, "A Parasztasas Vá Itozásas xix században," *Ethnographica*, LXXXVII, 143.

111. Thomas Hofer, "Changes in the Style of Folk Art and Various Branches of Folklore in Hungary During the 19th Century—An Interpretation," *Acta Ethnographica Academiae Scientiarum Hungaricae*, 29 (1980), 154–56.

112. See Ulrich Bauche, *Landtischler, Tischlerwerk und Intarsienkunst in den Vierlanden* (Hamburg, 1965), passim.

113. Petr Bogatyrev, *The Functions of Folk Costume in Moravian Slovakia* (The Hague: Mouton, 1971), pp. 46–56; Dégh, *Folktales and Society*, pp.20–25; Hofer, "Peasant Expressive Culture, 1800–1914: Tendencies of Separation and Mergence," paper delivered at the United States-Hungarian Conference on Industrialization, Budapest, August 23–25, 1982. For the Irish religious upsurge of the nineteenth century, see Emmit Larkin, "The Devotional Revolution in Ireland, 1850–75," *American Historical Review*, 77 (June, 1972), pp.625–52.

114. Kraljic, "Croatian Migration to and from the United States," p. 97; Hofer, "Peasant Expressive Culture, 1800–1914," pp. 2–6; Benkart, "Religion, Family, and Community among Hungarians," pp. 9–21.

115. Richard Blanke, "Bismarck and the Prussian Polish Policies of 1886," *Journal of Modern History*, 45 (New York: Columbia University Press, 1981).

116. See William W. Hagan, "National Solidarity and Organic Work in Prussian Poland, 1814–1914," *Journal of Modern History*, 44 (March, 1972), 38–64; Rusinski, "The Role of the Peasantry of Poznan in the Formation of the Non-Agricultural Labor Market," 509–24.

117. Monika Gletter, *Pittsburgh-Wien-Budapest Programm und Praxis der Nationalitaten Politik bei der Dus wanderung der Ungarischen Slowaken nach America un 1900* (Wien, 1980); Dirk Hoerder, "Prussian Agents Among Polish Americans, 1900–1917: A Research Note," *Polish-American Studies*, XXXVIII (Autumn, 1981), 84–88.

118. Sugar, *Industrialization of Bosnia-Hercegovina, 1878–1918*, passim; Blum, *The End of the Old Order in Rural Europe, pp*. 432–37; Drage, *Austria-Hungary*, pp. 316–17; Hočevar, *The Structure of the Slovenian Economy, pp*. 58–59, 63–68.

119. Tomašic, "Personality Development in the Zadruga Society," 251–58; Kraljic, "Croatian Migration to and from the United States Between 1900–1914," p. 97.

120. Rusinski, "The Role of the Peasantry of Poznan in the Formation of

the Non-Agricultural Labor Market," 51–56; Barton, *Peasants and Strangers*, pp.68–69.

121. See Frank Renkiewicz, "The Profits of Nonprofit Capitalism: Polish Fraternalism and Beneficial Insurance in America," in Scott Cummings, ed., *Self-Help in Urban America: Patterns of Minority Business Enterpirse* (Port Washington, N.Y.: Kennikat Press, 1980), p.117.

122. Rischin, *The Promised City*, pp.35–42; Irving Howe, *World of Our Fathers* (New York, 1976), pp.18–20.

123. Cinel, "The Seasonal Emigrations of Italians in the Nineteenth Century: From Internal to International Destinations," *Journal of Ethnic Studies*, 10 (Spring, 1982), 47; Jones, "The Background to Emigration from Great Britain in the Nineteenth Century," 8–9; Murdzek, *Emigration in Polish Social and Political Thought*, pp. 60–79; Glettler, *Pittsburgh-Wien-Budapest*, pp. 366–73.

124. Jones, "The Background to Emigration from Great Britain in the Nineteenth Century," 8–9; Chmelar, "The Austrian Emigration," 284–85, 338; Hvidt, *Flight to America*, pp. 17–21; Murdzek, *Emigration in Polish Social and Political Thought*, pp. 98–99.

125. George Prpic, *Croatian Immigrants in America* (New York: New American Library, 1971), p. 150; Chmelar, "The American Emigration," 335; Benkart, "Religion, Family, and Community among Hungarians Migrating to American Cities," p.23; Cizmic, Iseljenistvo i Suvremena Ekonomska Emigracija a Prodrucja Karlovca, pp. 300–10.

126. Blum, *The End of the Old Order*, pp.439–40; Bodnar, Simon, and Weber, *Lives of Their Own*, p. 46; Barton, *Peasants and Strangers*, pp. 77–78; Briggs, *An Italian Passage*, pp.7–10, 68; Benkart, "Religion, Family, and Community among Hungarians Migrating to American Cities," pp. 12–25.

127. Puskás, *Kivándorlo Magyarok az Egyesült Allamokban, 1880–1940*, pp.185–99, says 82 percent of emigrants from Hungary had relatives in America; Mira Balen, "Porodični Odnosi i Njihouo Menjanje u Naseije Jažabet," *Sociologija*, IV (1962), 254–84.

128. Bell, *Fate and Honor, Family and Village* (Chicago: University of Chicago Press, 1979), pp. 179–88; Vecoli, "Chicago's Italians Prior to World War I," p. 84; Cinel, "The Seasonal Emigrations of Italians in the Nineteenth Century," 47–48; Fejos Zoltan, *Kivándorlás Amerikába A Zemphlén Középsö Vidékeröl* (Miskolc, Hungary, 1980), pp. 298–307, reports of Hungarians who emigrated over ten times to improve their farm or acquire one.

129. See Edna Bonachich, "A Theory of Middlemen Minorities," *American Sociological Review*, 38 (Oct. 1973), 583–94; T. Shanin, "The Nature and Logic of the Peasant Economy," *Journal of Peasant Studies*, (1973), 68–80.

130. Hvidt, *Flight to America*, p.187; Kraljic, "Croatian Migration to and From the United States Between 1900 and 1914," p.165: Chmelar, "The Austrian Emigration, 1900–1914," p.335; Betty Boyd Caroli, *Italian Repatriation from the United States, 1900–1914* (New York: Center for Migration Studies, 1973); Jonathan Sarna, "The Myth of No Return: Jewish Return Migration to Eastern Europe, 1881–1914," *American Jewish History*, LXXI (Dec., 1981), 256–68.

131. Virtanen, *Settlement or Return: Finnish Emigrants in the International Overseas Return Migration Movement*, pp. 93, 108, 175–76; see also Cardoso, *Mexican Emigration to the United States, 1897-1931*, p.144.

132. Puskás, "The Conflicts of Adaptation of the Hungarian Emigrants in America," paper presented to the United States-Hungarian Conference on Industrialization, Budapest, Aug. 23–25, 1982, pp. 3–5.
133. Cinel, *From Italy to San Francisco*, pp. 57, 65–83.

CHAPTER 2

Families Enter America

1. John Bodnar, Roger Simon, and Michael Weber, *Lives of Their Own: Blacks, Italians and Poles in Pittsburgh, 1900–1960* (Urbana: University of Illinois Press, 1982), pp. 41–42; Maldwyn A. Jones, "The Background to Emigration From Great Britain in the Nineteenth Century," *Perspectives in American History*, VII (1973), 20; Robert C. Ostrergren, "Kinship Networks and Migration: A Nineteenth Century Swedish Example," *Social Science History*, 6 (1982), 293–320; *Pamietniki Emigrantow Stany Ziednoc Zone* (2 vols.; Warszawa: Ksiazka I wiedza, 1977), I, 33; Judith Ellen Smith, "Remaking Their Lives: Italian and Jewish Immigrant Family, Work and Community in Providence, Rhode Island, 1900–1940" (Ph.D. dissertation, Brown University, 1980), pp. 147, 223; Gary Mormino, "The Hill Upon the City: An Italo-American Neighborhood In St. Louis, Missouri, 1838–1955" (Ph.D. dissertation, University of North Carolina, 1977), p. 84; Jeremy Brecher, Jerry Lombardi, and Jan Stackhouse, comps. and eds., *Brass Valley: The Story of Working People's Lives and Struggles in an American Industrial Region* (Philadelphia: Temple University Press, 1982), pp. 10–40; William Hoglund, "Finnish Immigrant Letter Writers: Reporting from the U.S. to Finland, 1870's to World War I," in *Finnish Diaspora II: United States* (Toronto: Multicultural History Society of Ontario, 1981), p. 21; Carl Ross, "Finnish-American Women in Transition, 1910–1920," in ibid., p.239; Pauline Young, *Pilgrims of Russian-Town* (Chicago: University of Chicago Press, 1932), pp. 13–32; Francisco A. Rosales, "Mexican Immigration to the Urban Midwest During the 1920's" (Ph.D. dissertation, Indiana University, 1978), pp. 149–157, 174–75.
2. Edwin Fenton, *Immigrants and Unions, A Case Study: Italians and American Labor, 1870–1920* (New York: Arno Press, 1975), pp. 80–81; Rudolph J. Vecoli, "Chicago's Italians Prior to World War I" (Ph.D. dissertation, University of Wisconsin, 1963), pp. 89–90; Theodore Saloutos, "Causes and Patterns of Greek Emigration to the United States," *Perspectives in American History*, VII (1973), 405; Julianna Puskás, *Kivándorlo Magyarok az Egyesult Allamokban, 1880–1940* (Budapest, Hungary: Akademiai Kiadó, 1982), p. 35; Helen Zesse Papanikolas, "Toil and Rage in a New Land: The Greek Immigrants in Utah," *Utah Historical Quarterly*, 38 (Spring, 1970), 115–16; Edna Bonacich, "A Theory of Middleman Minorities," *American Sociological Review*, 38 (1973), 583–94.
3. Jerome Blum, *The End of the Old Order* (Princeton, N.J.: Princeton University Press, 1978), pp. 219, 228, 260; Witold Kula, Nine Assoroddorai-Kula, and Marian Kula, eds., *Listy Emigrantowz Brazylii i Stanow Zjed Noczonych, 1890–91* (Warsaw, Poland, 1973), p.314.
4. Samuel L. Bailey, "The Adjustment of Italian Immigrants in Buenos Aires and New York, 1870–1914," *American Historical Review* 88 (April,

1983), 284–88; Herbert S. Klein, "The Integration of Italian Immigrants into the United States and Argentina: A Comparative Analysis," ibid., 295–318. See Robert F. Harney, "Ambiente and Social Class in North American Little Italies," *Canadian Review of Studies in Nationalism*, 2 (1975), 208–24.

5. Peter R. Shergold, *Working-Class Life: The "American Standard" in Comparative Perspective, 1899–1913* (Pittsburgh: University of Pittsburgh Press, 1982), pp. 61–62, 212–13; Lawrence A. Cardoso, *Mexican Emigration to the United States, 1897–1931* (Tucson: University of Arizona Press, 1980), p.22. See Rowland Tappan Berthoff, *British Immigrants in Industrial America, 1790–1950* (Cambridge, Mass.: Harvard University Press, 1953), p. 66.

6. Virginia Yans-McLaughlin, *Family and Community: Italian Immigrants in Buffalo, 1880–1930* (Ithaca, N.Y.: Cornell University Press, 1977), p. 28; James K. Benson," Irish and German Families and the Economic Development of Midwestern Cities, 1860–1895: St. Paul, Minnesota as a Case Study" (Ph.D. dissertation, University of Minnesota, 1980), pp. 61–65, 282, 341; Irving Howe, *World of Our Fathers* (New York: Simon and Schuster, 1976), p.155; Gerd Korman, *Industrialization, Immigrants, and Americanizers: The View From Milwaukee* (Madison: State Historical Society of Wisconsin, 1967), pp. 35–36. See Krzysztor Groniowski, "Spor o model Kultury Polonijnej w Stanach zjednoczonych na Przelomie xix i xx wieku," in *Kultura Skupisk Polonijnych* (Warszawa: Bibliotera Narodowa Instytut Historii Pan, 1981), pp. 48–63.

7. Bodnar, Simon, and Weber, *Lives of Their Own*, pp. 56–58; Bodnar, "Immigration, Kinship, and the Rise of Working-Class Realism," *Journal of Social History*, 14 (Fall, 1980), 51–54; William De Marco, "Ethnics and Enclaves: The Italian Settlement in the North End of Boston" (Ph.D. dissertation, Boston College, 1980), pp. 167–68; John Ellsworth, *Factory Folkways* (New Haven, Conn.: Yale University Press, 1952), pp. 139–40: See James R. Barrett, "Work and Community in the Jungle: Chicago's Packing House Workers, 1894–1922" (Ph.D. dissertation, University of Pittsburgh, 1981), pp. 176–93; Leslie Woodcock Tentler, *Wage-Earning Women: Industrial Work and Family Life in the United States, 1900–1930* (New York: Oxford University Press, 1979), p. 17; Tamara K. Hareven, *Family Time and Industrial Time* (Cambridge, England: Cambridge University Press, 1982), pp. 85–86, 101, 113, 117–124. Hareven argues that, to an extent, kinship served as a surrogate for labor unions, but the experience of coal mining regions would suggest that unions and kinship at work were not mutually exclusive.

8. Caroline Manning, *The Immigrant Woman and Her Job* (New York: Arno Press, 1970), pp. 106–74; Dorothea De Schweintz, *How Workers Find Jobs: A Study of Four Thousand Hosiery Workers in Philadelphia* (Philadelphia: University of Pennsylvania Press, 1932); George Huganir, "The Hosiery Looper in the Twentieth Century: A Study of Family Occupational Processes and Adaptation to Factory and Community Change, 1900–1950" (Ph.D. dissertation, University of Pennsylvania, 1958) pp. 6–8. William Leiserson, *Adjusting Immigrant and Industry* (New York, 1924), p.31; Louise C. Odencrantz, *Italian Women in Industry: A Study of Conditions in New York City* (New York, 1919), p.283; Corrine Azen Krause, "Urbanization Without Breakdown: Italian, Jewish, and Slavic Immigrant Women in Pittsburgh, 1900–1945," *Journal of Urban History*, 4 (May, 1978), 296–97.

9. Theodore Hershberg, "A Tale of Three Cities: Blacks and Immigrants in Philadelphia: 1850– 1880, 1930 and 1970," *Annals of the American Academy of Political and Social Sciences*, 441 (Jan., 1979), 68; Clyde and Sally Griffen, *Natives and Newcomers: The Ordering of Opportunity in Mid-Nineteenth-Century Poughkeepsie* (Cambridge, Mass.: Harvard University Press, pp.67– 69; Laurence Glasco, "Ethnicity and Occupation in the Mid-Nineteenth Century: Irish, Germans and Native-born Whites in Buffalo, New York," in *Immigrants in Industrial America, 1850–1920*, ed. by Richard L. Ehrlich (Charlottesville: University Press of Virginia, 1977), pp. 151– 53; 61 Cong., 2nd Sess., S. Doc. 282, *Reports of the Immigration Commission, Occupations of the First and Second Generation of Immigrants in the United States, Fecundity of Immigrant Women* (Washington, 1911), pp. 19– 20; 61 Cong., 2nd Sess., S. Doc. 282, *Reports of the Immigration Commission, Immigrants in Cities* (2 vols.; Washington, 1911), I, 130– 31; II, 497ff.

10. Edward A. Zivich, "From Zadruga to Oil Refinery: Croatian Immigrants and Croatian-Americans in Whiting, Indiana, 1890– 1950" (Ph.D. dissertation, SUNY at Binghamton, 1977), pp. 37– 39; Rosara Lucy Passero, "Ethnicity in the Men's Ready-Made Clothing Industry, 1880– 1950: The Italian Experience in Philadelphia" (Ph.D. dissertation, University of Pennsylvania, 1978; Carolyn Golab, *Immigrant Destinations* (Philadelphia: Temple University Press, 1978), pp. 62– 63; Yans-McLaughlin, *Family and Community*, p. 46; Ivan H. Light, *Ethnic Enterprise in American Business and Welfare Among Chinese, Japanese, and Blacks* (Berkeley: 1972), pp. 9– 10; John Modell, *The Economics and Politics of Racial Accommodation: The Japanese of Los Angeles, 1900–1942* (Urbana: University of Illinois Press, 1977), p. 9; Harry H.L. Kitano, *Japanese Americans: The Evolution of a Subculture* (Englewood Cliffs, N.J.: Prentice Hall, pp. 104– 05; Louis C. Odencrantz, *Italian Woman in Industry, A Study of Conditions in New York City* (New York, 1919), pp. 36, 60; Mary Remiga Napolska, "The Polish Immigrant in Detriot to 1914," *Annals of the Polish Roman Catholic Union Archives and Museum*, X (1945–46), 34– 35; Joseph John Parot, "The American Faith and the Persistence of Chicago Polonia, 1870–1920" (Ph.D. dissertation, Northern Illinois University, 1971), passim; Niles Carpenter, *Immigrants and Their Children* (Washington, 1927), p. 297.

11. Thomas Dublin, *Women at Work: The Transformation of Work and Community in Lowell, Massachusetts, 1826–1860* (New York: Columbia University Press, 1979), pp. 2– 3, 26, 138– 62.

12. Daniel Nelson, *Managers and Workers: Origins of the New Factory System in the United, 1880–1920* (Madison: University of Wisconsin Press, 1975), pp. 3– 5; Walter Weyl and M. Sakolski, "Conditions of Entrance to the Principal Trades," *Bulletin of the Bureau of Labor*, No. 67 (Nov., 1906), 681– 91, 714– 19; Paul H. Douglass, *American Apprenticeship and Industrial Education* (New York, 1921), pp. 75– 81; Douglass, "Is the New Immigration More Unskilled than the Old," *Quarterly Publications of the American Statistical Association* (June, 1919), 396– 97.

13. Daniel Nelson, *Managers and Workers: Origins of the New Factory System in the United States, 1880–1920*, *p.*4; U. S. Dept. of Commerce, Bureau of the Census, *Sixteenth Census of the United States: 1940: Population, Comparative Occupational Statistics for the U.S., 1970–1940* (Washington, 1943), pp. 104– 06. See also Gertrude Bancroft, *The American Labor*

Force: Its Growth and Changing Composition (New York: John Wiley, 1958), pp. 24–35; and Clarence D. Long, *The Labor Force Under Changing Income and Employment* (Princeton, N.J.: Princeton University Press, 1958).

14. Bruce Laurie, Theodore Hershberg and George Alter, "Immigrants and Industry: The Philadelphia Experience, 1850–1880," *Journal of Social History*, 11 (Winter, 1976), 241–46; Clyde and Sally Griffen, *Natives and Newcomers: The Ordering of Opportunity in Mid-Nineteenth Century Poughkeepsie* (Cambridge, Mass.: Harvard University Press, 1978), pp. 183, 281–82. For an account of declining crafts and new demands for unskilled operatives at a particular plant see Howard M. Gitelman, *Workingmen of Waltham: Mobility in American Urban Industrial Development, 1850–1890* (Baltimore, Md.: Johns Hopkins University Press, 1974), pp. 54ff. See also Isaac A. Hourwich, *Immigration and Labor* (New York: G.P. Putnam, 1912), pp. 396–413.

15. See David Montgomery, "Immigrant Workers and Managerial Reform," in *Immigrants in Industrial America*, p.98; Richard C. Edwards, Michael Reich, and David M. Gordon, eds., *Labor Market Segmentation* (Lexington, Mass.: Lexington Books, 1973), pp. xi–xiii. Montgomery has argued that the new stress on efficiency and production at the expense of skills caused twentieth-century rank-and-filers to forge a "new unionism" which sought to initiate struggles for a greater control of production on the part of workers.

16. See Herbert Gutman, *Work, Culture, and Society in Industrializing America* (New York: Vintage Books, 1976), 5–41; Thomas Kessner, *The Golden Door: Italian and Jewish Immigrant Mobility in New York City, 1880–1915* (New York: Oxford University Press, 1977), pp. 24–44; Yans-McLaughlin, *Family and Community*, p. 36.

17. Caroline Golab, *Immigrant Destinations*, pp. 5–6. Jews may be an exception to this premise since they frequently were able to implement pre-migration skills; see Arcadius Kahan, "Economic Opportunity and Some Pilgrims' Progress: Jewish Immigrants from Eastern Europe in the U.S., 1890–1914," *Journal of Economic History*, XXXVIII (Mar., 1978), 237–45.

18. Susan E. Hirsch, *Roots of the American Working-Class: The Industrialization of Crafts in Newark, 1800–1860* (Philadelphia: University of Pennsylvania Press, 1978), pp. 47–50.

19. Berthoff, *British Immigrants in Industrial America, 1790–1950*, pp. 31–88; Hirsch, *Roots of The American Working-Class*, pp. 47–50; Amy Zahl Gottlieb, "The Influence of British Trade Unionists on the Regulation of the Mining Industry in Illinois," *Labor History*, 19 (Summer, 1978), 397; Montgomery, *Beyond Equality: Labor and the Radical Republicans, 1862–1872* (New York: Alfred A. Knopf, 1967), p.36.

20. Daniel J. Walkowitz, *Worker City, Company Town: Iron and Cotton Worker Protest in Troy and Cohoes, New York* (Urbana: University of Illinois Press, 1978), pp. 33–38; Kathleen Neils Conzen, *Immigrant Milwaukee: Accommodation and Community in a Frontier City* (Cambridge, Mass.: Harvard University Press, 1976), p. 101; Oscar and Mary F. Handlin, *The Wealth of the American People* (New York: McGraw-Hill, 1975), p. 149; Warren C. Scoville, *Revolution in Glassmaking, Entrepreneurship and Technological Change in an American Industry, 1880–1920* (Cambridge: Harvard University Press, 1948), pp. 31–34, 120–42, 222–23. Errol Wayne Stevens, "Heartland Socialism: The Socialist Party of America in Four Midwestern Communities,

1898–1920" (Ph.D. dissertation, Indiana University, 1978), p. 64; Brecher, Lombardi, and Stackhouse, *Brass Valley*, p. 5; Korman, *Industrialization, Immigrants, and Americanization*, pp. 24–25.

21. Vecoli, "Chicago's Italians," pp. 7–15; Mormino, "The Hill Upon the City," pp. 90, 138–54; Fenton, *Immigrants and Unions: A Case Study*, p. 37.

22. Joseph Stipanovich, "In Unity is Strength: Immigrant Workers and Immigrant Intellectuals and Progressive America: A History of the South Slav Social Democratic Movement, 1900–1918" (Ph.D. dissertation, University of Minnesota, 1978), p.128; Vera Laska, *The Czechs in America, 1633–1977* (Dobbs Ferry, N.Y.: Oceana Publications, 1978); Joseph Pauco, *75 Rokov Prvej Katolickei Slovenskej Jednoty* (Cleveland, 1965), pp. 6–9; Kahan "Economic Opportunity and Some Pilgrims' Progress: Jewish Immigrants from Eastern Europe in the U.S.," 237–45.

23. The "split-labor market" theory originated with Edna Bonacich, "A Theory of Ethnic Antagonisms: The Split Labor Market," *American-Sociological Review*, 37 (1972), 574–79; Bonacich, "A Theory of Middleman Minorities," *American-Sociological Review*, 38 (1973), 583–94. See Hilton, "The Split Labor Market and Chinese Immigration," 101; Modell, *The Economics and Politics of Racial Accommodation*, pp. 94–96; Robert Schoen, "Toward A Theory of the Demographic Implications of Ethnic Stratification," *Social Science Quarterly*, 59 (Dec., 1978), 477–78; William Petersen, "Chinese Americans and Japanese Americans," in *American Ethnic Groups*, ed. by Thomas Sowell (Washington, D.C.: Urban Institute, 1978), pp. 65–92.

24. Walter Licht, *Working For the Railroad: The Organization of Work in the Nineteenth Century* (Princeton, N.J.: Princeton University Press, 1983). Railroad shortages of labor during the period of railway construction seemed widespread. Supplies were plentiful once lines were operating. See Shergold, *Working-Class Life*, pp. 41ff.

25. Licht, *Working For the Railroad* p. 148; Korman, *Industrialization, Immigrants, and Americanizers*, pp. 28–39, 46–47; Alice Kessler-Harris, *Out To Work: A History of Wage-Earning Women in the United States* (New York: Oxford University Press, 1982), p. 161; Stanley Buder, *Pullman: An Experiment in Industrial Order and Community* (New York: Oxford University Press, 1967), p. 80; Yans-McLaughlin, *Family and Community*, pp. 43–44; Bodnar, Simon, and Weber, *Lives of Their Own*, p. 240; Vecoli, "Chicago's Italians Prior to World War I," pp. 344–46; David H. Katzman, *Seven Days a Week: Women and Domestic Service in Industrializing America* (New York: Oxford University Press, 1978), p. 70; Ross, "Finnish-American Women in Transition, 1910–1920," 244; Paul F. McGoldrick and Michael B. Tannen, "Did American Manufacturers Discriminate against Immigrants before 1914?" *Journal of Economic History* 37 (1977), 723–24.

26. The story of Mexican immigration is beginning to take shape in recent Chicano studies. See Richard Garcia, "Class Consciousness and Ideology: The Mexican Community of San Antonio, Texas: 1930–40," *Aztlan*, 9 (1978), 23–69; Albert Camarillo, *Chicanos in a Changing Society: From Mexican Pueblo to American Barrio in Santa Barbara and Southern California, 1848–1920* (Cambridge, Mass.: Harvard University Press, 1979), pp. 79–85, 89–97, 126: Cardoso, *Mexican Emigration to the United States*, pp. 22–31, 86; Mark Reisler, *By the Sweat of Their Brow: Mexican Immigrant Labor in the United States, 1900–1940* (Westport, Conn.: Greenwood, 1976); Mario T. Garcia, *Desert Immigrants: The Mexicans of El Paso, 1880–1920*

(New Haven: Yale University Press, 1981), pp. 68, 87–88; Gilberto Cardenas, "United States Immigration Policy toward Mexico: An Historical Perspective," *Chicano Law Review*, II (Summer, 1975), 66–80; Louis and Richard Parry, *A History of the Los Angeles Labor Movement* (Berkeley: University of California Press, 1963), pp. 71–73; Paul Taylor, *Mexican Labor in the United States: Chicago and the Calumet Region* (Berkeley: University of California Press, 1932), remains a valuable resource.

27. Hareven, *Family Time and Industrial Time*, pp. xi–xii, 1–5; Yans-McLaughlin, *Family and Community*, pp. 18–28; Bodnar, Simon, and Weber, *Lives of Their Own*, p. 89; Harry H.L. Kitano and Akemi Kikumura, "The Japanese-American Family," in *Ethnic Families in America*, ed. by Charles H. Mindel and Robert W. Habenstein (second edition; New York: Elsevier, 1981), pp. 41–60; Donna R. Gabaccia, "Houses and People: Sicilians in Sicily and New York" Ph.D. dissertation, University of Michigan, 1979); Maxine Schwartz Seller, ed., *Immigrant Women* (Philadelphia: Temple University Press, 1981); John C. Holley, "The Two-Family Economics of Industrialization: Factory Workers in Victorian Scotland," *Journal of Family History* 6 (Spring, 1981), 57–69.

28. Bodnar, Simon and Weber, *Lives of Their Own*, p. 189; Hareven, *Family Time and Industrial Time*, pp. 90–95.

29. Bodnar, Simon, and Weber, *Lives of Their Own*, p. 95.

30. Bodnar, *Workers' World: Kinship, Community and Protest in an Industrial Society* (Baltimore, Md.: Johns Hopkins University Press, 1982), p. 28.

31. Ibid., pp. 174–75; Hareven, *Family Time and Industrial Time*, p. 73.

32. Bodnar, *Workers' World*, p. 175.

33. Ibid., p. 176; Tentler, *Wage-Earning Women: Industrial Work and Family Life in the United States, 1900–1930*, pp. 74, 87–90; Dino Cinel, *From Italy to San Francisco: The Immigrant Experience* (Stanford, Calif.: Stanford University Press, 1982), pp. 194-95; Hasia Diner, *Erin's Daughters in America* (Baltimore, Md.: Johns Hopkins University Press, 1983), pp. 110–15.

34. Steven Dubnoff, "The Family and Absence from Work: Irish Workers in a Lowell, Massachusetts, Mill" (Ph.D. dissertation, Brandeis University, 1976), pp. 52–66; Hareven, *Family Time and Industrial time*, p. 117, also suggests that movement to industrial cities may have revived the authority of rural families.

35. Kitano and Kikomura, "The Japanese-American Family," pp. 42–52.

36. Kathleen Conzen, *Immigrant Milwaukee, 1836–1860* (Cambridge, Mass.: Harvard University Press, 1976), p. 73; Bodnar, "Beyond Ethnicity: Polish Generations in Industrial America," in *The Polish Presence in Canada and America*, ed. by Frank Renkiewicz (Toronto: Multicultural Historical Society of Ontario, 1982), p. 145; John Briggs, *An Italian Passage* (New Haven, Conn.: Yale University Press, 1978), p. 107.

37. Richard M. Bernard, *The Melting Pot and the Altar: Marital Assimilation in Early Twentieth-Century Wisconsin* (Minneapolis: University of Minnesota Press, 1980), pp. 117–24; Kitano and Kikumura, "The Japanese-American Family," 44–46; Cinel, *From Italy to San Francisco* p. 170; R.A. Burchell, *The San Francisco Irish, 1848–1880* (Berkeley: University of California Press, 1980), pp. 84–85; Bodnar, *Immigration and Industrialization: Ethnicity in an American Mill Town, 1870–1940* (Pittsburgh: University of Pittsburgh Press, 1977), p. 131.

38. Dubnoff, "The Family and Absence from Work," pp. 254–58; Claudia Goldin, "Family Strategies and the Family Economy in the Late Nineteenth Century; The Role of Secondary Workers," in *Philadelphia*, ed. by Theodore Hershberg (New York: Oxford University Press, 1981), pp. 284–304; Hareven, *Family Time and Industrial Time*, pp. 207–12; Karen Mason, Maris Vinovskis, and Tamara Hareven, "Women's Work and the Life Course in Essex County, Massachusetts, 1880," in *Transitions: The Family and Life Course in Historical Perspectives*, ed. by Hareven (New York: Academic Press, 1978), pp. 187–216.

39. Bodnar, "Schooling and the Slavic American Family," in *American Education and the European Immigrant*, ed. by Bernard J. Weiss (Urbana: University of Illinois Press, 1982), p. 86; Frances H. Early, "The French-Canadian Family Economy and the Standard of Living in Lowell, Massachusetts, 1870," *Journal of Family History*, 7 (Summer, 1982), 191; Barrett, "Work and Community in the 'Jungle,'" pp. 187–90; Oliver Zunz, *The Changing Face of Inequality: Industrial Development, and Immigrants in Detroit, 1880–1920* (Chicago: University of Chicago Press, 1982), pp. 220–34.

40. Harris, *Out to Work: A History of Wage-Earning Women in the United States*, p. 110; Hirsch, *Roots of the American Working-Class*, p. 58; Zunz, *The Changing Face of Inequality*, pp. 75–79; Cinel, *From Italy to San Francisco*, p. 183; Mark J. Stern, "Differential Fertility in Rural Erie County, New York, 1855," *Journal of Social History*, 16 (Summer, 1983), 49–64; Maris A. Vinovskis, "Socio-Economic Determinants of Interstate Fertility Differentials in the United States in 1850 and 1860," *Journal of Interdisciplinary History*, 6 (1976), 375–96.

41. Michael Haines, *Fertility and Occupations: Population Patterns in Industrialization* (New York: Academic Press, 1979), pp. 126–36, 245–48.

42. Tentler, *Wage-Earning Women: Industrial Work and Family Life in the United States*, pp. 59, 137–38, 142; Joan Younger Dickinson, *The Role of the Immigrant Women in the U.S. Labor Force, 1890–1910* (New York: Arno Press, 1980), pp. 1, 58, 122; Hareven, *Family Time and Industrial Time*, p. 190; Smith, "Remaking Their Lives: Italian and Jewish Immigrant Family, Work, and Community in Providence, Rhode Island, 1900–1940," p. 60; Joseph John Parot, "The 'Serdeczna Matko' of the Sweatshops: Martial and Family Crises of Immigrant Working Class Women in Late-Nineteenth Century Chicago," in *The Polish Presence in Canada and America*, ed. by Frank Renkiewicz (Toronto: Multicultural Historical Society of Ontario, 1982), pp. 155–84.

43. Ellen Horgan Biddle, "The American Catholic Irish Family," in *Ethnic Families in America*, ed. by Mindell and Habenstein, p. 95; Hareven, *Family Time and Industrial Time*, p. 198; Robert E. Kennedy, Jr., *The Irish: Emigration, Marriage, and Fertility* (Berkeley: University of California Press, 1973), pp. 7–9, 59–60; Diner, *Erin's Daughters in America*, p. 74.

44. Biddle, "The American Catholic Irish Family," pp. 94–96; Seller, ed., *Immigrant Women*, pp. 47–51; Cinel, *From Italy to San Francisco*, pp. 87–105, 107, 178–79; George A. Kourvetaris, "The Greek-American Family," in *Ethnic Families in America*, ed. by Mindell and Habenstein, pp. 178–79. Yans-McLaughlin, *Family and Community*, p. 92. See Christine Stansell, "Women, Children, and the Uses of the Streets: Class and Gender Conflict in New York City, 1850–1880," *Feminist Studies*, 8 (Summer, 1982), 309–35.

45. Hareven, *Family Time and Industrial Time*, pp. 202–05; Seller, ed.

Immigrant Women, pp. 86–122; Katzman, *Seven Days a Week: Women and Domestic Service in Industrializing America*, pp. 49–51; David Montgomery, *Workers' Control in America* (Cambridge, England: Cambridge University Press, 1979), p.39; Saloutos, "Causes and Patterns of Greek Emigration to the United States," p. 120. Garcia, *Desert Immigrants: The Mexicans of El Paso*, p. 91; Kessler-Harris, *Out to Work: A History of Wage-Earning Women*, pp. 123–27, 143; Yans-McLaughlin, *Family and Community*, p. 193; Julianna Puskás, *From Hungary to the United States, 1880–1914* (Budapest, Hungary: Akadémiai Kiadó, 1982), p. 142.

46. Diner, *Erin's Daughters in America*, pp. 70–75; Hareven, *Family Time and Industrial Time*, p. 78; Moses Rischin, *The Promised City: New York Jews, 1870–1914* (New York: Harper and Row, 1962), pp. 60–61, 81; William Toll, *The Making of an Ethnic Middle Class: Portland Jewry Over Four Generations* (Albany: SUNY Press, 1982), pp. 42–76; Bodnar, *Anthracite People: Families, Unions, and Work* (Harrisburg: Pennsylvania Historical and Museum Commission, 1983), p. 8.

47. Susan Kleinberg, "Technology and Women's Work: The Lives of Working Class Women in Pittsburgh, 1870-1900," *Labor History*, 17 (Winter, 1976), 71; Kessler-Harris, *Out to Work: A History of Wage-Earning Women in the United States*, p. 128.

48. Bodnar, Simon, and Weber, *Lives of Their Own*, pp. 98–100; Bodnar, *Workers' World*, pp. 48, 59; Bodnar, *Anthracite People*, pp. 11, 31.

49. Kourvetaris, "The Greek American Family," p. 176; Seller, ed., *Immigrant Woman*, p. 119, 137; Bodnar, *Anthracite People*, p. 13; Puskás, *From Hungary to the United States, 1880–1914*, p. 151; Brecher, Lombardi, and Stackhouse, *Brass Valley*, p.28; Fenton, *Immigrants and Unions, A Case Study: Italians and American Labor, 1870-1920*, p. 26; Phyllis Williams, *South Italian Folkways* (New York: Russell and Russell, 1938); Ross, *Finnish-American Women in Transition*, pp. 251–52; Hoglund, *Finnish Immigrant in America*, Safia F. Haddad, "The Women's Role in the Socialization of Syrian-Americans in Chicago," in *The Arab Americans: Studies in Assimilation*, ed. by Elain C. Habopian and Add Paden (Wilmette, Ill.: Medina University Press, 1969); Melford S. Weiss, *Valley City: A Chinese Community in America* (Cambridge, Mass.: Schenkman, 1974, p.77.

50. Herbert G. Gutman, *Work, Culture, and Society in Industrializing America* (New York: Vintage, 1976), p.77; Hareven, *Family Time and Industrial Time*, p.163; Conzen, *Immigrant Milwaukee*, pp. 52–56; Zunz, *The Changing Face of Inequality*, p.243; Bodnar, Simon, and Weber, *Lives of Their Own*, pp. 104–05; Yans-McLaughlin, *Family and Community*, pp. 64–65; Stanley Nadel, Kleindeutschland: New York City Germans, 1845–1880" (Ph.D. dissertation, Columbia University, 1981), pp. 171–72.

51. Hareven and John Modell, "Urbanization and the Malleable Household," *Journal of Marriage and the Family* (Aug., 1973), 467–77; Barrett, "Work and Community in the 'Jungle': Chicago's Packing-House Workers," p. 173; Gabaccia, "Sicilians in Space: Environmental Change and Family Geography," *Journal of Social History*, 16 (Winter, 1982), 53–66; Zunz, *The Changing Face of Inequality*, pp. 72–73.

CHAPTER 3

Workers, Unions, and Radicals

1. Anthony Coelho, "A Row of Nationalities: Life in a Working-Class Community: the Irish, English, and French-Canadians of Fall River, Massachusetts, 1850–1890" (Ph. D. dissertation, Brown University, 1980), pp. 152–62; Kathleen Conzen, *Immigrant Milwaukee: Accommodation and Community in a Frontier City* (Cambridge, Mass.: Harvard University Press, 1976), pp.111–13; Rowland Tappan Berthoff, *British Immigrants in Industrial America, 1790–1950* (Cambridge: Harvard University Press, 1953), p. 101.

2. Coelho, "A Row of Nationalities: Life in a Working-Class Community," pp. 172–73; Berthoff, *British Immigrants in Industrial America*, pp. 89–101.

3. Hartmut Keil, "The German Immigrant Working Class of Chicago, 1875–1890: Workers, Labor Leaders and the Labor Movement," in *American Labor and Immigration History, 1870–1920's: Recent European Research*, ed. by Dirk Hoerder (Urbana: University of Illinois Press, 1983), pp. 156–75. See also David Montgomery, *Beyond Equality: Labor and the Radical Republicans, 1862–1872* (New York: Alfred A. Knopf, 1967), p. 38; Warren C. Scoville, *Revolution in Glassmaking, Entrepreneurship and Technological Change in American Industry, 1880–1920* (Cambridge, Mass.: Harvard University Press, 1948), pp. 77–120; John Rowe, *The Hard-Rock Men: Cornish Immigrants and the North American Mining Frontier* (New York: Barnes and Noble, 1974), p. 274, for other examples of immigrants creating their own forms of labor organizations and activities.

4. Judith Ellen Smith, "Remaking Their Lives: Italian and Jewish Immigrant Family, Work, and Community in Providence, Rhode Island, 1900–1940" Ph.D., dissertation, Brown University, 1980), pp. 221–23.

5. Amy Zahl Gottlieb, "The Influence of British Trade Unionists on the Regulation of the Mining Industry in Illinois, 1872," *Labor History*, 19 (Summer, 1978), 397–400; Sally M. Miller, *The Radical Immigrant* (New York: Twayne, 1974), p. 103.

6. Steve Fraser, "Dress Rehearsal for the New Deal: Shop-Floor Insurgents, Political Elites, and Industrial Democracy in the Amalgamated Clothing Workers," in *Working-Class America*, ed. by Michael H. Frisch and Daniel J. Walkowitz (Urbana: University of Illinois Press, 1983), pp. 228–40. Edward Shorter and Charles Tilly, *Strikes in France, 1830–1968* (Cambridge, Mass.: Harvard University Press, 1974), felt that more sophisticated worker communities and organizations had to be established before strikes could be effective.

7. Daniel J. Walkowitz, *Worker City, Company Town: Iron and Cotton Worker Protest in Troy and Cohoes, New York, 1855–84* (Urbana: University of Illinois Press, 1978), pp. 9–31.

8. Ibid., pp. 101–37.

9. Henry B. Leonard, "Ethnic Cleavage and Industrial Conflict in Late 19th Century America: The Cleveland Rolling Mill Company Strikes of 1881 and 1885," *Labor History*, 20 (Fall, 1979), 542–48; Michael Allen Gordon, "Studies in Irish and Irish-American Thought and Behavior in Gilded Age New York City" (Ph. D. dissertation, University of Rochester, 1977), pp.

354–68; Nancy Scheper-Hughes, "Inheritance of the Meek: Land, Labor, and Love in Western Ireland," *Marxist Perspectives*, 5 (1979), 46–77. See Joshua B. Freeman, "Catholics, Communists, and Republicans: Irish Workers and the Organization of the Transport Workers' Union," in *Working-Class America*, ed. by Frisch and Walkowitz, pp. 256–60.

10. Gordon, "Studies in Irish and Irish-American Thought and Behavior," pp. 368–450.

11. Ibid., pp. 451–510; Montgomery, *Beyond Equality*, pp. 38–39.

12. Zeese Papanikolas, *Buried Unsung: Louis Tickas and the Ludlow Massacre* (Salk Lake City: University of Utah Press, 1982), pp. 71–79; Victor Greene, *The Slavic Community on Strike* (Notre Dame, Ind.: Notre Dame University Press, 1968), pp. 135–40. See Michael Nash, *Conflict and Accommodation: Coal Miners, Steelworkers, and Socialism, 1890–1920* (Westport, Conn.: Greenwood Press, 1982).

13. John Bodnar, *Anthracite People: Families, Unions and Work* (Harrisburg: Pennsylvania Historical and Museum Commission, 1983), pp. 4–6.

14. Ibid., p. 8.

15. Gerald Rosenblum, *Immigrant Workers* (New York: Basic Books, 1973), pp.130–38; Greene, *Slavic Community on Strike*.

16. Patricia Ann Cooper, "From Hand Craft to Mass Production: Men, Women, and Work Culture in American Cigar Factories, 1900–1919" (Ph. D. dissertation, University of Maryland, 1981), pp. 191–213.

17. Scoville, *Revolution in Glassmaking*, p. 228. Errol Wayne Stevens, "Heartland Socialism: The Socialist Party of America in Four Midwestern Communities, 1898–1920" (Ph. D. dissertation, Indiana University, 1978), p. 63.

18. Susan E. Hirsch, *Roots of the American Working-Class: The Industrialization of Crafts in Newark, 1800–1860* (Philadelphia: University of Pennsylvania Press, 1978), pp. 110–23.

19. Bruce Laurie, *Working People of Philadelphia, 1800–1850* (Philadelphia: Temple University Press, 1980), pp. 138–59.

20. Montgomery, "The Shuttle and the Cross: Weavers and Artisans in the Kennsington Riots of 1844," *Journal of Social History*, 5 (Summer, 1972), 411–46.

21. John T. Cumbler, *Working-Class Community in Industrial America: Work, Leisure and Struggle in Two Industrial Cities, 1880–1930* (Westport, Conn.: Greenwood Press, 1979), pp. 195–97.

22. Leonard, "Ethnic Cleavage and Industrial Conflict in Late 19th Century America," 526–40.

23. Colomba M. Furio, "Immigrant Women and Industry, A Case Study: The Italian Immigrant Women and the Garment Industry, 1880–1950" (Ph. D. dissertation, New York University, 1979), pp. 156–60; Ralph Mann, *After the Gold Rush: Society in Grass Valley and Nevada City, California, 1849–1870* (Stanford, Calif.: Staford University Press, 1982), pp. 178–79; David Brody, *Steelworkers in America: The Nonunion Era* (Cambridge, Mass.: Harvard University, Press, 1960), pp. 96–108, 247–48; Arthur F. Corwin, "Causes of Mexican Emigration to the United States: A Summary View," *Perspectives in American History*, VII (1973), 557–635.

24. Tamara K. Hareven, *Family Time and Industrial Time* (Cambridge, England: Cambridge University Press, 1982), pp. 146–50; John Bodnar, *Im-*

migration and Industrialization: Ethnicity in an American Mill Town (Pittsburgh: University of Pittsburgh Press, 1977), pp. 120–40; Bodnar, *Workers' World: Kinship, Community and Protest in an Industrial Society* (Baltimore, Md.: Johns Hopkins University Press, 1982), pp. 75–87; David Montgomery, *Workers' Control in America: Studies in the History of Work, Technology, and Labor Struggles* (Cambridge, England: Cambridge University Press, 1979), pp. 42–43; Barbara M. Posadas, "The Hierarchy of Labor and Psychological Adjustment in an Industrial Environment: Filipinos, The Pullman Company and the Brotherhood of Sleeping Car Porters," *Labor History*, 23 (Summer, 1982), 359–60; Mann, *After the Gold Rush*, pp. 183–84; Cooper, "From Hard Craft to Mass Productions: Men, Women, and Culture in American Cigar Factories," p. 254; Scoville, *Revolution in Glassmaking*, describes the resistance of skilled immigrant glassmakers.

25. Stephen Meyer, *The Five-Dollar Day: Labor Management and Social Control in the Ford Motor Company, 1908–1921* (Albany: SUNY Press, 1981), pp. 79–85; Hareven, *Family Time and Industrial Time*, pp. 218–19, found that the Amoskeag textile mills in New Hampshire had to hire 24,000 workers a year to maintain a work force of 13,700.

26. Meyer, *The Five-Dollar Day*, pp. 102–26.

27. Montgomery, *Workers' Control in America*, pp. 32–33; Stuart D. Brandes, *American Welfare Capitalism, 1880–1940* (Chicago: University of Chicago Press, 1976), pp. 59–60, 116–23; Gerd Korman, *Industrialization, Immigrants and Americanizers: The View from Milwaukee* (Madison: State Historical Society of Wisconsin, 1967), pp. 144–64; Bodnar, *Immigration and Industrialization*, pp. 99–100.

28. See Edwin Fenton, *Immigrants and Unions, A Case Study: Italians and American Labor, 1870–1920* (New York: Arno Press, 1975); Brody, *Steelworkers in America*; Greene, *The Slavic Community on Strike*; Bodnar, *Immigration and Industrialization*, p. 178; Leslie Hough, "The Turbulent Spirit: Violence and Coaction among Cleveland Workers, 1877–1899" (Ph. D. dissertation, University of Virginia, 1977).

29. Robert Asher, "Union Nativism and the Immigrant Response," *Labor History*, 23 (Summer, 1982), 325–48.

30. Ibid., 337–44; Bodnar, *Immigration and Industrialization*, pp. 35–50; Montgomery, *Workers' Control in America*, p. 43. Leon Fink, *Workingmen's Democracy: The Knights of Labor and American Politics* (Urbana: University of Illinois Press, 1983), pp. 187–88; Thomas J. Suhrbur, "Ethnicity in the Formulation of the Chicago Carpenters Union, 1855–1890," in *German Workers in Industrial Chicago, 1850–1910: A Comparative Perspective*, ed. by Hartmut Keil and John B. Jentz (DeKalb: Northern Illinois University Press, 1983), 86–101.

31. Melvyn Dubofsky, *We Shall Be All: A History of the Industrial Workers of the World* (Chicago: Quadrangle Books, 1969), p. 9; Richard A. Garcia, "Class Consciousness and Ideology: The Mexican Community of San Antonio, Texas: 1930–1940," *Aztlan*, 9 (1978), 23–69; Jeremy Brecher, Jerry Lombardi, and Jan Stackhouse, *Brass Valley: The Story of Working People's Lives and Struggles in an American Industrial Region* (Philadelphia: Temple University Press, 1982), pp. 78–79; Smith, "Remaking Their Lives: Italian and Jewish Immigrant Family, Work and Community in Providence, Rhode Island, 1900–1940," p. 49; Irving Howe, *World of Our Fathers* (New York:

Simon and Schuster, 1976), pp. 108–09; Deborah Dash Moore, *At Home in America: Second Generation New York Jews* (New York: Columbia University Press, 1981), pp. 53–55.

32. James R. Barrett, "Work and Community in the Jungle: Chicago's Packing-House Workers, 1894–1922" (Ph. D. dissertation, University of Pittsburgh, 1981), pp. 2–3, 195–265, 289, 305; David Brody, *The Butcher Workmen: A Study of Unionization* (Cambridge: Harvard University Press, 1964), p. 20. Brody felt that close contact on the killing floor helped to unite various ethnic groups in butcher unions while workers in places such as steel mills were more likely to be separated. See Neil Betten, "Polish-American Steelworkers: Americanization through Industry and Labor," *Polish-American Studies*, 23 (1976), 31–42.

33. Cumbler, *Working-Class Community in Industrial America: Work, Leisure and Struggle in Two Industrial Cities, 1880–1930*, pp. 169–76. See Carl Siracusa, *A Mechanical People: Perceptions of the Industrial Order in Massachusetts, 1815–1880* (Middletown, Conn.: Wesleyan University Press, 1979), p. 164.

34. Furio, "Immigrant Women and Industry: A Case Study," pp. 162–201.

35. Julianna Puskás, *From Hungary to the United States, 1880–1914* (Budapest: Akadémiai Kiadó, 1982), p. 147; Dubofsky, *We Shall Be All*, pp. 199–204.

36. Dubofsky, *We Shall Be All*, pp. 204–09.

37. Ibid., pp. 224–235.

38. Ibid., pp. 235–42.

39. William D. Haywood, *Bill Haywood's Book: The Autobiography of William D. Haywood* (New York: International Publishers, 1919), p. 249.

40. Furio, *Immigrant Women and Industry: A Case Study*, pp 176–78; Dubofsky, *We Shall Be All*, pp. 252–85; Miller, *The Radical Immigrant*, p. 111. Ethnic leaders and ethnic cooperation emerged again in Lawrence in 1919 in an even longer strike. Again, the city's elite and conservative labor and ethnic leaders opposed the strike, while labor leaders such as Anthony Craparo spearheaded the strike; see Rudolph J. Vecoli, "Anthony Craparo and the Lawrence Strike of 1919," in *Pane e Lavoro: The Italian American Working Class*, ed. by George E. Pozzetta (Toronto: Multicultural History Society of Ontario, 1980), pp. 3–27.

41. Milton Cantor, *The Divided Left: American Radicalism, 1900–1975* (New York: Hill and Wang, 1978), pp. 27–36.

42. Michael Karni, "Finnish-American Cooperativism: The Radical Years, 1917–1930," in *Self-Help in Urban America*, ed. by Scott Cummings (Port Washington, N.Y.: Kennikat Press, 1980), pp. 146–47.

43. Miller, *The Radical Immigrant*, pp. 19–77, 116–37.

44. Bruce Laurie, *Working People of Philadelphia, 1800–1850*, pp. 162–87.

45. Sally M. Miller, "Milwaukee: Of Ethnicity and Labor," in *Socialism and the Cities*, ed. by Bruce Stave (Port Washington, N.Y.: Kennikat Press, 1975),pp. 44–50; Thomas W. Gavett, *Development of the Labor Movement in Milwaukee* (Madison: University of Wisconsin Press, 1965), pp. 27–59.

46. Miller, "Other Socialists: Native-Born and Immigrant Women in the Socialist Party of America, 1901–1917," *Labor History*, 24 (Winter, 1983), 84–102.

47. Moses Rischin, *The Promised City, New York's Jews, 1870–1914* (New

York: Harper and Row, 1962), pp. 119, 133, 145–50, 160–74; Fenton, *Immigrants and Unions, A Case Study: Italians and American Labor*, p. 466.

48. George E. Pozzetta, "Italians and the Tampa General Strike of 1910," in *Pane e Lavoro: The Italian American Working Class*, ed. by Pozzetta (Toronto: Multicultural Historical Society, 1980), pp. 29–46; Furio, "Immigrant Women and Industry: A Case Study," pp. 160–64.

49. Glenna Matthews, "An Immigrant Community in Indiana Territory," *Labor History*, 23 (Summer, 1982), 374–94. See James Green, *Grass-Roots Socialism: Radical Movements in the Southwest, 1895–1943* (Baton Rouge: Louisiana State University Press, 1978), p. 204.

50. Fenton, *Immigrants and Unions: A Case Study*, pp. 154–69, 484–85, 528.

51. Puskás, *From Hungary to the United States, 1880–1914*, pp. 157–70.

52. Joseph Stipanovich, "In Unity Is Strength: Immigrant Workers and Immigrant Intellectuals in Progressive America: A History of the South Slav Social Democratic Movement, 1900–1918" (Ph. D. dissertation, University of Minnesota, 1978), pp. 108–22; Bodnar, *Immigration and Industrialization*, pp. 192–93. For Czech workers see Milan Dostalik, "Ceske Delnicke Hnuti ve Spojenych Sta tech za Hospodarske Krize et 1873–1878," in *Začiatky Českej A Slovenskej Emigrácie do USA*, ed. by Josef Polisensky (Bratislava, Czechoslovakia: Vydaatel'stovo Slovenskej Akademie, 1970), pp. 125–64.

53. Hoglund, *Finnish Immigrants in America, 1880–1920* (Madison: University of Wisconsin Press, 1960), pp. 113–14, has argued that American Finns were more politically conscious than suggested here. Recent scholarship, however, has tended to refute this view and stress the model of "hall socialism." See P. George Hummasti, "Working-Class *Herrat*: The Role of Leadership in the Finnish-American Socialist Movement in the Pacific Northwest," in *Finnish Diaspora II: United States* (Toronto: Multicultural History Society of Ontario, 1981), pp. 175–91; Auvo Kostiainen, "For or Against Americanization? The Case of the Finnish Immigrant Radicals," in *American Labor and Immigration History, 1870–1920's: Recent European Research*, ed. by Dirk Hoerder (Urbana: University of Ilinois Press, 1983), pp. 260–69; Michael G. Karni, Matti E. Kaups and Douglas J. Ollila, Jr., eds., *The Finnish Experience in the Western Great Lakes: New Perspectives* (Vammala, Finland, 1975), 180–85; Kostiainen, *The Forging of Finnish-American Communism, 1919–1924: A Study in Ethnic Radicalism* (Turku, Finland: Turun Yliopisto, 1978), pp. 30–33; Peter Kivisto, "The Decline of the Finnish American Left, 1925–1945," *International Migration Review*, 17 (Spring, 1983), 65–94.

54. Peter R. Shergold, *Working-Class Life: The "American Standard" in Comparative Perspective, 1849–1913* (Pittsburgh: University of Pittsburgh Press, 1982), pp. 29–32; 130–40.

55. Laurie, *Working People of Philadelphia, 1800–1850*, pp. 197–202.

56. Sean Wilentz, "Artisan Republican Festivals and the Rise of Class Conclift in New York City, 1788–1837," in *Working-Class America*, ed. by Michael H. Frisch and Daniel J. Walowitz (Urbana: University of Illinois Press, 1983), pp. 37–64.

57. Rischin, *The Promised City: New York Jews*, pp. 175–80; Pozzetta, "Italians and the Tampa General Strike of 1910," p. 407; Bodnar, Simon, and Weber, *Lives of Their Own*, pp. 246–47; Hummasti, "Working-Class *Herrat*:

The Role of Leadership in Finnish-American Socialist Movement in the Pacific Northwest," p. 181.

58. James S. Lapham, "The German-Americans of New York City, 1860–1890," (Ph. D. dissertation, St. John's University, 1977), p. 72; Laurie, *Working People of Philadelphia*, p. 124; Bodnar, *Anthracite People*, p. 61.

59. Gary Gerstle, "The Mobilization of the Working Class Community: The Independent Textile Union in Woonsocket, 1931–1946," *Radical History Review*, 17 (Spring, 1978), pp. 161–67; Vecoli, "Prelates and Peasants: Italian Immigrants and the Catholic Church," *Journal of Social History*, 2 (Spring, 1969) p. 227; Mark Stolarik, "Immigration and Urbanization: The Slovak Experience, 1870–1918" (Ph. D. Dissertation: University of Minnesota, 1974), p. 81; Milos Gusiorovsky, "Frantisek Pucher-Cier Novodsky a Robotnicke hnutie," in *Začiatry Ceskej A Slovenckej Emigrácie do USA*, ed. by Josef Polisensky, pp. 190–99; Interchurch World Movement, *Public Opinion and the Steel Strike* (New York; Harcourt, Brace, 1921), p. 233.

60. Howe, *World of Our Fathers*, pp. 519–31.

61. Humbert S. Nelli, *Italians in Chicago, 1880–1930: A Study in Ethnic Mobility* (New York: Oxford University Press, 1970), pp. 162, 168.

62. See Eric Foner, *Politics and Ideology in the Age of the Civil War* (New York: Oxford University Press, 1980), pp. 169–94; Michael F. Funchion, "Irish Chicago: Church, Homeland, Politics and Class in the Shaping of an Ethnic Group, 1870–1900,: in *Ethnic Chicago*, ed. by Peter d'A. Jones and Melvin G. Holli (Grand Rapids, Mich.: Eerdmans, 1981), pp. 8–39.

63. Paul Buhle, "Debsian Socialism and the 'New Immigrant' Worker," in *Insights and Parrallels: Problems and Issues of American Social History*, ed. by Wiliam L. O'Neil (Minneapolis: Burgess, 1973), pp. 249–30l; Rosenblum, *Immigrant Workers*, pp. 151–54; Stipanovich, "In Unity Is Strength: Immigrant Workers and Immigrant Intellectuals in Progressive America," pp. 140–48, 159; Puskás, *From Hungary to the United States, 1880–1914*, p. 166; Cantor, *The Divided Left: American Radicalism, 1900–1975*, p. 33; Miller, "Milwaukee: of Ethnicity and Labor," p. 56–61.

64. See Mike Davis, "The Barren Marriage of American Labor and the Democratic Party," *New Left Review*, 124 (Nov.-Dec. 1980), p. 46.

65. See David Montgomery, *Workers' Control in America* (Cambridge, England: Cambridge University Press, 1979); Peter Friedlander, *The Emergence of a UAW Local, 1936–1939* (Pittsburgh: University of Pittsburgh Press, 1975); Michael J. Piore, *Birds of Passage: Migrant Labor and Industrial Societies* (Cambridge: Cambridge University Press, 1979), pp. 135–57.

66. Bodnar, *Workers' World*, pp. 182–83.

67. See Friedlander, *The Emergence of a UAW Local, 1936–1939*, pp. 29–31, 103–110; Ronald Schatz, "Union Pioneeers: The Founders of Local Unions at General Electric and Westinghouse, 1933–1937," *Journal of American History* 66 (December, 1979), pp. 586–602.

68. Bodnar, *Workers' World*, pp. 187–94; Montgomery, *Workers' Control in America*, pp. 4–5; Alice and Staughton Lynd, ed., *Rank and File: Personal Histories by Working-Class Organizers* (Boston: Beacon Press, 1973), pp. 1–7, 52, 69; Sidney Fine, *Sit-down: The General Motors Strike of 1936–1937* (Ann Arbor: University of Michigan Press, 1969), pp. 199–201, 272.

69. See David M. Gordon, Richard Edwards, and Michael Reich, *Segmented Work, Divided Workers: The Historical Transformation of Labor in the United States* (Cambridge, England: Cambridge University Press, 1982).

CHAPTER 4

The Rise of an Immigrant Middle Class

1. See Milton Gordon, *Assimilation in American Life: The Role of Race, Religion and National Origin* (New York: Oxford University Press, 1964), pp. 63–80.

2. Conflict in immigrant communities has been attributed to a variety of causes. Timothy Smith saw it as a result of "voluntarism" with different groups pursuing their own agendas. Victor Greene stressed the role of ethnic "opinion leaders" in generating divisiveness and John Bucowkzyk has emphasized the role of class conflict. See Smith, "Lay Initiative in the Religious Life of American Immigrants, 1880–1950," *Anonymous Americans*, ed. by Tamara Hareven (Englewood Cliffs, N.J.: Prentice-Hall, 1971), pp. 214–19. Greene, "Becoming American: The Role of Ethnic Leaders—Swedes, Poles, Italians, and Jews," in *The Ethnic Frontier*, ed. by M. Holli and P. d'A. Jones (Grand Rapids, Mich., Eerdmanns, 1977), pp. 144–45: John Bukowkzyk, "Polish Factionalism and the Formation of the Immigrant Middle Class in Brooklyn, 1880–1929," unpublished paper in author's possession. See also Kathleen Neils Conzen, *Immigrant Milwaukee: Accommodation and Community in a Frontier City* (Cambridge, Mass.: Harvard University Press, 1976), pp. 3–4; Thomas N. Brown, *Irish-American Nationalism, 1870–1890* (Philadelphia: J.B. Lippincott, 1966).

3. Moses Rischin, *The Promised City: New York's Jews, 1870–1914* (New York: Harper and Row, 1962), pp. 95–105.

4. The examples of regionalism are numerous but see Albert Camarillo, *Chicanos in a Changing Society: From Mexican Pueblo to American Barrios in Santa Barbara and Southern California, 1848–1930* (Cambridge, Mass.: Harvard University Press, 1979), pp. 187–88; Trasa Wychodzstwa, "Z Geografll Osadnichtwa i Dzialat Nosci Kaszubow W Stanach Zjednoczonych," *Studia Polonijne* 4 (Lublin, Poland, 1981), 293–303. James S. Lapham, "The German-Americans of New York City, 1860–1890" (Ph.D. dissertation, St. John's University, 1977), p. 14; Guido Dobbert, *The Disintegration of an Immigrant Community: The Cincinnati Germans, 1870–1920* (New York: Arno Press, 1980), p. 22; Dino Cinel, *From Italy to San Francisco* (Stanford, Cal.: Stanford Univ. Press, 1982), p. 212; Deborah Padgett, "Settlers and Sojourners: A Study of Serbian Adaptation in Milwaukee, Wisconsin" (Ph.D. dissertation University of Wisconsin-Milwaukee, 1979), p. 248; *Brass Valley: The Story of Working People's Lives and Struggles in an American Industrial Region*, compiled and edited by Jeremy Brecker, Jerry Lombardi, and Jan Stackhouse (Philadelphia: Temple University Press, 1982), p. 10; Andrew T. Kopan, "Greek Survival in Chicago: The Role of Ethnic Education, 1890–1980," in *Ethnic Chicago*, pp. 87–88; J.D. Gould, "European Intercontinental Emigration, 1815–1914: Patterns and Causes," *Journal of European Economic History*, 8 (Winter, 1979), 593–613; John W. Briggs, *An Italian Passage: Immigrants to Three American Cities, 1890–1930* (New Haven, Conn.: Yale University Press, 1978), p. 81; Rudolph Vecoli, "The Formation of Chicago's Little Italies," *Journal of American Ethnic History*, 2 (Spring, 1983), 5–20.

5. Dobbert, *The Disintegration of an Immigrant Community*, pp. 27–42.

6. Conzen, *Immigrant Milwaukee*, p. 154–56; Dobbert, *The Disintegration of an Immigrant Community*, p. 34.

7. Helena Znaniecki Lopata, *Polish Americans: Status Competition in an Ethnic Community* (Englewood Cliffs, N.J.: Prentice-Hall, 1976); Ewa Morawska, "The Internal Status Hierarchy in the East European Immigrant Communities of Johnstown, Pennsylvania, 1890–1930," *Journal of Social History*, 16 (Fall, 1982), 86–89.

8. Irving Howe, *World of Our Fathers* (New York: Simon and Schuster, 1976), pp. 117, 139, 154; Harold Runblom and Hans Norman, *From Sweden to America: A History of the Migration* (Minneapolis: University of Minnesota Press, 1976), 231; Edwin Fenton, *Immigrants and Unions, A Case Study: Italians and American Labor* (New York: Arno Press, 1975), p. 94.

9. Julianna Puskás, *Kivándorlo Magyarok az Egyesült Allamokban, 1880–1940* (Budapest, Hungary: Akadémiai Kiadó, 1982), pp. 120–27, 161–78.

10. Josef J. Barton, *Peasants and Strangers: Italians, Rumanians, and Slovaks in an American City, 1890–1950* (Cambridge, Mass.: Harvard University Press, 1975), pp. 75–80.

11. Edward Zivich, "From Zadruga to Oil Refinery: Croatian Immigrants and Croatian-Americans in Whiting, Indiana, 1890–1950" (Ph.D. dissertation, SUNY at Binghamton, 1977), pp. 8, 80; Milos Vujnovich, *Yugoslavs in Louisiana* (Gretna, La.: Pelican, 1974) John C. Sciranka, "Diamond Jubilee Years of the Pennsylvania Slovak Catholic Union," in *Pennsylvania Slovak Catholic Union* (Pittston, Pa., 1968), p. 24. Church fraternities in Poland actually collected funds for funerals and sickness; see William Thomas and Florian Znaniecki, "The Polish Peasant in Europe and America (2 vols; New York: Octagon, 1974), II, 1588; Stephanie O. Husek, "Slovak American Fraternal, Cultural, and Civic Organizations to 1914," in *Slovak in America* (Middletown, Pa., 1976), p. 25.

12. Thomas and Znaniecki, *The Polish Peasant in Europe and America*, II, 1588–89.

13. Humbert Nelli, *Italians in Chicago, 1880–1930: A Study in Ethnic Mobility* (New York: Oxford University Press, 1970), pp. 170–71; Josef Barton, "Eastern and Southern Europeans," *Ethnic Leadership in America*, ed. by John Higham (Balitmore, Md.: Johns Hopkins University Press, 1978), 154–59.

14. Frank Renkiewicz, "The Profits of Non-profit Capitalism: Polish Fraternalism and Beneficial Insurance in America," in *Self-Help in Urban America*, ed. by Scott Cummings (Port Washington, N.Y.: Kennikat Press, 1980), p. 117; Briggs, *An Italian Passage: Immigrants to Three American Cities*, pp. 17–24; Fenton, *Immigrants and Unions*, pp. 15–16.

15. See Nelli, *Italians in Chicago*, p. 173; Edward R. Kantowicz, "Polish Chicago: Survival through Solidarity," in *The Ethnic Frontier*, 184–85; Barton, "Eastern and Southern Europeans," 168; John Bodnar, *Immigration and Industrialization: Ethnicity in an American Mill Town* (Pittsburgh: University of Pittsburgh Press, 1977), pp. 112–20.

16. See Sciranka, "Diamond Jubilee Year of the Pennsylvania Slovak Catholic Union," p. 24; *Ukrainian Workingmen's Association* (Scranton, Pa.: Ukrainian Workingmen's Association, 1961), pp. 198–99; Joseph Stipanovich, "In Unity Is Strength: Immigrant Workers in Progressive America: A History of the South Slav Social Democratic Movement, 1900–1918" (Ph.D. dissertation, University of Minnesota, 1978), pp. 5–6.

17. Vujnovich, *Yugoslavs in Louisiana*, 145–56.

18. Barton, "Eastern and Southern Europeans," pp. 161–69; Vujnovich, Yugoslavs in Louisiana, pp. 150–82; Dobbert, The Disintegration of an Immigrant Community, pp. 280–82.

19. Renkiewkz, "The Profits of Non-profit Capitalism: Polish Fraternalism and Beneficial Insurance in America," p. 125.

20. William Toll, "Mobility, Fraternalism, and Jewish Cultural Change: Portland, 1910–1930," in The Jews of the West: The Metropolitan Years, ed. by Moses Rischin (Waltham, Mass.: American Jewish Historical Society, 1979), pp. 86–106.

21. Samuel L. Bailey, "The Adjustment of Italian Immigrants in Buenos Aires and New York, 1870–1914," American Historical Review, 88 (Apr., 1983), 304–05; George E. Pozzetta, "The Italians of New York City, 1890–1914" (Ph.D. dissertation, University of North Carolina, 1971); Nelli, Italians in Chicago, p. 157; Cinel, From Italy to San Francisco, p. 225; Vera Laska, The Czechs in America, 1633–1977 (Dobbs Ferry, N.Y.: Oceana, 1978), p. 36.

22. Wasyl Halich, Ukrainians in the United States (Chicago, 1937), p. 80; Victor Greene, "Becoming American: The Role of Ethnic Leaders—Swedes, Poles, Italians, and Jews," 155.

23. Konstantin Čulen, Dejiny Slovakov Amerike (2 vols; Bratislava, Czechoslovakia, 1942), I, 197; Fifty Years of the First Catholic Slovak Union (Cleveland, Ohio, 1942), pp. 72–73.

24. See Edward R. Kantowicz, Polish-American Politics, pp. 35–36, 70; Angela T. Pienkos, A Brief History of Federation Life Insurance of America, 1913–1976 (Milwaukee: Haertlein Graphics, 1976); Victor Greene, For God and Country, pp. 130–38.

25. Walter C. Warzeski, Byzantine Rite Rusins in Carpatho-Ruthenia and America (Pittsburgh, Pa., 1971), pp. 112–113; Nelli, Italians in Chicago, p. 105; Halich, Ukrainians in the United States; Zivich, "From Zadruga to Oil Refinery," p. 82.

26. John Bodnar, "Ethnic Fraternal Benefit Associations: Their Historical Development, Character and Significance," in Records of Ethnic Fraternal Benefit Associations in the United States: Essays and Inventories (St. Paul, Minn.: Immigration History Research Center, 1981), pp. 5–14.

27. Thomas and Znaniecki, The Polish Peasant in Europe and America, 1577, 1588; Kantowicz, Polish-American Politics in Chicago, 1888–1940 (Chicago: University of Chicago Press, 1975); pp. 10–11; Lopata, Polish-Americans, pp. 56–57; Peter V. Rovnianek, Zapisky za Ziva Pochovaneho (Pittsburgh, 1924); Culen, Dejiny Slovakov v Amerike, I, 201ff.; Dobbert, The Disintegration of an Immigrant Community, p. 103.

28. Michael Roman, comp., Jubilee Almanac of the Greek Catholic Union of USA (Homestead, Pa., 1967), p. 34.

29. Vujnovich, Yugoslavs in Louisiana, p. 164; Roman, Jubilee Almanac of the Greek Catholic Union of USA, 50–53.

30. Renkiewkz, "The Profits of Non-profit Capitalism: Polish Fraternalism and Beneficial Insurance in America," p. 127.

31. Bodnar, "Ethnic Fraternal Benefit Associations: Their Historical Development, Character and Significance," 5–14; Radnik, Oct. 31, 1928, p. 1; Interchurch World Movement, Public Opinion and the Steel Strike (New York, 1921), pp. 221–41.

32. Muriel Sheppard, Cloud By Day: The Story of Coal, Coke and People

(Chapel Hill: University of North Carolina Press, 1947), p. 108; John Bodnar, Roger Simon, Michael Weber, *Lives of Their Own: Blacks, Italians, and Poles in Pittsburgh* (Urbana: University of Illinois Press, 1982), pp. 58, 80.

33. George Prpic, *South Slavic Immigration to America* (Boston: Twayne, 1978), pp. 108–09; 181–82; Barton, "Eastern and Southern Europeans," 161–68; David Stasa, "Comparative Study of Detroit and St. Louis Sokols" (Ph.D. dissertation, St. Louis University, 1975).

34. Bodnar, "Ethnic Fraternal Benefit Associations: Their Historical Development, Character, and Significance," pp. 5–14.

35. *Macedonians in North America* (Toronto, Ontario, 1960), pp. 8–11; *Souvenir Program of the National Slovak Society, 1946* (Pittsburgh, Pa., 1974), 35–37; *Proletarec*, May 1, 1927, p. 4. See J. David Greenstone, "Ethnicity, Class, and Discontent: The Case of Polish Peasant Immigrants," *Ethnicity*, 2 (1975), p. 8.

36. *American Srobobran*, Aug. 26, 1933, p. 26; "Program, Ukrainian Chorus, 1932," Yaremko Papers, Immigration History Research Center; *Jednota*, Feb. 12, 1936, p. 11; John C. Sciranka, *Slovaks Under the Stars and Stripes* (New York: Foreign Language Information Service, 1930), pp. 16–22.

37. *Jednota*, Jan. 13, 1937, p. 10; Jan. 4, 1939, p. 5.

38. *Zajednicar*, Oct. 16, 1940, p. 10.

39. See Dobbert, *The Disintegration of an Immigrant Community*, p. 252; Gerald J. Bobango, "The Union and League of Romanian Societies: An Assimilating Force Reviewed," *East European Quarterly*, XII (Spring, 1978), 85; Vujnovich, *Yugoslavs in Louisiana*, p. 158; Sophonisba P. Breckinridge, *New Homes for Old Americans* (New York, 1921), pp. 93–95; Angela T. Pienkos, *A Brief History of Federation Life Insurance of America, 1913–1976*, pp. 20–34.

40. Paul E. Johnson, *A Shopkeeper's Millennium: Society and Revivals in Rochester, New York, 1815–1837* (New York: Hill and Wang, 1978), pp. 20–23, 41–42.

41. Daniel J. Walkowitz, *Worker City, Company Town: Iron and Cotton Worker Protest in Troy and Cohoes, New York, 1855–84* (Urbana: University of Illinois Press, 1978), pp. 109–110, 260.

42. Clyde and Sally Griffen, *Natives and Newcomers: The Ordering of Opportunity in Mid-Nineteenth-Century Poughkeepsie* (Cambridge, Mass.: Harvard University Press, 1978), pp. 46–95. See Arno J. Mayer, "The Lower Middle Class as a Historical Problem," *Journal of Modern History*, 47 (Sept. 1975), 409–36.

43. Jenna Weissman Joselit, *Our Gang: Jewish Crime and the New York Jewish Community, 1900–1940* (Bloomington: Indiana University Press, 1983), pp. 22–23, 106–107; Francis Ianni, *A Family Business: Kinship and Social Control in Organized Crime: Italians and Syndicate Crime* (New York: Oxford University Press, 1976), pp. 66–79.

44. Stanley Nadel, "Kleindeutschland: New York City's Germans, 1845–1880" (Ph.D. dissertation, Columbia University, 1981), pp. 171–72; Dean R. Esslinger, *Immigrants and the City: Ethnicity and Mobility in a Nineteenth-Century Midwestern Community* (Post Washington, N.Y.: Kennikat Press, 1975), p. 105; Conzen, *Immigrant Milwaukee*, p. 18; Frank Serene, "Immigrant Steelworkers in the Monongahela Valley" (Ph.D. dissertation, University of Pittsburgh, 1979), pp. 85–86. Francisco A. Rosales, "Mexican Immigration to the Urban Midwest During the 1920s" (Ph.D. dis-

sertation, Indiana University, 1978), pp. 194–195; Frantisek Hrusovsky, *Slovensko-Rehole v. Amerike* (Cleveland: Slovensky Ustav Pri Opatstve, 1955), pp. 26–29, 166–76.

45. Timothy L. Smith, "New Approaches to the History of Immigration in Twentieth-Century America," *American Historical Review*, LXXI (July, 1966), 1271.

46. Mary P. Ryan, *Cradle of the Middle-Class: The Family in Oneida County, New York, 1790–1865* (Cambridge, England: Cambridge University Press, 1981) pp. 105–09. Ryan argues that revivals did not simply consolidate the cultural hegemony of industrialists but were also used for the regeneration of families so they could adopt proper modes of behavior.

47. Henry Feingold, *Zion in America* (New York: Twayne, 1974), pp. 77–78; Rischin, *The Promised City: New York's Jews*, pp. 51–56; Peter R. Decker, "Jewish Merchants in San Francisco: Social Mobility on the Uran Frontier," in *The Jews of the West: The Metropolitan Years*, ed. by Moses Rischin (Waltham, Mass.: American Jewish Historical Society, 1979), pp. 12–19; David A. Gerber, "Cutting Out Skylock: Elite Anti-Semitism and the Quest for Moral Order in the Mid-Nineteenth Century American Market Place," *Journal of American History*, 69 (Dec., 1982), pp. 615–17, 636; Michael N. Dobkowski, *The Tarnished Dream: The Basis of American Anti-Semitism* (Westport, Conn.: Greenwood Press, 1979); Toll, *The Making of an Ethnic Middle-Class: Portland Jewry Over Four Generations* (Albany: SUNY Press, 1982), pp. 17–20.

48. Briggs, *An Italian Passage: Immigrants to Three American Cities, 1890–1930* (New Haven, Conn.: Yale University Press, 1978), pp. 163–71; Demma Paoli Gumina, *The Italians of San Francisco, 1850–1930* (New York: Center for Migration Studies, 1978), pp. 143–51.

49. William De Marco, "Ethnics and Enclaves: The Italian Settlement in the North End of Boston" (Ph.D. dissertation, Boston College, 1980), pp. 138–39.

50. Lawrence A. Lovell-Troy, "Clan Structure and Economic Activity: The Case of Greeks in Small Business Enterprise," in *Self-Help in Urban America* (Port Washington, N.Y.: Kennikat, 1980), pp. 84–85.

51. Conzen, *Immigrant Milwaukee*, pp. 107–10.

52. Edna Bonacich and John Modell, *The Economic Basis of Ethnic Solidarity: Small Business in the Japanese American Community* (Berkeley: University of California Press, 1980), pp. 2–3; Ivan Light, "Asian Enterprise in America: Chinese, Japanese, and Koreans in Small Business," in *Self-Help in Urban America*, pp. 33–35.

53. Bonacich and Modell, *The Economic Basis of Ethnic Solidarity*, pp. 22–31; Ivan Light, *Ethnic Enterprise in America: Business and Welfare among Chinese, Japanese, and Blacks* (Berkeley: University of California Press, 1972).

54. Bonacich and Modell, *Economic Basis for Ethnic Solidarity*, pp. 47–63. See Harry H.L. Kitano, *Japanese Americans: The Evolution of a Sub-culture* (Englewood Cliffs, N.J.: Prentice-Hall, 1976), p. 27, claimed that a traditional expectation of many Japanese was to run their own business. Light, *Ethnic Enterprise in America*, concluded that the Japanese thrust into business originated not because of traditional values but because of the workings of traditional credit associations. Edna Bonacich argues that they

entered easy-to-liquidate trades because they wanted to return; see Bonacich, "A Theory of Middlemen Minorities," *American Sociological Review*, 38 (October, 1973), 583–94. Light, "Asian Enterprise in America," 37–43, found Koreans in Los Angeles in the 1970s overrepresented in small retail businesses because they found it difficult to get other jobs which required the ability to speak English and because they arrived with relatively high levels of capital compared, for instance, to Mexicans.

55. John Modell, *The Economics and Politics of Racial Accommodation: The Japanese of Los Angeles, 1900–1942* (Urbana: University of Illinois Press, 1977), pp. 8–10, 25; Grace Heilman Stimson, *Rise of the Labor Movement in Los Angeles* (Berkeley: University of California Press, 1955).

56. Smith, "New Approaches to the History of Immigration in Twentieth-Century America," 1270–71.

57. James F. Donnelly, "Catholic New Yorkers and New York Socialists in 1870–1920" (Ph.D. dissertation, New York University, 1982), pp. 59–60; Rowland Tappan Berthoff, *British Immigrants in Industrial America, 1790–1950* (Cambridge, Mass.: Harvard University Press, 1953), p. 177; Dennis Clark, "The Irish Catholics: A Postponed Perspective," in Randall J. Miller and Thomas J. Marzik, *Immigrants and Religion in Urban America* (Philadelphia: Temple University Press, 1977), p. 59; John W. Briggs, *An Italian Passage: Immigrants to Three American Cities, 1890–1930* (New Haven, Conn.: Yale University Press, 1978), p. 168; Julianna Puskás, *From Hungary to the United States*, pp. 173–75; Richard Garcia, "Class Consciousness and Ideology: The Mexican American Community of San Antonio, Texas: 1930–1940," *Aztlan*, 9 (1978), 42–43. Similar separations among Puerto Ricans in New York City are described in Virginia E. Sanchez Korrol, *From Colonia to Community: The History of Puerto Ricans in New York City, 1917–1948* (Westport, Conn.: Greenwood Press, 1983), p. 57.

58. Ulf Beijbom, *Swedes in Chicago: A Demographic and Social Study of the 1846–1880 Immigration* (Stockholm: Laromedelsforlagen and Chicago Historical Society, 1971), pp. 266–83.

59. R.A. Burchell, *The San Francisco Irish, 1848–1880* (Berkeley: University of California Press, 1980), p. 77.

60. Cinel, *From Italy to San Francisco*, pp. 228–30.

61. Modell, *The Economics and Politics of Racial Accommodation*, pp. 13–15; Stipanovich, "In Unity Is Strength," pp. 97–102.

62. Garcia, "Class Consciousness and Ideology: The Mexican Community of San Antonio," pp. 48–53.

63. Lapham, "The German-Americans of New York City," pp. 135–41, 156, 221.

64. Jeffrey S. Gurock, *When Harlem Was Jewish, 1870–1930* (New York: Columbia University Press, 1979), pp. 86–97, 112–13; John Higham, ed., *Ethnic Leadership in America* (Baltimore, Md.: Johns Hopkins University Press, 1978), pp. 20–21; Feingold, *Zion in America*, pp. 142–53.

CHAPTER 5

Church and Society

1. Andrew T. Kopan, "Greek Survival in Chicago: The Role of Ethnic Education, 1890–1980," in *Ethnic Chicago*, ed. by Peter d'A. Jones and Melvin G. Holli (Grand Rapids, Mich.: Eerdmans, 1981), p. 95; Rudolph J. Vecoli, "Prelates and Peasants: Italian Immigrants and the Catholic Church," *Journal of Social History*, 2 (Spring, 1969), 218.

2. Stephen Shaw, "Chicago's Germans and Italians, 1903–1939: The Catholic Parish as a Way Station of Ethnicity and Americanization" (Ph. D. dissertation, University of Chicago, 1981), p. 174. Clifford Geertz, *The Interpretation of Cultures: Selected Essays* (New York, 1973); Timothy L. Smith, "Religion and Ethnicity in America," *American Historical Review*, 83 (Dec., 1978), 1155–81; Abner Cohen, ed., *Custom and Politics in Urban Africa: A Study of Hausa Migrants in Yoruba Towns* (Berkeley: University of California Press, 1969), pp. 190–94. Charles F. Keyes argues that the belief in shared descent is crucial but an often contrived aspect of functional ethnicity in "Towards a New Formulation of the Concept Ethnic Group," *Ethnicity*, 3 (1976), 203–06. See also Vecoli, "Prelates and Peasants," 218; Michael Hechter, "The Political Economy of Ethnic Change," *American Journal of Sociology*, 79 (1974).

3. James S. Lapham, "The German-Americans of New York City, 1860–1890" (Ph.D. dissertation, St. John's University, 1977) pp. 50–62; Frederick Luebke, "The Germans," in *Ethnic Leadership in America*, ed. by John Higham (Baltimore, Md.: Johns Hopkins University Press, 1978), pp. 68–69.

4. Lapham, "The German-Americans of New York City," pp. 87–98. See Alan N. Graebner, "The Acculturation of an Immigrant Church: The Lutheran Church-Missouri Synod, 1917–1924" (Ph.D. dissertation, Columbia University, 1965), pp. 83–130.

5. Keith P. Dyrud, "The Establishment of the Greek Catholic Rite in America as a Competition to Orthodoxy," in *The Other Catholics*, ed. by Dyrud, Michael Novak, and Rudolph J. Vecoli (New York: Arno Press, 1978), pp. 190–96; Myron Bohdon Kuropas, "Ukrainian Chicago: The Making of a National Group in America," in *Ethnic Chicago*, ed. Jones and Holli, pp. 145–46; Walter Warzeski, *Byzantine Rite Rusins* (Pittsburgh, Pa.: Byzantine Seminary Press, 1971) p. 102.

6. Dyrud, "The Establishment of the Greek Catholic Rite in America as a Competition to Orthodoxy." pp. 211–21.

7. See Alan Graebner, *Uncertain Saints: The Laity in the Lutheran Church-Missouri Synod, 1900–1970* (Westport, Conn.: Greenwood Press, 1975), pp. 3–10.

8. Judith Ellen Smith, "Remaking their Lives: Italian and Jewish Immigrant Family, Work, and Community in Providence, Rhode Island, 1900–1940" (Ph. D. Dissertation, Brown University, 1980), pp. 213–14; Dolan, *The Immigrant Church*, pp. 19–20.

9. See Chrysie Mamalakis Constantakos, *The American-Greek Subculture* (New York: Arno Press, 1980); Josef Barton, *Peasants and Strangers: Italians, Rumanians, and Slovaks in an American City, 1890–1950* (Cambridge, Mass.: Harvard University Press, 1975), p. 70.

10. Ellen Horgan Biddle, "The American Catholic Irish Family," in *Ethnic Families in America*, ed: by Charles Mindell and Robert W. Habenstein (New York: Elsevier, 1976), pp. 104–06; Jay Dolan, "Philadelphia and the German Catholic Community," in *Immigrants and Religion in Urban America*, ed. by Randall Miller and Thomas D. Marzik (Philadelphia: Temple University Press, 1977), p. 71; Joseph Barton, "Religion and Cultural Change in Czech Immigrant Communities, 1850–1920, " *Immigrants and Religion in Urban America*, p. 15; R.A. Burchell, *The San Francisco Irish, 1848–1880* (Berkeley: University of California Press, 1980), pp. 92–93; Joseph Parot, *Polish Catholics in Chicago, 1850–1920* (DeKalb: Northern Illinois University Press, 1983), p. 87; Kathleen Conzen, *Immigrant Milwaukee: Accommodation and Community in a Frontier City* (Cambridge, Mass.: Harvard University Press, 1976), p. 161; Philip Gleason, *The Conservative Reformers: German-American Catholics and the Social Order* (Notre Dame, Ind.: University of Notre Dame Press, 1968), p. 90; Richard Linkh, *American Catholicism and European Immigrants, 1900–1924* (New York: Center for Migration Studies, 1975), pp. 91–97; Silvano Tomasi, *Piety and Power* (New York: Center for Migration Studies, 1975), p. 137; George A. Kourvetaris, "The Greek American Family," in *Ethnic Families in America*, p. 171.

11. Dolan, *The Immigrant Church: New York's Irish and German Catholics* (Baltimore: Johns Hopkins University Press, 1975), pp. 72–92; Lapham, "The German-Americans of New York City," p. 3: Dolan, "Philadelphia and the German Catholic Community," in *Immigrants and Religion in Urban America*, p. 71; Conzen, *Immigrant Milwaukee: Accommodation and Community in a Frontier City*, p. 161.

12. Dolan, *The Immigrant Church*, p. 71; Philip Gleason, *The Conservative Reformers: German-American Catholics and the Social Order*, pp. 32–34; Vecoli, "Peasants and Prelates," *Journal of Social History*, 2 (September, 1969), 262; Robert Cross, *The Emergence of Liberal Catholicism in America* (Chicago, 1968), pp. 29–39, 88–94.

13. Robert D. Cross, "The Irish," in *Ethnic Leadership in America*, ed. by Higham, pp. 180–84; Emmet Larkin, "The Devotional Revolution in Ireland, 1850–1875," pp. 104–06; Lawrence B. Davis, *Immigrants, Baptists, and the Protestant Mind in America* (Urbana: University of Illinois Press, 1973), p. 5; Dennis J. Clark, "The Irish Catholics: A Postponed Perspective," in Miller and Marzik, *Immigrants and Religion in Urban America*, pp. 54–59.

14. Clark, "The Irish Catholics: A Postponed Perspective," pp. 55–59; Ann Taves, "Lay Catholic Piety in Mid-Nineteenth Century America," *American Catholic Studies Newsletter*, 9 (Spring, 1983), 7–8; Larkin, "The Devotional Revolution in Ireland, 1850–75," 625–37; Dolan, *The Immigrant Church*, p. 151.

15. Stanley Nadel, "Kleindeutschland: New York City's Germans, 1845–1880" (Ph. D. dissertation, Columbia University, 1981), pp. 185–90.

16. Donna Merwick, *Boston Priests, 1848–1910: A Study of Social and Intellectual Change* (Cambridge, Mass.: Harvard University Press, 1973), pp. 7, 147, 157; Dolan, *The Immigrant Church*, pp. 164–69; Clark, "The Irish Catholics: A Postponed Perspective," p. 60; Daniel Callahan, *The Mind of the Catholic Layman* (New York: Charles Scribner, 1963), p. 29.

17. Linkh, *American Catholicism and European Immigrants, 1900–1924*, p. 104; Julianna Puskás, *Kivándorlo Magyarok az Egyesült Allamokban,*

1880–1940 (Budapest, Hungary: Akadémiai Kiadó, 1982); Tomasi, *Piety and Power*, 75–77; Monika Glettler, *Pittsburgh Wien-Budapest: Programm und Praxis der Nationalitaten politik bei der ungarischen Slowaken Nach Amerika um 1900* (Wein: Der Osterreichichischen Akademie der Wissenschaften, 1980), pp. 220–28.

18. See Lawrence D. Orton, *Polish Detroit and the Kolasinski Affair* (Detroit: Wayne State University Press, 1981), and Hieronim Kubiak, *The Polish National Catholic Church in the United States, 1897–1965* (Kraków, Poland: Naki Uniwersyetu Jagiellonskiego, 1982).

19. Tomasi, *Piety and Power*, pp. 141–48; David A. Gerber, "Modernity in the Service of Tradition: Catholic Lay Trustees at Buffalo's St. Louis Church and the Transformation of European Communal Traditions, 1829–1855," *Journal of Social History* (Summer, 1982), 655–58. See Patrick Carey, "Two Episcopal Views of Lay Clerical Conflicts, 1785–1960," *Records of the American* Catholic History Society, LLXXXVII (1976), 85–114; Edwin Fenton, *Immigrants and Unions, A Case Study: Italians and American Labor, 1870–1920* (New York: Arno Press, 1975), pp. 4–5.

20. Vecoli, "Cult and Occult in Italian American Culture: The Persistence of a Religious Heritage," in *Immigrants and Religion in Urban America*, ed. by Miller and Marzik, pp. 25–46; Dino Cinel, *From Italy to San Francisco: The Immigrant Experience* (Stanford, Calif.: Stanford University Press, 1982), p. 207; Richard Varbero, "Urbanization and Acculturation: Philadelphia's South Italians, 1918–1933" (Ph.D. dissertation, Temple University, 1975), pp. 208–12. See Davis, *Immigrants, Baptists and the Protestant Mind in America*, p. 112; Barbara Lés, "Funkcje Polskich Zborow baptystycznych w Srodowisku Polonii Amerykanskiej," *Przeglad Polonijny*, VI, No. 1 (1980), 19–32.

21. Vecoli, "Prelates and Peasants: Italian Immigrants and the Catholic Church," p. 268; Tomasi, *Piety and Power*, pp. 33, 74–120.

22. Robert P. Swierenga, "Local-Cosmopolitan Theory and Immigrant Religion: The Social Basis of Antebellum Dutch Reformed Schism," *Journal of Social History*, 14 (Fall, 1980); James D. Bratt, "The Reformed Churches in Acculturation," in *They Came to Stay: Dutch Immigration and Settlement in the Nineteenth and Twentieth Centuries*, ed. by Robert Swierenga (New Brunswick, N.J.: Rutgers University Press, forthcoming).

23. Lapham, "The German-Americans of New York City, 1860–1890," p. 98; Nadel, "Kleindeutschland: New York City's Germans, 1845–1880," pp. 193–217.

24. Conzen, *Immigrant Milwaukee*, pp. 161–70.

25. Nora Faires, "Ethnicity in Evolution: The German Community in Pittsburgh and Allegheny City, Pennsylvania, 1845–1885" (Ph.D. dissertation, University of Pittsburgh, 1981), pp. 325–52, 605–612.

26. John J. Bukowczyk, "Polish Factionalism and the Formation of the Immigrant Middle Class in Brooklyn, 1880–1919," unpublished paper in author's possession.

27. Bukowczyk, "Polish Factionalism and the Formation of the Immigrant Middle Class in Brooklyn"; Mark Stolarik, "Immigration and Urbanization: The Slovak Experience, 1870–1918" (Ph.D. dissertation, University of Minnesota, 1974), pp. 86–88, 94–95. See Milos Gosiorovsky, "Frantisek Pucher-Cernovodsky-a roboinick hnutie," in *Zacestky Ceskej a Slovenskej*

emigracie do USA, ed. by Josef Polisensky (Bratislava, Czechoslovakia, 1970), pp. 197–207.

28. Anthony J. Kuzniewski, *Faith and Fatherland: The Polish Church War in Wisconsin, 1896–1918* (Notre Dame, Ind.: University of Notre Dame Press, 1980), pp. 29–31.

29. Ibid., pp. 36–39.

30. Ibid.

31. Ibid.

32. *Kuyer Polski*, June 3, 5, 30,1896, quoted in ibid.

33. Kuzniewski, *Faith and Fatherland*, pp. 41, 43.

34. Ibid., pp. 52–57.

35. Ibid., pp. 60–70, 102.

36. Ibid., p. 102.

37. Miecislaus Haiman, *Ziednoczenie Polskie Rzymski-Katolickie W. Ameryce 1873–1948* (Chicago, 1948), pp. 25ff. See Victor Greene, *For God and Country: The Rise of Polish and Lithuanian Ethnic Consciousness in America, 1880–1910* (Madison: State Historical Society of Wisconsin, 1975), pp. 66–84.

38. Joseph John Parot, *Polish Catholics in Chicago, 1850–1920* (DeKalb: Northern Illinois University Press, 1981), pp. 36–98; Barbara Lés, *Kosciol w Procesie Asymilacji Polonii Amerykanskiej* (Warsaw: Zaklad Narodowy Imienia Ossolinskich Wydawnictwo, 1981), pp. 133–73.

39. Parot, *Polish Catholics in Chicago, 1850–1920*, pp. 71–98; Anthony J. Kuzniewski, "Wenceslaus Kruszka and the Origins of Polish Roman Catholic Separatisms in the United States," in *The Polish Presence in Canada and America*, ed. by Frank Renkiewicz (Toronto: Multicultural History Society of Ontario, 1982), pp. 97–116.

40. Parot, *Polish Catholics in Chicago, 1850–1920*, pp. 36–98.

41. S. J. Alexander, "Slovaks in Pittsburgh," unpublished paper in author's possession; Alexander, "The Immigrant Church and Community: The Formation of Pittsburgh's Slovak Religious Institutions, 1880–1914" (Ph.D. dissertation, University of Minnesota, 1980), pp. 300–37.

42. Alexander, "Slovaks in Pittsburgh."

43. Ibid.

44. Ibid.

45. Ibid.

46. Ibid.

47. See Bodnar, "Schooling and the Slavic-American Family," in *American Education and the European Immigrant*, ed. by Bernard Weiss (Urbana: University of Illinois Press, 1982), pp. 78–95.

48. Roger Daniels, "The Japanese," in *Ethnic Leadership in America*, ed. by Higham, pp. 41–44; Dirk Hoerder, "Prussian Agents Among Polish Americans, 1900–1917: A Research Note," *Polish-American Studies*, XXXVIII (Autumn, 1981), 84–88.

49. Puskás, *From Hungary to the United States* (Budapest: Akadémiai Kiadó, 1982), pp. 109–39.

50. Glettler, *Pittsburg-Wien-Budapest*, pp. 80–89, 109–39; Puskás, *From Hungary to the United States*, p. 197; Paul C. Nyholm, *The Americanization of the Danish Lutheran Churches in America* (Minneapolis: Augsburg, 1963), pp. 91–93.

CHAPTER 6

Immigrants and the Promise of American Life

1. Thomas Kessner, *The Golden Door: Italian and Jewish Mobility in New York City, 1880–1915* (New York: Oxford University Press, 1977), p. 11.

2. Kathleen Neils Conzen, *Immigrant Milwaukee: Accommodation and Community in a Frontier City* (Cambridge, Mass.: Harvard University Press, 1976), p. 73; Clyde and Sally Griffen, *Natives and Newcomers: The Ordering of Opportunity in Mid-Nineteenth Century Poughkeepsie* (Cambridge, Mass.: Harvard University Press, 1978), p. 69; Olivier Zunz, *The Changing Face of Inequality: Urbanization, Industrial Development, and Immigrants in Detroit, 1880–1920* (Chicago: University of Chicago Press, 1982), p. 37; R.A. Burchell, *The San Francisco Irish, 1848–1880* (Berkeley: University of California Press, 1980), p. 59; Stephan Thernstrom, *The Other Bostonians: Poverty and Progress in the American Metropolis, 1880–1970* (Cambridge, Mass.: Harvard University Press, 1973), p. 115; John Bodnar, Roger Simon, and Michael Weber, *Lives of Their Own: Blacks, Italians, and Poles in Pittsburgh* (Urbana: University of Illinois Press, 1982), p. 138; Ricardo Romo, *East Los Angeles: History of a Barrio* (Austin: University of Texas Press, 1983), p. 113.

3. Robert P. Swierenga, "Dutch International Migrations and Occupational Change: A Structural Analysis of Multinational Linked Files," paper presented at the Social Science History Association, Bloomington, Indiana, Nov., 1982; Griffen and Griffen, *Natives and Newcomers*, pp. 68–70; Thernstrom, *The Other Bostonians*, pp. 117–19; Thernstrom, *Poverty and Progress: Social Mobility in a Nineteenth Century City* (Cambridge, Mass.: Harvard University Press, 1964), p. 100; Kessner, *The Golden Door*, p. 114; Albert Camarillo, *Chicanos in a Changing Society: From Mexican Pueblos to American Barrios in Santa Barbara and Southern California, 1848–1930* (Cambridge, Mass.: Harvard University Press, 1979), p. 175; Romo, *East Los Angeles*, p. 123; Dean R. Esslinger, *Immigrants and the City: Ethnicity and Mobility in a Nineteenth Century Midwestern Community* (Port Washington, N.Y.: Kennikat Press, 1975), p. 82; Tamara Hareven, *Family Time and Industrial Time* (Cambridge, England: Cambridge University Press, 1982), p. 259; Gordon W. Kirk, *The Promise of American Social Mobility in a Nineteenth Century Immigrant Community, Holland, Michigan, 1847–1894* (Philadelphia: American Philosophical Society, 1978).

4. See Griffen and Griffen, *Natives and Newcomers*; Esslinger, *Immigrants and the City*; Thernstrom, *The Other Bostonians*, p. 137; Kessner, *The Golden Door*, pp. 82,80; Josef Barton, *Peasants and Strangers: Italians, Rumanians, and Slovaks in an American City, 1890–1950* (Cambridge, Mass.: Harvard University Press, 1975); Bodnar, Simon, and Weber, *Lives of Their Own*.

5. Griffen and Griffen, *Natives and Newcomers*, p. 73; Thernstrom, *The Other Bostonians*, p. 150.

6. Thernstrom, *The Other Bostonians*, p. 137; Kessner, *The Golden Door*, p. 90; Bodnar, Simon, and Weber, *Lives of Their Own*, p. 36; Mitchell Gelfand, "Progress and Prosperity: Jewish Social Mobility in Los Angeles in the Booming Eighties," in *Jews of the West: The Metropolitan Years*, ed. by Moses Rischin (Waltham, Mass.: American Jewish Historical Society, 1979), pp. 44–45.

7. Esslinger, *Immigrants and the City*, pp. 82-122; Guido Dobbert, *The Disintegration of an Immigrant Community: The Cincinnati Germans, 1870–1920* (New York: Arno Press, 1980), pp. 26-33; Griffen and Griffen, *Natives and Newcomers*, pp. 69, 169; Conzen, *Immigrant Milwaukee*, pp. 96–97; Hartmut Keil, "Chicago's German Working Class in 1900," in *German Workers in Industrial Chicago, 1850–1910*, ed. by Keil and John B. Jentz (DeKalb: Northern Illinois University Press, 1983), p. 23.

8. Barton, *Peasants and Strangers*, p. 112; Bodnar, *Immigration and Industrialization: Ethnicity in an American Mill Town* (Pittsburgh, Pa.: University of Pittsburgh Press, 1977), p. 168; Thernstrom, *The Other Bostonians*, p. 134; Griffen and Griffen, *Natives and Newcomers*, p. 72.

9. Anthony Coelho, "A Row of Nationalities: Life in a Working Class Community: the Irish, English, and French-Canadians of Fall River, Massachusetts, 1850–1890" (Ph.D. dissertation, Brown University, 1980), p. 78; Kessner, *The Golden Door*, p. 123; Barton, *Peasants and Strangers*, p. 112. See Edward P. Hutchinson, *Immigrants and Their Children* (New York: Wiley, 1956); Stanley Lieberson, *A Piece of the Pie: Blacks and White Immigrants* since 1880 (Berkeley: University of California Press, 1980).

10. Griffen and Griffen, *Natives and Newcomers*, pp. 72, 182, 193, 281–82; Thernstrom, *The Other Bostonians*, p. 97; Bruce Laurie, Theodore Hershberg, and George Alter, "Immigrants and Industry: The Philadelphia Experience, 1850–1880," *Journal of Social History*, 9 (Winter, 1975), pp. 219–67; Peter R. Decker, *Fortunes and Failures: White-Collar Mobility in Nineteenth-Century San Francisco* (Cambridge, Mass.: Harvard University Press, 1978), pp. 189–92; Gelfand, "Progress and Prosperity: Jewish Social Mobility in Los Angeles in the Booming Eighties," p. 43; Dobbert, *The Disintegration of an Immigration Community*, p. 33.

11. Thernstrom, *Poverty and Progress*, p. 96; Kessner, *The Golden Door*, p. 143; Esslinger, *Immigrants and the City*, p. 43; Conzen, *Immigrant Milwaukee*, p. 42; Bodnar, *Immigration and Industrialization*, p. 58.

12. See Ulf Beijbom, *Swedes in Chicago: A Demographic and Social Study of the 1846–1880 Immigration* (Stockholm: Laromedelsforlagen and the Chicago Historical Society, 1971), p. 131; Romo, *East Los Angeles*, p. 125.

13. Hareven, *Family Time and Industrial Time*, pp. 236–39; Coelho, "A Row of Nationalities," pp. 27–52; Camarillo, *Chicanos in a Changing Society*; Burchell, *The San Francisco Irish*, p. 34; Decker, *Fortunes and Failures*, pp. 23, 81, 170–71, 211–15; Branko Mita Colakovic, *Yugoslav Migrations to America* (San Francisco: R and E, 1973), pp. 144–45; Gary Ross Mormino, "The Hill Upon the City: An Italo-American Neighborhood in St. Louis, Missouri, 1880–1955" (Ph.D. dissertation, University of North Carolina, 1977), p. 71.

14. Ulf Beijbom, *Swedes in Chicago: A Demographic and Social Study of the 1846–1880 Immigration* (Stockholm, 1971), pp. 70–117.

15. Zunz, *The Changing Face of Inequality*, pp. 59–87.

16. Stanley Nadel, "Kleindeutschland: New York City's Germans, 1845–1880" (Ph.D. dissertation, Columbia University, 1981), pp. 58–59; Theodore Hershberg, et al., "A Tale of Three Cities: Blacks, Immigrants and Opportunity in Philadelphia, 1850–1880, 1930, 1970," in *Philadelphia*, ed. by Theodore Hershberg (New York: Oxford University Press, 1981), pp. 468–69; Dino Cinel, *From Italy to San Francisco* (Stanford, Calif.: Stanford University

Press, 1983), pp. 108–22; Albert Camarillo, *Chicanos in a Changing Society: From Mexican Pueblos to American Barrios in Santa Barbara and Southern California, 1848–1930* (Cambridge, Mass.: Harvard University Press, 1979), pp. 144–55; David Ward, *Cities and Immigrants* (New York: Oxford University Press, 1971), p. 107; Sam Bass Warner and Colin Burke, "Cultural Change and the Ghetto," *Journal of Contemporary History*, 4 (October, 1969), pp. 173–77; Thomas Philpott, *The Slum and the Ghetto* (New York: Oxford University Press, 1978), pp. 141–43.

17. Hershberg, et al., "A Tale of Three Cities," pp. 473–74; Zunz, *The Changing Face of Inequality*, pp. 60–87.

18. See Edwin Fenton, *Immigrants and Unions: A Case Study: Italians and American Labor, 1870–1920* (New York: Arno Press, 1975), pp. 40–41; Rudolph J. Vecoli, "Chicago's Italians Prior to World War I" (Ph.D. dissertation, University of Wisconsin, 1963), pp. 156–66, 186.

19. Jeffrey S. Gurock, *When Harlem was Jewish, 1870–1930* (New York: Columbia University Press, 1979), pp. 6–65; Deborah Dash Moore, *At Home in America: Second Generation New York Jews* (New York: Columbia University Press, 1981), p. 76.

20. Jeremy Brecher, Jerry Lombardi, and Jan Stackhouse, *Brass Valley: The Story of Working People's Lives and Struggles in an American Industrial Region* (Philadelphia: Temple University Press, 1982), pp. 30–31; Bodnar, Simon, and Weber, *Lives of Their Own* pp. 72–80; Camarillo, *Chicanos in a Changing Society*, pp. 147–53; Conzen, *Immigrant Milwaukee*, p. 145; Moore, *At Home in America*, pp. 61–65, 87; Judith Ellen Smith, "Remaking Their Lives: Italian and Jewish Immigrant Family, Work, and Community in Providence, Rhode Island, 1900–1940" (Ph.D. dissertation, Brown University 1980), pp. 150–52; James Borchert, "Urban Neighborhood and Community: Informal Group Life, 1850–1870," *Journal of Interdisciplinary History*, XI (Spring, 1981), pp. 608, 817. Christiane Harzig, "Chicago's German Northside, 1880–1900: The Structure of a Gilded Age Ethnic Neighborhood," in *German Workers in Industrial Chicago, 1850–1910*, ed. by Keil and Jents, p. 142.

21. Robert G. Barrows, "Beyond the Tenement: Patterns of American Urban Housing, 1870–1930," *Journal of Urban History*, 9 (Aug., 1983), pp. 402–18.

22. Roger D. Simon, "The City-Building Process: Housing and Services in New Milwaukee Neighborhoods, 1880–1910," *Transactions of the American Philosophical Society*, 68 (July, 1978); Thernstrom, *Poverty and Progress*, pp. 117, 156–57; Conzen, *Immigrant Milwaukee*, p. 78; Zunz, *The Changing Face of Inequality*, pp. 152–53; Barton, *Peasants and Strangers*, pp. 102; Bodnar, Simon, and Weber, *Lives of Their Own*, p. 256; Kenneth T. Jackson "The Spatial Dimension of Social Control: Race, Ethnicity, and Government Housing Policy in the United States, 1916–1968," in *Modern Industrial Cities: History, Policy, and Survival*, ed. by Bruce Stave (Beverly Hills, Calif.: Sage, 1981), pp. 79–128; James A. Barrett, "Work and Community in the 'Jungle': Chicago's Packing House Workers, 1894–1922" (Ph.D. dissertation, University of Pittsburgh, 1981), p. 180; Stanley Buder, *Pullman: An Experiment in Industrial Order and Community* (New York: Oxford University Press, 1967), pp. 81–82; Daniel Luria, "Wealth, Capital and Power: The Social Meaning of Home Ownership," *Journal of Interdisciplinary History*, 7 (Autumn, 1976), 278.

23. Bodnar, Simon, and Weber, *Lives of Their Own*, pp. 160–67; Frank Renkiewicz, "The Profits of Non-Profit Capitalism: Polish Fraternalism and Beneficial Insurance in America," in *Self-Help in Urban America* ed. by Scott Cummings (Port Washington, N.Y.: Kennikat, 1980), pp. 122–27; Burchell, *The San Francisco Irish*, pp. 41–45; Zunz, *The Changing Face of Inequality*, pp. 170–71.

24. Homeownership at the expense of children's education is suggested in Thernstrom, *Poverty and Progress: Social Mobility in a Nineteenth Century City*, pp. 154–57; David Hogan, "Education and the Making of the Chicago Working Class, 1880–1930," *History of Education Quarterly*, 18 (Fall, 1978), 244. The Providence study was described in Joel Perlmann, "Working Class Homeownership and Children's Schooling in Providence, Rhode Island, 1880–1905," *History of Education Quarterly*, 23 (Summer, 1983), 175–93.

25. James K. Benson, "Irish and German Families and the Economic Development of Midwestern Cities, 1860–1895: St. Paul, Minnesota, as a Case Study" (Ph.D. dissertation, University of Minnesota, 1980), pp. 384–85; Jeffrey G. Williamson, *Late Nineteenth Century American Development: A General Equilibrium History* (London, England: Cambridge University Press, 1974), p.221; B. Block, R. Fels, and M. McMahon, "Housing Surplus in the 1920s?" *Explorations in Economic History*, 8 (Spring, 1971), 259–83.

26. Bodnar, Simon, and Weber, *Lives of Their Own*, pp. 153–55; Zunz, *The Changing Face of Inequality*, p. 153; Donna R. Gabaccia, *From Italy to Elizabeth Street: Housing and Social Change Among Italian Immigrants, 1880-1930* (Albany: SUNY Press, 1983). In a study of Czech farmers and Mexican laborers in Texas between 1880 and 1930, Josef Barton discovered Czech families pursued the acquisition of property while Mexicans, with links to families in Mexico, wandered as laborers, a suggestion that property loomed large as an extension of family interests among permanent settlers. See "Land, Labor, and Community in Nueces," in *Ethnicity on the Great Plains*, ed. by Frederick C. Luebke, (Lincoln: University of Nebraska Press, 1980), pp.190–209.

CHAPTER 7

America on Immigrant Terms: Folklife, Education, and Politics

1. Lawrence W. Levine, *Black Culture and Black Consciousness* (New York: Oxford, 1977), pp. 63, 445. For views of "living culture" as opposed to "traditional culture" see Robert B. Klymasz, "From Immigrant to Ethnic Folklore: A Canadian View of Process and Transition," *Journal of the Folklore Institute*, X (Dec., 1973), pp. 131–40; Richard Bauman, "Differential Identity and the Social Base of Folklore," *Journal of American Folklore*, 84 (Jan.-Mar., 1971), pp. 31–41; Richard Dorson, *American Folklore* (Chicago: University of Chicago Press, 1959), pp. 137–41; Dorson, "Is There a Folk in the City," in *The Urban Experience and Folk Traditions*, ed. by A. Paredes and E. Stekert (Austin: University of Texas Press, 1971), pp. 48–54; Barbara Kirshenblatt-Gimblett, "Culture Shock and Narrative Creativity," in *Folklore in the Modern World*, ed. by Dorson (The Hague: Mouton, 1978), pp. 109–22.

2. A. William Hoglund, *Finnish Immigrants in America, 1880–1920* (Madison: University of Wisconsin Press, 1961), pp. 24–33; Svatava Pirkova-Jakobson, "Harvest Festivals Among Czechs and Slovaks in America," *Journal of American Folklore* (July-Sept., 1956), pp. 266–80; Leo Papp, *The Portuguese-Americans* (Boston: Twayne, 1981), pp. 188–96; Stewart Culin, "Customs of the Chinese in America," *Journal of American Folklore*, III (Jan.-Mar., 1890), pp. 191–200; Robert F.G. Spier, "Tool Acculturation Among 19th Century California Chinese," *Ethnohistory*, 5 (1958), pp. 97–117; Phyllis H. Williams, *South Italian Folkways in Europe and America* (New York: Russell and Russell, 1938), pp. 94, 152, 178; Roy Rosenzweig, *Eight Hours for What We Will: Workers and Leisure in an Industrial City, 1870–1920* (Cambridge, England: Cambridge University Press, 1983), pp. 82, 153–56.

3. See Mick Moloney, "Irish Traditional Music in America," *Sing Out*, 25, No. 4 (1977), 3–5; George Korson, *Minstrels of Mine Patch* (Hatboro, Pa.: Folklore Associates, 1964), pp. 232, 264; Kenneth A. Thigpen, "Folklore and the Ethnicity Factor in the Lives of Romanian-Americans" (Ph.D. dissertation, Indiana University, 1974), pp. 192–94; Andrew Vazsonyi, "The Cicisbeo and the Magnificent Cuckold: Boardinghouse Life and Lore in Immigrant Communities," *Journal of American Folklore*, 91 (Apr.-June, 1978), 641–56; Susan G. Davis, "Utica's Polka Music Tradition," *New York Folklore*, 4 (Summer-Winter, 1978), 103–24; Albert J. Pike, "Transitional Aspects of Polish American Music," *The Polish Review*, III (Autumn, 1958), 104–11; Hoglund, *Finnish Immigrants in America*, p. 33; Estelle Schneider and Bob Norman, "'I Felt it in My Own Bones,' Yiddish Songs of a Jewish Rank and Filer," *Sing Out*, 25, No. 5 (1977), 5–11; Americo Paredes, "Tributaries to the Mainstream: The Ethnic Groups," in *Our Living Traditions*, ed. by Tristram Potter Coffin (New York: Basic Books, 1968), pp. 70–82.

4. See Maxine Seller, *To Seek America: A History of Ethnic Life in the United States* (New York: Jerome Ozer, 1977), pp. 181–86; Stanley L. Cuba, "Polish Amateur Theatricals in America: Colorado as a Case Study," *Polish-American Studies*, 28 (Spring, 1981), 23–24; Lawrence Pisani, *The Italian in America* (New York: Exposition, 1975), pp. 175–76' David Lifson, *Epic and Folk Plays of the Yiddish Theater* (New York, 1975), passim; Irving Howe, *World of Our Fathers* (New York: Simon and Schuster), pp. 460-67; E. Ewen, "City Lights: Immigrant Women and the Rise of the Movies," *Signs*, (Spring, 1980), 545–65.

5. Thigpen, "Folklore and the Ethnicity Factor in the Lives of Romanian-Americans," pp. 97–114; Emma Gee, "Poems of Angel Island," *Amerasia Journal*, 9 (Fall, 1982), 88; Vazsonyi, "The Cicisbeo and the Magnificent Cuckold: Boardinghouse Life and Lore in Immigrant Communities," pp. 642–43; Hoglund, *Finnish Immigrants in America*, pp. 24–26; Carla Bianco, "Migration and Urbanization of a Traditional Culture: An Italian Experience," in *Folklore in the Modern World*, ed. by Richard M. Dorson (The Hague: Mouton, 1978), p.59; Carla Bianco, *The Two Rosetos* (Bloomington: Indiana University Press, 1974), Robert A. Georges, "Greek-American Folk Beliefs and Narratives: Survivals and Living Tradition" (Ph.D. dissertation, Indiana University, 1964), pp. 121–22. See Naomi Katz and Eli Katz, "Tradition and Adaptation in American Jewish Humor," *Journal of American Folklore* 84 (Apr.-June, 1971), pp. 215–20.

6. John F. McClymer, "The Americanization Movement and the Education of the Foreign-born Adults, 1919–1925," in *American Education and the European Immigrant, 1840–1940*, ed. by Bernard J. Weiss (Urbana: University of Illinois Press, 1982), pp. 96–116; Richard A. Varbero, "Urbanization and Acculturation: Philadelphia's South Italians, 1918–1932" (Ph.D. dissertation, Temple University, 1975), p.156.

7. See Alexander Field, "Education Expansion in Mid-Nineteenth Century Massachusetts," *Harvard Educational Review*, 46 (1976), pp. 521–52; Marvin Lazerson, *Origins of the Urban School: Public Education in Massachusetts, 1870–1915* (Cambridge, Mass.: Harvard University Press, 1971), pp. 214–15; Ronald D. Cohen and Raymond A. Mohl, *The Paradox of Progressive Education: The Gary Plan and Urban Schooling* (Port Washington, N.Y.: Kennikat Press, 1979), pp. 84–85.

8. Martin E. Dann, "Little Citizens: Working Class and Immigrant Childhood in New York City, 1890–1915" (Ph.D. dissertation, City University of New York, 1978), pp. v, 337; Carl Kaestle, *The Evolution of an Urban School System* (Cambridge, Mass.: Harvard University Press, 1973; Stanley K. Schultz, *The Culture Factory: Boston Public Schools, 1789–1860* (New York: Oxford University Press, 1973), pp. 55–67.

9. Cohen and Mohl, *The Paradox of Progressive Education*, pp. 87–95; Mario T. Garcia, *Desert Immigrants: The Mexicans of El Paso* (New Haven, Conn.: Yale University Press, 1981), pp. 110–12; Sherry Gorelick, *City College and the Jewish Poor: Education in New York, 1880 and 1924* (New Brunswick, N.J.: Rutgers Unversity Press, 1981), p.56; Michael B. Katz, "The Origins of Public Education: A Reassessment," *History of Education Quarterly*, 16 (Winter, 1976), pp. 381–407.

10. See Dobbert, *The Disintegration of an Immigrant Community* (New York: Arno Press, 1980), pp. 264–69; Walter H. Beck, *Lutheran Elementary Schools in the United States* (St. Louis, Mo.: Concordia, 1965), p.1; Cohen and Mohl, *The Paradox of Progressive Education*, pp. 104–05; Jeffrey S. Gurock, *When Harlem was Jewish, 1870-1930* (New York: Columbia University Press, 1979), pp. 164–65; David Hogan, "Education and the Making of the Chicago Working Class," *History of Education Quarterly*, 18 (Fall, 1978), pp. 8–9.

11. Cohen and Mohl, *The Paradox of Progressive Education*, pp. 88–97.

12. Carl Kaestle and Maris Vinovskis, *Education and Social Change in Nineteenth Century Massachusetts* (Cambridge, England: Cambridge University Press, 1980), pp. 55–56; John W. Briggs, *An Italian Passage: Immigrants to Three American Cities, 1890–1930* (New Haven, Conn.: Yale University Press, 1978), p.55; Timothy Smith, "Immigrant Social Aspiration and American Education, 1880–1930," *American Quarterly*, 21 (Fall, 1969), pp. 522–25.

13. Kaestle and Vinovskis, *Education and Social Change in Nineteenth-Century Massachusetts*, pp. 36–37; Mark Stolarik, "Immigration and Urbanization: The Slovak Experience, 1870–1918" (Ph.D. dissertation, University of Minnesota, 1974), p. 269; Dann, "Little Citizens: Working Class and Immigrant Childhood in New York City," p. 334; Hogan, "Education and the Making of the Chicago Working Class," pp. 8–10; Michael R. Olneck and Marvin Lazerson, "The School Achievement of Immigrant Children, 1900–1930," *History of Education Quarterly*, 15 (Winter, 1974), 453–82; Bodnar, "Mate-

rialism and Morality: Slavic-American Immigrants and Education," *Journal of Ethnic Studies*, 3 (Winter, 1976), 11; Cohen and Mohl, *The Paradox of Progressive Education*, pp. 102–03.

14. Conzen, *Immigrant Milwaukee*, p. 92; Varbero, "Urbanization and Acculturation: Philadelphia's South Italians, 1918–1932," pp. 156, 173; Rudolph J. Vecoli, "Prelates and Peasants: Italian Immigrants and the Catholic Church," *Journal of Social History* 12 (Spring, 1969), 249; Leslie Woodcock Tentler, *Wage-Earning Women: Industrial Work and Family Life in the United States, 1900–1930* (New York: Oxford University Press, 1979), p. 99; Guadalupe San Miguel, "The Struggle Against Separate and Unequal Schools: Middle-Class Mexican-Americans and the Desegregation Campaign in Texas, 1929–1957," *History of Education Quarterly*, 23 (Fall, 1983), 344–45.

15. Dennis Clark, *The Irish in Philadelphia* (Philadelphia: Temple University Press, 1973), pp. 89–96; Jay P. Dolan, *The Immigrant Church: New York's Irish and German Catholics* (Baltimore, Md.: Johns Hopkins University Press, 1975), pp. 104–110; Burchell, *The San Francisco Irish*, pp. 162–70.

16. James W. Sanders, *The Education of an Urban Minority: Catholics in Chicago, 1833–1965* (New York: Oxford University Press, 1977), pp. 3–19; Philip Gleason, "Immigrants and American Catholic Higher Education," in *American Education and the European Immigrant*, pp. 161–75; Richard M. Linkh, *American Catholicism and European Immigrants, 1900–1924* (New York: Center for Migration Studies, 1975), pp. 111–14.

17. Varbero, "Urbanization and Acculturation: Philadelphia's South Italians," p. 171; Stolarik, "Immigration, Education, and the Social Mobility of Slovaks, 1870–1930," in *Immigrants and Their Religion in Urban America*, ed. by Randall M. Miller and Thomas D. Marzik (Philadelphia: Temple University Press, 1977), p. 111; quotation is from Bodnar, "Materialism and Morality," p. 9.

18. Beck, *Lutheran Elementary Schools in the United States*, pp. 101–25.

19. See Rolland G. Paulston, *Other Dreams, Other Schools: Folk Colleges in Social and Ethnic Movements* (Pittsburgh, Pa., 1980); Cohen and Mohl, *The Paradox of Progressive Education*, p. 107; Andrew T. Kopan, "Greek Survival in Chicago: The Role of Ethnic Education, 1890–1980," in *Ethnic Chicago*, ed. by Peter d'A. Jones and Melvin G. Holli (Grand Rapids, Mich.: Berdmans, 1981), pp. 126–84.

20. Gorelick, *City College and the Jewish Poor*, pp. 48–61, 113–18, 133; Selma Berrol, "Public Schools and Immigrants: The New York City Experience," in *American Education and the European Immigrant*, p. 35; Deborah Dash Moore, *At Home in America: Second-Generation New York Jews* (New York: Columbia University Press, 1981), p. 91; Berrol, "Education and Economic Mobility: The Jewish Experience in New York City, 1880–1920," *American Jewish Historical Quarterly*, 65 (Mar., 1976), p.260.

21. Arthur A. Goren, *New York Jews and the Quest for Community: The Kehillah Experiment, 1908–1922* (New York: Columbia University Press, 1970), pp. 2–3, 110–13, 122–23, 186–95.

22. See Paul Kleppner, *The Third Electoral System, 1853–1892* (Chapel Hill: University of North Carolina Press, 1979), pp. 11–13.

23. Ibid., pp. 19–20; David Montgomery, "The Shuttle and the Cross," *Journal of Social History*, 5 (Summer, 1972), pp. 411–46.

24. Kleppner, *The Third Electoral System*, pp. 198–237.

25. R.A. Burchell, *The San Francisco Irish, 1848–1880* (Berkeley: University of California Press, 1980), pp. 100–27.

26. Michael F. Holt, *The Formation of the Republican Party in Pittsburgh, 1848–1860* (New Haven, Conn.: Yale University Press, 1969), pp. 107–46; Burchell, *The San Francisco Irish*, pp. 100–27.

27. Richard Jensen, *The Winning of the Midwest: Social and Political Conflict, 1888–1896* (Chicago: University of Chicago Press, 1971), pp. 58–123.

28. David Noel Doyle, *Irish Americans, Native Rights, and National Empires* (New York: Arno Press, 1976), pp. 264–67.

29. Jensen, *The Winning of the Midwest*, pp. 278–92; Kleppner, *The Cross of Culture: A Social Analysis of Midwestern Politics, 1850–1900* (New York: Free Press, 1970), p.368.

30. Edward J. Rose, *Henry George* (New York: Twayne, 1968), pp. 119–27; James S. Lapham, "The German-Americans of New York City, 1860-1890" (Ph.D. dissertation, St. John's University, 1977), pp.119–27; James F. Donnelly, "Catholic New Yorkers and New York Socialists in 1870 and 1920" (Ph.D. dissertation, New York University, 1982), pp. 244–67; Michael Allen Gordon, "Studies in Irish and Irish American Thought and Behavior in Gilded Age New York City" (Ph.D. dissertation, University of Rochester, 1977), p. 493.

31. David Ward, *Cities and Immigrants* (New York: Oxford University Press, 1971), pp. 6–7; Varbero, "Urbanization and Acculturation: Philadelphia's South Italians, 1918–1932," pp. 279–90; Edward R. Kantowicz, *Polish-American Politics in Chicago, 1888-1940* (Chicago: University of Chicago Press, 1975), pp. 189–209; John L. Shover, "Ethnicity and Religion in Philadelphia Politics, 1924–1940," *American Quarterly*, XXV (Dec., 1973), 499–515; Allan J. Lichtman, *Prejudice and the Old Politics: The Presidential Election of 1928* (Chapel Hill: University of North Carolina Press, 1979), pp. 94–95, 108, 167, 179.

32. Dobbert,"The Disintegration of an Immigrant Community," pp. 49–62.

33. Gary Dean Best, *To Free A People: American Jewish Leaders and the Jewish Problem in Eastern Europe, 1890–1914* (Westport, Conn.: Greenwood Press, 1982), pp. 15–35, 114–45; Morton Tenzer, "The Jews," in *The Immigrants' Influence on Wilson's Peace Policies*, ed. by Joseph O'Grady (Lexington: University of Kentucky Press, 1967), p.317; O'Grady, ed., *The Immigrants' Influence on Wilson's Peace Policies*, pp. 5–6; Ronald H. Bayor, *Neighbors in Conflict: The Irish, Germans, Jews and Italians of New York City, 1929–1941* (Baltimore, Md.: Johns Hopkins University Press, 1978), pp. 57–59; Howe, *World of Our Fathers, pp. 391–93*.

34. O'Grady, ed., *The Immigrants' Influence on Wilson's Peace Policies*, pp. 5–6, 21; O'Grady, "The Irish," in ibid. p.67; John B. Duff, "The Italians," in ibid., pp. 111, 123.

35. Bayor, *Neighbors in Conflict*, pp. 57–147; Cinel, *From Italy to San Francisco*, p. 253.

36. See Ira Katznelson, *City Trenches: Urban Politics and the Pattern of Class in the United States* (New York: Pantheon, 1981), pp. 6–15, 208–12, for an extended discussion on the division of political interests between workplace and community issues.

37. Donnelly, "Catholic New Yorkers and New York Socialists in 1870–1920," pp. 54–65; see Perry R. Duis, *The Saloon: Public Drinking in Chicago and Boston, 1880–1920* (Urbana: University of Illinois Press, 1983), pp. 118–20, 147.

38. Lapham, "The German-Americans of New York City, 1860–1890" (Ph.D. dissertation, St. John's University, 1977), p. 243; Kantowicz, *Polish-American Politics in Chicago*, pp. 180–96; Hans L. Trefousse, *Carl Schurz*, A *Biography*, pp. 180–96; Donnelly, "Catholic New Yorkers and New York Socialists in 1870–1920," p. 234; Varbero, "Urbanization and Acculturation," pp. 289–91; Briggs, *An Italian Passage*, p. 176; Gary Mormino, "The Hill Upon the City: An Italo-American Neighborhood in St. Louis, Missouri, 1880–1955" (Ph.D. dissertation, University of North Carolina, 1977), pp. 273–75.

39. Raymond E. Wolfinger, "The Development and Persistence of Ethnic Voting," in American Ethnic Politics, ed. by Lawrence H. Fuchs (New York: Harper, 1968), pp. 164–66.

CHAPTER 8

Conclusion: The Culture of Everyday Life

1. See two works by Oscar Handlin: *Boston's Immigrants* (Cambridge, Mass.: Harvard University Press, 1941) and *The Uprooted* (Boston: Little, Brown, 1951). Handlin's work, of course, dominated immigration history for several decades and continues to influence the popular and scholarly imagination. A recent text on American economic history, Robert L. Heilbroner, *The Economic Transformation of America* (New York: Harcourt Brace Jovanovich, 1977) contained the Handlin view essentially intact.

2. Herbert Gutman, *Work, Culture and Society in Industrializing America* (New York: Vintage Books, 1977), pp. 3–78; Thomas J. Archdeacon, *Becoming American: An Ethnic History* (New York: Macmillan, 1983).

3. John Higham, "Current Trends in the Study of Ethnicity in the United States," *Journal of American Ethnic History*, 2 (Fall, 1982), 5–15.

4. Gabriel Kolko, *Main Currents in Modern American History* (New York: Harper and Row, 1976), pp. 69–70; Henry Glassie, *Passing the Time in Ballymenone: Culture and History of an Ulster Community* (Philadelphia: University of Pennsylvania Press, 1982).

5. See Fernand Braudel, *The Structures of Everyday Life* (New York: Harper and Row, 1982), pp. 28, 51–70; James A. Henretta, "Social History as Lived and Written," *American Historical Review*, 84 (Dec., 1979), 1300–01; Norman Birnbaum, "The Crises in Marxist Sociology," in *Radical Sociology*, ed. by J. David Colfax and Jack L. Roach (New York: Basic Books, 1971), pp. 109–22; Pierre Bourdieu, "Marriage Strategies as Strategies of Social Reproduction," in *Family and Society: Selections from Annales*, ed. by R. Forster and O. Ranum (Baltimore, Md.: Johns Hopkins University Press, 1975), pp. 129–31.

6. See Clifford Geertz, *The Interpretation of Cultures* (New York, 1977); Patrick H. Hutton, "The History of Mentalities: The New Map of Cultural History," *History and Theory*, XX (1981), 237–59.

7. See Herbert Marcuse, *One Dimensional Man: Studies in the Ideologies of Advanced Industrial Society* (Boston: Beacon Press, 1964), pp. 193, 208–10; Barrington Moore, *Social Origins of Dictatorship and Democracy* (Boston: Beacon Press, 1966), p. 486.

8. Hermann Rebel, *Peasant Classes: The Bureaucratization of Property and Family Relations under Early Hapsburg Absolutism, 1511–1636* (Princeton, N.J.: Princeton University Press, 1983), pp. 118–19, 170–80.

9. See Fernand Braudel, *The Mediterranean and the Mediterranean World in the Age of Philip II*, trans. by Sian Reynolds (2 vols.; New York: Harper & Row, 1972), I, pp. 20–22; Lawrence Stone, "The Revival of Narrative Reflections as a New Old History," *Past and Present*, 85 (Nov., 1979), 143–41.

10. See Harriet Friedman, "Household Production and the National Economy: Concepts for the Analysis of Agrarian Formations," *Journal of Peasant Studies*, 7 (Jan., 1980), 158–84; Chaya S. Piotrkowski, *Work and the Family System* (New York: Free Press, 1978).

11. Abner Cohen, ed., *Urban Ethnicity* (London: Tavistock, 1974), p. xiii.

12. See John Cammett, *Antonio Gramsci and the Origins of Italian Communism* (Stanford, Calif.: Standord University Press, 1967).

Selected Bibliography

AKERMAN, SUNE. "Swedish Migration and Social Mobility: The Tale of Three Cities." *Social Science History*, 1 (Winter, 1977), 178–209.
——, and HANS NORMAN. "Political Mobilization of the Workers: The Case of the Worcester Swedes." In *American Labor and Immigration History, 1870–1920: Recent European Research*, ed. by Dirk Hoerder, 235–58. Urbana: University of Illinois Press, 1983.
ANDERSON MICHAEL. "Household Structure and Industrial Revolution: Mid-Nineteenth Century Preston in Comparative Perspective." In *Household and Family in Past Time*, ed. by Peter Laslett, 215–35. Cambridge, England: Cambridge University Press, 1972.
APP, AUSTIN J. "The Germans." In *The Immigrants' Influence on Wilson's Peace Policies*, ed. by Joseph P. O'Grady, 30–35. Lexington: University of Kentucky Press, 1967.
ASHER, ROBERT. "Union Nativism and the Immigrant Response." *Labor History*, 23 (Summer, 1982), 325–48.
BAILEY, SAMUEL L. "The Adjustment of Italian Immigrants in Buenos Aires and New York, 1870–1914." *American Historical Review*, 88 (April, 1983), 281–305.
BAKER, T. LINDSAY. *The First Polish Americans*. College Station: Texas A&M University Press, 1979.
BARANY, GEORGE. "The Magyars." In *The Immigrants' Influence on Wilson's Peace Policies*, ed. by Joseph P. O'Grady, 140–72. Lexington: University of Kentucky Press, 1967.
BARRETT, JAMES R. "Work and Community in the Jungle: Chicago's Packing House Workers, 1894–1922." Ph.D. dissertation, University of Pittsburgh, 1981.
BARROWS, ROBERT G. "Beyond the Tenement: Patterns of American Urban Housing, 1870–1930." *Journal of Urban History*, 9 (August, 1983), 395–420.
BARTON, JOSEF J. "Eastern and Southern Europeans." In *Ethnic Leadership in America*, ed. by John Higham, 150–75. Baltimore: John Hopkins University Press, 1978.
——. *Peasants and Strangers: Italians, Rumanians, and Slovaks in an American City, 1890–1950*. Cambridge, Mass.: Harvard University Press, 1975.
——. "Religion and Cultural Change in Czech Immigrant Communities, 1850–1920." In *Immigrants and Religion in Urban America*, ed. by Randall M. Miller and Thomas D. Marzik, 3–24. Philadelphia: Temple University Press, 1977.
BAYOR, RONALD. *Neighbors in Conflict: The Irish, Germans, Jews, and Italians of New York City, 1929–1941*. Baltimore, Md.: John Hopkins University Press, 1978.
BECK, WALTER H. *Lutheran Elementary Schools in the United States*. St. Louis: Concordia, 1965.
BEIJBOM, ULF. *Swedes in Chicago: A Demographic and Social Study of the 1946–1880 Immigration*. Stockholm: Läromedelsförlagen and Chicago Historical Society, 1971.

[267

BELL, RUDOLPH M. *Fate and Honor: Family and Village*. Chicago: University of Chicago Press, 1979.

BENKART, PAULA KAYE. "Religion, Family, and Community among Hungarians Migrating to American Cities, 1880–1930." Ph.D. dissertation, John Hopkins University, 1975.

BENSON, JAMES K. "Irish and German Families and the Economic Development of Midwestern Cities, 1860–1895: St. Paul, Minnesota, as a Case Study." Ph.D. dissertation, University of Minnesota, 1980.

BEREND, IVAN, AND GYÖRGY RANKI. *Economic Development in East-Central Europe in the Nineteenth and Twentieth Centuries*. New York: Columbia University Press, 1974.

BERKNER, LUTZ K. "The Stem Family and the Development Cycle of the Peasant Household: An Eighteenth Century Austrian Example." *American Historical Review*, 77 (April, 1972) 398–418.

BERNARD, RICHARD M. *The Melting Pot and the Altar: Marital Assimilation in Early Twentieth-Century Wisconsin*. Minneapolis: University of Minnesota Press, 1980.

BERTHOFF, ROWLAND TAPPAN. *British Immigrants in Industrial America, 1790–1950*. Cambridge, Mass.: Harvard University Press, 1953.

———. "Peasants and Artisans, Puritans and Republicans: Personal Liberty and Communal Equality in American History." *Journal of American History*, 69 (December, 1982), 579–98.

BEST, GARY DEAN. *To Free A People: American Jewish Leaders and the Jewish Problem in Eastern Europe, 1890–1914*. Westport, Conn.: Greenwood Press, 1982.

BIDDLE, ELLEN HORGAN. "The American Catholic Irish Family." In *Ethnic Families in America*, ed. by Charles Mindel and Robert W. Habenstein, 89–123. New York: Elsevier, 1976.

BIRNBAUM, NORMAN. "The Crisis in Marxist Sociology." In *Radical Sociology*, ed. by J. David Colfax and Jack L. Roach, 109–22. New York: Basic Books, 1971.

BLOCH, HARRIET HALL. "Household Economy and Entrepreneurial Activity in a Polish Peasant Village." Ph.D. dissertation, Columbia University, 1973.

BLUM, JEROME. *The End of the Old Order in Rural Europe*. Princeton, N.J.: Princeton University Press, 1978.

BODNAR, JOHN, ROGER SIMON, AND MICHAEL P. WEBER. *Lives of Their Own*. Urbana: University of Illinois Press, 1982.

BODNAR, JOHN. "Materialism and Mortality: Slavic American Immigrants and Education, 1890–1940". *Journal of Ethnic Studies*, 3 (Winter, 1976), 1–19.

———. *Workers' World: Kinship, Community and Protest in an Industrial Society*. Baltimore, Md.: John Hopkins University Press, 1982.

BOGATYREV, PETR. *The Functions of Folk Costume in Moravian Slovakia*. The Hague, The Netherlands: Mouton, 1971.

BONACICH, EDNA, AND JOHN MODELL. *The Economic Basis of Ethnic Solidarity: Small Business in the Japanese American Community*. Berkeley: University of California Press, 1980.

BORCHERT, JAMES. "Urban Neighborhood and Community Informal Group Life, 1850–1970." *Journal of Interdisciplinary History*, XI (Spring, 1981), 607–31.

Selected Bibliography

BRANDES, STUART D. American Welfare Capitalism, 1880–1940. Chicago: University of Chicago Press, 1976.

BRATT, JAMES D. "The Reformed Churches in Acculturation." In They Came To Stay: Dutch Immigration and Settlement in America, ed. by Robert Swierenga. New Brunswick, N.J.: Rutgers University Press, forthcoming.

BRAUDEL, FERNAND. Capitalism and Material Life, 1400–1800. New York: Harper & Row, 1973.

BRECHER, JEREMY, JERRY LOMBARDI, AND JAN STACKHOUSE, compilers and editors. Brass Valley: The Story of Working People's Lives and Struggles in an American Industrial Region. Philadelphia: Temple University Press, 1982.

BRIGGS, JOHN W. An Italian Passage: Immigrants to Three American Cities, 1890–1930. New Haven, Conn.: Yale University Press, 1978.

BRODY, DAVID. The Butcher Workmen: A Study in Trade Union Organization. Cambridge, Mass.: Harvard University Press, 1964.

——. Steelworkers in America, The Nonunion Era. Cambridge, Harvard University Press, 1960.

BROZEK, ANDRZEJ. Polonia Amerykaska: The American Polonia. Warsaw, Poland: Interpress Publications, 1980.

BRZESKI, ANDRZEJ. "Industrialization and Peasantry: An Economist's View." East European Quarterly, III (1970), 406–19.

BUDER, STANLEY. Pullman: An Experience in Industrial Order and Community Planning. New York: Oxford University Press, 1967.

BUHLE, PAUL. "Debsian Socialism and the 'New Immigrant' Worker." In Insights and Parallels: Problems and Issues of American Social History, ed. by William L. O'Neil, 249–304. Minneapolis, Minn.: Burgess, 1973.

BUJAK, FRANCISZEK. Galicya. Two volumes. Lwów Galicia: Nakladem Ksiegarni H. Altenberga, 1908–1910.

——. Limanowa: Miasteczko Powiatowe w Zachodniej Galicyi, Stan Spoeczny I Gospodarczy. Kraków, Galicia: G. Gebethner I Spoka, 1902.

BUKOWCZYK, JOHN J. "Polish Factionalism and the Formation of the Immigrant Middle Class in Brooklyn, 1880–1929." Unpublished paper in author's possession.

——. "The Politics of Parish Formation: Intra-Clerical Rivalry in Brooklyn's Polish Settlements." Paper delivered at Organization of American Historians meeting, Philadelphia, April 2, 1982.

BURCHELL, R.A. The San Francisco Irish, 1848–1880. Berkeley: University of California Press, 1980.

BURSTEIN, ALAN N. "Immigrants and Residential Mobility: The Irish and Germans in Philadelphia, 1850–1880." In Philadelphia, ed. by Theodore Hershberg, 174–203. New York: Oxford University Press, 1981.

CAMARILLO, ALBERT. Chicanos in a Changing Society: From Mexican Pueblos to American Barrios in Santa Barbara and Southern California, 1848–1930. Cambridge, Mass.: Harvard University Press, 1979.

CANTOR, MILTON. The Divided Left: American Radicalism. 1900–1975. New York: Hill and Wang, 1978.

CARDOSA, LAWRENCE. Mexican Emigration to the United States. 1897–1931. Tucson: University of Arizona Press, 1980.

CHIROT, DANIEL. Social Change in a Peripheral Society: The Creation of a Balkan Colony. New York: Academic Press, 1976.

Selected Bibliography

CHMELAR, JOHANN. "The Austrian Emigration, 1900–1914." *Perspectives in American History*, VII (1973), 275–378.

CINEL, DINO. *From Italy to San Francisco*. Stanford, Calif.: Stanford University Press, 1982.

——. "The Seasonal Emigration of Italians in the Nineteenth Century: From Internal to International Destinations." *Journal of Ethnic Studies*, 19 (Spring, 1982), 43–68.

CIZMIC, IVAN. *Iseljenistvo i Suvremena Ekonomska Emigracija a Prodrucja Karlovca*. Zagreb, Yugoslavia: Matica Hrvatska, 1973.

CLARK, DENNIS. *The Irish in Philadelphia*. Philadelphia: Temple University Press, 1973.

——. "The Irish Catholics: A Postponed Perspective." In *Immigrants and Religion in Urban America*, ed. by Randall M. Miller and Thomas D. Marzik, 48–68. Philadelphia: Temple University Press, 1977.

COELHO, ANTHONY. "A Row of Nationalities: Life in a Working-Class Community: The Irish, English, and French Canadians of Fall River, Massachusetts, 1850–1890." Ph.D. dissertation, Brown University, 1980.

COHEN, ABNER, editor. *Urban Ethnicity*. London, England: Tavistock, 1974.

COHEN, MIRIAM. "Changing Education Strategies among Immigrant Generations: New York Italians in Comparative Perspective." *Journal of Social History*, 15 (Spring, 1982), 443–66.

COHEN, RONALD D., AND RAYMOND A. MOHL. *The Paradox of Progressive Education: The Gary Plan and Urban Schooling*. Port Washington, N.Y.: Kennikat Press, 1979.

COLAKOVIC, BRANKO MITA. *Yugoslav Migrations to America*. San Francisco: R & E Research, 1973.

COLE, JOHN W., AND ERIC R. WOLF. *The Hidden Frontier: Ecology and Ethnicity in an Alpine Valley*. New York: Academic Press, 1974.

CONWAY, ALAN. "The Welsh Emigration to the United States." *Perspectives in American History*, VII (1973), 177–271.

CONZEN, KATHLEEN NEILS. "Immigrants, Immigrant Neighborhoods, and Ethnic Identity: Historical Issues." *Journal of American History*, 66 (December, 1979), 603–15.

——. *Immigrant Milwaukee: Accommodation and Community in a Frontier City*. Cambridge, Mass.: Harvard University Press, 1976.

COOPER, PATRICIA ANN. "From Hand Craft to Mass Production: Men, Women, and Work Culture in American Cigar Factories, 1900–1919." Ph.D. dissertation, University of Maryland, 1981.

CORWIN, ARTHUR F., "Causes of Mexican Emigration to the United States: A Summary View." *Perspectives in American History*, VII (1973), 557–635.

——, editor. *Immigrants and Immigrants: Perspectives on Mexican Labor Migration to the United States*. Westport, Conn.: Greenwood Press, 1978.

CUMBLER, JOHN T. *Working-Class Community in Industrial America: Work, Leisure and Struggle in Two Industrial Cities, 1880–1930*. Westport, Conn.: Greenwood Press, 1979.

CUMMINGS, SCOTT. "Collectivism: The Unique Legacy of Immigrant Economic Development." In *Self-Help in Urban America*, ed. by Scott Cummings, 5–29. Port Washington, N.Y.: Kennikat Press, 1980.

CZAP, PETER. "The Perennial Multiple Family Household, Mishino, Russia, 1782–1858." *Journal of Family History*, 7 (Spring, 1982). 5–26.

DANN, MARTIN E. "Little Citizens: Working Class and Immigrant Childhood in New York City, 1890–1915." Ph.D. dissertation, City University of New York, 1978.

DAVIS, LAWRENCE B. *Immigrants, Baptists, and the Protestant Mind in America*. Urbana: University of Illinois Press, 1973.

DECKER, PETER R. *Fortunes and Failures: White-Collar Mobility in Nineteenth-Century San Francisco*. Cambridge, Mass.: Harvard University Press, 1978.

———. "Jewish Merchants in San Francisco: Social Mobility on the Urban Frontier." In *The Jews of the West: The Metropolitan Years*, ed. by Moses Rischin, 12–33. Waltham, Mass.: American Jewish Historical Society, 1979.

DEGH, LINDA. *Folktales and Society: Story-Telling in a Hungarian Peasant Community*. Bloomington: Indiana University Press, 1969.

DeMARCO, WILLIAM. "Ethnics and Enclaves: The Italian Settlement in the North End of Boston." Ph.D. dissertation, Boston College, 1980.

DICKINSON, JOAN YOUNGER. *The Role of the Immigrant Women in the U.S. Labor Force, 1890–1910*. New York: Arno Press, 1980.

DINER, HASIA R. *Erin's Daughters in America*. Baltimore, Md.: Johns Hopkins University Press, 1983.

DOBBERT, GUIDO A. *The Disintegration of an Immigrant Community*. New York: Arno Press, 1980.

DOLAN, JAY P. "Philadelphia and the German Catholic Community." In *Immigrants and Religion in Urban America*, ed. by Randall M. Miller and Thomas D. Marzik, 69–83. Philadelphia: Temple University Press, 1977.

———. *The Immigrant Church: New York's Irish and German Catholics*. Baltimore, Md.: Johns Hopkins University Press, 1975.

DONNELLY, JAMES F. "Catholic New Yorkers and New York Socialists in 1870–1920." Ph.D. dissertation, New York University, 1982.

DORSON, RICHARD M. *American Folklore*. Chicago: University of Chicago Press, 1959.

DOYLE, DAVID NOEL. *Irish Americans, Native Rights, and National Empires*. New York: Arno Press, 1976.

DRAGE, GEOFFREY. *Austria-Hungary*. London, England: Murray, 1909.

DUBLIN, THOMAS. *Women at Work: The Transformation of Work and Community in Lowell, Massachusetts, 1826–1860*. New York: Columbia University Press, 1979.

DUBNOFF, STEVEN. "The Family and Absence from Work: Irish Workers in a Lowell, Massachusetts, Mill." Ph.D. dissertation, Brandeis University, 1976.

DUBOFSKY, MELVYN. *We Shall Be All: A History of the Industrial Workers of the World*. Chicago: Quadrangle Books, 1969.

DUCKER, JAMES H. *Men of the Steel Rails: Workers on the Atchison, Topeka and Santa Fe Railroad, 1869–1900.*. Lincoln: University of Nebraska Press, 1983.

DYRUD, KEITH P. "The Establishment of the Greek Catholic Rite in America as a Competitor to Orthodoxy." In *The Other Catholics*, ed. by Keith P. Dyrud, Michael Novak, and Rudolph J. Vecoli, 190–226. New York: Arno Press, 1978.

EARLY, FRANCES H. "The French-Canadian Family Economy and Standard of Living in Lowell, Massachusetts, 1870." *Journal of Family History*, 7 (Summer, 1982), 180–99.

EASTERLIN, RICHARD A., et al. *Immigration*. Cambridge, Mass.: Harvard University Press, 1982.

——. "Population Issues in American Economic History: A Survey and a Critique." In *Recent Developments in the Study of Business and Economic History*, ed. by Robert E. Gallman, 131–58. Greenwich, Conn.: JAI Press, 1977.

——. *Population, Labor Force, and Long Swings in Economic Growth*. New York: National Bureau of Economic Research, 1968.

EDSON, C.H. "Immigrant Perspectives on Work and Schooling: Eastern European Jews and Southern Italians." Ph.D. dissertation, Stanford University, 1979.

EDWARDS, RICHARD, Michael Reich, and David Gordon. *Labor Market Segmentation*. Lexington, Mass.: D.C. Heath, 1973.

ERICKSON, CHARLOTTE, editor. *Emigration From Europe, 1815–1914: Select Documents*. London, England: Adam & Black, 1976.

——. *Invisible Immigrants: The Adaptation of English and Scottish Immigrants in Nineteenth-Century America*. Coral Gables, Fla.: University of Miami Press, 1972.

ESSLINGER, DEAN R. *Immigrants and the City: Ethnicity and Mobility in a Nineteenth-Century Midwestern Community*. Port Washington, N.Y.: Kennikat Press, 1975.

FAIRES, NORA. "Ethnicity in Evolution: The German Community in Pittsburgh and Allegheny City, Pennsylvania, 1845–1885." Ph.D. dissertation, University of Pittsburgh, 1981.

FENTON, EDWIN. *Immigrants and Unions, A Case Study: Italians and American Labor, 1870–1920*. New York: Arno Press, 1975.

FONER, ERIC. *Politics and Ideology in the Age of the Civil War*. New York: Oxford University Press, 1980.

FRASER, STEVE. "Dress Rehearsal for the New Deal: Shop-Floor Insurgents, Political Elites, and Industrial Democracy in the Amalgamated Clothing Workers." In *Working-Class America*, ed. by Michael H. Frisch and Daniel J. Walkowitz, 212–55. Urbana: University of Illinois Press, 1983.

FREEMAN, JOSHUA B. "Catholics, Communists, and Republicans: Irish Workers and the Organizations of the Transport Workers Unions." In *Working-Class America*, ed. by Michael R. Frisch and Daniel J. Walkowitz, 256–83. Urbana: University of Illinois Press, 1983.

FRIEDMANN, HARRIET. "Household Production and the National Economy: Concepts for the Analysis of Agrarian Formations." *Journal of Peasant Studies*, 7 (January, 1980), 158–84.

FURIO, COLOMBA M. "The Cultural Background of the Italian Immigrant Woman and Its Impact on her Unionization in the New York City Garment Industry, 1880–1919." In *Pane e Lavoro: The Italian-American Working-Class*, ed. by George E. Pozetta, 81–98. Toronto, Canada: Multicultural Historical Society, 1980.

——. "Immigrant Women and Industry: A Case Study: The Italian Immigrant Women and the Garment Industry: 1880–1950." Ph.D. dissertation, New York University, 1979.

GABACCIA, DONNA R. *From Italy to Elizabeth Street*. Albany: SUNY Press, 1983.

———. "Sicilians in Space: Environmental Change and Family Geography." *Journal of Social History*, 16 (Winter, 1982), 53–56.

GALOS, ADAM, AND KAZIMIERZ WAJDA. "Migrations in the Polish Western Territories Annexed by Prussia (1815–1914)." In *Employment-Seeking Emigration of the Poles World Wide, XIX and XX Centuries*, ed. by Celina Bobinska and Andrzej Pilch, 53–56. Kraków, Poland: Panstowe Wydawni Naukowe, 1975.

GAMINO, MANUEL. *El Inmigrante Mexicano: La Historia de su Vida*. Mexico City: Universidad Nacional Autónoma de México, 1969.

GARCIA, MARIO. *Desert Immigrants: The Mexicans of El Paso, 1880–1920*. New Haven, Conn., Yale University Press, 1981.

GARCIA, RICHARD A. "Class, Consciousness, and Ideology—The Mexican Community of San Antonio, Texas: 1930–1940." *Aztlan*, 9 (1978), 23–69.

GAVAZZI, MILOVAN. "The Extended Family in Southeastern Europe." *Journal of Family History*, 7 (Spring, 1982), 89–102.

GAVETT, THOMAS W. *Development of the Labor Movement in Milwaukee*. Madison: University of Wisconsin Press, 1965.

GELFAND, MITCHELL. "Progress and Prosperity: Jewish Social Mobility in Los Angeles in the Booming Eighties." In *The Jews of the West: The Metropolitan Years*, ed. by Moses Rischin, 24–49. Waltham, Mass.: American Jewish Historical Society, 1979.

GENOVESE, EUGENE D. *Roll, Jordan, Roll: The World the Slaves Made*. New York: Pantheon, 1972.

GEORGE, PETER. *The Emergence of Industrial America: Strategic Factors in American Economic Growth since 1870*. Albany: SUNY Press, 1982.

GEORGES, ROBERT A. "Greek-American Folk Beliefs and Narratives: Survivals and Living Tradition." Ph.D. dissertation, Indiana University, 1964.

GERBER, DAVID A. "Modernity in the Service of Tradition: Catholic Lay Trustees at Buffalo's St. Louis Church and the Transformation of European Communal Traditions, 1829–1855." *Journal of Social History*, 15 (Summer, 1982), 655–84.

———. "Cutting Out Skylock: Elite Anti-Semitism and the Quest for Moral Order in the Mid-Nineteenth-Century American Market Place." *Journal of American History*, 69 (December, 1982), 615–37.

GLEASON, PHILIP. *The Conservative Reformers: German-American Catholics and the Social Order*. Notre Dame, Ind.: University of Notre Dame Press, 1968.

GLETTLER, MONIKA. *Pittsburgh-Wien-Budapest: Programm und Praxis der Nationalitatenpolitik bei der Auswanderung der ungarischen Slowaken Nach Amerika um 1900*. Wein: Der Osterreichischen Akademic der Wissenschaften, 1980.

GOLDEN, CLAUDIA. "Family Strategies and the Family Economy in the Late Nineteenth Century: The Role of Secondary Workers." In *Philadelphia*, ed. by Theodore Hershberg, 277–310. New York: Oxford University Press, 1981.

GORDON, MICHAEL ALLEN. "Studies in Irish and Irish-American Thought and Behavior in Gilded Age New York City." Ph.D. dissertation, University of Rochester, 1977.

GORELICK, SHERRY. *City College and the Jewish Poor: Education in New York, 1880–1924*. New Brunswick, New Jersey: Rutgers University Press, 1981.

Selected Bibliography

GOREN, ARTHUR A. *New York Jews and the Quest for Community: The Kehillah Experiment, 1908–1922*. New York: Columbia University Press, 1970.

GOTTLIEB, AMY ZAHL. "The Influence of British Trade Unionists on the Regulation of the Mining Industry in Illinois, 1872." *Labor History*, 19 (Summer, 1978), 397–415.

GOULD, J.D. "European Inter-Continental Emigration 1815–1914: Patterns and Causes." *Journal of European Economic History*, 8 (Winter, 1979), 593–679.

GRAFF, HARVEY J. *The Literacy Myth: Literacy and Social Structure in the Nineteenth-Century City*. New York: Academic Press, 1979.

GRAY, MALCOLM. "Scottish Emigration: The Social Impact of Agrarian Change in the Rural Lowlands, 1775–1875." *Perspectives in American History*, VII (1973), 95–174.

GRIFFEN, CLYDE AND SALLY. *Natives and Newcomers: The Ordering of Opportunity in Mid-Nineteenth-Century Poughkeepsie*. Cambridge, Mass.: Harvard University Press, 1978.

GRIGG, DAVID. *Population Growth and Agrarian Change: A Historical Perspective*. Cambridge, England: Cambridge University Press, 1980.

GUMINA, DEANNA PAOLI. *The Italians of San Francisco, 1850–1930*. New York: Center for Migration Studies, 1978.

GUNDA, BELA. "The Ethno-Sociological Structure of the Hungarian Extended Family." *Journal of Family History*, 7 (Spring, 1982), 40–51.

GUROCK, JEFFREY. *When Harlem Was Jewish, 1870–1930*. New York: Columbia University Press.

HACKER, LOUIS M. *The Course of American Economic Growth and Development*. New York: John Wiley, 1970.

HAINES, MICHAEL. *Fertility and Occupation: Population Patterns in Industrialization*. New York: Academic Press, 1979.

HALPERN, JOEL M. "Town and Countryside in Serbia in the Nineteenth Century: Social and Household Structure as Reflected in the Census of 1860." In *Household and Family in Past Time*, ed. by Peter Laslett, 401–27. Cambridge, England: Cambridge University Press, 1972.

HAMMEL, E.A. "The Zadruga as Process." In *Household and Family in Past Time*, ed. by Peter Laslett, 335–73. Cambridge, England: Cambridge University Press, 1972.

HANDLIN, OSCAR. *Boston's Immigrants: A Study in Acculturation*. Cambridge, Mass.: Harvard University Press, 1941.

——. *The Uprooted*. Boston: Little, Brown and Company, 1951.

HANSEN, MARCUS LEE. *The Atlantic Migration, 1607–1960*. Cambridge, Mass.: Harvard University Press, 1940.

HANZLIK, J. "Zaciatky Vystahovalectva Zo Slovenska do USA a jeho priebeh az do roku 1918, jeho priciny a následky." In *Zaciatky Ceskej a Slovenskej Emigracie do USA*, ed. by Josef Polisenský, 49–96. Bratislava, Czechoslovakia: Vydavatelstvo Slovenskej Akademie Vied, 1970.

HAREVEN, TAMARA K. *Family Time and Industrial Time: The Relationship Between the Family and Work in a New England Industrial Community*. Cambridge, England: Cambridge University Press, 1982.

HARRIS, RUTH ANN M. "The Nearest Place Which Wasn't Ireland: A Study of Pre-Famine Irish Circular Migration to Britain." Ph.D. dissertation, Tufts University, 1980.

HECHTER, MICHAEL. "The Position of Eastern European Immigrants to the

United States in the Central Division of Labor: Some Trends and Prospects." In *The World-System of Capitalism: Past and Present*, ed. by Walter L. Goldfrank, 111–30. Beverly Hills, Calif.: Sage Publications, 1979.

HEILBRONNER, ROBERT L. *The Limits of American Capitalism*. New York: Harper and Row, 1966.

HERSHBERG, THEODORE, ALAN N. BURSTEIN, EUGENE P. ERICKSEN, STEPHANIE W. GREENBERG, AND WILLIAM L. YANCEY. "A Tale of Three Cities: Blacks, Immigrants, and Opportunity in Philadelphia, 1850–1880, 1930, 1970." In *Philadelphia*, ed. by Theodore Hershberg. New York: Oxford University Press, 1981.

HIGGS, ROBERT. *The Transformation of the American Economy, 1865–1914*. New York: John Wiley, 1971.

HIGHAM, JOHN. *Send These Unto Me: Jews and Other Immigrants in Urban America*. New York: Atheneum, 1975.

——, editor. *Ethnic Leadership in America*. Baltimore: Johns Hopkins University Press, 1978.

HINKA, JOHN PAUL. "Priests and Peasants: The Greek Catholic Pastor and the Ukrainian National Movement in Austria, 1867–1900." *Canadian Slavonic Papers*, xxi (March, 1979), 1–14.

HIRSCH, SUSAN E. *Roots of the American Working Class: The Industrialization of Crafts in Newark, 1800–1860*. Philadelphia: University of Pennsylvania Press, 1978.

HOČEVAR, TOUSSAINT. *The Structure of the Slovenian Economy, 1848–1963*. New York: Studia Slovenica, 1965.

HOERDER, DIRK. "Prussian Agents Among Polish Americans, 1900–1917: A Research Note." *Polish-American Studies*, XXXVIII (Autumn, 1981), 84–88.

HOFER, TOMAS. "Changes in the Style of Folk Art and Various Branches of Folklore in Hungary During the Nineteenth Century—An Interpretation." *Acta Ethnographica Academiae Scientiarum Hungaricae*, 29 (1980), 149–65.

——. "Peasant Expressive Culture, 1800–1914: Tendencies of Separation and Mergence." Paper delivered to conference of American and Hungarian Historians, August 23–26, 1982, Budapest.

HOGAN, DAVID. "Education and the Making of the Chicago Working-Class." *History of Education Quarterly*, 18 (Fall, 1978), 227–70.

HOGLUND, A. WILLIAM. *Finnish Immigrants in America, 1880–1920*. Madison: University of Wisconsin Press, 1960.

——. "Finnish Immigrant Letter Writers: Reporting from the U.S. to Finland, 1870's to World War I." In *Finnish Diaspora II: United States*, ed. by Michael Karni, 13–32. Toronto: Multicultural History Society of Ontario, 1981.

HOLT, MICHAEL. *Forging a Majority: The Formation of the Republican Party in Pittsburgh, 1848–1860*. New Haven, Conn.: Yale University Press, 1969.

HOWE, IRVING. *World of Our Fathers*. New York: Simon and Schuster, 1976.

HUMMASTI, P. GEORGE. "Working-Class *Herrat*: The Role of Leadership in Finnish-American Socialist Movement in the Pacific Northwest." In *Finnish Diaspora II: United States*, ed. by Michael Karni, 175–91. Toronto: Multicultural History Society of Ontario, 1981.

HUMPHRIES, STEPHEN. *Hooligans or Rebels: An Oral History of Working-Class*

Childhood and Youth, 1889–1939. Oxford, England: Basil Blackwell, 1981.

HVIDT, KRISTIAN. *Flight to America: The Social Background of 300,000 Danish Emigrants*. New York: Academic Press, 1975.

JACKSON, KENNETH T. "The Spatial Dimensions of Social Control: Race, Ethnicity and Government Housing Policy in the United States, 1916–1969." In *Modern Industrial Cities: History, Policy, and Survival*, ed. by Bruce Stave. Beverly Hills, Calif.: Sage Publications, 1981.

JANOWSKA, HALINA. "An Introductory Outline of the Mass Movement of Polish Emigrants: Their Directions and Problems, 1870–1945." In *Employment-Seeking Emigration of the Poles World Wide, XIX and XX Centuries*, ed. by Celina Bobinska and Andrzej Pilch, 121–44. Kraków, Poland: Panstowe Wydawni Naukowe, 1975.

JELAVICH, BARBARA. *History of the Balkans*. Two volumes. Cambridge, England: Cambridge University Press, 1983.

JENSEN, RICHARD. *The Winning of the Midwest: Social and Political Conflict, 1888–1896*. Chicago: University of Chicago Press, 1971.

JOHNSON, PAUL E. *A Shopkeeper's Millennium: Society and Revivals in Rochester, New York, 1815–1837*. New York: Hill and Wang, 1978.

JONES, MALDWYN A. "The Background to Emigration From Great Britain in the Nineteenth Century." *Perspectives in American History*, VII (1973), 3–92.

KAESTLE, CARL F., and Maris A. Vinovskis. *Education and Social Change in Nineteenth-Century Massachusetts*. Cambridge, England: Cambridge University Press, 1980.

KAMPHOEFNER, WALTER. "Transplanted Westfalians: Persistence and Transformation of Socioeconomic and Cultural Patterns in the Northwest German Migration to Missouri." Ph.D. dissertation, University of Missouri, 1978.

KANTOWICZ EDWARD R. *Polish-American Politics in Chicago, 1880–1940*. Chicago: University of Chicago Press, 1975.

KARNI, MICHAEL. "Finnish-American Cooperativism: The Radical Years, 1917–1930." In *Self-Help in Urban America*, ed. by Scott Cummings. Port Washington, N.Y.: Kennikat Press, 1980.

KATZ, MICHAEL B. "The Origins of Public Education: A Reassessment." *History of Education Quarterly*, 16 (Winter, 1976), 381–407.

KATZMAN, DAVID M. *Seven Days a Week: Women and Domestic Service in Industrializing America*. New York: Oxford University Press, 1978.

KATZNELSON, IRA. *City Trenches: Urban Politics and the Patterning of Class in America*. New York: Pantheon, 1981.

KEIL, HARTMUT. "The German Immigrant Working-Class of Chicago, 1875–1890: Workers, Labor Leaders, and the Labor Movement." In *American Labor and Immigration History, 1877–1920's: Recent European Research*, ed. by Dirk Hoerder, 156–75. Urbana: University of Illinois Press, 1983.

KENNEDY, ROBERT E. *The Irish: Emigration, Marriage, and Fertility*. Berkeley: University of California Press, 1973.

KESSLER-HARRIS, ALICE. *Out to Work: A History of Wage-Earning Women in the United States*. New York: Oxford University Press, 1982.

KESSNER, THOMAS. *The Golden Door: Italian and Jewish Immigrant Mobility in New York City, 1880–1915*. New York: Oxford University Press, 1977.

KITANO, HARRY H.L., AND AKEMI KIKUMURA. "The Japanese American Family." In *Ethnic Families in America: Patterns and Variations*, ed. by Charles H. Mindel and Robert W. Habenstein, 41–60. New York: Elsevier, 1976.

KLEIN, HERBERT S. "The Integration of Italian Immigrants into the United States and Argentina: A Comparative Analysis." *American Historical Review*, 88 (April, 1983), 306–29.

KLEPPNER, PAUL. *The Cross of Culture: A Social Analysis of Midwestern Politics, 1850–1900.* New York: Free Press, 1970.

——. *The Third Electoral System, 1853–1892.* Chapel Hill: University of North Carolina Press, 1979.

KNODEL, JOHN E. *The Decline of Fertility in Germany, 1871–1939.* Princeton, N.J.: Princeton University Press, 1974.

KÖLLMANN, WOLFGANG, AND PETER MARSCHALCK. "German Emigration to the United States," translated by Thomas C. Childers. *Perspectives in American History*, VII (1973), 499–554.

KOLOSSA, TIBOR. "The Social Structure of the Peasant Class in Austria-Hungary: Statistical Sources and Methods of Research." *East European Quarterly*, III (1970), 120–137.

KOPAN, ANDREW T. "The Role of Ethnic Education, 1890–1980." In *Ethnic Chicago*, ed. by Peter d'A. Jones and Melvin G. Holli, 80–139. Grand Rapids, Mich.: Eerdmans, 1981.

KORMAN, GERD. *Industrialization, Immigrants, and Americanizers: The View From Milwaukee.* Madison: State Historical Society of Wisconsin, 1967.

KOSTIAINEN, AUVO. "For or Against Americanization? The Case of the Finnish Immigrant Radicals." In *American Labor and Immigration History, 1870–1920's: Recent European Research*, ed. by Dirk Hoerder, 259–75. Urbana: University of Illinois Press, 1983.

KOURVETARIS, GEORGE A. "The Greek American Family." In *Ethnic Families in America: Patterns and Variations*, ed. by Charles H. Mindel and Robert W. Habenstein, 168–88. New York: Elsevier, 1976.

KRALJIC, FRANCES. "Croatian Migration To and From the United States Between 1900 and 1914." Ph.D. dissertation, New York University, 1975.

KRIEDTE, PETER, et al. *Industrialization Before Industrialization.* Cambridge, England: Cambridge University Press, 1981.

KUROPAS, MYRON BOHDON. "Ukrainian Chicago: The Making of a Nationality Group in America." In *Ethnic Chicago*, ed. by Peter d'A. Jones and Melvin G. Holli, 141–79. Grand Rapids, Mich.: Eerdmans, 1981.

KUZNETS, SIMON. "The Contribution of Immigration to the Growth in America." In *The Reinterpretation of American Economic History*, ed. by Robert Fogel and Stanley Engerman, 396–401. New York: Harper, 1971.

——. "Immigration of Russian Jews to the United States: Background and Structure." *Perspectives in American History*, IX (1975), 35–124.

KUZNIEWSKI, ANTHONY J. *Faith and the Fatherland: The Polish Church Wars in Wisconsin, 1896–1918.* Notre Dame, Indiana: University of Notre Dame Press, 1980.

LAM, PHILIP A. "The Creation and Demise of San Francisco Chinatown Freedom Schools: One Response to Desegregation." *Amerasia Journal*, 5 (1978), 57–74.

LAPHAM, JAMES S. "The German-Americans of New York City, 1860–1890." Ph.D. dissertation, St. John's University, 1977.

LARKIN, EMMET. "The Devotional Revolution in Ireland, 1850–1875." *American Historical Review*, (June, 1972), 625–52.

LASLETT, PETER. "Family and Household as Work Groups: Areas of Traditional Europe Compared." In *Family Forms in Historic Europe*, ed. by Richard Wall et al. Cambridge, England, Cambridge University Press, 1972.

——, and Richard Wall, editors. *Household and Family in Past Time*. Cambridge, England: Cambridge University Press, 1972.

LAURIE, BRUCE. *Working People of Philadelphia, 1800–1850*. Philadelphia: Temple University Press, 1980.

LAZERSON, MARVIN. *Origins of the Urban School: Public Education in Massachusetts, 1870–1915*. Cambridge: Harvard University Press, 1971.

LEES, LYNN HOLLEN. *Exiles of Erin: Irish Migrants in Victorian London*. Ithaca, N.Y.: Cornell University Press, 1979.

LEONARD, HENRY B. "Ethnic Cleavage and Industrial Conflict in Late 19th Century America: The Cleveland Rolling Mill Company Strikes of 1882 and 1885." *Labor History*, 20 (Fall, 1979), 542–48.

LÉS, BARBARA. *Kościol W. Procesie Asymilacji Polonii Amerykanskiej*. Warsaw, Poland: Zaklad Narodowy Imienia Ossolinskich Wydawnictwo, 1981.

LEVINE, DAVID. *Family Formation in an Age of Nascent Capitalism*. New York: Academic Press, 1977.

LEVINE, LAWRENCE W. *Black Culture and Black Consciousness*. New York. Oxford University Press, 1977.

LICHT, WALTER. *Working For the Railroad: The Organization of Work in the Nineteenth Century*. Princeton, N.J.: Princeton University Press, 1983.

LIEBERSON, STANLEY. *A Piece of the Pie: Black and White Immigrants Since 1880*. Berkeley: University of California Press, 1980.

LIGHT, IVAN. "Asian Enterprise in America: Chinese, Japanese and Koreans in Small Business." In *Self-Help in Urban America*, ed. by Scott Cummings, 33–54. Port Washington, N.Y.: Kennikat Press, 1980.

LINKH, RICHARD M. *American Catholicism and European Immigrants, 1900–1924*. New York: Center for Migration Studies, 1975.

LIVI-BACCI, Massimo. *A History of Italian Fertility During the Last Two Centuries*. Princeton: Princeton University Press, 1977.

LIVINGSTON, JOHN. "The Industrial Removal Office, The Galveston Project, and the Denver Jewish Community." In *The Jews of the West: The Metropolitan Years*, ed. by Moses Rischin, 50–74. Waltham, Massachusetts: American Jewish Society, 1979.

LOUKINEN, MICHAEL M. "Second Generation Finnish-American Migration from the Northwoods to Detroit, 1920–1950." In *Finnish Diaspora II: United States*, ed. by Michael Karni, 107–26. Toronto: Multicultural History Society of Ontario, 1981.

LOVELL-TROY, LAWRENCE A. "Clan Structure and Economic Activity: The Case of Greeks in Small Business Enterprise." In *Self-Help in Urban America*, ed. by Scott Cummings, 58–85. Port Washington, New York: Kennikat Press, 1980.

LUEBKE, FREDERICK C., editor. *Ethnic Voters and the Election of Lincoln*. Lincoln: University of Nebraska, 1971.

MacDONAGH, OLIVER. "The Irish Famine Emigration to the United States." *Perspectives in American History*, X (1976), 357–446.

MALASKA, H.O. "A Description of the Nature and Development of Adult Education among the Finnish Immigrants in the United States, 1880–1930." Ph.D. dissertation, Indiana University, 1978.

MANN, ARTHUR. *The One and the Many: Reflections on the American Identity.* Chicago: University of Chicago Press, 1979.

MANN, RALPH. *After the Gold Rush: Society in Grass Valley and Nevada City, California, 1849–1870.* Stanford, Calif.: Stanford University Press, 1982.

MARCUSE, HERBERT. *One Dimensional Man: Studies in the Ideology of Advanced Industrial Society.* Boston: Beacon Press, 1964.

MATTHEWS, GLENNA. "An Immigrant Community in Indian Territory." *Labor History,* 23 (Summer, 1982), 374–94.

MCCORMICK, RICHARD L. "Ethno-Cultural Interpretations of Nineteenth-Century American Voting Behavior." *Political Science Quarterly,* 89 (June, 1974) 351–77.

MERWICK, DONNA. *Boston Priests, 1848–1910, A Study of Social and Intellectual Change.* Cambridge, Mass.: Harvard University Press, 1973.

MEYER, STEPHEN. *The Five Dollar Day: Labor Management and Social Control in the Ford Motor Company, 1908–1921.* Albany: SUNY Press, 1981.

MILLER, SALLY M. "Milwaukee: of Ethnicity and Labor." In *Socialism and the Cities,* ed. by Bruce Stave, 41–47. Port Washington, N.Y.: Kennikat Press, 1975.

——. "Other Socialists: Native-Born and Immigrant Women in the Socialist Party of America, 1901–1917." *Labor History,* 24 (Winter, 1983), 84–102.

——. *The Radical Immigrant.* New York: Twayne, 1974.

MIRAK, ROBERT. "The Armenian Orthodox and Armenian Protestant Churches in the New World to 1915." In *Immigrants and Religion in Urban America,* ed. by Randall M. Miller and Thomas D. Marzik, 136–60. Philadelphia: Temple University Press, 1977.

MITTERAUER, MICHAEL, AND ALEXANDER KAGAN. "Russian and Central European Family Structure: A Comparative View." *Journal of Family History,* 7 (Spring, 1982), 103–31.

——, AND REINHARD SIEDER. *The European Family: Patriarchy to Partnership, 1400 to the Present.* Chicago: University of Chicago Press, 1982.

MODELL, JOHN. "An Ecology of Family Decisions: Suburbanization, Schooling, and Fertility in Philadelphia, 1800–1920." *Journal of Urban History,* 6 (August, 1980), 397–418.

——. *The Economics and Politics of Radical Accommodations: The Japanese of Los Angeles, 1900–1942.* Urbana: University of Illinois Press, 1977.

MOKYR, JOEL. "Industrialization and Poverty in Ireland and the Netherlands." *Journal of Interdisciplinary History,* X (Winter, 1980), 429–58.

MONTGOMERY, DAVID. *Beyond Equality: Labor and the Radical Republican, 1862–1872.* New York: Alfred A. Knopf, 1967.

——. "Nationalism, American Patriotism, and Class Consciousness among Immigrant Workers in the United States in the Epoch of World War I." Paper delivered at the United States-Hungarian Conference on Industrialization, Budapest, August, 1982.

——. *Workers' Control in America: Studies in the History of Work, Technology and Labor Struggles.* Cambridge, England: Cambridge University Press, 1979.

MOORE, BARRINGTON. *Injustice: The Social Bases of Obedience and Revolt.* White Plains, N.Y.: M.E. Sharpe, 1978.

Selected Bibliography

——. *Social Origins of Dictatorship and Democracy: Lord and Peasant in the Making of the Modern World*. Boston: Beacon Press, 1966.

MOORE, DEBORAH DASH. *At Home in America: Second Generation New York Jews*. New York: Columbia University Press, 1981.

MORAWSKA, EWA. "The Internal Status Hierarchy in the East European Immigrant Communities of Johnstown, Pa., 1890–1930's." *Journal of Social History*, 16 (Fall, 1982), 75–108.

MORMINO, GARY ROSS. "The Hill Upon the City: An Italo-American Neighborhood in St. Louis, Missouri, 1880–1955." Ph.D. dissertation, University of North Carolina, 1977.

——. "We Worked Hard and Took Care of Our Own: Oral Histories of Italians in Tampa." *Labor History*, 23 (Summer, 1982), 395–415.

MURDZEK, BENJAMIN P. *Emigration in Polish Social-Political Thought, 1870–1914*. New York: Columbia University Press, 1977.

NADEL, STANLEY. "Kleindeutschland: New York City's Germans, 1845–1880." Ph.D. dissertation, Columbia University, 1981.

NAKANE, CHIE. "An Interpretation of the Size and Structure of the Household over Three Centuries." In *Household and Family in Past Time*, ed. by Peter Laslett and Richard Wall, 518–43. Cambridge, England: Cambridge University Press, 1972.

——. *Kinship and Economic Organization in Rural Japan*. London: Athlone Press, 1967.

NELLI, HUMBERT S. *Italians in Chicago, 1880–1930: A Study in Ethnic Mobility*. New York: Oxford University Press, 1970.

NILSSON, FRED. *Emigrationen fran Stockholm till Nordamerika 1880–1893: En Studie i Urban Utvandring*. Stockholm, Sweden: Studia Historica Upsaliensia, 1970.

NUGENT, WALTER. *Structures of American Social History*. Bloomington: Indiana University Press, 1981.

O'GRADY, JOSEPH P., editor. *The Immigrants' Influence on Wilson's Peace Policies*. Lexington: University of Kentucky Press, 1967.

OLNECK, MICHAEL R., and MARVIN LAZERSON. "The School Achievement of Immigrant Children, 1900–1930." *History of Education Quarterly*, 15 (Winter, 1974), 453–82.

OLSON, AUDREY L. *St. Louis Germans, 1850–1920: The Nature of an Immigrant Community and its Relation to the Assimilation Process*. New York: Arno Press, 1980.

PADGETT, DEBORAH. "Settlers and Sojourners: A Study of Serbian Adaptation in Milwaukee, Wisconsin." Ph.D. dissertation, University of Wisconsin, 1979.

PAPANIKOLAS, ZEESE. *Buried Unsung: Louis Tikas and the Ludlow Massacre*. Salt Lake City: University of Utah Press, 1982.

PARMET, ROBERT D. *Labor and Immigration in Industrial America*. Boston: Twayne Publishers, 1981.

PAROT, JOSEPH JOHN. *Polish Catholics in Chicago, 1850–1920: A Religious History*. DeKalb: Northern Illinois University Press, 1981.

PILCH, ANDREZEJ. "Migrations of the Galician Populace at the Turn of the Nineteenth and Twentieth Centuries." In *Employment-Seeking Emigration of the Poles World Wide, XIX and XX Centuries*, ed. by Celina Bobinska and Andrzej Pilch, 77–102. Krakow, Poland: Panstowe Wydawni Naukowe, 1975.

Selected Bibliography

PIORE, MICHAEL J. *Birds of Passage: Migration Labor and Industrial Societies*. Cambridge, England: Cambridge University Press, 1979.

PIOTR, TARAS. "Problem Kulturowej Tozsamosci Ethnicznego Getta." *Studia Polonijne*, 4 (Lublin, 1981), 127–57.

PIRKOVA-JAKOBSON, SVATAVA. "Harvest Festivals among Czechs and Slovaks in America." *Journal of American Folklore, (July-September, 1956)*, 266–80.

PLAKANS, ANDREJS. "Ties of Kinship and Kinship Roles in an Historical Eastern European Peasant Community: A Synchronic Analysis." *Journal of Family History*, 7 (Spring, 1982), 52–75.

POSADAS, BARBARA M. "The Hierarchy of Color and Psychological Adjustment in an Industrial Environment: Filipinos, The Pullman Company, and the Brotherhood of Sleeping Car Porters." *Labor History*, 23 (Summer, 1982), 349–73.

POUNDS, NORMAN J. *The Upper Silesian Industrial Region*. Bloomington: Indiana University Press, 1958.

POZZETTA, GEORGE E. "Italians and the Tampa General Strike of 1910." *In Pane e Lavoro: The Italian American Working Class*, ed. by George E. Pozzetta, 29–46. Toronto, Canada: Multicultural Historical Society, 1980.

PRPIC, GEORGE J. "The South Slavs." In *The Immigrants Influence on Wilson's Peace Policies*, ed. by Joseph O'Grady, 173–203. Lexington: University of Kentucky Press, 1967.

PUSKÁS, JULIANNA. "The Conflicts of Adaptation of the Hungarian Emigrants in America." Paper presented to the United States-Hungarian Conference on Industrialization, Budapest, August 23–25, 1982.

——. *Kivándorlo Magyarok az Egyesült Allamokban, 1880–1940*. Budapest, Hungary: Akadémiai Kiadó, 1982.

RACZ, ISTVÁN. A *Paraszti Migráció és Politikia Megítélése Magyaroszágon, 1849–1914*. Budapest, Hungary: Akadémiai Kiadó, 1980.

RAPHAEL, MARC LEE. *Jews and Judaism in a Midwestern Community: Columbus, Ohio, 1840–1975*. Columbus: Ohio Historical Society, 1979.

REBEL, HERMANN. *Peasant Classes: The Bureaucratization of Property and Family Relations under Early Hapsburg Absolutism 1511–1636*. Princeton, N.J.: Princeton University Press, 1983.

RENKIEWICZ, FRANK. "The Profits of Non-profit Capitalism: Polish Fraternalism and Beneficial Insurance in America." In *Self-Help in Urban America*, ed. by Scott Cummings, 113–29. Port Washington, N.Y.: Kennikat, 1980.

RISCHIN, MOSES. *The Promised City: New York's Jews, 1870–1914*. New York: Harper and Row, 1962.

RODGERS, DANIEL T. *The Work Ethnic in Industrial America, 1850–1920*. Chicago: University of Chicago Press, 1978.

ROMO, RICARDO. *East Los Angeles: History of a Barrio*. Austin: University of Texas Press, 1983.

ROSALES, FRANCISCO A. "Mexican Immigration to the Urban Midwest During the 1920's." Ph.D. dissertation, Indiana University, 1978.

ROSE, EDWARD J. *Henry George*. New York: Twayne, 1968.

ROSENBLUM, GERALD. *Immigrant Workers*. New York: Basic Books, 1973.

ROSS, CARL. "Finnish American Women in Transition: 1910–1920." In *Finnish Diaspora II: United States*, ed. by Michael Karni, 239–55. Toronto: Multicultural History Society of Ontario, 1981.

Selected Bibliography

Rowe, John. *The Hand-Rock Men: Cornish Immigrants and the North American Mining Frontier*. New York: Barnes and Noble, 1974.

Runblom, Harold, and Hans Norman. *From Sweden to America: A History of the Migration*. Minneapolis: University of Minnesota Press and Uppsala: Acta Universitatis Upsaliensis, 1976.

Rusinski, Wladyshaw. "The Role of the Peasantry of Poznan (Wielkopolska) in the Formation of the Non-Agricultural Labor Market." *East European Quarterly*, III (1970), 509–24.

Ryan, Mary P. *Cradle of the Middle Class: The Family in Oneida County, New York, 1790–1865*. Cambridge, England: Cambridge University Press, 1981.

Saloutos, Theodore. "Causes and Patterns of Greek Emigration to the United States." *Perspectives in American History*, VII (1973), 381–437.

Sanders, James W. *The Education of an Urban Minority: Catholics in Chicago, 1833–1965*. New York: Oxford University Press, 1977.

Sanders, Zinta. "Latvian Education in the United States: Antecedents and Development of Secondary Schools." *Journal of Ethnic Studies*. 7 (Spring, 1979), 31–42.

Schneider, Jane, and Peter Schneider. *Culture and Political Economy in Western Sicily*. New York: Academic Press, 1976.

Schultz, Stanley K. *The Culture Factory: Boston Public Schools, 1789–1860*. New York: Oxford, 1973.

Seller, Maxine, editor. *Immigrant Women*. Philadelphia: Temple University Press, 1981.

——. "The Education of Immigrants in the United States: An Introduction to the Literature." *The Immigration History Newsletter*, 13 (May, 1981), 1–8.

——. *To Seek America: A History of Ethnic Life in the United States*. New York: Jerome Ozer, 1977.

Serene, Frank H. "Immigrant Steelworkers in the Monongahela Valley: Their Communities and the Development of a Labor Class Consciousness." Ph.D. dissertation, University of Pittsburgh, 1979.

Shergold, Peter R. *Working-Class Life: The American Standard in Comparative Perspective, 1899–1913*. Pittsburgh: University of Pittsburgh Press, 1982.

Shover, John L. "The Emergence of a Two Party System in Republican Philadelphia, 1924–1936." *Journal of American History*, LX (March, 1974), 985–1002.

——. "Ethnicity and Religion in Philadelphia Politics, 1924–1940." *American Quarterly*, XXV (December, 1973), 499–515.

Sieder, Reinhard, and Michael Mitterauer. "The Reconstruction of the Family Life Course: Theoretical Problems and Empirical Results. In *Family Forms in Historic Europe*, ed. by Richard Wall, et al. Cambridge, England: Cambridge University Press, 1983. 309–45.

Smith, Judith Ellen. "Remaking Their Lives: Italian and Jewish Immigrant Family, Work and Community in Providence, Rhode Island, 1900–1940." Ph.D. dissertation, Brown University, 1980.

Smith, Timothy L. "New Approaches to the History of Immigration in Twentieth-Century America." *American Historical Review*, LXXI (July, 1966), 1265–79.

——. "Religion and Ethnicity in America." *American Historical Review*, 83 (December, 1978), 1155–85.

STANKIEWICZ, ZBIGNIEW. "The Economic Emigration from the Kingdom of Poland Portrayed on the European Background." In *Employment-Seeking Emigration of the Poles World Wide, XIX and XX Centuries*, ed. by Celina Bobinska and Andrzej Pilch, 27–54. Krakow, Poland: Panstwowe Wydawni Naukowe, 1975.

STERN, MARK J. "Differential Fertility in Rural Erie County, New York, 1855." *Journal of Social History*, 16 (Summer, 1983), 49–64.

STIPANOVICH, JOSEPH. "Collective Economic Activity among Serb, Croat, and Slovene Immigrants in the United States." In *Self-Help in Urban America*, ed. by Scott Cummings. Port Washington, New York: Kennikat Press, 1980.

——. "In Unity Is Strength: Immigrant Intellectuals in Progressive America: A History of the South Slav Social Democratic Movement, 1900–1918." Ph.D. dissertation, University of Minnesota, 1978.

STOLARIK, MARK. "Immigration and Urbanization: The Slovak Experience, 1870–1918." Ph.D. dissertation, University of Minnesota, 1974.

——. "Immigration, Education and the Social Mobility of Slovaks, 1870–1930." In *Immigrants and Religion in Urban America*, ed. by Randall M. Miller and Thomas D. Marzik. Philadelphia: Temple University Press, 1977.

SUGAR, PETER F. *Industrialization of Bosnia-Hercegovina, 1878–1918*. Seattle: University of Washington Press, 1963.

SWIERENGA, ROBERT P. "Dutch Immigrant Demography, 1820–1880." *Journal of Family History*, 5 (Winter, 1980), 390–405.

——. "Dutch International Migration and Occupational Change: A Structural Analysis of Multinational Linked Files." Paper presented at Social Science History Association, Conference, Bloomington, Indiana, November, 1982.

——. "Dutch Immigration Patterns in the Nineteenth and Twentieth Centuries." In *They Came to Stay: Essays on Dutch Immigration and Settlement in America*, ed. by Robert Swierenga. New Brunswick, N.J.: Rutgers University Press, forthcoming.

——. "Local-Cosmopolitan Theory and Immigrant Religion: The Social Bases of the Antebellum Dutch Reformed Schism." *Journal of Social History*, 14 (Fall, 1980), 113–35.

TAJTÁK, L. "K začiatkom Amerikánsko-Slovenských Novín." Začiatky *Ceskej a Slovenskej emigrácie do USA*, ed. by Josef Poliènský, 186–96. Bratislava, Yugoslavia: Vydavateľstvo Slovenskej Akadémie Vied, 1970.

TAVES, ANN. "Lay Catholic Piety in Mid-Nineteenth Century America." *American Catholic Studies Newsletter*, 9 (Spring, 1983), 7–8.

TEMIN, PETER. "Labor Scarcity in America." *Journal of Interdisciplinary History*, 1 (Winter, 1971), 251–64.

TENTLER, LESLIE WOODCOCK. *Wage-Earning Women: Industrial Work and Family Life in the United States, 1900–1930*. New York: Oxford University Press, 1979.

TENZER, MORTON. "The Jews." In *The Immigrants' Influence on Wilson's Peace Policies*, ed. by Joseph O'Grady, 287–317. Lexington: University of Kentucky Press, 1967.

Selected Bibliography

THERNSTROM, STEPHAN. *The Other Bostonians: Poverty and Progress in the American Metropolis, 1880–1970*. Cambridge, Harvard University Press, 1973.

——. *Poverty and Progress: Social Mobility in a Nineteenth Century City.* Cambridge: Harvard University Press, 1964.

THIGPEN, KENNETH A. "Folklore and the Ethnicity Factor in the Lives of Romanian-Americans." Ph.D. dissertation, Indiana University, 1974.

THISTLETHWAITE, FRANK. "Migration from Europe Overseas in the Nineteenth and Twentieth Centuries." *Rapports: XIe Congress International des Sciences Historiques*, 5 (Stockholm, 1960), 40–69.

TOLL, WILLIAM. *The Making of an Ethnic Middle-Class: Portland Jewry Over Four Generations.* Albany: SUNY Press, 1983.

——. "Mobility, Fraternalism and Jewish Cultural Change: Portland, 1910–1930." In *The Jews of the West: The Metropolitan Years*, ed. by Moses Rischin, 75–107. Waltham, Massachusetts: American Jewish History Society, 1979.

TOMASI, SYLVANO. *Piety and Power*. New York: Center of Migration Studies, 1975.

TOMAŠIĆ, DINKO. "Personality Development in the Zadruga Society." *Psychiatry*, V (May, 1948), 229–61.

TREFOUSSE, HANS L. *Carl Schurz: A Biography*. Knoxville: University of Tennessee Press, 1982.

USELDING, PAUL. *Studies in the Technological Development of the American Economy During the First Half of the Nineteenth Century.* New York: Arno Press, 1975.

VARBERO, RICHARD A. "Urbanization and Acculturation: Philadelphia's South Italians, 1918–1932." Ph.D. dissertation, Temple University, 1975.

VASSADY, BELA. "The 'Homeland Cause' as Stimulant to Ethnic Unity: The Hungarian American Response to Károlyi's 1914 American Tour." *Journal of American Ethnic History*, 2 (Fall, 1982), 39–64.

VECOLI, RUDOLPH J. "Anthony Capraro and the Lawrence Strike of 1919." In *Pane e Lavoro: The Italian American Working Class*, ed. by George E. Pozzetta, 3–27. Toronto: Multicultural History Society of Ontario, 1980.

——. "Chicago's Italians Prior to World War I." Ph.D. dissertation, University of Wisconsin, 1963.

——. "Cult and Occult in Italian-American Culture: The Persistence of a Religious Heritage." In *Immigrants and Religion in Urban America*, ed. by Randall M. Miller and Thomas D. Marzik, 25–47. Philadelphia: Temple University Press, 1977.

——. "Prelates and Peasants: Italian Immigrants and the Catholic Church." *Journal of Social History*, 2 (Spring, 1969), 217–68.

VIRTANEN, KEIJO. *Settlement or Return: Finnish Emigrants (1860–1930) in International Overseas Return Migration.* Helsinki: Finnish Historical Society, 1979.

VOLGYES, IVAN. "Economic Aspects of Rural Transformation in Eastern Europe." In *The Process of Rural Transformation*, ed. by Ivan Volgyes, Richard E. Lonsdale, and William P. Avery, 89–127. New York: Pergamon, 1980.

WAKATSUKI, YASUO. "The Japanese Emigration to the United States, 1866–1924: A Monograph." *Perspectives in American History*, XII (1979), 389–516.

WALKER, MACK. *Germany and the Emigration, 1816–1885.* Cambridge, Mass.: Harvard University Press, 1964.

WALKOWITZ, DANIEL J. *Worker City, Company Town: Iron and Cotton Worker Protest in Troy and Cohoes, New York, 1855–1884.* Urbana: University of Illinois Press, 1978.

WALLERSTEIN, IMMANUEL. *The Modern World-System.* New York: Academic Press, 1974.

WARD, DAVID. *Cities and Immigrants.* New York: Oxford University Press, 1971.

WEISS, BERNARD J., editor. *American Education and the European Immigrant, 1840–1940.* Urbana: University of Illinois Press, 1982.

WILENTZ, SEAN. "Artisan Republican Festivals and the Rise of Class Conflict in New York City, 1788–1837." In *Working-Class America,* ed. by Michael H. Frisch and Daniel J. Walkowitz, 37–77. Urbana: University of Illinois Press, 1983.

WILLIAMS, PHYLLIS H. *South Italian Folkways in Europe and America.* New York: Russell and Russell, 1938.

WILLIAMSON, JEFFREY G. *Late Nineteenth-Century American Development: A General Equilibrium History.* London, England: Cambridge University Press, 1974.

WOLF, ERIC R. *Europe and the People Without History.* Berkeley: University of California Press, 1982.

WOLFINGER, RAYMOND E. "The Development and Persistence of Ethnic Voting." In *American Ethnic Politics,* ed. by Lawrence H. Fuchs, 163–93. New York: Harper, 1968.

YANS-MCLAUGHLIN, VIRGINIA. *Family and Community: Italian Immigrants in Buffalo, 1880–1930.* Ithaca, N.Y.: Cornell University Press, 1977.

ZIVICH, EDWARD. "From Zadruga to Oil Refinery: Croatian Immigrants and Croatian-Americans in Whiting, Indiana, 1890–1950." Ph.D. dissertation, SUNY, Binghamton, 1977.

ZUNZ, OLIVER. *The Changing Face of Inequality: Urbanization, Industrial Development, and Immigrants in Detroit, 1880–1920.* Chicago: University of Chicago Press, 1982.

Index

Index

and labor movement, 93–94, 104
Polish bishop issue, 160–61
and Rusins, 146–47
Russian Orthodox vs. Roman, 146–47
schools, 194
and socialism, 109–10
and social mobility, 171–72
see also Church
Central Labor Union, 90
Cermak, Anton, 204
Chicago "Swede Town," 176–77
Chicanos
folk culture, 188
as workers, 70–71
Child labor
family economy and, 76–77, 193
and schooling, 190–91, 193
Chinese immigrants, folk culture of, 186, 189
Church, 144–68
centralization of, 152–53
competing leadership in, 156–57
discord and divisions in, 157–65
ethnicity and, 150–56
homeland governments' interference in, 166
role in immigrant society, 144–50
schooling and, 193–97
social services of, 148–50
trusteeism issue, 154
see also Catholicism; Protestantism
Cigar industry, 93
Cinel, Dino, 13
Čizmić, Ivan, 44
Class distinctions, 118–20
Clergy
competition among, 156–67
labor activity by priests, 104, 109–10
Cleveland, Grover, 204
Clustering of families, 62–66
Coal mine safety legislation, 87–88
Cohoes, N.Y., as example of industrial town, 89–90
Commercial agriculture. See Agriculture, commercial
Communal associations, 89
Community divisions among immigrants, 117–20
Contadini, 32
Conzen, Kathleen, 120
Cooperation, and family, 72–77
Cooperative associations, 26, 86
Craftsmen
displacement by capitalism, 30–34, 64–65

social status of, 170–75
and unions, 86–87, 94
Craft unions, 94
Crime, and entrepreneurship, 132
Croatia, emigration from, 10–12
Croatian fraternals, 122, 126–28
Cudahy, Patrick, 69
Culen, Konstantin, 125
Culture
of everyday life, 206–16
folk, of immigrants, 184–89
"peasant" or rustic, and nationalism, 46–50
Czech immigrants, folk culture, 186

Dance, immigrant folk, 186–88
DeLeon, Daniel, 105, 110
Democratic Party, 198–201
Denmark
regional variations in emigration, 8–9
social level and emigration, 17
Diaz, Porfirio, 22
Dougherty, Dennis, 153
Drascovich, Michael, 124
Dubnoff, Steven, 74
Dutch, regional variations in emigration by, 9
Dutch Reformed Church, 155
Dyniewicz, Ladislaus, 162

Easterlin, Richard, 2
Economic activity, and migration, 2–3
Economy, family, 71–83
Education
and child labor, 190–93
of immigrant children, 189–97
parochial schools, 157–65
vocational, 190, 192
Ejidos, 22
Emancipation of peasants, 24–25
Emigration
commercial agriculture and, 23–30
by craftsmen, 30–34
by family networks, 57–71
family structure and, 38–43
internal transiency and, 43–45
literacy and, 23
motivation for, 1–3, 52–53
nationalism and, 46–50
population expansion and, 34–37
pragmatism and, 45–54
regional variations in, 3–23
from rural societies, 51–52
and social level, 13–22
structure of, 1–23
see also Immigrants

288]

Index

Index

Minority identity, and nationalism, 48
Mitchell, John, 88
Mobility
  geographical, 175–79
  social, 169–75
Molba, 122
Molly Maguires, 187
Moore, Barrington, 211
Mortgages, 181–82
Mundelein, George, 192
Murgas, Jozef, 157
Mussolini, Benito, 202

Napieralska, Emily, 124
Nationalism
  emigration and, 46–50
  immigrant involvement in homeland,
    200–02
  labor movement and, 111
Nazism, 201, 202
Nelson, Daniel, 64
Networks of migration, 57–71
New Deal, 114
Newmanich, Anton, 132
Newspapers, Socialist, 110
1930s, immigrant workers in, 112–15
Nowiny Polskie, 158–60
Nuclear family, 39, 82–83

Occupational concentrations, 63–64
Occupational status, and mobility,
  170–75
O'Connell, William Henry, 152
Ottendorfer, Oswald, 141

Paderewski, Ignace, 201
Pale, Jews from, 20
Parochial schools, 157–65
Peasants
  emancipation of, 24–25
  and national culture, 46–49
Peretz, I.L., 49
Philadelphia, ethnic and cultural divisions in, 94–95
Picavet, Luis, 104
Piore, Michael, 113
Pius IX, Pope, 154
Pogorelec, Charles, 107
Poles, emigration patterns, 12–13
Polish Catholic Union, 127
Polish Educational Society (PES), 157–58
Polish immigrants
  and the church, 153, 156–62
  folk culture of, 187–88
  fraternals, 127
Polish National Alliance (PNA), 126

Polish Peasant in Europe and America,
  122
Polish Roman Catholic Union (PRCU),
  126, 161
Political bosses, 202–04
Politics of immigrants, 197–04
Poppenhusen, Conrad, 132, 141
Population expansion, 34–37
Portuguese immigrants, folk culture of,
  186
Powderly, Terence, 111
Priests
  labor activity by, 104, 109–10
  see also Clergy
Protestantism
  clash with Catholicism, 92–94, 197–98
  divisions and tensions within, 155
  social mobility and, 171–72
Prussia
  emigration from, 21, 26
  see also Germany
Public schooling, 189–97
Puskás, Julianna, 25

Racz, Istvan, 10
Radic, Anton, 49
Radic, Stephan, 49
Radicalism
  immigrant workers and, 103–04, 116
  see also Socialism
Raffeiner, Johann, 146
Redemptionists, 152
Regional factionalism among immigrants,
  118–20
Regional variations in emigration, 3–23
Religion
  politics and, 197
  schooling and, 157–65
  see also Church
Reppucci, Louis, 136
Republican Party, 95, 109, 110, 198
Resurrectionists, 161–62
Return migration, 53–54
Revivalism, and labor movement, 94–95,
  109
Rischin, Moses, 31
Rocco, Angelo, 104
Rockefeller, John D., 99
Romanian immigrants, folk culture of,
  187, 189
Roosevelt, Franklin D., 200, 202
Rosenblum, Gerald, 93
Rosenwald, Julius, 134
Rovnianek, Peter, 125, 127, 214
Rusins, and the church, 146–47
Russian Orthodox Church, 146–47

Index

and premigration traditions, 85–88
skilled workers and, 86–92
see also Labor movement
United Anthracite Miners (UAM), 91–92
United Hebrew Trades, 106
United Mine Workers of America, 88, 100, 114
Unskilled vs. skilled workers. See Skill differences

Vecoli, Rudolph, 154
Vereins, 119
Vocational training, 190, 192

Wages
differentials between U.S. and British, 60–61
and labor shortages, 29–30
Wales
regional variations in emigration, 4
social level and emigration, 16
see also Great Britain
"Walking delegates," 86
Walkowitz, Daniel, 89

Weaver, Daniel, 88
Weaver, Thomas, 88
Webb, Thomas, 86
Weydemeyer, Joseph, 105
Wilson, Woodrow, 201
Wirt, William, 191–92
Wise, Stephen, 201
Women
employment of married, 78–80
influence and power of, 80–82
kinship networks and, 62
and labor strikes, 90–92

Yiddish, 118
Yiddishkeit, 49
Youth of immigrants, 75
Yudin, Feigel, 188
Yugoslav socialists 107–08, 127
Yuhasz, Michael, 124

Zadruga, 122
Zatkovich, Gregory, 201
Zunz, Olivier 177

DATE DUE
